The Allotment Plot

NICOLE TONKOVICH

The Allotment Plot

Alice C. Fletcher, E. Jane Gay,
and Nez Perce Survivance

University of Nebraska Press   Lincoln

© 2012 by the Board of Regents of
the University of Nebraska
All rights reserved
Manufactured in the United States of America

Library of Congress Cataloging-in-Publication
Data

Tonkovich, Nicole.
The allotment plot: Alice C. Fletcher, E. Jane Gay,
and Nez Perce survivance / Nicole Tonkovich.
p. cm.
Includes bibliographical references and index.
ISBN 978-0-8032-7137-1 (cloth: alk. paper)
ISBN 978-1-4962-3036-2 (paperback)
1. Nez Percé Indians—Land tenure. 2. Nez
Percé Indians—History—19th century. 3. Nez
Percé Indians—Government relations. 4. Indian
allotments—Idaho—Nez Percé Indian Reservation—History—19th century. 5. Allotment of
land—Idaho—Nez Percé Indian Reservation—
History—19th century. 6. Fletcher, Alice C. (Alice
Cunningham), 1838–1923—Correspondence.
7. Gay, E. Jane, 1830–1919—Photograph
collections. 8. Nez Percé Indian Reservation
(Idaho) I. Title.
E99.N5T66 2012
979.5004'974124—dc23
2012011621

Set in Sabon.

Contents

List of Illustrations [vii]
Preface [xi]
Acknowledgments [xv]

Introduction: *Allotment and Nimiipuu Survivance* [1]

PART ONE. BEGINNINGS

Introduction: *After the End of Nez Perce History* [41]
1. A False Beginning [55]
2. Another Beginning [73]

PART TWO. LAND

Introduction: *Map and Territory, Space and Place* [95]
3. "The Square Idea" [103]
4. Ethnographic Knowledge and Native Cartography [135]

PART THREE. CITIZENS

Introduction: *E Pluribus Unum* [167]
5. Technologies of Citizenship [175]
6. Fictions of Coherence [199]

PART FOUR. ENDINGS

Introduction: *"If the Work Is Ever to Be Finished"* [221]
7. Irresolutions and Incompletions [225]
8. The Ends of Nez Perce Allotment [251]

PART FIVE. AFTERWARD

  Introduction: *"Double Pictures Have Met Us All along the Way"* [271]
9. After-Words [279]
10. After-Images [299]

   Notes [335]
   Bibliography [389]
   Index [409]

Illustrations

1. "Chief Joseph with Alice C. Fletcher," by E. Jane Gay [2]
2. Map of Nez Perce country [9]
3. Crayon drawing of Alice C. Fletcher, 1888, by E. H. Miller [16]
4. Alice C. Fletcher, by Napoleon Company, Barcelona, ca. 1900 [17]
5. James Reubens, Mark Williams, James B. Monteith, and Archie B. Lawyer, ca. 1878 [45]
6. "Christian women of Joseph's band, now returned to their old home" [48]
7. "Council at Kamiah," 22 July 1889, by E. Jane Gay [70]
8. "They Donned War Bonnets," Stephen Reubens and James Reubens at Cold Spring ID, 10 Aug. 1889, by E. Jane Gay [75]
9. "James Reuben and Archie Lawyer," by E. Jane Gay [76]
10. Josiah Redwolf, 1970 [91]
11. David P. Thompson, Nez Perce Reservation, Township 32 North, Range 2 East, 22 Oct. 1873 [106]
12. "Clearwater River at Kamiah," by E. Jane Gay [113]
13. Edson D. Briggs, survey map, Nez Perce Reservation, Township 32 North, Range 3 East, July–August 1890 [117]
14. "Squirrel Camp," by E. Jane Gay, at full size [118]
15. "Squirrel Camp," 4–15 July 1889, by E. Jane Gay, in *Choup-nit-ki* [119]
16. Lewiston, Idaho, probably 28 May 1889, by E. Jane Gay [122]

17. "Lewiston," as included by E. Jane Gay in *Choup-nit-ki* [122]
18. Fort Lapwai, by E. Jane Gay [124]
19. "North Fork of the Clearwater," by E. Jane Gay [125]
20. "The Damp Thermopylae," ca. September 1890, by E. Jane Gay [126]
21. Edson D. Briggs, survey map, Nez Perce Reservation, Township 33 North, Range 3 East, July–August, 1891 [127]
22. "Where Dick Fell," November 1891, by E. Jane Gay [128]
23. "Where We Gathered Indian Songs," [by E. Jane Gay], cover [130]
24. "Where We Gathered Indian Songs," [by E. Jane Gay], interior [130]
25. "Camp Bearing Tree," by E. Jane Gay [132]
26. "Clearwater River—Nicodemus' Home on the Left," by E. Jane Gay [141]
27. Edson D. Briggs, detail, Nez Perce Reservation, Township 32 North, Range 4 East, September 1889 [142]
28. Edson D. Briggs, detail, Nez Perce Reservation, Township 32 North, Range 3 East, September 1889 [142]
29. Patent Receipt No. 1631, of Wa sin me sa kart sa, or Nicodemus [144]
30. Patent Receipt No. 1633, of Kar yokts, or Nancy Nicodemus [145]
31. "The Nez Perce Country," as drawn by Kew-kew'-lu-yah, July 1891 [146]
32. "Old Billy Williams," June 1891, by E. Jane Gay [150]
33. "Weippe Prairie in 1885 by Corbett Lawyer," 1965 [162]
34. Weippe Prairie Map, overlay by Gene Eastman [163]
35. Accounts of 4 July 1890 [176]
36. "Camp at Lapwai. Tal-lik-lykt. July 4," by E. Jane Gay [184]
37. "Women's Work in Savagery," 1893 Columbian Exposition exhibit [190]
38. "Behold the Cook!" by E. Jane Gay [191]
39. "Spalding Town 1902–1935," Landscape report map [230]
40. Map of Spalding, Idaho, ca. 1900 [231]
41. "Nez Perce Wallets etc. Henry Fair, Lewiston, Idaho" [247]
42. Box [Cox] Case, by E. Jane Gay, image 1 [264]

43. Box [Cox] Case, by E. Jane Gay, images 3 and 4 [265]
44. James Stuart and Harriet Mary Stuart [272]
45. Silas Whitman standing by a tipi [273]
46. "Camp Meeting at Lapwai, July 4," by E. Jane Gay [274]
47. Tepees at Nespelem, July 4 celebration, ca. 1900–1905, by Edward H. Latham [276]
48. Native American women riding horses, ca. 1900–1905, by Edward H. Latham [276]
49. Sam Morris (Sik-Um-Chets-Kun-In), Paul Eneas, and Billy Carter [280]
50. Starr J. Maxwell and family members [283]
51. Pile of Clouds and Tah'mawiinúnmy, ca. 1910 [291]
52. E. Jane Gay, page from draft manuscript of *Choup-nit-ki* [305]
53. "Salmon Feast," July 1890, by E. Jane Gay [307]
54. "The Barbecue," from *Choup-nit-ki* [307]
55. List of Photographs from *Choup-nit-ki* [308]
56. *Choup-nit-ki*, page 396 [309]
57. Katherine Cloud and Bert Cloud, ca. 1905 [311]
58. Funeral of James Stuart, 1929 [312]
59. The Dickson-Cloud family, ca. 1915 [313]
60. Home built by James Stuart for his sister Nancy [314]
61. "Remember this? It was fun wasn't it?" [315]
62. Dickson-Cloud family album [316–17]
63. "Indians when they had their 4 of July last year. 1911" [319]
64. "At Spalding / July sure hot" [320]
65. Cloud family at Dickson Ranch, ca. 1915 [322]
66. "Nez Percé Indian Family—World War I" [323]
67. Harriet Stuart and Annie Parnell Little, by E. Jane Gay [324]
68. Unidentified Nez Perce women [325]
69. "'Reubens Bro's' Nesperce Tribe," by Major Lee Moorhouse [326]
70. Portrait of Harriet Mary, by John N. Choate [328]
71. James Dickson at Carlisle Indian School [329]
72. Clayton Dickson and the Chilocco Indian Agricultural School baseball team [330]
73. Clayton Dickson at Chilocco Indian Agricultural School [331]
74. Horse procession [332]

Preface

Since the early eighteenth century the federal government of the United States of America has exercised a unilateral and presumptive right to manage the sovereign Native groups classified by the Marshall Supreme Court in 1831 as "domestic dependent nations."[1] Since the nineteenth century the secretary of the interior has served as the trustee of record and has exercised the right to manage monies derived from Indian lands but has not, until relatively recently, been held legally liable for failing to produce a formal accounting for the management of those funds. In fact, not until 1987 was the Department of the Interior required by statute to "audit and reconcile" its tribal accounts and to report the results of its trust fund management to its Indian clients.[2]

By that time the task of fully reconciling nearly two hundred years of inaccurate and incomplete records had become utterly daunting, and the department temporized.

Seven years later, in 1994, Congress passed the American Indian Trust Fund Management Reform Act to force compliance, but the Bureau of Indian Affairs "admitted that it was incapable of complying with the [congressional] mandates" and hired a professional accounting firm, Arthur Andersen, to perform the task. After an initial survey Andersen reported that to prepare the "full and complete historical accountings, audits, and reconciliations" would cost

$280 million. Unsurprisingly, Andersen and the government reached a compromise: Andersen audited the accounts for a twenty-year period (1972–1992), at a cost of $21 million (a price tag that was nearly double their initial estimate for that twenty-year year audit).[3]

In the face of these egregious failures on the part of the BIA, Native activist Eloise Cobell filed a historic lawsuit in 1996. *Cobell v. Salazar* charged the federal government with breach of trust and demanded acknowledgment, action, and financial redress on behalf of nearly three hundred thousand individual Indian money account holders. Recognizing that the fiduciary responsibility could be astronomical should Cobell win the lawsuit, the federal government quickly moved to establish a date—31 December 2006—beyond which lawsuits could no longer be brought in these matters. On 28 December 2006, just three days before the date that would limit federal liability, the Nez Perce Tribe filed a class-action lawsuit conjointly with eleven other tribes to demand a "full and complete [accounting] from the federal government for hundreds of tribal trust fund accounts worth billions of dollars."[4] *Nez Perce Tribe, et al. v. Kempthorne, et al.* joined hundreds of similar suits, all seeking to hold a paternalistic federal entity to fair and just standards.

These cases have their roots in a succession of disastrous policies by which the federal government has attempted to manage its relationship with Native peoples. Chief among these infamous policies was the Dawes General Allotment Act of 1887. The Nez Perces were among the first to be subjected to that law. The Dawes Act intended to expropriate Natives of their lands, extinguish tribal governments, and transform tribal cultures into disaggregated, atomized, individual citizens. Funds related to the sale and transfer of lands under Dawes were, of course, to be held in trust by federal guardians on the presumption that Natives would be incompetent managers of their properties and would be unable to keep track of where and how their monies had been invested and disbursed. The irony is too apparent to require comment.

The ironic mode, in fact, seems the appropriate voice in which to analyze the events associated with the application of the Dawes Act on the Nez Perce Reservation that are the subject of this book.

Here I have sought to bring together the topics of Native sovereignty, which has its roots in land, citizenship, and control of cultural property; the bungled federal attempts to erase that sovereign identity; the archive of records of that interaction; and the historical accounts drawn from those archives that have narrated the encounter.

Because the matter of federal attempts to manage Indian tribes and monies antedated the Dawes Act, this book begins *in medias res*. Although the federal government attempted to close the issue at the end of 2006, lawsuits such as *Nez Perce v. Kempthorne* insisted that such a closure was premature. Even should *Cobell v. Salazar* reach a settlement, these supplementary suits, which intend to pursue a full accounting and a full settlement, will keep the matter open. Hence, this book lacks a formal ending. In place of a tidy narrative resolution, I have offered after-words and after-images, in the anticipation that here, as in the lawsuits currently active, the Nez Perces will have—and should have—the final word(s).

Acknowledgments

This book owes its existence to a network of generous researchers, archivists, and friends. Three deserve special thanks, for they shared with me large numbers of primary sources that they had gathered and processed. At the very beginning of this undertaking, while I was still thinking of this book simply as a study of Jane Gay's photographs, Elizabeth Jacox loaned me four boxes of files she had amassed over several years of researching Gay's biography. Later, as Alice Fletcher entered the picture, Caroline Carley shared with me her notes and transcriptions of Fletcher's nearly illegible field diaries, and these became the foundation of my further forays into the little books collected in series 10, box 12A at the National Anthropological Archives. As I began to try to locate Nez Perce–authored documents in the archive, Dennis Baird furnished many letters and documents that he had gathered in his own research expeditions. To him I owe special thanks, for he is a superb researcher, archivist, and activist.

From early on, Joanna Scherer has been a gracious mentor and colleague. Our acquaintance began as I worked as a visiting senior scholar at the National Museum of Natural History under her sponsorship. During that icy Washington DC winter, she also housed and fed me and drove me to and from the archives, and in the process of our conversations, she taught me a great deal about the politics and

ACKNOWLEDGMENTS

processes of photographic collection and conservation. Since that time she has several times furnished crucial missing pieces of documentary evidence upon which my arguments have depended. Her student interns Marie Wisecup, Kayleigh Stack, and Abigail Yerxa have searched out and copied several key documents for my use.

A network of archivists and librarians deserve thanks for their wisdom and patience. Among the many others, I want to name several who exemplified the ideal balance between protecting their collections and guiding curious scholars through them. The librarians at the University of Idaho special collections located dozens of obscure records, almost as if by magic. Carolyn Bowler, who was the photographic curator of the Idaho State Historical Society during most of the time I worked on this project, was immensely helpful in contributing her expert knowledge about the Jane Gay photographic collection. At the Peabody Museum, Susan Haskell and Pat Kervick were wise guides; and as I was finishing the documentation of the book, Pat Kervick generously helped me with citational forms. At the National Archives in Seattle, Patty McNamee's guidance and expertise were invaluable. At the National Anthropological Archives, Jeannie Sklar, Vyrtis Thomas, and Stephanie Christensen also provided wise guidance. At the University of Washington, Nicolette Bromberg was a valuable interlocutor about northwest-area photographs and photographers.

Under the auspices of the federal Sabbatical in the Parks Program, I was able to spend several months living and working in the Spalding area at the Nez Perce National Historical Park Archives. The hospitality and warmth of the staff there are remarkable, and I am especially grateful to Marc Blackburn, then-director Gary Somers, and Jason Lyon for welcoming me into their work spaces and patiently answering my questions. It would be difficult for me to find enough ways to thank Robert Applegate for his friendship, his wisdom, his patience, his local knowledge, and his generous help. Robert allowed me to learn by doing: under his guidance I prepared the catalog for a new accession to the park that contained hundreds of records pertinent to this study. Douglas Nash, the donor of that collection, has kindly given me permission to reproduce and quote from some of these materials, although access to the collection is still restricted.

As I worked at the park, I became friends with many Nez Perce tribal members. Two of them—scholars and archivists—have been especially central to this book. Diane Mallickan's commitment to recovering the history of Nez Perces is well demonstrated in her publications and in her work with the Northwest Historical Manuscripts Series; Diane was and is also a generous friend who has shared with me her family collections, her photographs, and her understanding of Starr Maxwell and James Stuart. Nakia Williamson-Cloud has an artist's eye and a historian's encyclopedic knowledge. His mental archive of Native photographs left me in awe and repeatedly brought me back to him for advice, for identifications, and for good conversation. He, too, was willing to share with me his own family's photographic archive; many of these images have enriched the book.

Other Idaho friends contributed the significant resources of friendship, hospitality, and insightful conversation: Louise Barber, another appreciator of Jane Gay's work, and Lynn N. Baird, librarian and archivist extraordinaire, deserve special mention. Other friends inhabit the virtual world but have nevertheless been marvelous interlocutors: Gene Eastman, a cartographer and scholar, and Dick Storch, photo historian and collector, added invaluable last-minute materials to this work.

Closer to my academic home, at a particularly difficult time in my conceiving how to unite the various threads of this study, Maureen Konkle served as a most helpful interlocutor. Her work inspired me, and she directed me to several foundational studies. Lisa Logan likewise offered humor and warm support. I have been particularly fortunate to have advised dozens of talented graduate students over the years I have worked on this book, and several of them have cut their archival teeth by helping me transcribe Fletcher's very bad handwriting. For aid in this regard I thank Deborah Tokars, Melisa Klimaszewski, and Jason Homer. Jake Mattox got to know the *Christian Register* better than he could have imagined. Ben Chapin managed my bibliography with good humor and great professionalism. Special

ACKNOWLEDGMENTS

thanks go to Lisa M. Thomas, advisee, friend, editor, and scholar, who copyedited and proofed this book.

Working with the University of Nebraska Press on this book has been a pleasure. Matt Bokovoy and Elisabeth Chretien patiently and promptly responded to my e-mail questions, Sabrina Stellrecht shepherded the project through the production process, and Sally Antrobus edited the manuscript with a clear eye, a marvelous sense of humor, and a solid understanding of alterations that would make the text more reader-friendly.

Funding to support this research came from a number of generous grants from academic senate funds of the University of California, San Diego, and from the Schlesinger Library on the History of Women in America, the National Park Service's Sabbatical in the Parks Program, and the National Endowment for the Humanities.

As always, members of my own family became part of the dense network of emotional and intellectual support upon which I have always depended. Jennifer Hoffman was a constant voice of rationality and was always happy to try to track down the most arcane sources. Ashley Hoffman and Amy Hoffman, both visual artists, were my travel companions and research assistants. Ashley's photographic skills and Amy's eye for the landscape have informed every page of this book. Gary Hoffman, my fellow traveler, map guru, guide, and patient partner, read drafts, wrangled computer programs, took photographs, asked questions, and, at the end, patiently and uncomplainingly delinked footnotes. He is my North Star.

The Allotment Plot

Introduction
Allotment and Nimiipuu Survivance

In late June 1890, during the second of four summers devoted to assigning lands in severalty to the Nez Perces, Alice C. Fletcher, the government allotting agent, posed for a photograph with Chief Joseph and James Stuart, her interpreter.[1] Segments of this image, shown here in full in figure 1, often illustrate accounts of the allotment era in general histories of the American West and of Native America, for the photograph gives visual form to the major assumptions undergirding the Dawes General Allotment Act of 1887, a piece of legislation Fletcher had helped to conceptualize.[2] In this photograph a Native leader who had recently engaged the United States in an armed encounter stands in an open field conversing with a middle-aged white woman. A second Native man, Stuart, kneels, facing Fletcher. The encounter seems to be civil, perhaps even friendly. Joseph looks benignly at Fletcher; Stuart has assumed a pose that suggests submissiveness. Both men wear western working attire, not fringed buckskins and feather headdresses. The image implicitly promises a lasting peace, wherein this woman, a federal agent, might stand in a place that had recently been a killing field, discussing with a revered Native leader the policy she imagined would transform him and his followers into citizen-farmers.

The static, even statuesque, triangulated poses of the three belie the image's underlying titillation. Its nineteenth-century viewers

FIG. 1. "Chief Joseph with Alice C. Fletcher, Gov't Allotting Agent when the Nez Perce Reservation was thrown open. James Stewart kneeling," by E. Jane Gay, ca. 26 June 1890. ISHS 3771, Idaho State Historical Society Library and Archives.

would have remembered vividly Joseph's part in one of the era's last armed Native resistances. A photograph of this hero so dressed, apparently listening attentively to a diminutive white woman, reinforced his widely circulated announcement at the close of the Nez Perce War in October 1877 that he would "fight no more forever."[3] Yet Nimiipuu accounts of the end of the war establish otherwise.[4] And as details in E. Jane Gay's photograph make clear, his well-known declaration did not signal a capitulation.[5] Joseph carries a blanket and wears his long hair braided with an upswept forelock, details signaling his resistance to assimilation. Although Stuart kneels, he does so not in submission either to Joseph or to Fletcher but because the photographer had posed him thus, "to break the line of 3 standing."[6] Indeed, the two men represent generational and ideological divisions that presented Fletcher with great challenges, for Stuart exemplified what a Nez Perce man might become, given the rights of citizenship, the advantages of white education, and the franchise, while Joseph, unwilling to be transformed, embodied efficacious nonviolent resistance.

Allotment to the Nez Perces, one of the first tribal groups to be subjected to a policy designed to eliminate Native polities and cultures, proceeded on the assumption that their violent resistance was a thing of the past.[7] Such presumptive tranquility meant a woman could be appointed to oversee the legal imperatives enabling the United States to consolidate its continental land holdings at the end of the nineteenth century. Alice Fletcher and Jane Gay, her ad hoc expedition photographer, came into the field armed not with rifles and swords but with pen and ink, maps and tracing paper, cameras and tripods. "Tender violence," Laura Wexler's apt phrase, might thus describe Fletcher's tasks, but the label should not be taken to diminish their force, for "the Empress of all the Indias," as Gay playfully called Fletcher, was fully backed by the will of the federal government she represented.[8]

Jane Gay accompanied Fletcher into the field during each of four summers between 1889 and 1892 and made several hundred photographs of the allotment. Unlike the men who pursued the so-called grand endeavors of salvage ethnography and photography who were her contemporaries, Gay did not make images to preserve a disappearing culture.[9] Rather, she documented a federal policy of enforced pacification. Thus she made few photographs of traditionally dressed Nimiipuu celebrating ceremonial occasions or riding in parades. She sited her images in the mountainous and forested Idaho landscape, terrain presumptively awaiting the farmer's plow and the developer's axe; she took photographs of tidy log cabins surrounded by fenced pastures, or of surveyors, chainmen, and clients standing in fenced fields.[10] In each case the fences demonstrate that the rectilinear logic of equivalent land ownership could rationalize even this rugged place.

Alice Fletcher sent a print of the photograph of herself, Stuart, and Joseph with a letter to her close friend Electa Sanderson Dawes, the wife of the senator for whom the Allotment Act was named. Of it she wrote, in part, "Chief Joseph was here for the first time since the Nez Perce War. . . . Equally accountable and punishable . . . he presented a most interesting blending of the old and the new—all of which I greatly enjoyed. . . . He is yet in the prime of life and full of power to work but I doubt if he is ever able to go much further in progressive ideas. He has done well and is a hero in many ways."[11] In this letter, as in so many others she wrote from the field, Fletcher intended to demonstrate the challenges of her work. She emphasizes the degree to which the "progressive ideas" she promulgated might be impeded by her clients' loyalties to "the old," but she betrays no doubt of succeeding in her tasks: to divide the Nez Perce Reservation into equivalent plots of land and to assign those plots to individual owners who would "work" the land and develop skills of capitalist production and mercantile exchange appropriate to their transformed status as enfranchised citizens. Her letter is one of tens of thousands of documents that record and justify the transformation. These documents, preserved in state-sponsored archives, join with and are supplanted by cultural artifacts that make a similar argument. The feather headdresses, armaments, and items of traditional dress deposited for anthropological study in public and privately sponsored museums implied that their makers had abandoned their traditional lifeways to embrace civilization.

In Gay's photograph we might well mark those who are not visible: the photographer, of course, remains apart from the image she has made, her presence not even suggested by a shadow. Because she is effaced, she assumes the silent authority of the documentarian. Fletcher may stand alone, but she stands for an invisible network of interested federal, church, and academic institutions that supported allotment. As well, she stands for, or represents, a number of powerful white women who had been involved in articulating and effecting national policies of expansion, racial identification, and political consolidation, even though they themselves did not yet enjoy the franchise. Photographs, of course, can capture only the instant of their making. They obscure the events that preceded them and do not betray what will happen in the moments to follow. In June 1890, for example, Joseph did not live in Kamiah, where this image was made, but on the Colville Reservation, two hundred miles to the northwest. Only recently had he and his followers returned from an eight-year internment in Indian Territory, their release the result of his years-long public relations campaign. Although he stands with his interlocutors in an open field within the Nez Perce Reservation, he continued to refuse to accede to allotment. Just days after Gay made this photograph, Joseph led the war procession at a Fourth of July celebration at Fort Lapwai and then returned to Nespelem. Until the end of his life he continued to demand that the United States honor its agreement to secure the Wallowa Valley to his people.

Although his posture belies it, James Stuart also embodied significant power, for he translated the negotiations by which allotment proceeded. He mediated between Fletcher and the local agent, between Fletcher and her clients, and among disparate groups of Nimíipuu. By all accounts Stuart unfailingly supported Fletcher in her work, and because she trusted him, he was able to accomplish many of his own aims without his employer's notice. After allotment closed, Stuart became a powerful political figure who used his diplomatic acumen and his considerable knowledge of federal policy to establish procedures and programs by which the Nez Perces began to reclaim lands, monies, and cultural patrimonies that allotment had attempted to extinguish.

In this study I demonstrate how, by skillful resistances and negotiations, the Nez Perces effected the modification of allotment policies on their home ground and, despite the law's dismal effects on their lands and peoples, continued to exist as a sovereign body. I analyze the major goals of allotment, which sought to transform and absorb Native lands, peoples, and histories. I examine the means by which the U.S. government intended to realize those goals, exemplified in Alice Fletcher's efforts; and I show how and why she failed to accomplish these tasks. In so doing I depend upon a broad archive, comprising not only the documents buttressing this federal policy but an unruly assemblage of oral, performative, and documentary sources, testimonies often occluded by state power. Thus, in place of the standard historical and biographical narratives about how allotment proceeded in northwestern Idaho, I present a different story—indeed, many different stories—about this policy and its effects. I construct a multivocal counter-narrative challenging the standard history of national consolidation and modifying its most recent versions that foreground the involvement of white women in the operations of so-called manifest domesticity.[12]

In *The Allotment Plot* I extend the work of scholars such as J. Diane Pearson, who, in *The Nez Perces in the Indian Territory: Nimiipuu Survival*, has begun to extend Nez Perce history beyond its supposed end in 1877, and who, as a part of that project, asserts the importance of Nimiipuu ownership of land and stories, two key components of sovereign identity.[13] My study begins where Pearson's concludes, with the initial stages of allotment between 1889 and 1892. Of that policy Vine Deloria Jr. observes, "Nearly all Indian writers adopt the interpretation that *the [Dawes] act itself* allotted the reservations. . . . [but a]lmost all of the tribes who made agreements with the United States secured some additional legal rights, generally unique to their own situation, in these negotiations."[14] Following Deloria, I assert that on the Nez Perce Reservation, people—Native and white, engaged with one another in active and occluded encounters—accomplished allotment. Those who administered the policy followed an abstract theoretical plan. They quickly found themselves to be in active negotiation with Nez Perces, whose interventions forced them to modify their plans and the policy itself in ways that would recognize specific details of Nez Perce history, territory, and culture.

Allotment, like many other federal Indian policies, was meant to apply to all Native peoples, sovereign nations whom the Marshall decisions of the 1830s had lumped together as undifferentiated Indian wards of the nation. By focusing on a single case study, I implicitly argue that the law was not and could not be so generally applied, and that its ongoing revisions and ultimate failure resulted from specific Native interventions. As I demonstrate, the unique circumstances following the Nez Perce War of 1877 led the federal government to target the Nez Perce peoples as one of the first groups who would undergo allotment. Having instigated and helped theorize the Dawes General Allotment Act, Alice C. Fletcher left the legislative chambers of Washington DC and personally supervised the allotment on the Nez Perce Reservation. The story of how she attempted to do so exemplifies the marvelously ironic circumstance in which a theorist actually attempted to carry out the policy she had helped to conceptualize. Fletcher worked within a specific place and interacted with actual human subjects whose needs and wishes she and her fellow legislators and reformers had resolutely ignored as they drafted the Allotment Act. Fletcher herself declared to the Board of Indian Commissioners in 1885 her disdain for Native reactions to the idea of allotment: "The work must be done for them whether they approve or not." The Nez Perces did not approve, and as Fletcher strove mightily to do the work "for [or despite] them," they negotiated wisely, resisted strategically, and thus secured additional legal rights for themselves, in the process forcing her to make revisions to the law that lessened some of its negative impacts on their specific situation.[15]

In presenting this account of allotment, I take the idea of intersubjectivity to its widest application and endeavor to account for the multiple agencies, groups, and people whose interests were at stake in allotment. These include federal and state partisans who attempted to use the policy to consolidate land holdings and to further business interests in the Pacific Northwest, church interests, private networks of women reformers whose assumptions and interests determined allotment's ideological valences, intellectual proponents of anthropological theory, and builders of academic programs of study whose ideas seemed to justify the new policy and whose institutional identities were bolstered thereby. The records of those interest groups constitute an archival complex I call "memory palaces": state-sponsored libraries, archives, and museums and the similar privately funded holdings of university-affiliated anthropological museums, libraries, and collections, all of which had their institutional identities enhanced by the documents produced and the artifacts gathered as a part of allotment's application.[16]

Allotment's Failure

In 1873 Edward P. Smith, commissioner of Indian affairs opined, "Where everything is held in common . . . individual progress is rendered very improbable."[17] As his remarks suggest, discussions of Native assimilation were ongoing long before the passage of the Dawes General Allotment Act in 1887. That law sought to separate Native peoples from the land base that comprised their sovereign status as a precondition to their becoming enfranchised citizens. Communally held lands were to be divided into standard plots and an equivalent amount of land was to be assigned to each recipient. These potential owners, however, first had to fulfill a twenty-five-year period of apprentice citizenship, during which time the federal government would hold their properties in trust. Ultimately, with full title to their land, these allottees would also receive the franchise. Proponents of the legislation claimed that it benefited Native clients by giving them legal title to their lands; at the same time, it reduced the size of Indian reservations, opening them to commercial development and to railroad routes that would bind east coast to west.[18] Properties that remained after members of a given tribe had all received allotments would be publicly sold and the profits given to the tribe. As Loring Benson Priest makes clear, "the fact remained that undisputed title to a definite portion of land was to be gained only by surrendering any claim to the rest."[19] Allotment decimated Native lands. For example, more than 70 percent of the Nez Perce Reservation land, as it had been defined by the Treaty of 1863, passed from tribal control, reducing the total acreage of the reservation from 756,960 acres to 175,026 acres by 1895.[20]

The numbers of acres lost to allotment, how much money changed hands in the process, and the means by which Natives became citizen-owners of lands on which their ancestors had lived for centuries are vexed and dismal topics. These abuses happened because the federal government approved a law designed to extinguish entire cultures. Under the alibi of enlightened and charitable reeducation, the Dawes Act stipulated procedures for merging individualized Native subjects into the American body politic and erasing their histories while documenting the entire process in state-sponsored institutions of memory. Moreover, the law accorded with the most advanced scientific thinking of the day. Everyone stood to benefit: Native peoples would receive legal rights and the franchise, the

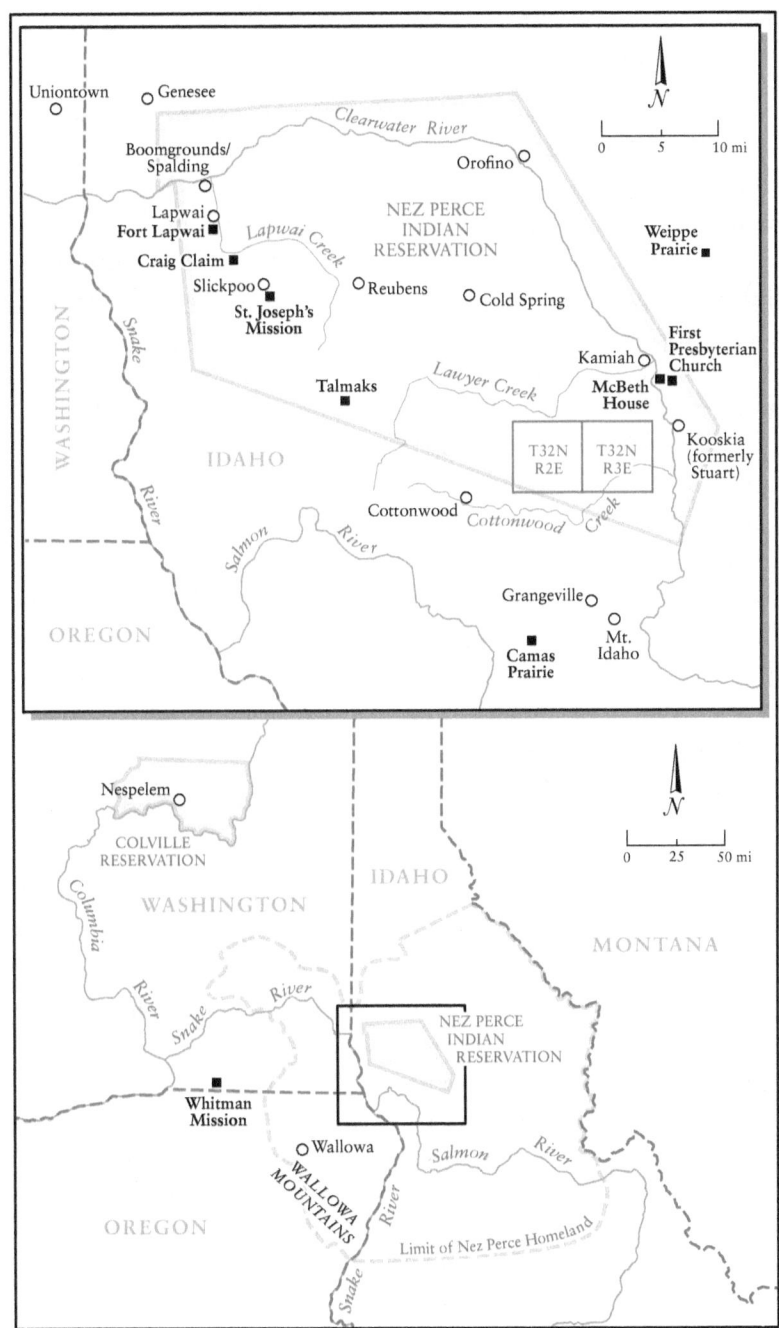

FIG. 2. Nez Perce country

nation would gain a broadened tax base and assume control of lands that had heretofore constituted uncomfortable *imperia in imperium*, and students of the human sciences would find their developmental narrative confirmed as they watched Native cultures progress from savagery to civilization. Most happily, the process did not call for violence and loss of life, for bureaucrats, missionaries, educators, and other representatives of disinterested charity would ensure its fair and rational administration.

Allotment failed in its actual application because the bureaucratic imaginary did not match the local histories, places, or peoples it intended to transform. This mismatch called forth a series of clarifications, modifications, and amendments.[21] For several years before the Dawes General Allotment Act became law, legislators, lobbyists, and reformers discussed, debated, resisted, and revised its details.[22] During the half century of its application, Congress and the Office of Indian Affairs continued to amend it.[23] Originally, for example, the law had specified that allottees were to receive plots of land equivalent in size; it gave no heed to the land's fertility, location, or mineral content. Almost immediately, legal stipulations sought to correct the error and to account for the different potential value of equivalent parcels of land. Allottees whose lands would support only grazing, for example, received larger allotments than those whose lands supported farming. Lands enriched by mineral deposits, with access to water for irrigation or transport, or that abounded in fish and game quickly disappeared from the roster of available properties. As Acting Commissioner of Indian Affairs A. C. Belt informed Alice Fletcher early in the process, "[M]ineral lands should not be allotted to Indians. The allotment of such lands is not contemplated by the severalty act. . . . The Indians, under their present title, have no right to work mines, or in any manner to dispose of minerals found within the Reservation." Almost as an afterthought, Belt added, "It would be well to report the description of all mineral lands found during your work, for the information of this office."[24]

Of course, equivalency of land varied according to the recipient's race. According to William T. Hagan, "If the land were valuable for timber or minerals, the government's policy was for the Indians to surrender it for White exploitation; however, the sum received by the Indians in exchange for giving up their rights in the land was estimated in terms of its use as agricultural land, a markedly lower figure than if it had been estimated in terms of its timber and mineral resources."[25] Initially the Dawes Act stipulated that only heads of families were to receive land. In 1891, however, it was amended to include all Native men, women, and children. The twenty-five-year probationary period, during which apprentice citizens were to farm the land before they could own it outright, was shortened almost immediately (first in 1891, and repeatedly thereafter) to allow Native allottees to lease their lands to white settlers.[26] In 1906 the Burke Act abbreviated the period of probation and allowed "competent" allottees to sell their lands. Competency, like equivalence, rested on racist assumptions. Federally appointed commissions routinely held that allottees who possessed a portion of white blood were competent — that is, able to alienate their property; they frequently required those whose blood was unmixed to fulfill the twenty-five-year probation.

By presenting a detailed study of how and why allotment failed on a single reservation, I demonstrate how policies imagined within the mid-nineteenth-century legislative chamber were challenged by specific lands and lifeways. Numerous local details of topography, geography, history, and custom elicited ongoing amendments designed to adjust the Dawes Act to the Nez Perce Reservation. For example, although the principles of rectilinear survey sufficed to apportion lands on the Great Plains, surveyors in northwestern Idaho devised new methods for mapping, dividing, describing, and evaluating the high plateaus, deep forested canyons, riverine valleys, and mineral-bearing mountains of the territory they mapped. Focusing my study on a single reservation, I demonstrate in detail how Fletcher and her workers sought to apply the law and how the Nez Perces aided in the application of, negotiated, and resisted the policy. On the Nez Perce Reservation allotment did not eliminate tribal government, nor did it expunge Nimiipuu culture; it did not, as its more sanguine proponents imagined it would, absorb Nez Perces into the surrounding communities of whites. It failed because of the active resistance of those it intended to subjugate. Long acquainted with the habits and vices of white settlers, they used the occasion of allotment to settle previous boundary disputes, to demand the payment of long-ignored treaty payouts, to oust a corrupt agent, to hire qualified school personnel, to retain sovereign control of tribal membership, and to preserve important ceremonial sites. They did so by sending petitions, ambassadors, and written appeals to Washington DC; by exchanging cultural artifacts and stories for advantageous land concessions; and by simple, stubborn, and sustained resistance. Above all, they kept their own records, wrote their own histories, and used those records as the basis of their ongoing negotiations with the federal government over lands and unresolved concessions long after Alice C. Fletcher had left the area.

The Gendered Work of Domestic Colonialism

Allotment followed the presumptive military conquest and containment of Native cultures with a program of benevolent pacification and assimilation. As Eric N. Olund asserts, such "ostensibly liberal" policies effectively "erased colonialism from American political discourse."[27] Yet investigations of such colonial aggressions, topics that now occupy the attention of scholars engaged in post-nationalist American Studies, have focused largely on similar means and modes of conquest being pursued extra-nationally, even as the evidence of their failure became amply apparent at home. Such post-nationalist work resists a dominant narrative of westward expansion and Manifest Destiny as a means of drawing attention to other vectors of settlement and conquest.[28] In so doing, as Michael A. Elliott argues, it has "shifted attention away from the ongoing colonial relationships between the U.S. and the American Indian tribes within its borders."[29] Despite its announced intent to resist "the teleological narrative that imperialism tells about itself, the inexorable westward march of empire," post-nationalist scholarship has not questioned the markers it claims to resist, markers with teleologies barely hidden in such phrases as "the closing of the frontier" and "the last Indian wars."[30] Yet as Philip J. Deloria has demonstrated in *Indians in Unexpected Places*, such contrivances of historical narration have occluded ongoing acts of violence against indigenous peoples. "Pacification," the policy that followed Wounded Knee, Deloria claims, "laid the cultural conditions for the new expectations of the early twentieth century. Harmlessness, ... assimilation replacing Indian national distinctiveness, a white American national memory laced through with conquest, ... added up to either complete domination ... or a complete freedom to ignore Indian people altogether" (*IUP*, 50).

For all its strengths, post-nationalist scholarship assumes a de facto consolidated national identity guaranteed by military conquest, land cessions, and assimilation/erasure of Native polities.[31] It fails to account for the fact that Indian nations did not, in fact, yield their sovereignty, either as a result of war or because of less bellicose means of legal pacification. Thus the nation whose post-histories preoccupy current scholars might be said to be an imaginary construct, for as Arjun Appadurai observes, the nation is "the ideological alibi of the territorial state."[32] All-inclusive USAmerican nationhood, founded on a consolidated and contiguous geography, has precariously maintained its existence in an ongoing set of policies—the Indian Reorganization Act, termination, relocation, and Self-Determination—that have attempted to perfect allotment's original aim of totally assimilating Native nations.[33]

Post-national scholarship has also given close attention to the cultural work of gendered subjects, most notably for this book in the concept of "manifest domesticity," technologies of benevolent conquest that expose the "spatial and political interdependence of home and empire."[34] Here I exemplify, extend, and challenge this concept by attending to local, specific details connecting domestic conquest to gendered ideals. I investigate the precise place and the exact conditions under which the putative conquest occurred, and I mark the limits of its efficacy in the face of Native resistance. Because I understand allotment to have been neither an inevitability nor an objective and impersonally applied policy, I have tried to attend to the ongoing tensions that marked Fletcher's and Gay's involvement in projects of colonial domestication. As Jacki Thompson Rand

[13]

argues, colonialism is not the rational, coherent, and effective instrument described in theoretical formulations such as manifest domesticity, for such accounts "[exaggerate] historic colonial power and [grant] it a consistency and uniformity of purpose and action that is assumed rather than an accurate reflection of local conditions." In this study I take "local conditions" to include the presumptions about gender that guided those who theorized and applied allotment in Idaho. Rand continues, "Colonizers were exploitive and destructive, but they also exhibited anxieties, limitations, and inadequacies that interfered with the rational plan. It was not necessarily the best and brightest who peopled the front lines of expansion, carried out colonial administration, fought tribes, and implemented policies. Colonizers could be dependent on the people they aspired to overcome, and even, at times, at their complete mercy."[35]

In this book I show that resistant Nimiipuu recognized and exploited Fletcher's "anxieties" as an aspiring ethnological scholar and "limitations" as a woman holding a federal appointment. As a professional anthropologist Fletcher often delimited her scholarly work by relating it to her gender. She published a series of monographs about the Omaha peoples that bore titles such as "Personal Studies of Indian Life. Politics and Pipe-Dancing." In such a title the topic — politics — is conventionally masculine, yet Fletcher overtly claimed to be offering a "personal" and feminized insight into the issue. Similarly, she approached many of her Nimiipuu informants through family networks and on the basis of personal friendships. She made womanly identity foundational to her allotting work, as well, for she refused bribes of money and offers of political preferment. She thus seemed to be a welcome antidote to the "not necessarily . . . best and brightest" administrators who had preceded her.[36] Yet Fletcher's objectivity was compromised, for she skillfully exploited private networks of religious and financial backers to serve her own personal and professional aspirations.

In its conception and in its application, allotment, a technology of domestic colonialism, depended upon dominant cultural understandings of gender. Apparently unaware of the irony of her words, Alice Fletcher described allotment as a policy meant "to bring . . .

manhood" to a group who had recently been figured as ferocious warriors, as recorded in E. Jane Gay's *Choup-nit-ki* (C, 113). In *A Stranger in Her Native Land*, Fletcher's biographer Joan Mark called her "Mother to the Indians."[37] Fletcher presented herself as the embodiment of feminine probity, an intentional self-fashioning most apparent in figure 3, a portrait she commissioned and gave to the Peabody Museum in 1889, just before she departed for Idaho.[38] E. H. Miller's crayon drawing presents Fletcher, then fifty-one years old, as a slightly chubby girl with a firmly set chin, her neck swathed in feminine ruffles. This diffidence and self-effacement she strategically balanced with a gentle but determinedly firm public presence, suggested by her rigid posture, regal bearing, and formal attire documented in a second portrait, figure 4, made about ten years later in Barcelona.[39] The combination of feminine modesty and masculine determination recommended her to a broad and supportive network of religious donors, scientific professionals, and feminine reformers. She held the appointment of special Indian agent, a position commonly awarded to white men, for which she received a handsome salary. And if the documentary record is accurate, she approached her tasks with a manly determination and confidence. For example, Edson Briggs, Fletcher's surveyor, recalled that when she presented the details of allotment to the Nez Perces gathered at Kamiah, she "talked to the Indians 'like a man and a brother'" (C, 105).

Nor was she manifestly domestic. Fletcher, Gay, and other women (especially Presbyterian missionary Susan McBeth) who furthered the policies of civilization on the Nez Perce Reservation strategically and publicly detached themselves from domestic duties and carved out spaces for themselves as legislators, thinkers, teachers, scholars, and writers. They assigned the minutiae generally thought to be women's province to lesser agents—often racialized men—who attended to the tasks of cooking and laundry, of translating, transcribing, and record keeping. As both Fletcher and McBeth wrote their ethnographic and linguistic studies they depended heavily on Native men who acted as informants, translators, and interpreters; rarely did they credit these men as collaborators.[40]

FIG. 3. (*above*) Crayon drawing of Alice C. Fletcher, 1888, by E. H. Miller. Courtesy of the Peabody Museum of Archaeology and Ethnology, Harvard University. 88-56-10/84070, Digital file #60741949.

FIG. 4. (*right*) Alice C. Fletcher, Carte de visite, ca. 1900, by Antonio and Emilio Fernandez of the Napoleon Company, Barcelona. Ms. 4558, Box 33, PACF, National Anthropological Archives, Smithsonian Institution.

The instability of gendered identity characterizes Jane Gay's epistolary accounts of allotment as well. Here she figures herself both as a masculine Photographer and a feminized Cook. She refers to Alice Fletcher in similarly fluid terms as "Her Majesty" and as "the Allotting Agent," a gender-neutral identity.[41] The various performances involved in discussing, enforcing, and resisting the gendered ideals of allotment offer a striking critique of what we think domesticity means, and can demonstrate that gender is a disciplinary force, tactically claimed, inconsistently manifested, and easily disavowed and that its performances are situationally determined.

By foregrounding gender as a crucial component of the "local conditions" of allotment, I demonstrate that manifest domesticity's effect was constrained and, at best, limited. We know that allotment failed; but the story of how its failure resulted from the methods of its application—in specific places and times by gendered agents with multiple and sometimes conflicting alliances—is a complicated one. That study perforce recognizes the importance of indigenous resistance. Long before Alice Fletcher stepped from the Northern Pacific Railroad palace car that brought her to northwest Idaho in May 1889, Nimiipuu men and women had lived cheek by jowl with missionaries who had applied brutal force to elicit their compliance. They had jostled with settler colonists intent on appropriating their lands and minerals; they had studied at white boarding schools and entered into business relationships with white partners; they had applied their facility in the technologies of legal discourse, reading, writing, and argumentation to the cause of resisting any further diminution of their sovereign cultural identities. They were not surprised by, nor did they yield to, Fletcher's plans.[42]

Allotment's Agents

On 17 April 1889, the U.S. secretary of the interior appointed Alice Fletcher to oversee the allotment of lands within the Nez Perce Reservation.[43] Fletcher has been characterized by Siobhan Senier as "easily one of the most influential—and dangerous—people in the history of allotment."[44] Her appointment as special Indian agent was the logical result of her relentless pursuit of affiliative support. Because her father died when she was but an infant, Fletcher grew up in a series of ad hoc families. Thus she learned early in life to rely on networks of friends and, later, colleagues.[45] As a young woman she worked for an extended period as a governess and companion to the daughters of Claudius Buchanan Conant, a Brooklyn merchant. After his daughters were grown, Conant supported Fletcher financially until she was well over thirty years old. When he died in 1877, Fletcher, who had not married, was forced to find work to support herself.

In New York she joined Sorosis, the first organization of professional women in the United States; with the help of members of that group she launched a career as a public lecturer on topics related to the nascent sciences of American archaeology and anthropology. She sought information to supplement her lectures from F. W. Putnam, the newly appointed head of Harvard's Peabody Museum of American Archaeology and Ethnology, who became her lifelong mentor.[46] On the lecture circuit she met Suzette La Flesche and Thomas Henry Tibbles, who in 1879 were touring to protest federal attempts to relocate the Ponca peoples to Indian Territory. This encounter suggested to Fletcher a new field for her endeavors. She could pursue relationships with Native people rather than depend on Putnam for all of her information; living among them in affiliative relationships, she could gather such information herself, a research method now known as participant observation. In 1881 she made her first visit to the Omahas, and over the next several years she established close ties with the powerful La Flesche family, members of which gave her valuable ethnological data that established her as an eminent early anthropologist. Francis La Flesche, brother of Suzette, became Fletcher's lifelong collaborator. For her part, Fletcher advocated for the Omahas in the capital, aiding them to secure title to their lands and to resist removal upon the occasion of Nebraska's incipient statehood. She joined several Washington DC reform groups, including the Indian Rights Association and Women's Indian Association, organizations that wielded a powerful influence in shaping federal allotment policy. Because of her activism, the secretary of the interior appointed her to supervise the partitioning and allotment of Omaha and Winnebago lands. Fletcher also wrote a massive federal *Report on Indian Education and Civilization*, a work Mark describes as "a comprehensive survey of United States government and Indian relations, past and present" (SNL, 115). The *Report* established her as an expert in Indian affairs.

By 1885 Fletcher had begun to investigate the uses of photography in ethnographic research. She published a short essay in *Science*, "Composite Portraits of American Indians," based on Francis Galton's techniques of eugenic photography, a system of superimposing multiple facial photographs to yield a visible racial or sociological typology.[47] She used photography more fully during her tenure as the planner and executor of the Bureau of Indian Affairs display at the New Orleans World's Industrial and Centennial Cotton Exposition. On that occasion she found it difficult to acquire the scale models of Omaha dwellings and tribal artifacts that she had hoped to exhibit. Instead, she organized the display, "Indian Civilization," around a series of sixteen before-and-after photographs of Omaha peoples. Lacking images of the supposedly primitive past of this culture, Fletcher arranged for "her friends among the Omahas . . . to dress in old-time costumes and to be photographed showing their past customs" (Mark, SNL, 111). These surrogated images she placed in contrast to others "showing the Omahas enjoying their new way of life." While the contrasts surely demonstrated change over time, Fletcher nevertheless directed their interpretation in a series of well-attended "Noon Talks" (Mark, SNL, 114). She also distributed a booklet, *Historical Sketch of the Omaha Tribe of Indians in Nebraska*, containing engraved reproductions of several of the photographic images and summarizing her remarks. Pleased with the success of her exhibit, she "concluded to buy a photographic apparatus & learn how to take pictures & take the camera" on her next expedition to Nebraska.[48] Eventually Fletcher did learn to take photographs, but she probably never used the cumbersome equipment in the field.[49] Instead, she arranged for others to furnish her with the images she would need.

[20]

Fletcher's accumulated experience in field work, advocacy, research, and government service earned her the support of a network of powerful friends in Washington DC and led to her appointment as a special agent charged with allotting lands to the Nez Perces under provisions of the Dawes Act. Joan Mark's *A Stranger in Her Native Land* offers the fullest account to date of how Fletcher carried out that assignment. Yet Mark devotes just three of the twenty-four chapters of her book to the Nez Perce allotment.[50] In writing of her subject's work among the Nez Perces, the biographer emphasizes Fletcher's disinterested and principled application of policy, presenting her as a woman intent on "carry[ing] out her sworn duty" (176). Although I am greatly indebted to Mark's path-breaking archival work, I have found in my reading of those same records, supplemented with other primary sources related to allotment, that what Fletcher saw as her "duty" might also be described as self-interest. My interpretation of her work between 1889 and 1895 sees this pioneering woman anthropologist and activist as culpable, sometimes scheming, and certainly always partisan. I endeavor to keep in mind that she was carrying out a federal policy she and her associates had helped to theorize. Mark does not ask whether Fletcher's indebtedness to and awareness of her political, financial, and intellectual supporters shaped her actions and decisions. I show that at every moment, Fletcher was aware of the interests of her wide-ranging partisan networks. She sought to carry out the best interests of the Presbyterian Church, embodied in her mentors, William and Mary Thaw, whose money generously supported Presbyterian causes and charitable work among the Indians.[51] Following William Thaw's death in 1889, his wife made a number of direct and indirect bequests to Fletcher. She established a fund guaranteeing lifelong financial support to her friend; these monies eventually supported an endowed chair for Fletcher at Harvard University. As well, while she was in the field, Fletcher remained in close contact with her intellectual mentor, F. W. Putnam, with whom she consulted about her decisions, her research interests, and her personal life, and upon whose sponsorship her continued professional development depended. To her efforts he lent his personal tutelage and the authority of Harvard University and the Peabody Museum, giving substance to work that, because done by a woman, might have been seen as amateur dabbling.

Fletcher's friend and companion E. Jane Gay wrote the major record upon which those who have studied allotment on the Nez Perce Reservation depend. The editor of the *Red Man* described her as "a lady well known in the Army and in Washington society," yet little verifiable biographical information is available about Gay.[52] Born into a large New Hampshire family, she, like Fletcher, did not marry and lived her adult life in a series of ad hoc families. While Fletcher sought the support of powerful men, however, Gay established her closest relationships with women who, like her, were educators, social workers, and independent thinkers.[53] With Catherine Melville, she established and taught in boarding schools in Tennessee and in Kentucky, where Melville was socially connected with the family of Andrew Johnson (Lincoln's vice-president and later the seventeenth president of the United States).[54] Like Fletcher, Gay and Melville established and exploited affiliative connections in the nation's capital, where patronage was a usual means of doing business. In 1862 Melville sought employment for herself and "Miss Gay" in "writing or copying . . . *plats*, such as the Land Office or Coast Survey gives to ladies in Washington."[55] During the Civil War the two women served as volunteer nurses, and Gay later worked as a clerk in the Dead Letter office, employment she reportedly referred to as "seventeen years in the penitentiary."[56] Thus Gay had an insider's understanding of, and even contempt for, the intricacies of bureaucratic procedure. Not surprisingly, she also became connected with women involved in reform work, most notably those who styled themselves Friends of the Indian. These included Henrietta Bradley, whom Gay called "Nettie" and addressed as "N" in her correspondence. Like Gay and Fletcher, Bradley was a member of the Women's Indian Rights Association. Bradley and Gay visited Europe together three years after Catherine Melville died in 1880. In the Washington DC home where the unmarried Bradley lived with her paternal family, Gay occupied a "large room . . . specially for [her], where she had her carpenter's tools and could do her expert cabinet-making."[57]

Gay and Fletcher likely first became acquainted because they were interested in how photography could further government work.[58] Both associated with a cadre of federal workers involved in western exploration and expansion, anthropological investigations, and Indian issues. Gay's professional and avocational interests would have made her a likely candidate for Fletcher's attentions. Familiar with federal bureaucratic procedures, including those related to western territories, she was also a skilled cook, carpenter, and taxidermist. Gay's first documented relationship with Fletcher began in early 1888.[59] In a frequent correspondence over the next months it is likely (although no reliable evidence exists) that the two women agreed that Gay would learn photography and join Fletcher in the field as her photographer. In October 1888 she arrived on the Winnebago Reservation, where Fletcher was allotting lands. There, and in Washington DC during the winter of 1888–89, the two continued to discuss and experiment with the possibilities of photography.[60] Gay's relation with Fletcher was itself a participant-observer investigation, for she wrote of Fletcher's work and photographically documented her life, both during the Winnebago and Nez Perce allotments and for more than ten years to follow, as she shared Fletcher's home in Washington DC.

Fletcher's assignment on the Nez Perce Reservation did not include funding for an official photographer, probably because an increasingly parsimonious Congress had deemed such staff to be extraneous.[61] Her assignment, after all, took her to territory presumptively known through earlier federal surveys. Nevertheless, Fletcher knew the value of the visual record for documentation, for publicity, and for the anthropological researches she intended to pursue while among the Nez Perces. Gay accompanied her as a friend, a cook and companion, and as her ex officio photographer. She did not intend to assemble her photographs in large folio albums, present them to federal officials, or preserve them in national archives. Yet both women agreed that photographs had enough potential value to warrant Gay's involvement, apparently at her own expense, in the allotment project. The unofficial photographic and written documents produced by Gay became an important part of how Fletcher's nongovernmental supporters understood her work and have subsequently become a major tool for historians and scholars who seek to understand the human and intersubjective dimensions of allotment.

It could be argued that the activities of Fletcher and Gay on the Nez Perce Reservation exemplify manifest domesticity. Agents of the state, embodying its liberal promises of citizenship although themselves disfranchised, they advocated and carried forth a disastrous policy in service of an expansionist internal colonial effort. However, as I demonstrate, myriad conditions determined, directed, and limited their agency. Unmarried women lacking family support, they perforce became self-sufficient within professions that, because they were nascent, were more accepting of women—on the condition, of course, that they conform to gendered expectations. Neither Gay nor Fletcher was a women's rights woman.[62] Both, however, were part of and depended for support and promotion of their ideas on networks of women partisans. These networks were both public and overtly political, such as the women involved with various Indian rights associations and private, sentimental friendships, often with women who enjoyed personal or affiliative access to powerful men.

Nor was their work on the Nez Perce Reservation an uncontested success. Living and working among a cultural group who valued the advice of elder women, they may have found their presence and message to be more readily received.[63] Yet Nimiipuu commitment to family and culture, a loyalty uniting a group otherwise divided by factional disputes, challenged their gendered message: that allotment required a manly self-interested individualism. Fletcher and Gay also inaccurately presumed that the Nez Perces had been defeated, that they did not understand their relationship to the federal government, and that they were unwilling to accept change. Over the course of four summers, as they interacted with nearly every person who received allotted land and gathered people's family histories, they gradually modified those misconceptions and developed complex and long-lasting relationships with several of their informants. Four such Nimiipuu men, all of whom interacted regularly with Fletcher, exemplify the fact that Native people, like their white counterparts, dealt with the forces of modernity and were not "corralled on isolated and impoverished reservations [where they had] almost dropped out of history itself."[64] They, and others like them, creatively and effectively dealt with the forces of technology, the growth of industry and commerce in the Pacific Northwest, and the competitive individualization imagined by federal policy.[65]

These "modern" Indian subjects included, of course, Chief Joseph. Although he did not live on the Nez Perce Reservation, he exemplified the efficacy of principled resistance to allotment's agendas. As he demonstrated to the allotting party, a traditional partisan might nevertheless be well traveled and adept at using personal appearances, mass communication, and diplomatic negotiation to advance his causes.[66] Near Fort Lapwai Fletcher met another skillful diplomat, James Moses, who had cultivated successful working relationships with white missionaries and agency administrators. Moses presented a great threat to Fletcher because of his strategic nonalignment. Bilingual, at ease with Christian and traditional Nimiipuu alike, he had worked alongside agency personnel and thus understood the politics, patronage, and bureaucratic procedures used by whites to deal with the Nez Perces. His skills made him an adept mediator. His alliance with the agency caused Fletcher a good deal of trouble upon her arrival and established him as a formidable foe. Moses initially led the group who opposed allotment, suggesting and then helping them carry out tactics that eventually forced Fletcher to remove her base of operations to Kamiah, as far away from the agency as she could go and still remain on the reservation.

Two other Nimiipuu men, James Reubens and James Stuart, were more closely aligned with Fletcher, and she understood them to be her supporters.[67] Educated at white-sponsored schools, both were articulate, skilled translators, and popular public speakers and generally enjoyed the respect of white settlers in the area. The *Nez Perce News* described Reubens in words that would apply to Stuart as well, calling him "a representative of the higher type of Indians."[68] Their language and diplomatic skills furthered Fletcher's work. Both understood the intricacies of allotment law and exemplified the competitive self-interest Fletcher saw as characterizing allotment's subjects; nevertheless, as she came to realize, they were principled and effective advocates for their people as well. James Reubens's family had long lived among white settlers. The elder Reubens, a Nimiipuu headman and brother-in-law to Chief Joseph, had owned properties in the area of present-day Lewiston, where according to his son, "he welcomed all weary white travelers into his house and treated the strangers with great kindness. He gave that country to have a town build there, and also allowed certain whites to locate themselves along the banks of the Clearwater and take up farms."[69] As a young man Reubens became an assistant teacher at the Fort Lapwai Agency school, and during the Nez Perce War he was a translator and scout for U.S. forces. He later served as an interpreter for Nimiipuu prisoners of war at Fort Vancouver.[70]

In 1880 Reubens and two Nimiipuu Presbyterian ministers went to Indian Territory to work with the incarcerated prisoners there. Reubens had charge of the agency schools. Instrumental in gaining the release of the prisoners, he personally led an advance group of them back to Lapwai in 1883. Newspapers in Indian Territory praised him as "one of the most intelligent Indians in the Nation," noting that he had "read all the standard modern and ancient histories, as well as the biographies of our most prominent men."[71] When Fletcher arrived on the Nez Perce Reservation in 1889, Reubens was one of the first Nimiipuu she met, and during the four years that followed, he became her friend, adviser, informant, and sometime opponent. He consulted with her about allotment's meaning for his people, advocated for the sale of the surplus lands in 1895, and until his death in 1897 continued to serve as a liaison between the on-reservation Nimiipuu and those who lived at Colville.

James Stuart had been educated at the Chemawa Indian School in Oregon. He may, in fact, have heard Alice Fletcher speak there in 1886 as she was en route to Alaska. He became her interpreter and her most reliable employee. In addition to guiding and translating for Fletcher and Gay, he advised them on practical details of outdoor life, camping, and the care and feeding of draft animals. As with all such cultural intermediaries, Stuart's translations exceeded the merely linguistic. He explained tribal history, customs, and the current political situation to the allotting agent; he interpreted, as well, the motivations of her clients. He secured ethnographic interviews for Fletcher with two of her most valuable elder informants, Nancy Corbett and Kew-kew'-lu-yah (Billy Williams), who explained to her the intricacies of Nimiipuu history, culture, and political structure. Fletcher incorrectly considered Stuart to be a less independent thinker than Reubens. Although Stuart reliably supported her, he did not fully embrace the changes allotment promised to introduce into Nez Perce culture. His wife Harriet had been among those interned in Indian Territory, and he remained cognizant that allotment only deepened divisions among his people and threatened their cultural patrimonies.

After Fletcher departed the reservation in 1892, and in the three years leading to the sale of surplus lands in 1895, Stuart advocated for the land sale, arguing that it would bring an immediate infusion of much-needed cash to impoverished Nez Perces. Jane Gay reports that before 1904, Stuart was "President of the Board of Trade of the town of Stuart" (present-day Kooskia) and that he had visited Washington DC at least once to call upon the Idaho congressional delegation on behalf of the Nez Perces (C, 448). As the new century began, however, Stuart took action to alleviate the disastrous effects of allotment. Deciding that local action would yield more immediate, practical, and lasting relief than ongoing appeals for federal aid, in 1923 Stuart helped establish the Nez Perce Home and Farm Association, the nexus of a tribal council organized in 1927. The association carried out a five-year plan to reclaim Nimiipuu children, recover tribal lands that had been leased or sold to whites, and ultimately to recuperate tribal sovereignty. Its founding members, chaired by Stuart, later drafted the first tribal constitution. This group, according to tribal historian Allen P. Slickpoo, was "the Nez Perces' first permanent executive body."[72] Thus, in the last years of his life, James Stuart again became a relay point, or conduit, uniting disparate and scattered portions of the tribe under a constitution that is the present foundation of tribal sovereignty.

"[H]ow the Indians have been treated by the Whiteman"

Most of the books that recount Nez Perce history adopt the same chronological boundaries. These studies present detailed, ethnographically based accounts of a rich and powerful culture whose

INTRODUCTION

end supposedly came in 1877, when Chief Joseph and General Nelson A. Miles ceased hostilities.[73] Alvin M. Josephy's foundational *The Nez Perce Indians and the Opening of the Northwest*, for example, concludes: "With their defeat the history of the Nez Perces as an independent people came to an end."[74] To his massive 633-page history Josephy appends a ten-page "Epilogue," of which two pages summarize the subsequent history of the tribe as "a bypassed and largely ignored people" lacking the resources to join "the mainstream of American life."[75] Only recently have scholars begun systematically to investigate tribal history after 1877. J. Diane Pearson's *The Nez Perces in the Indian Territory* documents the history of members of Joseph's band who were interned in Oklahoma and subsequently returned to the Northwest.[76] Emily Greenwald's *Reconfiguring the Reservation* presents a comparative study of the Nez Perce and the Jicarilla Apache allotments. Basing her study on land records, maps, and deeds, Greenwald demonstrates that Nez Perce allottees made strategic choices of land as a way of preserving sites central to tribal culture. Her work suggests the importance of reading this history with close attention to the vast archive of allotment records but does not consider the question I seek to answer in this study: How were these choices made as a result of intersubjective negotiations between agents, both federal and tribal?

Of these published histories, only one, *Noon Nee-Me-Poo*, was written by a Nez Perce scholar. A generation before Slickpoo, however, James Reubens wrote a brief history that has been less widely circulated. In October 1880, while he was in Indian Territory, Reubens penned the following history to be placed in the cornerstone of the newly constructed Ponca Agency School. As in all the documents quoted, errors in quoted passages are precise transcriptions. In 1934 the Reubens history was reprinted with other documents in the *Chronicles of Oklahoma*. Because this document supports my claim that Native voices and ideas can be located in counter-archival sources, I use an extended segment of that manuscript document to summarize the key events in Nimiipuu history prior to allotment, as they were understood by a Nimiipuu thinker and writer:

[28]

History of Nez Perce Indians from 1805 up to the present time. Nez Perces formerally lived in Idaho Territory where they were discovered by Lewis and Clark in 1805.[77] At that time the tribe numbered from 6000 to 7000 and conquered all the surrounding tribes of Indians. Nez Perces lived by hunting expeditions east of the Rocky Mountains in large numbers sometimes, as high as 4,000 and leave the rest of the tribe to remain at their own country to protect it from being invaded by some other tribe of Indians.

They lived and enjoyed the happiness and freedom and lived just as happy as any other Nation in the World.

But alas, the day was coming when all their happy days was to be turned into day of sorrow and moening Their days of freedom was turned to be the day of slavary. Their days of victory was turned to be conquered, and their rights to the country was disregarded by another nations which is called "Whiteman" at present day.

In 1855 a treaty was made between the Nez Perce Nation and United States.

Wal-la-mot-kin (Hair tied on forehead) or Old Joseph, Hullal-ho-sot, or (Lawyer) were the two leading Chiefs of Nez Perce Nation in 1855. both of these two Chiefs consented to the treaty and accordingly Nez Perce sold to the United States part of their country.

In 1863 another treaty was made in which Lawyer and his people consented but Joseph and his people refused to make the second treaty from that time Joseph's people were called None-treaty Nez Perces.

The treaty Nez Perces numbered 1800

None-treaty numbered 1000

The Nez Perse decreased greatly since 1805 up to 1863. The smallpox prevailed among the tribe which almost destroyed the tribe.

Lawer's people advanced in civilization. and became farmers ec. They had their children in schools. While Joseph's people refused all these things and lived outside what was called Nez Perce Reservation. In 1877 Government undertook to move Young Joseph people on the Res. At this date . . . there was Nez Perce War bloody one. nine great battles were fought, the last battle lasted five days which Joseph surrendered with his people with his people 1000. Indians had went

INTRODUCTION

> on the war path but when Joseph surrendered there was only 600, 400 killed during the wars or went to other tribes. after the capture Joseph was brought to this Territory as captives. . . .
>
> I wrote this about my own people. I am a member of Nez Perce tribe and Nephew of Chief Joseph at present I am employed by the Government Interpreter and Teacher for my People. . . .
>
> When this is opened and read may be understood how the Indians have been treated by the Whiteman.
>
> Writer
> James Reuben
> "Nez Perce Indian."[78]

Acknowledging pre-contact history, but implying that dealings with whites produced the intratribal divisions he enumerates, Reubens takes 1855 as his point of beginning. He emphasizes the tribe's cosmopolitan knowledge and trading prowess, linking their dealings with the "[nation] . . . called 'Whiteman'" to that nation's disregard for Nimiipuu sovereign "rights to the country." He traces the intertwined but divergent histories of treaty and non-treaty bands, for although Reubens interpreted for federal forces in the Joseph War, he here asserts his political solidarity and filiative connections with the incarcerated people he later helped to repatriate and for whose rights he continued to advocate until his death in 1897. Reubens clearly expected his history to continue to be relevant to those who would read it when the cornerstone was opened. His foresight exemplifies what Gerald Vizenor calls survivance, "an active sense of presence, the continuance of native stories, not a mere reaction, or a survivable name. Native survivance stories are renunciations of dominance, tragedy, and victimry. Survivance means the right of succession or reversion of an estate, and in that sense, the estate of native survivancy."[79] I use the term to refer to texts such as Reubens's, for it depends on a figure of speech for which the referents are property in land and in (hi)stories, two cornerstones of sovereign identities.

Reubens's history is among the records not yet brought to bear on the dominant "Whiteman" accounts of Nimiipuu history. Written by a Native intellectual whose allegiances were complex and shifting, the account stands as a record of what he understood to be the key events in his people's history. It asserts, as well, that despite several decades of white attempts to dispossess them of their culture, land, and stories, Nimiipuu partisans practiced active resistance to these incursions and left articulate and compelling written records of their work. Their archive is centrally important to this book.

Allotment's Archives

The Dawes Act did not allot the reservations, nor did the archive collect the records of allotment. Policies of collecting, preserving, and curating are intersubjective, contingent, and ideologically determined. As Antoinette Burton has observed, "historical and ethnographic work has followed if not the flag, then the archive."[80] Those who introduced allotment to the Nez Perce Reservation produced a plethora of written documentation: census rolls; maps and plats; policy memos; weekly, monthly, and yearly reports; genealogical notes; and legal and financial records, all in support of the eventual sale of so-called excess reservation lands and the cultural assimilation of Nez Perce peoples. These, the official federal records, were mirrored in public discourse by Alice Fletcher's written and oral reports to reform associations who supported her work and in her occasional essays, published in periodicals such as Carlisle Indian School's *Red Man* and *Morning Star*, the *Christian Register*, the *Southern Workman*, and *Lend a Hand*. Record Groups 48, 75, and 95 of the National Archives of the United States (a collection so vast that it must be stored in several geographically dispersed repositories) contains the federal record of allotment; the National Anthropological Archives holds Fletcher's personal records. These two collections, however, capacious as they are, do not constitute a definitive archive. Within the mass of documents that one might imagine to be held in these places, many key items seem not to exist, and their absences point to the larger epistemological lacunae and happenstance construction of archives generally. These missing documents may simply be misfiled or misplaced, despite the best efforts of dedicated archivists to keep them in order. Some have been destroyed, as were most of Fletcher's letters to Francis La Flesche.

Others may have been intentionally hidden, misfiled, taken by researchers for their own collections, or withdrawn because they contain evidence that is too complex or too damaging to be included in the official accounts.[81] Still other records have been so damaged as to be nearly illegible: they are letterpress copies, torn, stained, water-damaged, missing key pages, and perhaps intentionally mutilated. Other sources point to these gaps and can sometimes supplement them. For example, the letters Jane Gay wrote between 1889 and 1892 recount events that remain unmentioned in Alice Fletcher's official reports and personal correspondence. Because Gay was not a government employee, her letters contained highly personalized and often acerbic critiques of allotment's more blatant failures. They offer a useful corrective to Fletcher's accounts, but their value as evidence is modified by the conditions under which Gay wrote, circulated, and preserved them.

Gay apparently intended to publish a collection of her letters from Idaho as a travel book or series of journalistic reminiscences illustrated with her photographs, perhaps resembling those written by her friend Frank Hamilton Cushing ("My Adventures in Zuñi") or by Fletcher ("Personal Studies of Indian Life"), both of which first appeared in *Century* magazine. That scheme never materialized. Rather, Gay ultimately included a selection of her public and private letters in a handcrafted two-volume scrapbook, *Choup-nit-ki: With the Nez Perces*, which she and her niece Emma J. Gay prepared between 1895 and 1909. As the two women worked on this project, Jane Gay edited, rearranged, and amended the letters and selected several hundred black-and-white photographs that illustrate the album.[82] These albums remained in the family until 1951, when another of Gay's nieces, Jane Gay Dodge, deeded them to the Schlesinger Library on the History of Women in America.

In 1981 Frederick E. Hoxie, in collaboration with Joan T. Mark, published an edition of Gay's letters, titled *With the Nez Perces: Alice Fletcher in the Field, 1889–1892*. This edition does not completely reproduce *Choup-nit-ki*. It omits what the editors deemed to be "repetitious and overlong descriptive passages" (xxxvi), contains only thirty-nine of the hundreds of striking images that enhance the scrapbook volumes, and is marred by occasional but serious errors in transcription. As the title implies, the editors made choices about which segments of Gay's letters to include, choices seemingly determined by whether their content illuminated Fletcher's character, since Mark was Fletcher's biographer and published *A Stranger in Her Native Land* seven years later. Happily, scholars can now consult the full text of the scrapbooks and view several related photo albums compiled by Gay, thanks to an electronic reproduction sponsored by the Schlesinger Library on the History of Women in America as a part of Harvard University's Open Collections Program.

Yet *Choup-nit-ki* by no means represents all of Gay's written output during this period. She wrote reports of Fletcher's work that were published in the *Red Man*, *Lend a Hand*, and the *Christian Register*, all of which recount information beyond that contained in the scrapbooks. Nor is it likely that all of Gay's writings from the Idaho period have yet been located. *Choup-nit-ki*, profusely illustrated as it is, does not contain all of Gay's photographs. The E. Jane Gay Photograph Collection and the Swayne Collection of the Idaho State Historical Society and the photographic collections of the University of Idaho hold many more images made by Gay on the Nez Perce Reservation, but these archives do not include photographic work she pursued after Fletcher declared herself to have finished the allotment. The Schlesinger Library and the National Anthropological Archives each own some of these post-1892 images, but most of the later photographs were destroyed after Gay's death.[83] New images continue to emerge, many of them now in possession of descendants of the Nez Perces or the missionaries to whom Gay gave copies of her images. I have based this study on every available public record and photograph produced by Gay, and in the process of writing it, I have located several new sources—columns published in the *Christian Register* and in *Lend a Hand*, and several loose photographs and albums recently donated to and as yet under restricted access at the Nez Perce National Historical Park Archives in Accession 632, the Lawyer Collection.

Both women's records, although produced at the time and in the place of which they speak, are significant not only for what they make apparent but also for what they do not say or show. In her letters Gay often intentionally omitted information, such as details of how Nimiipuu partisans challenged and negotiated with Fletcher. Because she wrote for eastern readers who shared her reform sensibilities, she chose details that allowed her to emplot intriguing narratives in which Fletcher emerged triumphant, vindicated by her devotion to duty. In writing this study I have assumed all the data—whether documentary, epistolary, or photographic—to be in some degree consciously crafted, self-interested, partisan, and incomplete. I have read these records comparatively and have used them to construct a multivocal and often contradictory account of selected events related to the allotment.

As a copious documentary record demonstrates, Nez Perce peoples sought to understand, clarify, modify, and resist the policies unilaterally urged upon them. These records, collected and sometimes difficult to find in the official archive, provide evidence for revising and reframing the dominant understanding of allotment and its assumption that Native cultures were, after the 1890s, absorbed into a USAmerican polity. Within the official and private letters of white missionaries, administrators, and agents lie accounts of Nez Perce actions and resistances. Within state archives—scattered, unindexed, hidden, and/or misfiled—lie documents written by Nez Perces who were involved in allotment's agendas and plots. Tidy ranks of acid-free boxes contain their letters requesting clarification of policies, their sworn affidavits, and their petitions bearing hundreds of names, demanding the rights promised by law and by treaty and protesting the ongoing venality and downright criminality of white agents entrusted to oversee tribal lands and monies. Much of that Native testimony may be indexed and cross-referenced within a byzantine tangle of archival documentation, once useful to federal workers but now largely obstructive to hurried archival researchers. Other parts of it emerge only serendipitously.

Native voices have narrated the transcribed myths and legends that now grace the anthropological archive. Nimiipuu informants told Fletcher a number of origin tales, narrated stories of pre-contact events, and explained to her the political structures that emerged from settlement patterns. She wrote two monographs based upon this information, which remained unpublished until the mid-1990s. Thus once that story was "taken," to borrow the words of Carolyn Steedman, "it was not returned to [them], not even in the formulaic [ethnographic monograph], but rather left behind, in [the field notes,] the case books, and the Archive."[84] These Native records can yield powerful evidence of a vibrant culture engaged in steady, carefully planned, and highly effective resistance to the best-laid plans of church and state.

Other archives exist that are not the properties of state and academic memory palaces. As Native peoples learned early on, white collectors, anthropologists, schoolteachers, and special government agents predictably misinterpreted the stories they had "taken" and, in the process, impoverished the culture whence they had originated. Thus they compiled their own archives—privately held assemblages of traditional items of material culture as well as scrapbooks and collections of clippings, photographs, and letters. In these records lies the most powerful evidence of allotment's failure. They document the involvement of individual tribal members in shaping accounts of their history as well as the persistence of Nimiipuu identity as a political, sovereign reality.

Moreover, nonwritten sources such as ceremonies, parades, dances, songs, and oral narration necessarily comprise an expanded historical record. As cultural historian Arturo J. Aldama asserts, such performances insist on a past that is not lost or buried; these performances are *collective*, not individuated, events that challenge chronological borders.[85] Turning to this expanded archive, in the five parts of this book I present accounts of Independence Day celebrations in Nespelem, Lewiston, Lapwai, and Kamiah, considering these intercultural gatherings to be occasions upon which countermemories manifest themselves in action and demonstrate how Native resistance to allotment policy enabled the survivance of tribal cultures and protected the sovereignty of the Nimiipuu even during the darkest years immediately following the allotment period.[86]

[35]

INTRODUCTION

Allotment's Plots

In investigating the intersubjective means by which allotment proceeded on the Nez Perce Reservation, I wish to resist the model of linear history for which the outcome was a foregone conclusion predicated by Manifest Destiny.[87] In such teleological, causal, and progressive story forms, the present seems to be the only possible outcome of the past. In structuring this book I am particularly interested in the craft of historical emplotment. *Plot* is a particularly modern notion, related both to real estate and to texts. Plots divide both land and stories into segments — beginnings, middles, ends, chapters, verses, and acts, to name a few — to be given measurable exchange value, to be owned, and to be sold. Thus allotment and narrative theory share a common vocabulary in words such as *plot, property, individual,* and *commodification.* As Lennard J. Davis has demonstrated, "The origin of the word 'plot' is related first to a plot of land, and subsequently to the describing of that bit of land. . . . '[P]lot' in English seems related to property," whether in land, in fiction, or in historical narratives, all of which I consider here.[88] Histories, like stories, follow plots; they have beginnings and endings. Like stories, their middles unfold causally and feature individuated agents whose development moves them from ignorance to enlightenment.[89] And finally, the ownership of stories is an important component of sovereign identity.

Local histories, such as those of Native nations, have frequently been absorbed by larger narratives, the causality of which assumes the consolidated USAmerican nation to be "the center and the end of history" and presumes that allotment, albeit a failed policy by every account, nevertheless extirpated Native polities and peoples, making them a part of the larger national project.[90] Historian Arif Dirlik advocates countering such progressive histories with resistant narratives originating from "places, the locations for everyday life, where people tell stories that are intimately linked with the necessities of existence and survival against the abstract demands of states and capital."[91] What I write here does not aspire to be a history. It is, rather, a collection of place-based stories about the first

[36]

years of allotment. Some of these stories originate in the place of Nimiipuu sovereignty; others emerge from the space of the state archive, which often supports a dominant historical narrative. I engage these sources in a conversation, or a collaboration, seeking to respect the positions of the multiple agents engaged in these activities. I have arranged these conversations in a loose, episodic chronology, wherein I examine the interplay of the various records, emphasizing their tenuousness rather than assuming their place in a "manifest"—that is, necessary and foreordained—outcome.

In *The Allotment Plot* I have not written a chronological history of allotment, nor have I tried to trace the intricacies of individual cases or claims, except as they represent general trends or illustrate how allotment proceeded.[92] In each chapter I suggest several possible narratives about a given theme related to the history of allotment. As a result, I have tried to resist the teleologically progressive assumptions undergirding Alice C. Fletcher's acts as she sought to extinguish Nez Perce claims on their ancestral lands and to assimilate individual Nez Perce peoples. In parts 1 and 4 I focus on the narrative devices of beginnings and conclusions, seeking to show the ideological assumptions encoded in these markers. In parts 2 and 3 I attend to the specific aims of allotment—to appropriate land and to transform, assimilate, and erase Native cultures. I demonstrate how Fletcher pursued these aims and how the Nimiipuu resisted them. And in part 5 I look beyond the putative ending of allotment and, with the aid of counter-archival sources, show how Nimiipuu agents have represented themselves and preserved their sovereign cultural identities.

Part One

Beginnings

Introduction

After the End of Nez Perce History

Presbyterian missionary George L. Deffenbaugh found the celebration held on 4 July 1885 at the Nez Perce Agency in Lapwai, Idaho, to be a notable one. In his annual report to the commissioner of Indian affairs, Deffenbaugh remarked on "the absence of the usual drunkenness and horse-racing" that had characterized celebrations in past years, and reported that the occasion had been distinguished by a week-long Presbyterian "camp meeting" attended by nearly a thousand people from the area and from "adjacent tribes." He continued, "In the midst of the week's meetings they suspended their usual daily services to celebrate *the natal day of our country and theirs*, and I suppose that the day was not any more patriotically observed anywhere by the citizens of the nation. There were processions, speeches, dinner, plays, and in the evening fireworks; and with it all the best of order and the most hearty good-will." Enhancing the holiday atmosphere was the presence of a large group of exiled tribal members who had, until recently, been interned in prison camps in Kansas and in the Indian Territory since the conclusion of the 1877 war. As a part of the Fourth of July celebration, Deffenbaugh noted, eighty of "the returned Nez Percés" were "received . . . to the membership of the reservation churches."[1]

This auspicious occasion has figured centrally in accounts concerned with allotment on the Nez Perce Reservation. Deffenbaugh's phrase "[T]he natal day of our country and theirs" suggests a moment of new beginning for the Nez Perces. For example, according to Frederick E. Hoxie and Joan T. Mark, "In 1885 the exiled Nez Perces from the war of 1877 arrived home from Indian Territory on July 4 and were welcomed at the Lapwai camp meeting in a restrained but moving ceremony. . . . Thereafter the Fourth of July was a symbol both of the white Christian nation the missionaries represented and of the return from exile of those who had resisted the white man."[2] Several years later, in her biography of Alice Fletcher, Mark expanded on the connection, claiming, "[F]uture celebrations of the holiday . . . came to symbolize the unity of the Nez Perces, their pride in their past, and their resistance to the white people" (SNL, 189). For these scholars, the return and the rapprochement it seemed to represent signaled an era of amicable unity on the Nez Perce Reservation. Armed conflict over disputed lands was at an end, amity in the churches prevailed, and Nez Perces who had been divided were reunited.

Beginnings, however, are rarely as tidy as fictional or historical narratives would seem to promise. The return of the internees, for example, might as easily be read as an ending—to their unjust incarceration. Beginnings are an artifice of narrative, establishing the necessary conditions from which the story that follows will commence. In seeing the Fourth of July of 1885 as a beginning of a new period in Nez Perce history, Hoxie and Mark overlook several important details. First, "the exiled Nez Perces" who "were welcomed at the Lapwai camp meeting" were, in fact, fewer than half of the group who had returned. Moreover, they had not arrived on July 4 but about a month earlier. These are not minor points but contribute to the interpretation of allotment these scholars use to introduce *With the Nez Perces* and pursued and elaborated by Mark in *A Stranger in Her Native Land*. In both cases, these books presume that after 4 July 1885, the Nez Perces were once again a polity united by their Presbyterian affiliation. The implications are that a unity of tribal opinion is desirable, and that Presbyterian church interests were a major ally to Alice C. Fletcher as she sought to begin the work of allotment on the Nez Perce Reservation.

Other modes of telling, however, can yield different stories. I argue that Nez Perces, not always in perfect agreement with one another, nevertheless effected an end to the internment. The two occasions of return, both occurring after the putative end of Nez Perce history in 1877, prefigure other ways of beginning the story of allotment, in which Nez Perces actively determine when and under what conditions Fletcher might begin her work.

To call the holiday celebration of 1885 a symbol of the unity of the Nez Perces greatly overstates the case, as Allen P. Slickpoo makes clear. He declares, "The 'heathens'' return caused many problems for the agent, the missionaries, and the Presbyterian Nez Perces. The Fourth became a pivotal point of that conflict."[3] Here Slickpoo trenchantly summarizes the tensions that surfaced publicly and annually at these summer celebrations and points to the complex divisions and rapprochements among the various groups of Nimiipuu. On the reservation, those who were affiliated with the Presbyterian Church and who followed an agrarian lifestyle lived in the Kamiah area, while those who lived within traditional religious and sociopolitical structures and who were hunters, fishers, and ranchers lived sixty miles to the west, in the Lapwai area.[4] Catholic Nimiipuu, most of whom followed traditional religious and cultural patterns, also lived on the western side of the reservation in the vicinity of St. Joseph's Mission. When the exiles returned in 1885, those who had embraced Presbyterian Christianity while in Indian Territory were welcomed on the Nez Perce Reservation; those who remained committed to resisting white religion and culture settled on the Colville Reservation in Washington.[5] Despite the geographical, political, and religious divisions, however, none of these groups was willing to yield claim to the lands that comprised Nimiipuu sovereign identity.

Rather than connect the exiles' return to the USAmerican celebration of independence from Great Britain, I emphasize that the reunion festivities in 1885 included rituals common to summer gatherings since long before the advent of the first white missionaries in the Northwest. That event celebrated Nimiipuu survivance. As Joseph Roach's study of strategic performances suggests, such repeated ceremonial occasions, especially when they are held at the same "[site] of memory," invoke and solidify collective identification. At the same time they enable change, since each repeated occasion necessarily includes modifications and substitutions—of attire, performers, ritual, or other details. Despite these alterations, those who participate in such celebrations observe the occasion with reference to earlier, similar events that have been held in the same place and that now open the possibility for "cultural self-invention through the restoration of behavior"—albeit under now quite different circumstances—within that place and within that enduring history.[6]

The 268 exiles who returned from Indian Territory in early June 1885 were not, in fact, the first to be released from internment. Two years earlier, led by James Reubens, a smaller party of about thirty elders, widows, and orphans had preceded them. To recognize this earlier arrival is to focus on the complex motives of Reubens, a protagonist whose allegiances were multiple, strategic, and mutable. The son of a Nimiipuu headman, he had been educated at the Fort Lapwai Agency school and at "a private school at The Dalles."[7] During the Nez Perce War he had served as a scout for General O. O. Howard. Yet three years after the war's end, with Archie Lawyer and Mark Williams, he went as a federal appointee to Indian Territory, where he established a school, worked as a translator, and actively petitioned for the group to be returned to their homelands. Figure 5, a formal studio portrait probably made in 1878, shows the three young men, seated and wearing formal attire, with James B. Monteith, then the Nez Perce agent. Reubens is seated at the left of the group of three.

The release of the first group of internees directly resulted from an alliance between James Reubens and Chief Joseph.[8] Although they had taken different sides in the recent war, and although they differed on matters of policy and religion, both applied their considerable rhetorical skills to accomplish the return of all the internees to the Northwest.[9] Joseph had argued that his people's attachment to their ancestral lands made it impossible for them to live anywhere else. He contended that the internment was an unjust condition to which he had not agreed, and he insisted that lands in the Wallowa area not be sold or ceded to white settlement. For his part, Reubens

FIG. 5. James Reubens (*left*), Mark Williams, and Archie B. Lawyer are seated, with James B. Monteith standing, ca. 1878. A handwritten annotation describes Lawyer, Williams, and Reuben as "all *full* Nez Perce Indians commissioned or appointed by the Indian Department at Washington as teachers to Chief Joseph's Nez Perces in the Indian Territory, reaching there in Dec. 1878" and says James taught at the boarding school at Lapwai. NEPE-HI-0179. Courtesy of National Park Service, NPNHP.

enlisted support from white Presbyterian activists, emphasizing that the internees had embraced Christianity. In his public petitions on their behalf he framed the argument by encouraging sympathetic identification, emphasizing the similarities between the internees and white reformers.[10] He wrote, for example, "If any man has human feeling toward his fellow men he is bound to sympathise with his people, who have been oppressed, wronged and mistreated."[11]

Presbyterian church groups took up the cause of the internees, in the process arguing that the Nez Perces (as well as other Native groups) needed to have legal title to their lands. Both strands of this logic structure Commissioner Hiram Price's 1882 *Report of the Commissioner of Indian Affairs*. He wrote, "The deep-rooted love for the 'old home,' which is so conspicuous among them . . . can never be eradicated. . . . I am constrained to believe that the remnant of this tribe should be returned to Idaho." But since permission for the return had not yet been granted, he continued, "But if Congress should decide that the best interests of all concerned will be best subserved by retaining these Indians where they are now are, it will be necessary to have such legislation as will perfect the title to the lands which have been selected for them and upon which they now reside."[12]

It was a short step from recommending Joseph's band be given title to lands in Indian Territory to including the entire reunited tribe on the list of initial allottees under the Dawes Act.[13] Such an initiative was overdue, according to some white settlers in Idaho. As the return of Joseph's people became a real possibility, the *Lewiston Teller* editorialized, "Had the government fixed the conditions so that every Indian in this nation could acquire title to his land and other property in severalty before the proposed return of these warriors to Idaho, there would have been something to hang a permanent hope upon of a permanent peace."[14] As these examples suggest, supporters of allotment reasoned that Indians' only recourse for survival in the face of an overwhelming and almost ungovernable tidal wave of land-hungry white settlers was for them to take individual title to (a greatly reduced portion of) their lands.[15]

The Nimiipuu, Presbyterian, and federal parties who brokered the return of this initial small group stipulated the details by which it was to be accomplished.[16] Perhaps not coincidentally, the party included one or more relatives of James Reubens.[17] The Lapwai Presbyterian congregation also was involved, voting on 15 October 1882 to accept the group of "13 widows, 13 children and five orphans" back into the fold.[18] When Agent Charles E. Monteith reported this approval to the commissioner of Indian affairs, he also offered his opinion about whom the group should include, suggested a date of departure, and recommended an appropriate mode of transport and route of travel.[19]

These first returnees reached Lapwai on or about 4 July 1883.[20] Their arrival was observed by Kate C. McBeth, a Presbyterian missionary living on the reservation, who recounted it in a letter she sent to the *Saturday Review* later that year. McBeth was no friend of Reubens, who had not been among the young men trained by her sister Susan as Presbyterian pastors and missionaries. Nor did she approve of traditional ceremonial activities, especially as they were practiced on the Fourth of July. In point of fact, since her arrival on the reservation four years earlier, Kate McBeth had endeavored to replace horse racing, gaming, and the war procession with hymns, sermons, and a picnic. In her letter she disapprovingly emphasized Reubens's command of the occasion: "I knew well there was to be an imposing scene when told that fifty horse men had met them at Thunder Hill, but were sent back by James [Reubens], saying he would not shake hands with any one until he reached Lapwai."[21] More than twenty years later she expanded upon this account in her history, *The Nez Perces since Lewis and Clark*, adding these details: "James appeared around a bend in the road, on a fine, fresh horse, and with a dark blue business suit on. Cartridge belt and pistol in its place! As free from dust as if he had but crossed the street! Where did he make his toilet? was the question. After him rode the weariest, dustiest, most forlorn band of women with blankets and belongings behind each woman on her horse."[22] In front of the agency building Reubens made a speech expressing the group's joy at their return. McBeth does not recount the content of that address.

Most subsequent secondary sources follow and even intensify McBeth's emphasis on James Reubens's control of the details of the arrival, his apparent care with his appearance, and his oratory. In her biography of Alice Fletcher, for example, Mark writes, "With the dramatic flair for which he was famous, Reuben timed the arrival of their caravan to coincide with the Fourth of July celebration" (SNL, 188). While Reubens may indeed have embraced the opportunity to return this group to their homelands during the summer celebration, many other factors determined when they arrived. The agents at Lapwai and Oakland had debated the timing of their release; the secretary of the interior approved the date. The duration of their journey from Indian Territory to Lapwai depended on railroad schedules and weather conditions. Moreover, had "non-Native settlers" not prevented fresh horses from Lapwai from reaching the group, they would likely have arrived at least two weeks earlier.[23]

FIG. 6. "Christian women of Joseph's band, now returned to their old home." *Foreign Missionary* 44, no. 9 (Feb. 1886): 422.

Neither McBeth nor Mark considers that Reubens gave attention to details that would mark the occasion, especially since the group arrived during a celebration being observed in a place of ceremonial significance. As was appropriate, he donned clean attire and brushed his horse. To demonstrate that this group did not return under bellicose terms, and to emphasize the church affiliation of its members, he dressed not in Native regalia but in a western-style suit, as had Joseph before him when he "attend[ed] Presbyterian functions."[24] Those who accompanied Reubens also wore clothing that signaled their Christian affiliation, as is apparent in figure 6, an engraving depicting the "Christian women of Joseph's band," that illustrated F. F. Ellinwood's "Descriptive Sketch" of the Nez Perce Mission in the *Foreign Missionary*, a publication of the Presbyterian Board of Foreign Missions.[25]

Reubens's cartridge belt and pistol emblematized his role as protector of this visibly defenseless group of women, children, and ailing elder men and established him as an equal to the "detachment of troopers" who had escorted the party to Lapwai from Kelton, Utah, where they had transferred from train to horseback.[26]

Finally, rather than shake hands with those sent out to meet them at Thunder Hill, he delayed such ceremonies until the party had arranged themselves appropriately on the meeting grounds near the Lapwai Agency, where their friends and relatives had gathered to receive them. As the occasion demanded, and as had become customary at other Fourth of July celebrations held in this location, Reubens, a skilled public speaker, delivered an oration. According to Slickpoo's official tribal history, written some seventy years after the occasion, Reubens's address included these sentiments: "Language cannot express our joy when we remember that our feet will soon tread again our native land, and our eyes behold the scenes of our childhood. The undying love for home, which we have cherished in our hearts so long, has caused our tears to flow for years, but now we are but one step from that home."[27] Slickpoo provides no documentary source for the speech, but his choice to attribute these words to Reubens honors that leader's purposes and strategically emphasizes the uninterrupted connection of this group to the land on which they stood. In restoring voice to this leader, the official tribal history reclaims the occasion as a part of Nimiipuu history, not USAmerican or Presbyterian history.

Two years passed before the remaining internees returned. The details of their release show how federal agencies and Presbyterian leaders sought to control these prisoners even after they departed Indian Territory.[28] Yet a fuller record reveals, as well, that Joseph and other leaders defied such control. Fewer than half of the returnees from the Oakland Agency (118, according to Agent Charles Monteith), actually came to the Nez Perce Reservation.[29] Of these, most were professedly Presbyterian. The greater portion of exiles (150 of them), those most closely associated with Joseph, had been separated at Wallula Junction and sent to the Colville Reservation in Washington.[30] Accounts vary as to the reasons for this division. It is likely Joseph himself had never intended to return to the Lapwai area. While still in Indian Territory, according to Robert H. Ruby and John A. Brown, he had sent three men to Chief Moses "asking permission to live on the Colville [Reservation]. They would recognize Moses as chief; and in case Moses should die first, Joseph would succeed him. Moses sent back word that the exiles would be welcome."[31] The 1885 *Annual Report of the Commissioner of Indian Affairs* confirms this, stating, "The reason for sending these Indians to two separate agencies was partly on account of their own desire in the matter." To forestall accusations of too much heed being given to Indian preferences, the report noted that the separation was "principally on account of indictments said to be pending in Idaho against Chief Joseph and some of his immediate followers."[32]

Other factors were also at play. Yellow Wolf, one of the returnees sent to the Colville Reservation, recollected, "[R]eligion had to do with where they placed us.... Because we respected our [Washani or Seven Drums] religion, we were not allowed to go on the Nez Perce Reservation. When we reached Wallula, the interpreter asked us, 'Where you want to go? Lapwai and be Christian, or Colville and just be yourself?'"[33] Yellow Wolf's account is borne out by Deffenbaugh, who told the commissioner in 1885, "[I]t was ... a very proper thing to make a distinction between the subdued and unsubdued, and send the latter to a point remote from the scenes of their dastardly deeds and wanton depredations."[34] Deffenbaugh's comments emblematize the ill will of church interests on the reservation toward those who insisted on maintaining their principled opposition to forcible or strategic conversion.

The reception of those who went to the Colville Reservation is only sparsely documented. Pearson summarizes it in a sentence: "Supervised by a military escort, the wagon train to Colville was not greeted by any welcoming ceremonies, happy families, or considerate agency officials" (*NPIT*, 291). By contrast, the arrival of the others on 1 June 1885 at Lapwai was widely noted. Deffenbaugh, an eyewitness observer, reported it to the commissioner of Indian affairs; he also published a detailed account of the occasion that has dominated subsequent histories. To the *Foreign Missionary* he wrote an effusive description that starkly contrasts with his dismissive treatment of the Joseph band. He proclaimed, "They have come! We have just witnessed the scene of a century—yes, of a century."[35] The details of his record suggest that this occasion closely resembled the earlier group's welcome in 1883. The returnees formed a circle and heard ceremonial speeches. If the speakers emphasized the importance of land to these "returned wanderers," as had Reubens two years earlier, Deffenbaugh did not note it. Rather, he summarizes an address delivered by Tom Hill, one of the group, who "referred gratefully to the interposition of the Church and the law in their behalf, and closed with the announcement that their only desire now is to be henceforth law-abiding people and believers in the God of heaven." Then a semi-circle of welcoming Nez Perces "filed past and took the hand of every man, woman and child" of the returning prisoners. Deffenbaugh continues: "It was very touching . . . to hear the glad expressions. . . . 'Is it you, father!' or 'Is that you, brother!' Only one who had a heart of stone could have stood by and not entered with spirit into the joys of the occasion. . . . Our white ladies here could not restrain tears of sympathy as mothers and sisters sat down to mourn for those whom they hoped to find, but who, they learned, were lying in far-off graves."[36] The details of this account focus on the shared feelings that Reubens and Joseph had so skillfully manipulated as they brokered this return. For Deffenbaugh, the import of the occasion could best be measured not by its effect on those who were being reunited after eight years' separation but by the "tears of sympathy" shed by white women observers with whom Presbyterian reformers could most fully identify.

For other interested parties in the Lewiston/Lapwai area, the exiles' arrival caused heightened concern. Many local white residents had resisted the return, among them Aaron F. Parker, editor of Lewiston's *Nez Perce News*, who announced: "[W]e have come to the conclusion that we need their room more than their company. . . . Their return here would introduce the leaven of discontent to such an extent that Satan alone knows where the ferment would end."[37] Parker continued to publish inflammatory editorials through the spring of 1885, reminding the local populace of their real and imaginary issues with this group. Despite these anxieties, peace prevailed, for according to a historian's account, "no more than fifteen [of the 118 who returned to Lapwai] could be classified as able-bodied men."[38]

Kate McBeth shared Parker's premonitions of discord and "ferment." Rather than celebrate the return of spouses, children, and

[51]

friends of her congregants, she assumed the worst: that the exiles' return would tempt the weaker members of her flock to participate in "heathen" activities. She confided to her diary, "I do not much wonder that [the Kamiah Nez Perces] Wanted to go [to Lapwai] for the exiles from Indian Ter. Will be there." The potential reunification and its attendant possibility for recidivism prompted her to worry, "[T]his 4th . . . seems the One in which there is most to be anxious about the cause of Christ & Ourselves" and to sponsor an alternative celebration near her home in Kamiah. She spent July 3 "baking all forenoon . . . 200 cookies & snaps" for the next day's dinner, but admitted to herself that "perhaps few will be under the great tent which I see is set up back of the church."[39]

A specific logic connects the exiles' return to Idaho, Joseph's renewed presence, the involvement of Presbyterian sponsors, and the successful inception of allotment. That causal reasoning is perhaps best represented by these sentences from Allen Morrill and Eleanor Morrill's history of the McBeth sisters: "It was almost impossible to convince the Nez Perces of the necessity for individual land ownership. The majority of the tribe agreed with Chief Joseph, who opposed the Severalty Act, asserting that since all the land belonged to the tribe anyway, there was no sense in parceling it out among individuals. Without the endorsement given the project by the McBeths, much more time would have been required to persuade the Indians to apply for their allotments. When at last the break that Miss Fletcher had been seeking came, it was directly traceable to the McBeths."[40] This inaccurate and ideologically skewed account offers no support for its contention that "a majority of the tribe" agreed with Joseph. The degree to which his stand influenced reservation politics is difficult to measure. In the Morrill history the Kamiah Presbyterian congregation, prepared by their missionaries and in defiance of the more traditional and resistant group at Lapwai, bravely took the first allotments and thus opened the way for Fletcher's success. While this telling does correctly suggest the importance of the sponsorship of the Presbyterian Church in the process of allotment, it also implies a kind of divine sanction to the undertaking, aligning it with the inevitable civilization of the West by heroic missionaries and brave white women, pioneers of church and government service, Indian policy, and professionalized anthropology.

In the next two chapters I demonstrate that Fletcher's and Gay's reports of their attempts to begin allotment work at Lapwai intentionally obscured several tactical errors Fletcher made that brought her work to a virtual standstill and resulted in her decision to remove herself and her party to Kamiah. Here she was able to begin the allotment in earnest, an inception Gay credits to the aid of Presbyterian missionaries and the goodwill of their congregants. An account of Fletcher's initial missteps must be supplemented by other, even more obscured records that point to the effectual involvement of Nimiipuu — both individually and collectively — in determining how and when allotment would commence. This story focuses on how they decided to agree to allotment and emphasizes the logic, the means, and the outcomes of the resistance of leaders at Lapwai and at Kamiah who, despite their differences, saw the new federal policy as an opportunity to resolve serious current and longstanding issues that the Indian agency had ignored.

1. A False Beginning

By the end of the nineteenth century the rationalized extension of 160-acre individually owned homesteads into western territories seemed to demand that Native lands, enclosed in reservations thought to be too generously sized, should be similarly apportioned. In northern Idaho, where the boom-and-bust mining economy fed a climate of boosterism and "go-ahead" spirit, local newspapers routinely urged the federal government to pass an allotment law. An 1882 editorial in Lewiston's *Nez Perce News* declared, "Nothing will transform this city from a sleepy hollow to an active, booming business center but the opening of the reservation."[1] After the Dawes General Allotment Act was passed in February 1887, these same papers touted the land's potential and anxiously chronicled the preparations for the "opening" of the reservation. A headline in the *Grangeville Free Press* trumpeted "The Coming Boom!" and urged, "The People of Camas Prairie Should Prepare For It." "[T]he Almighty," the newspaper trumpeted, "never planned a piece of country . . . with less waste land. . . . [P]rosperity lies at the doorstep of every man who has the good fortune to own a quarter section of this fertile soil. Tickle it with a plow and it will laugh you a harvest of flour. . . . The railroad is coming. Do not trust to it alone to enhance the value of your land so that you can sell out on the boom, but cultivate your place and put in a crop."[2] The Nez Perce Reservation was seen as enclosing "a vast quantity of taxable property" that could provide homes for hundreds of new settlers, enrich territorial coffers, and increase population to a number that would allow Idaho to claim statehood.[3] The *Free Press* fretted that the reservation's boundaries "hindered the development of this region more than if it were a desert."[4] The next month the same newspaper revisited the theme, asserting, "The slow growth of Lewiston and Camas prairie and all the Clearwater country is due solely to the fact that the key to it is sealed territory in the possession of the Nez Perce Indians."[5] Extending railroad lines through the Camas Prairie would bring new settlers and benefit current residents by allowing commodities to flow more easily from plateau farms via railroad and river to Pacific ports.

Linking allotment to Idaho's growth, economic development, and eventual statehood follows the familiar emplotment of Manifest Destiny: the policy seemed to promise the inevitable success of westward expansion, driven by visionary investors, white entrepreneurs, and hardy, virtuous yeoman farmers. This story characterizes Native peoples—in this case, the Nez Perces—as static, resistant to change, obstinately refusing to embrace progress, and insistent upon maintaining collective ownership. Such assumptions are given the lie when measured against the fact that within the boundaries of the Nez Perce Reservation some form of allotment had been in place for the past thirty years, as stipulated in the treaties of 1855 and 1863.[6] The early surveys mandated by these treaties had delineated the boundaries of numerous twenty-acre plots, most of them in the river valleys.[7] Many Nimiipuu had already fenced their fields, were farming these lands, and were selling their produce to gold miners.

Long before Alice C. Fletcher arrived in Idaho, allotment had been actively discussed, debated, and experimented with on the Nez Perce Reservation. Some Nimiipuu men who had attended federal boarding schools, as had James Stuart, hoped to establish working farms with the help that had been promised them. In 1886 Stuart wrote to the commissioner of Indian affairs, "I have seen some of the reports saying that all the graduates from the Trainning Schools will be helped with such things they need." Desiring "to work and improve [his] land," he requested that the local agent be directed to issue him a harness and plow.⁸ Early in 1887 Agent George W. Norris wrote to Washington DC asking "whether the Department will sustain me in assigning to the individual indians of this tribe upon their application 160 acres, 320 acres, or such other quantity of land as the indians applying for will themselves fence and occupy." He reasoned, "Many would like to obtain the 20 acres already in possession, and take up more land at a distance, some for pasturage others for cultivation."⁹ Such a request suggests that at least some Nez Perce landowners considered allotment to be key to expanding their farms and ranches.

Nez Perce farmers and ranchers had good reasons for wanting a secure title to their lands. For years white cattlemen had allowed their stock to graze on the reservation. These stockmen often increased their herds by strategically acquiring (rustling) cattle belonging to their Native neighbors, sometimes with the excuse that they were merely "confiscat[ing] . . . the property of 'hostiles'—i.e. Nez Perces who were in the Joseph war of 1877!"¹⁰ Washington responded by ordering the local agent to enforce the boundaries, but these attempts generally failed.¹¹ In April 1889 for example, a month before Fletcher arrived on the reservation, the commissioner of Indian affairs once again instructed then agent Henry Heth to secure the boundaries. Heth complied, posting this notice in the *Teller*:

> TO WHOM IT MAY CONCERN.—I am directed by the President of the United States, to notify all persons who have cattle or stock of any kind, upon this reservation that they are required to remove the same without delay or military force will be sent, not only to remove the stock but to hold the offenders responsible, legally, to the utmost extent. If the stock belonging to white men, and now grazing on this reservation, are not removed in ten days I shall, as required, advise the department of the fact, and ask for military aid to carry out the orders of the Chief Magistrate of the Nation.¹²

The warning did not pass without resistance. Several weeks later the *Teller*'s editor protested, voicing an argument that had become common: "For twenty years and more the Indians and whites have dwelt here in the most neighborly and reciprocal manner, sharing with each other the use and occupancy of the whole country in common of pasture, with scarcely a murmur. . . . It has been a recognized fact by the Indians that the presence of the whites has afforded means of traffic whereby many have grown rich and opulent."[13] The *Teller*'s suggestion of a reciprocity between Indian and white stockmen contained a kernel of truth: many whites had been enriched by the practice, and Indian-owned cattle did graze outside reservation boundaries. But the rejoinder did not consider the issue of degree. Few Nez Perce ranchers held large herds; when their cattle slipped the boundaries, they were restrained by the fences of white ranchers.[14] The opposite was not true. Alice Fletcher explained the stakes in this disagreement to her friend Isabel Barrows: "I find every man . . . raising what ever he can on his land, but turning all his stock upon the reservation. . . . By this method the settlers raise stock on little cash and can carry a large number of head & become moderately prosperous. but if the reservation is cut off as a herding ground and the settler forced to maintain his cattle on his own land, the struggle for a livelihood becomes a serious matter."[15] As Fletcher makes clear, the resources of the reservation were crucial to the local economy. Her letter outlines the reasons underlying local white farmers' and ranchers' misinterpretations of the Dawes Act as well. They eagerly anticipated having access to reservation lands, overlooking the stipulation that reservation boundaries would be established and the land's Native owners would be deeded properties to sustain them, at least potentially, as the economic equals of their white neighbors.

It might seem that the story of allotment would begin with Alice Fletcher's welcome by both groups when she arrived in Idaho in May 1889. Whites would benefit from the eventual opening of reservation lands; Nez Perces would obtain secure title to their properties. This was not the case. Fletcher's work began only sporadically; she did not report significant success for several months following her arrival. The standard account of this critical three-month period, as given in Hoxie and Mark's introduction to *With the Nez Perces* and echoed in Mark's biography of Fletcher, depends upon Gay's and Fletcher's letters but does not question their framing, probe their omissions, or investigate the actions, motives, and negotiations of the Nez Perces. Neither woman fully credited the Nez Perces as equal negotiators, and both obscured or obfuscated certain details surrounding the delay and the initial allotments. Yet, as I have demonstrated, Nimiipuu had long been familiar with the general concept, and many of them had also read and considered how the Dawes Act would impact them.

In the version of the story based on Fletcher's and Gay's accounts, Fletcher was delayed for more than two months because the Lapwai-area Nez Perces were ignorant of the law's provisions and refused to meet with Fletcher to discuss its application or to take allotments. Only after Fletcher moved her base of operations to Kamiah, and only with the support of Susan McBeth and the Presbyterian Nez Perces, was she able to begin her work in earnest. This, as I demonstrate, is a false beginning. A counter-narrative based on these same sources might claim that a sovereign coalition of Nimiipuu including leaders from both Lapwai and Kamiah agreed to resist Fletcher's work until they had obtained certain concessions from Washington. These concessions would establish a fair and unambiguous beginning to allotment. The Nimiipuu councils demanded that Native scouts who had served in the 1877 conflict be paid for their work and repatriated exiles be reimbursed for the lands and stock they had left behind in Indian Territory. These actions would resolve issues resulting from the recent war. They insisted that reservation boundaries be resurveyed and stock belonging to white ranchers be removed. These concessions would force the federal government to recognize Nimiipuu control over a territory guaranteed by prior—and thus far flouted—treaty agreements.

By far the most important stipulation upon which Nimiipuu cooperation was based, however, was that Washington rescind the appointment of the reviled Charles E. Monteith as agent. Over the years of his bureaucratic association with the Nez Perce Agency—as agency clerk from 1871 to 1879 and as agent from 1882 to 1886—Monteith had alienated both Indians and whites. As early as 1882, on the occasion of his first appointment as agent, local residents had questioned his fitness for the office. In the *Nez Perce News*, "Publicus" asked: "[W]hat special fitness has Mr. Monteith ever displayed that he should be appointed to such a responsible position as that of Indian Agent? Is it because he is a Presbyterian? or because he is the son of his father? or because his brother was formerly agent at Lapwai? . . . [W]hat is the use of appointing a man as Indian Agent whose name is received by the Indians with terror. As I am told, the Indians held a council a short time ago on this subject and took a vote which proved that there were opposed to any change."[16] In 1886 a group of more than sixty Nez Perce men signed a petition addressed to President Grover Cleveland that "represent[ed] the unanimous opinion of our people against Charles E. Monteith's reappointment . . . as our agent" and suggesting that Alfred T. Beall be appointed instead.[17] The *Free Press* attributed those "animosities now existing between the agent, and the citizens and Indians . . . entirely to the acts of Mr. Monteith himself in the exercise of arbitrary power."[18] Thus, in 1889, Monteith's second appointment as agent was an almost universally unpopular move, questioned in area newspapers and adamantly opposed by the Nez Perces.[19]

It was widely known that Fletcher's work was encountering initial delays. The *Lewiston Teller* reported, "Miss Fletcher . . . has been deterred and delayed from commencing the work and prosecuting it, as we understand, not from the pressure and council of Indians, but by contrary representations of the existing state of facts made by whites."[20] Presumably the "contrary representations" were those furnished by agency personnel and interested parties, some of whom supported Monteith, and others who opposed him and wished to have the position for themselves. Affairs at the Nez Perce Agency had been chaotic even before Monteith's appointment was announced, resulting in a succession of five agents or temporary administrators since January 1 of that year.[21] Some of these had been accused of drunkenness on the job and of employing unqualified family members as school matrons and teachers.[22] Nimiipuu parents had complained to the local agents and to the Office of Indian Affairs that children who attended the agency school, then under the direct supervision of the agent, had been abused, neglected, and exposed to cold, hunger, disease, and unsanitary conditions.[23] A debate raged about whether the school should be administered by the agent, the superintendent, or church officials. The ongoing and unresolved problem of cattle grazing had also become conflated with the issue of the agent's appointment, for as Acting Agent Heth tried to rid the reservation of white men's cattle, he had discovered that Charles Monteith had profited from illegally breaching reservation boundaries. Monteith did not, of course, run cattle under his own name, but in partnership with William Caldwell, who as proprietor of a mail station was allowed to use reservation lands for these purposes. Heth brought charges that "C. E. Monteith's cattle run with Wm. Caldwell's stock, under his brand."[24] Monteith denied the allegation and had Heth arrested.

"Ferment" among reservation employees was not unusual, but this particular set of quarrels had escalated. In her first letter from Idaho, Jane Gay reported "that internecine war is raging among the [agency] officials. Three of them are on trial here in the county court for assault with intent to kill and for false imprisonment of each other. They all go armed and even the women of their families are accused of 'fighting with fists'" (C, 6).[25] This contretemps also touched allotment, since Fletcher's letter of appointment had specified that she was to perform her duties "in conjunction with the Agent."[26] Within the first week of her arrival, each of the main contenders for the agent's position had met with Fletcher and outlined his case to her, as had several powerful local white businessmen and ranchers.[27]

Fletcher was an astute and experienced bureaucrat. As a lobbyist and as an allotting agent she had seen the infightings and machinations of the agency system, and she was aware of the heightened tension surrounding lucrative federal appointments. She also understood that the timing of her arrival had been unfortunate and that her work threatened to become conflated with the local infighting. She wrote to Commissioner Thomas Jefferson Morgan in early June that Monteith's "appointment and my advent coming about the same time are classed together as indicative that the Government means to oppress and wrong the Nez Perce. This belief makes my position one of delicacy and difficulty and seems likely to promise complications in the future."[28]

Fletcher made an initial misstep (which she did not report as such) that threatened to confirm local suspicion about her being in league with the agency. Anxious to begin her work, she made a series of initial allotments, most of them to Nez Perce employees and to the Nez Perce wives of agency workers. On 20 June 1889 she informed the commissioner that she had "already started out groups of Indians [to] make selections" of land in the area north of the Clearwater River, close to the agency.[29] Yet she did not again mention these initial allotments (perhaps as many as a hundred of them). The reason for her silence becomes clear in light of Monteith's report to the commissioner, dated 26 August. He wrote, "I think all white men who married Nez Percé women have come upon the reserve and made selections for the benefit of their wives and children. The Indians move slow, generally, and in this their tardy action has given said whites opportunity to come in and select lands which reservation Indians had contemplated taking. This has caused considerable feeling."[30] Were Fletcher to have persisted in allotting land in Lapwai—and in this case, the most fertile and desirable land on the reservation—to Native women with white spouses who were agency employees, she would indeed seem to be complicit in yet another form of white exploitation.[31]

Rather than continue to allot lands in the Lapwai area, she decided to remove herself from the scene of such infighting. Exactly a week after her arrival at the agency, she "[w]rote Miss Sue McB [the Presbyterian missionary] offering to rent [her] home at Kamiah."[32] At that strategic remove, sixty miles to the east, she would be geographically, politically, and ideologically distanced from the agency. Her immediate departure, however, seems to have been delayed by federal bureaucracy and agency ineptitude—real or strategic—for she could not gather the necessary pack horses, harnesses, and wagons to support her move.

Fletcher publicly refused to align herself with any group of white interests in the Lapwai area. Gay tells of white cattlemen who apparently tried to bribe her and departed "evidently nonplussed, for, as they mounted their horses . . . one mutter[ed], 'Why in thunder did the Government send a woman to do this work? We could have got a holt on a man'" (C, 14). Fletcher had little to gain from conventional political bribery, since she did not drink, was well-paid, and as a woman, was unlikely to receive a political appointment more powerful than the one she currently held. Although she kept herself above local entanglements, she was beholden to other interests, chief among them the Presbyterian Church, as her initial work in the Lapwai area suggests.

Very early on, she turned her attention to the Langford claim, prime acreage the *Teller* had called "the richest and best situated piece of property on the reserve," and a site highly interesting to the Presbyterian Church as well.[33] Its boundaries were ambiguous and its ownership was contested. In 1848 the Nez Perces had given this tract to the first Presbyterian missionary in Idaho, Henry Spalding, as a mission site; in the years that followed, the claim, much enlarged, had passed to W. G. Langford, a local and powerful judge. Langford's understanding of the claim's boundaries greatly exceeded the amount of land given Spalding by the Nez Perces and now included some agency buildings, the Presbyterian missionary's home, and the Native church. As Kate McBeth wrote, "[T]his was not a matter simply of the families who would have been put out of their homes. but the changing the place of Worship with all its sacred memories. All the christian Nez Perce were touched when it came to this spot."[34] As well, Fletcher noted, lands comprising this claim were "regarded as a favorable point for a town site, as there [were] expectations that a railroad [would] one day pass along the Clearwater and the people living on the Lapwai and its tributaries could find easy access to a town situated at the mouth of the creek."[35]

Fletcher's attention to the Langford claim thus resurrected a divisive local debate. At first glance it suggests her naiveté about the ease with which she could begin her work. But Fletcher was not an inexperienced government employee, and her interest in this valuable land signals an alliance that would determine her conduct of allotment throughout the four years she was in Idaho. Just two weeks after her arrival she had written to J. C. Lowrie, secretary of the Presbyterian Board of Foreign Missions, asking him to send her all the information he had at his disposal concerning the Langford claim. She asked, "under what law did Mr. Spalding take the claim—for what purpose—what title was acquired, by what authority, and in whom was it vested. How did Judge Langford come into possession."[36] This letter suggests that Fletcher's initial instructions may have come from the church as well as the state, the church having asked her to assure their ownership of the land on which the mission buildings stood. A month later she queried Langford's attorney, E. O'Neill, asking for details about the claim, and sent her surveyor to verify the boundaries "set forth in Mr. Langford's deed."[37] These actions brought an immediate injunction from O'Neill, forbidding her to make allotments on the claim.[38] Fletcher then wrote to F. F. Ellinwood, a member of the Presbyterian Board of Foreign Missions, "I think there will be no difficulty in setting apart 160 acres for each mission station, but I am quite sure that it will be difficult if not impossible to secure the land in a compact form, in the points you designate."[39] The Langford claim continued to plague Alice Fletcher for the next four years; its boundaries and ownership remained unresolved when she left Idaho for the last time in 1892, and the case was resolved only when allotment was legally completed.[40]

Perhaps because her initial allotments seemed to favor white interests, and surely because of the injunction against allotting land on the Langford claim, Fletcher's work soon stalled. Jane Gay wrote in the *Red Man*, "I'd like to tell you something about the work of allotment" but then turned her account to an explanation of why allotment was *not* proceeding apace: "You start from Washington with instructions which read easy. 'Any body can allot Indians,' said a callow youth to me one day. I did not argue with him. I only said, 'I suppose you first catch your Indians.' . . . I saw by his eye that he expected to find them all in a row at the Agency waiting in immovable patience for him to label them in consecutive order and ticket them according to the nicely photographed plats furnished by the Department, for the most part drawn from imagination."[41]

As Gay and Fletcher soon discovered, "your Indians" were nowhere to be found. Mark explains that their absence was due to their custom of "mov[ing] out in the summer to hunt and gather root crops for the winter" (*SNL*, 171). While it is possible that some had indeed begun to leave for the camas harvest, the major hunting migrations did not begin until autumn. An accumulation of documentary evidence suggests another possibility. "[W]e are being boycotted," Gay finally wrote on 30 June (*C*, 44). In the initial optimism about allotment, it seems, none of its proponents, Fletcher included, had anticipated the "immovable patience" of the Nimiipuu, who stonewalled Fletcher's every opening gambit. The "council" Monteith had referred to was only one of several such meetings at which Native leaders planned how they might delay the inception of allotment as a bargaining point in seeking resolution to several matters of concern. At one such council meeting, James Reubens was chosen to represent their position to Washington DC. Until he returned, the Nez Perces would refuse to cooperate with Fletcher.[42]

Fletcher had already attended at least one of these council meetings on 8 June and made an important compromise.[43] She had "agree[d] to run out the border lines of the reservation and correct the encroachments of the white settlers," after which "there must be no more delay."[44] A second narrative of the meeting, given three years later by James Moses to Inspector W. W. Junkin, agrees in the main about these details: "When Miss Fletcher first came here my people told her to go around the boundary of the reservation, and after she done this to come back and talk with us. Her answer was that she would do so. She said if I find any white man on the reservation I will put them off and will give the Indians their places."[45] These details suggest that the delays Fletcher encountered at Lapwai were neither the result of Native ignorance nor because the locals had left the area for the autumn hunt. Fletcher's compromises might more precisely be called concessions, made in an effort to secure Nimiipuu cooperation.

In the absence of Indian clients, Fletcher obfuscated, using her weekly reports to direct the attention of the Office of Indian Affairs to other items. She asked for several clarifications of key portions of the Dawes Act.[46] She requested a census and the field notes of earlier surveys, claiming to have discovered that these key records were missing from local office files.[47] By making these requests, Fletcher was able to draw the attention of Washington officials to the incompetence of local administrators without directly accusing the current agent of mismanagement. Conditions that Fletcher could only hint at became the stuff of Gay's humor. To readers of the *Red Man*, she described the lack of support: "You go to the office, and look for a census roll. You do not find one. The office has a deserted appearance. The dust is over all. The inkstands are dry, the pens rusted, the paper soiled, the floor dirty. The stove has been used as a spittoon from time immemorial. . . . You sit down upon the wood-box and meditate. Where are the Indians? You ask the Agent and he says, 'Oh, about.'"[48] Gay's account, addressed to an audience of reform-minded Friends of the Indian who were already predisposed to believe the worst about the bureaucratic incompetencies of the reservation system, emphasized practices that allotment would redress when performed by a virtuous woman who knew her duty and was devoted to it.

In her requests for information from Washington, Fletcher misrepresented, to a certain extent, the local conditions she had encountered. For instance, she exaggerated the degree to which the provisions of the Dawes Act were misunderstood, and by whom. She reported general ignorance: "Upon my journey toward Lewiston I heard the people talking of 'the opening of the reservation,' and they evidently were unacquainted with the Severalty Act. It was the received opinion that as soon as the Indians were allotted all the remainder of the reservation would be thrown open as public lands. . . . No one in Lewiston seemed to be acquainted with the provisions of the law governing allotments."[49] Fletcher's impression was borne out by her initial encounters with area ranchers—"bold highwaymen," Gay called them (C, 24)—and with "fully 100 intending settlers," eager to avail themselves of the potential of "this latest and best Oklahoma," who had positioned themselves on the borders of the reservation to be ready to claim property as soon as the allotment should be completed.[50] Some had already built cabins and begun to plant crops within the reservation boundaries. Yet the full text of the Dawes General Allotment Act had been printed in the *Lewiston Teller* at least three times, and its provisions had been discussed in numerous editorials and reports.[51] It is likely that in reporting these blatant attempts to profit from the new law as "misunderstandings" or "ignorance," Fletcher was carefully alerting the Indian Office to the considerable degree of fraud, graft, and corruption being fed by the boosterism of the local papers. She surely also meant to signal that such blatant and willful misunderstandings were hindering her work.

Fletcher claimed, as well, that the Nez Perces "knew no more than the white people, except a few returned students from Oklahoma and Carlisle Schools who have read the Act of Feb. 8, 1887."[52] While misunderstandings surely existed, her assertion seriously misrepresents the extent to which allotment had been discussed and was understood by the Nez Perces. As I have already demonstrated, for several years prior to the passage of the Dawes Act, various agency officials had discussed the concept of severalty in councils with the local Nimiipuu leaders and had received—or at least reported—the impression of their general agreement with its premises. Thus, while it is unlikely that every person on the reservation had full command of the fine points of the current iteration of the Severalty Act, it is likely that many claimed to be ignorant of its provisions as a way of forestalling the beginning application of a law so apparently welcomed—and already being strategically misinterpreted—by white cattlemen, railroad developers, and squatters.

According to Fletcher, she needed to instruct the people of northwestern Idaho—both white and Indian—in the finer points of allotment law. The claim fortuitously furnished her with an acceptable and not entirely false explanation for why her work was not yet under way. Gay reported to the *Red Man* that Fletcher had "open[ed] a peripatetic school of instruction [to] inform the actual settler, who is in Egyptian darkness as to the provisions of the Severalty Act." Instructing the Nez Perces confirmed Fletcher's understanding that education was part of her duties as allotting agent. Thus she "talk[ed] and talk[ed] and then talk[ed] some more" to the Indians, and was "questioned and cross-questioned" by them.[53]

[67]

In this fashion, nearly six weeks passed. On 1 July, the first day of Charles E. Monteith's official appointment, Fletcher and Gay left the agency. In her account of their removal from Lapwai to Kamiah, Gay strategically uses biblical figures for humor. But the biblical allusion also establishes the allotments Fletcher made at Kamiah as the *first* allotments, and figure the beginning of allotment (at Kamiah) as a genesis of sorts, the dawning of a new era. She writes, "Our friend the Missionary has told us that the progressive Indians have their homes in Kamiah.... 'Kamiah is a Paradise,' said the Missionary, and we have determined to go to Paradise" (C, 44). Gay did not explain why it took the women seventeen days to make a journey that could have been accomplished in less than three. While she recounts their intermediate trip along the southern border of the reservation, and makes clear the extent to which white squatters had gathered, she does not suggest in any way that the leisurely pace may have been an intentional delay as Fletcher awaited news of James Reubens's return from Washington DC.

Unlike Adam and Eve, Fletcher and Gay did not sin, fall, and suffer an expulsion from Paradise. Rather, after escaping the hellish conditions at the agency, where at dawn "[t]he pine wood of the porch ... was literally broiling in the rays of the sun," they fell *into* Paradise, making a dangerous and precipitous descent in a violent thunderstorm into the edenic Clearwater Valley (C, 48, 51–52). There, Adam's curse—to till the soil by the sweat of his brow—was to be transformed into a promise, secured by allotment, of individual plots of land deeded to their Christian Nez Perce farmer/owners, whom Susan McBeth had prepared to accept both land and citizenship. "She [Susan McBeth] has sent us from Mt. Idaho ... a welcome to her house and a 'God bless you' on our work. How can we but start out hopefully?" Gay asks (C, 79). In Gay's account, then, the work "starts out" at Kamiah; Presbyterian Nez Perces are the first to accept their allotments, and their cooperation opens the way for the rest of the tribe to receive the entitlements of private ownership of property.

As Gay's story has it, Fletcher used the Presbyterian Sunday service (on 21 July) to announce her arrival in Kamiah. On the follow-

A FALSE BEGINNING

ing day she held a meeting to explain the details of the program, and on Tuesday she began to register allottees. At the Monday meeting Fletcher's explanations of the new law convinced the hesitant congregants to "take their land in severalty, because it is the law and is best for them" (C, 112). According to Gay, "She tells them she has come to bring them manhood, that they may stand up beside the white man in equality before the law." This argument is the lynchpin, and especially suggestive in light of Monteith's report, which makes it clear that the initial allotments in Lapwai were made to Nez Perce women with white husbands. Some of the listeners relented, and the meeting ended with Fletcher's invitation "to call at the cabin and be registered and talk about the land" (C, 113).

As the congregation exited the church, Gay waited with her camera to "[catch] the people as they group themselves about the door. The Indians are pleased to have their photographs taken and some press forward to be in front. . . . The Photographer shows some of the old men the pictures on the ground glass, whereat they laugh and wonder. One notices that the image is reversed; the rest fail to perceive it" (C, 114). Gay's image and accompanying commentary aptly demonstrate my contention through a different lens, as it were. Those she photographed were familiar with the technology of her camera and tripod, just as they understood the machinery of allotment. At least one seems to have understood the process of image making to the point of noting that the photographic field was reversed.[54] Figure 7 shows an undifferentiated line of Native clients posed at the side of the church, Fletcher standing at the far left. The structure of the image parallels the logic of allotment: the law will set into motion a process by which this undifferentiated population, a group that heretofore could be rationalized only by a simple census, or counting, will be transformed into discrete individuals by the bureaucratic technologies associated with allotment. The process, like the photograph, will reverse these men's outlooks and lives.

In documenting this meeting for their immediate constituencies, both women emphasized the religious dimensions of the remarkable reversal. Fletcher reported to the commissioner of Indian affairs, "This meeting was held in their church building and opened by

[69]

FIG. 7. "Council at Kamiah," 22 July 1889, by E. Jane Gay. Alice Fletcher stands at the far left; James Stuart, wearing a white shirt, tie, and hat, is seated on the steps toward the right; and Edson Briggs is standing at Stuart's right. In *Choup-nit-ki* Gay cropped the image at the lines indicated on this print (114). ISHS 63-221.66E, Idaho State Historical Society Library and Archives.

prayer by the Native pastor Rev. Robert Williams. . . . . The congregation . . . embrac[es] all the inhabitants of this region except a few families who represent the non progressive and old-time element."[55] In the *Red Man* Gay waxed more poetic: "There at last, clustered on benches on the floor, packed close together she finds her Indian. . . . So it was 1800 years ago—that . . . the not wise, not mighty, the common people listened . . . looking for a life in death which should open a way to, they did not know exactly what—but to something . . . freer, above all else to the protection of some Great Being who cared for them, and would see justice done at last."[56] Both women imply that a higher power, whether a benevolent federal program or a Presbyterian god, would secure a better life to the allottees. Whichever the case, it was clear that Presbyterian missionary teaching had prepared this people for the civilizing blessings of allotment.

Gay's account continues, naming "Robert Williams, the native Pastor of Kamiah" as the first to be registered, followed by "Robert's wife and the fathers and mothers of both and of brothers and sisters a goodly number. And the next day, 'Old Billy,' Robert's father, came and he made a new point of departure and Luke his brother started a new circle and then other Indians dropped in, one by one ... to be registered" (C, 116). These reports—read by private sponsors such as Fletcher's friend Mary Thaw, whose generous support of Presbyterian causes would figure centrally in the course of allotment over the next three summers—elicited substantial financial reward, both for the Nez Perces who supported allotment and for Alice Fletcher, as I detail in the chapters that follow.

Despite their overt address to the church interests who lobbied for, sponsored, and stood to gain materially by allotment's outcome, these accounts point suggestively to other tellings, other voices, and other actions: pressures, concessions, and negotiations. In her initial letter reporting the Kamiah meeting to the commissioner of Indian affairs, Fletcher wrote, "[M]any questions were asked me as to the future effect of the Act upon the status of the allotted Indian and the forms of government they would then be subject to. . . . [T]hey were desirous of knowing if after they were citizens they could not organize a local government under the county where they reside. . . . I was asked, when they would cease to be under an Agent? . . . I explained that I could not say."[57] These details belie Fletcher's earlier accounts of the Indians' ignorance of the law and suggest the limits of her own ability to predict the outcomes of her work. These initial allottees did not accept land in severalty out of simple faith and childlike trust in the advice of their missionary mentors. Their questions to Fletcher stemmed from their wish to understand allotment's local implications, and their mention of the future status of agency governance demonstrates their intent to retain sovereign control of their local affairs. The questions suggest, as well, that those who lived at Kamiah were aware of conditions at Lapwai and shared the general concern that appointment of Charles E. Monteith as agent was likely not an indicator that the Indian Office had the best interests of the Nez Perce peoples at heart.

2. Another Beginning

A week or so after the meeting at the Kamiah Presbyterian Church, Fletcher announced she would establish a base camp in the field where she would meet allottees upon their lands and finalize their deeds. The allotting party—Fletcher, Gay, James Stuart, the surveyor Edson Briggs, and his workers—headed west to Cold Spring, near the present-day town of Reubens, where according to Gay's account, "many of the Kamians had expressed a desire to be allotted" (C, 132). Provisioned for six days, the party split: the surveyors went into the field, leaving the others at the base camp (C, 133). A few potential allottees dropped by, but the Kamians did not materialize. The women later discovered their clients "had gone to the mines [to sell summer produce] and would not be back for two or three weeks" (C, 144). Gay wrote, "In this way a week passes, then another, the Surveyor running out land farther and farther from the camp, until at length [the women and their interpreter] are left to the solitude of their own reflections, and still the Kamians came not" (C, 137–38). Their food dwindled to nothing and they began to fear they would starve. Then, miraculously, appeared a party of young Indian men from Lapwai:

> They had ridden sixty miles to find the Allotting Agent that they might consult with her about their land *which they were now ready to take.*

> They were jolly young fellows who sang and told stories about the camp-fire and those among them who were "returned students" spoke good English.
>
> Learning the perplexities of the Cook, they went out at daybreak with their shot guns and, on rising, we found a brace of grouse laid at the tent door.
>
> ... They did their best to make our weary waiting endurable; they donned war bonnets and posed for the Photographer; ... [A]t last, tired of low rations, they formed in line ... bade us an affectionate farewell ... [and] rode cheerfully away. (C, 139–40; emphasis added)

Gay's charming story takes additional energy from its resemblance to other beginnings—those recounted in foundational national myths, for example—in which benevolent Natives rescue improvident whites. Every school child knows the tale of how Squanto taught the early New England settlers to plant corn and kept them from starving; every school child knows, as well, how Pocahontas rescued Captain John Smith. Both stories persist, and are persistently mistold, because they perpetuate an agreeable delusion: white settlers were providentially welcomed, rescued, fed, and nurtured by friendly Natives who taught them how to survive in the new world. Told in this context, the old story seems again to reassure its readers that the Nez Perces would eventually recognize that whites' incursions on their lands and cultures were ultimately for everyone's best advantage. Their offerings of food function as a kind of sacrament that seals the compact.

Figure 8, the photograph Gay took of the posing men, is arguably one of her best-known images, if only because it graces the cover of the paperback edition of her letters. It shows two mounted warriors. One wears a full-length eagle feather headdress and carries a pole topped with an eagle feather, likely an honor pole. The other man wears a smaller feather headdress, has an ermine skin over his right shoulder, and carries a folded blanket and rifle. They pose in a clearing, looking as if they have materialized from the misty forest behind them.[1]

Despite its wide circulation, within Gay's oeuvre, this image is an

FIG. 8. "They Donned War Bonnets," Stephen Reubens (*left*) and James Reubens at Cold Spring ID, 10 August 1889, by E. Jane Gay, *Choup-nit-ki*, 140. See also figure 6 of Gay's album "Where We Camped," where this photograph is captioned "The Nez Percé War Pole" (SLHWA). The Idaho State Historical Society's captioning, "War Poles," follows that title. ISHS 63-221.18, Idaho State Historical Society Library and Archives.

anomaly.[2] Since the purpose of her photography was to document the success of a program designed to civilize the Nez Perces, most of her portraits do not show Native peoples in regalia or in traditional attire. It might seem, then, that the most appropriate image to have resulted from this occasion would be one similar to the dual portrait of James Reubens and Archie Lawyer shown in figure 9. In this image both men are dressed in jackets, cravats, boots, and hats; Lawyer holds a rolled and tied document, perhaps the deed to his allotment. The two sit in a clearing in front of a wooden building, likely the McBeth cabin in Kamiah. All the details of the image—the seated poses, the clothing, the setting in proximity to the missionary's home—combine to offer the impression that these are

[75]

FIG. 9. "James Reuben and Archie Lawyer," by E. Jane Gay, *Choup-nit-ki*, 274. ISHS 63-221.86, Idaho State Historical Society Library and Archives.

two successfully assimilated allottees. The contrast of this photograph with "They Donned War Bonnets" thus raises several questions: Who were these un-named mounted men? If they had come from Lapwai, how had they known where to find Fletcher? Why were they "now ready to take" their allotments? And why had they brought with them war bonnets and an honor pole?

The answers to these questions support my contention that a counter-narrative of beginnings can establish the active agency of Nimiipuu leaders in the allotment process. Alice Fletcher's private documents, including her field diary entries for early August, provide a brief, if suggestive, corrective to Gay's account of the Cold Spring episode:

Friday, August 9:
   Clear.
   Broke camp early & started for Cold Spring. Reached there at 10.30 A.M. Photograph arrival at camp—a lovely spot.[3]

Jas Ruben Jas Maxwell Fitch Phinney & the Henry's here in P.M.
The hens lay eggs.
Jas. Maxwell brings us two grouse.
Saturday, August 10:
Clear.
The men all register & as there are several claimants for land I appoint Tuesday to meet Mr Briggs here.
Miss G. photographed Jas Ruben in his war dress on horseback Stephen Ruben also. Takes them charging.
Mr. McCormick arrived.
Wrote F. & sent all my mail by Mr. Henry.
Slight rain all night
2 more grouses given us for food.

These two entries, quoted here in their entirety, demonstrate the degree to which Gay's account was crafted and strategically emplotted. The women were never in danger of starving. They had brought tame laying hens with them, and presumably their interpreter could have found game in the forest. Moreover, the men from Lapwai reached them on the afternoon of their arrival at Cold Spring, bringing with them even more food. So it would seem that Gay's story of providential and friendly Natives has diverted the narrative from centering on the more serious purposes of the Cold Spring rendezvous. James Reubens, who had been a leader of the resistance and delay at Lapwai, and who had gone to Washington DC to present the petitions against Monteith, had now come willingly to take his allotment. Again, as at Lapwai in 1883, he was appropriately attired for a significant occasion, this time in ceremonial regalia.

The encounter at Cold Spring is both an ending and a beginning. It concludes a carefully obscured story in which Fletcher arrived on the reservation and, in attempting to accommodate the interests of the Presbyterian church, made a false beginning to allotments there. By granting land to Native women married to white men who also were agency employees, she dangerously aligned herself with the graft, disorder, and corruption of that administrative regime. Hoping to cover her error, she blamed Native ignorance of the law, rather

[77]

than acknowledge the concerns of several tribal council meetings that had resulted in Reubens's ambassadorial visit to Washington. Until he returned, she could not work, and thus she waited on the borders of the reservation, overseeing the resurvey of its boundaries. Reubens's arrival at Cold Spring ended the impasse, signaled the tribal councils' approval, and allowed the work to begin. To identify Cold Spring as a beginning highlights the extent to which Native negotiators succeeded in forcing the federal government to acknowledge them as active participants in their own futures. In this telling Reubens becomes a protagonist, an active agent rather than an accidental savior of two hapless white campers. He plays a centrally important part in making it possible for Fletcher's work to begin, a cooperation for which she had bargained and upon which her success depended. The counter-narrative reads like this:

Allotment began in earnest when James Reubens said it could. As a spokesman for the several tribal councils that had already petitioned Washington for Monteith's dismissal, and as an informed and interested individual intent on securing an advantageous allotment for himself and for his extended family, Reubens had occupied a key position in the initial negotiations. His involvement was undoubtedly the result of his prior experience as a tribal intermediary (evidenced by his part in securing the exiles' return), his ongoing interest in policy matters and reservation politics, and his connections with both white and Nimiipuu power elites. Upon her arrival Fletcher had recognized him as an important potential ally. Although Fletcher and Gay carefully obscured the details of their connection to Reubens, other documentary evidence reveals a suggestive connection that establishes Reubens's centrality to allotment's beginnings.

In her field diary Fletcher lists by name many (but not all) of the local power brokers she met upon her arrival in Idaho. On Monday, May 27, before she even arrived in Lewiston, a "Mr. Cannon" "gave [her the] names of Mr. Volmer" and other influential businessmen in Lewiston. J. P. Vollmer, "the richest man in the county," was president the local Board of Trade, a major investor in the Northern Pacific Railroad, and proprietor of a trading post at the Lapwai Agency.[4] According to a local historian, he was also "a staunch friend" of James Reubens.[5] In her field diary Fletcher does not mention having met Vollmer, but he was apparently one of her key local contacts. Evidence for this contention comes from an unlikely source: Charles Monteith. A man of hot temper, lacking Fletcher's sense of diplomacy, Monteith wrote an angry letter to the commissioner of Indian affairs, charging that "Upon her arrival [Vollmer] endeavored to prejudice Miss Alice C Fletcher, Special U.S. Indian Agent, against me, as also her companion a Miss Gay." In this letter protesting the renewal of Vollmer's license as an agency trader, Monteith was fighting to retain his own appointment. He fulminates, "Vollmer is my bitterest enemy.... He was one of the parties who encouraged James Reuben . . . to go to Washington last month, to ask my recall, and I am told that he furnished said Reuben with part of the money used in paying his expenses."[6]

Fletcher did not mention James Reubens by name in her field diary until 13 June, more than two weeks after she arrived. The entry reads: "Mr. Monteith to arrive to take Agency on 14. Talk to Jas R. Inds have wired money to send him to Wash. Wrote F. Sen. Washburn." By this time the two had surely begun to negotiate. At one of the three tribal council meetings of which Fletcher and Gay were aware, Nimiipuu leaders made it clear to Fletcher that they would not cooperate with the allotment until they had federal assurance that several outstanding issues had been resolved, and that they intended to send Reubens to Washington to communicate their concerns. Many of these issues—Monteith's reappointment chief among them—were beyond Fletcher's immediate authority and control. However, she could—and did—offer what appeared to be an important concession: "To fix the outboundaries where whites have crowded. All agree to that."[7] These diary entries suggest new explanations of Fletcher's initial actions. The day after the June 10 council she wrote to the commissioner, "Upon the north there are at least two sets of blazed lines and upon the East and South and West the lines have been moved so as to throw some of the Indians who have lived for years on their claims outside the reservation and in one instance the line has been moved in 28 rods for a distance of two miles taking from the Indians a valuable spring."[8] She dispatched her newly hired surveyor, Edson Briggs, "for Northern boundary in P.M."[9] Resurvey of the existing reservation boundaries was in actuality a procedure mandated by Fletcher's orders but subject to her judgment. She had been instructed to "do such re-tracing of lines and re-establish such monuments as may be found requisite."[10] A skilled negotiator, she parlayed this part of her duties into an apparent concession that would demonstrate her good faith.

Fletcher also was aware of and cooperated with James Reubens's visit to the capital, a fact not mentioned by Gay, nor noted by Fletcher's biographer. As the brief notations in her diary suggest, upon learning of his impending departure, she "[W]rote F. [Francis La Flesche]," her Omaha protégé and collaborator, then living in Washington, to inform him of Reubens's plans.[11] Her letter to Senator Washburn may also have been intended to introduce Reubens. For his part, Reubens kept Fletcher informed—while he was gone and when he returned—about the progress of his negotiations regarding Monteith. At some time during his stay in the capital he made contact with La Flesche, writing to Fletcher that he had "met Frank . . . he has been a great deal of service to me, and has interduced me to many of your friends. I like Frank very much, he is real Indian in very way, he has not got that high-toned actions which education gives to young Indians. But Frank knows the feelings of his race."[12]

With him Reubens carried "a petition bearing several hundred names . . . protesting against Monteith."[13] The document represented the concerns of three consecutive meetings of the tribal council, a sovereign body engaged in standard diplomatic negotiations. Even Fletcher (privately and strategically) acknowledged the diplomatic nature of his mission, writing to the commissioner: "In reply to the stimulating picture of citizenship, they say: 'If the Government wishes to make us like white men, they should give us some of the consideration shown white men. We have asked but one thing [the removal of Monteith], asked it by petitions bearing the name of nearly every man in the tribe and what heed has been paid to our voice? When the government wants us to do anything it promises much & we are to be white men. When we ask one favor, we are only Indians not worth hearing.'"[14] The terms in which Fletcher describes these particular difficulties make it clear that she and the various tribal councils had—separately and in conference—discussed allotment's promises of citizenship, due process, and democratic representation. These letters make it abundantly clear that the degree to which these promises would be realized might be severely tested were Monteith to be reappointed.

The petition, Reubens's personal appeal, and the commissioner's own knowledge of Monteith's record seem to have convinced John W. Noble, then secretary of the interior, that the appointment was a mistake. On June 22, Noble wrote to the commissioner of Indian affairs requesting "a short report to me whether you deem it to the good of the service that he [Monteith] should be continued in office. I am impressed by his own statement that he thinks the Indians have too much good pasture."[15] Five days later, Reubens wrote to Fletcher, "Commissioner Indian Affairs has already recommended to the Hon. Sect. of Interior that Monteith *should not stay there*, and submitted all the papers with this recommendations. What action the Sec. will take, remains to be seen by Saturday."[16]

Reubens had other agenda items as well. These he summarized in a letter he sent to the commissioner of Indian affairs after he had arrived in Washington DC and after he had conferred with Francis La Flesche. I quote it here in full:

Dear Sir:

I beg leave, and most respectfully, submit, the following, with the earnest requests of your favorable considerations, and with Official and written reply.

1st   Is there any money due the Nez Perce Indians, in the "U.S. Treasury"?

2nd   Is there any Law, by which U.S. Government could issue patent, to the Nez Perce Indians, for their surplus land, after the "Allotment" was completed?

As in the case with Omoha Indians, who hold patent for their surplus land, after their "Allotments" were taken, some years ago.

3rd   It was provided in the "Treaties" especially in 1863, that Government shall have right to keep mail stations long on the reservation, on public roads &c. &c.

But it was not understood, by the Indians, that said stations shall become extensive farms and stock raising places.

There are three stations on the reservation:

"Jack Grier's" place, has about 80 acres, on Clear-water river, has stock.

"White's station," has over 400. acres under fence, and cultivates about 100. acres & keep the rest for pasturing their cattle and horses.

Bill Caldwell's place, cultivates, at least 80 acres, has over 100. acres under fence, has about 300. cattle & horses. he has often branded stock belonging to Indians, and even branding cattle belonging to Indian Department.

Now by what right, are these white men allowed so much land on the reservation?

4th It is the desire of the Nez Perce's, that they be furnished with improved farming implements, such as wagons, threshing machines, reapers, mowers, sulky-plows, harness, harrows, and cooking-stoves.

There is no encouragement to them, when they have to cut their grain, with cradles and scythes, and then tramp it out with horses to save their grain.

5th During Chief Joseph's war in 1877, some 30. Nez Perces were employed as scouts, by Gen. Howard, they never got their pay. is there any way them to get their pay now?[17]

6th Have the Nez Perce Indians under the Laws full right to hunt and fish, outside the reservation? in the Mountains? and on Government unoccupied lands? In behalf of Nez Perce Indians,

Yours humble sert.
James Reubens
Nez Perce Indians[18]

This letter, a comprehensive summary of current issues the tribal council wished to have resolved, contains no reference to Fletcher, throwing into doubt Gay's implication that Reubens had gone to the capital to check on Fletcher's credentials and suggesting that the story was fabricated to excuse her delay in beginning the allotment. Reubens clearly demonstrates the extent to which the Nez Perces understood allotment, and not merely in the theoretical way the Dawes Act had outlined it, nor in the practical details of its immediate application, as Fletcher understood it. Rather, his letter—with its doubled signature "James Reubens/Nez Perce Indians" establishing his words as representing the tribal councils' concerns—suggests that the Nimiipuu saw the occasion of Reubens's visit to Washington as a chance to clarify and resolve issues the government had resolutely ignored. The questions deal with the details of prior treaties: the queries about hunting and fishing rights granted by the Treaty of 1863 but endangered by white hysteria about perceived Indian threats following the War of 1877; and the limits of benefits accruing to the keepers of mail stations. They ask for resolution of more recent issues: the reimbursement of scouts who had served Howard in the war. They seek to clarify how allotment would affect the Nimiipuu: Would they have "improved farming implements" with which to work their land? Finally, they anticipate issues unresolved even today, regarding land-based resources of wildlife, mineral deposits, and water and timber rights. They ask whether monies were owing the tribe.[19] Notably, this issue comes first on Reubens's list, suggesting that even at this relatively early date, Nez Perces had begun to question federal accountability in matters of tribal monies.

Reubens had long worried about what would follow when allotment ended, an issue about which he was much more prescient than Alice Fletcher. According to the *Teller*, "It has been known that Reuben ... was ambitious to maintain all of the Nez Perce reservation for the use of the Indians, that he delivered a substance of his desire in a speech several years ago at Lapwai, stating that it was true that the present generation of Indians could not occupy and improve the lands of the reservation but that he wanted the government to retain it as the property of the Indians to be parceled out as it was needed and would be needed by the tribe in generations yet unborn."[20] He had already proposed a solution to a problem not anticipated by allotment, the fractionated holdings that have continued to plague the descendants of original allottees. In his letter to the commissioner Reubens approached the question again. His mention of the Omaha allotment makes it clear that he had discussed his concerns with Fletcher and/or La Flesche and received an answer based on that precedent.

Alice Fletcher's actions while Reubens was away from the reservation, then, take on new resonance. Knowing full well the tribal council had determined not to cooperate with her until Reubens returned, and that a beginning to allotment—whether in Lapwai or in Kamiah—would depend on Monteith's withdrawal, she did what she could, within the limits of what she considered to be appropriate professionalism, to assure that another agent would be appointed. Maintaining an outward air of detachment, even to the point of removing herself from the agency headquarters, she nevertheless found a way to let the Indian Office know—indirectly, but nevertheless effectively—how matters stood.

She wrote two strategically important letters. The first was an uncharacteristically frank and forceful private letter to her friend Richard Henry Pratt, beginning with this overt admission: "I now write you to complain." Because she considered Pratt to be a "trusty man, . . . acquainted with Indians and Indian affairs, . . . who can gain the ear of the President & Sec'y," she writes in damning detail of "Mr. C. E. Monteith," a man she characterizes as "cold, calculating, uncommunicative [who] never forgets or ceases to pursue one whom he is adverse to. [H]e is arbitrary by nature and of the stuff tyrants are made of. I do not know what he has done in full. I only know that I never saw a tribe so censorious in their dislike distrust and aversion to a man . . . He is not in sympathy with having school . . . outside the reservation. He has opposed and has said he will oppose the Indian going away to gain knowledge." It is clear that Fletcher chose these details to convince Pratt, a champion of boarding school education for Indians, that his causes would likely also suffer were Monteith to be appointed. She then opines: "[T]here is no real opposition of any moment to allotment but—The Indians know that the Gov't and the white people are anxious for allotment, and they propose to ask that if they are quickly allotted, doing as the Gov't asks they also be granted this one request—the removal of C. E. Monteith. *They are trying to freeze me out.* I can't get an Indian chainman. They may lean on accidents, I recognize their tricks and am using all my power to placate." Fletcher concludes her long and detailed letter by urging Pratt to exert his considerable political influence to ensure that Monteith's appointment be rescinded, and suggesting an acceptable replacement. "Surely if the Pres't knows the feeling here, he would not force Monteith on these people. . . . There is an excellent man here Republican . . . Edward McConville. . . . [H]e is known, loved, & trusted by the people . . . put him in! Everything becomes plain and calm."[21]

Fletcher was a skillful persuader, one who carefully framed arguments to suggest that those she asked for support would benefit from cooperating with her requests. But the candor of her letter to Pratt, even when tempered with her characteristic self-effacement, is nearly unique in her correspondence from this period.[22] It stands in stark contrast to her second letter on the same subject, written a day later to the commissioner of Indian affairs. In the guise of a weekly report, she suggested, "The difficulties incidental to the incoming Agent, whose presence is resented by the tribe, considerably affects my work. The Indians feel aggrieved by the indifference shown toward their appeals and they distrust the good faith of the government in its laws. . . . It is sincerely to be hoped that the Government will make no mistake and force an issue which all would regret."[23]

Fletcher wrote both these letters while she lingered at Lapwai. The background they contain illuminates her initial movements: why she did not go immediately to Kamiah in early June, when she had written to Susan McBeth arranging to rent her cabin; why it took her more than two weeks to arrive there once she had left Lapwai. Along the way, she was overseeing Briggs's resurvey of the south and southwest boundaries, to be sure; she was also visiting with and taking the measure of squatter incursion along the Camas Prairie boundary. By the evidence of her field diary, she loitered: reading, visiting Susan McBeth in Mt. Idaho, and working on her own research and writing. In straightforward terms, she was delaying, awaiting Reubens's return, awaiting word about Monteith, and awaiting an indication that the tribal council had relented.[24]

Reubens's letters constitute an important but heretofore overlooked resource. They make it apparent that he went to Washington with Fletcher's knowledge and support. They illuminate the nature of his negotiations with federal officials. They make clear his success in receiving assurances that Monteith would be removed. They establish that before he returned to Idaho Reubens knew procedures for Monteith's recall had been set in motion. Finally, they quite fully discredit several secondary accounts of Reubens's trip that dismiss his diplomacy as a failure. According to Morrill and Morrill, for example, the commissioner had refused Reubens's plea: "In Washington James had again learned of the invincible power of the white man to take what he coveted."[25] Their conclusion seems to be based on reports in local newspapers, where Reubens's trip had been closely followed. Both the Office of Indian Affairs and Reubens were careful not to disclose the outcome of their talks until a case against Monteith could convincingly be made. Upon his return Reubens spoke carefully, knowing that to proclaim success would spark even more tension. The *Lewiston Teller* reported: "It is plainly evident, admitting that the report of Reuben to the Indians on the morning after his return be true, he has no heart in the further resistance to the government in reference to taking lands in severalty.... [H]e either became convinced ... of the utter uselessness of further efforts to oppose the orders of the government ... or became inspired with new hopes of the good which the allotment would make ... and thus has induced him to entirely change his programme of efforts."[26] True, Reubens had changed his mind and announced he would support allotment. But the *Teller*'s interpretation was flawed, limited by white presumptions about Native powerlessness. Reubens had not altered his "programme." Rather, he knew Monteith would be removed and had told Fletcher she could now proceed.

By Tuesday, July 16, Fletcher, still camped on the reservation border but once again "at work on [the] Langford claim," had broken camp and headed for Kamiah.[27] By July 22 she had begun to meet with the Kamiah Presbyterian Nez Perces, those who had initially demurred, telling Fletcher, "We must wait for our people in Lapwai to consent" (C, 112). On July 25 the *Teller* told its readers "that news has been sent over from Boise to this place that there is to be a change in the agency."[28] Monteith denied the report and continued to protest and resist removal until he was finally released from duty on 13 September.[29] Only after Monteith's appointment was rescinded and only after the consent of the tribal council did allotment begin in earnest.

On July 28 "Jas. Ruben called" on Fletcher in Kamiah; a week later she sent her surveyor "to locate Jas R. over by Genesee," and five days after that Reubens and his brother arrived at the Camp at Cold Spring to register for their allotments.[30] As his allotment, Reubens requested land immediately abutting the Langford claim. As early as 1875 he had written to the commissioner of Indian affairs to report the tribe's dissatisfaction with "the trouble given to us by Mr. Langford on our Reservation." The issue was that Langford had "claimed our mill which [had been] daily used for the Indians before Langford claimed it." Reubens's letter, written on behalf of his father, then a head chief, and a nine-man tribal council, concluded: "[W]e want the mill to be returned and all connect with it for the use of the Indians. Our Agent has told us not to talk about the matter but that all would be settled at Washington. So we send to you."[31] The area comprising and surrounding the Langford claim had originally been part of the Reubens family land. The elder Reubens had operated a ferry across the Clearwater in the early 1860s; he also kept a warehouse along the river's banks in the area that later became the town of Lewiston.[32] James Reubens apparently hoped to establish a definitive and legal claim to it under the allotment act. Five days after Gay made her photograph of the Reubens brothers at Cold Spring, the *Teller* reported, "Indian Reuben is one of the parties who has made choice of the ground near [Catholic gulch on the north side of the Clearwater] and intends changing his residence to that point."[33]

An intriguing series of events hints at the negotiations between Fletcher and Reubens regarding his choice of land. When Reubens sought out Fletcher in late July in Kamiah, after both were sure Monteith would be replaced, they seem to have had an extended series of conversations, some of them having to do with Fletcher's ethnographic researches. As she recorded in her field diary, he "stayed all night," "sang some Ind. songs," and apparently offered to obtain "ten Eagle feathers for F." for which Fletcher paid him "$4."[34]

[87]

The presumptive outcome of this visit is that the two agreed to meet at Cold Spring to finalize the details of Reubens's deed. The meeting may have spurred Fletcher to see in Reubens a young man with the potential to become another Francis La Flesche, one who could be educated, advocate in Washington and at home for his people, and, along the way, be a valuable informant and collaborator in her ethnographic researches. Shortly after he departed Fletcher wrote F. W. Putnam that she had "[found] . . . many myths here that I knew East of the Mts." This is surely the outcome of her recent conversations with Reubens. In this same letter she wrote, "One fine fellow I mean to educate for the law."[35]

After Reubens took his allotment, Fletcher began in earnest to make good on her plan. She wrote to Henry Heth, the former special agent at Lapwai who had since returned to Washington, informing him of her plans and enlisting him to help her raise money and arrange Reubens's enrollment at the Columbian Law School.[36] Heth, who had known Reubens in Idaho, agreed to help. He reported to Fletcher in October:

> I saw the Secretary of the Interior this morning, and asked him to give James Rubins a position as Messenger at a salary of say from 6 to 800 per annum in order to partly defray his expenses during his stay in W. attending the Law School. The Secretary said he would do so—provided you would make the application, accompanying same by a request from some members of his tribe—and also a letter from some of the citizens of Lewiston that James Rubins is a man worthy of his (the Secty) going out of the usual line in such matters—The Comer of Indian Affairs has promised if I could make the above arrangement with the Secty, that he would give 164\frac{00}{}$ per annum towards James education and defray his [travel] expenses [to Washington].[37]

Fletcher wrote to others as well, including Mary Thaw, who replied that she "[would] give . . . $1000 for Jas. Ruben."[38] She asked her friend John Wesley Powell, then director of the U.S. Geological Survey and head of the Bureau of Ethnology, to hire Reubens as an assistant while he was in Washington. Her request interwove ethnographic concerns, political preferment, and federal policy: "I find that the myths etc. of the Nez Perces are fast dying out. All the old customs are now obsolete and some difficult to recover. James Ruben ... has quite a store of knowledge and more than all possessed of native talent & ability—and capable of serving science intelligently. Trusting you may be able to employ him, others make it possible for him to secure his legal course of study and thus serve not only James Ruben but his deserving tribe."[39]

Despite Fletcher's considerable efforts, James Reubens did not attend law school. It is unclear why, although a letter from Heth suggests one important reason: "The Secretary, said Monteith had given James R. a terrible character, a drunkard, a libertine, and a gambler!"[40] Heth and Fletcher sought documentation to counter Monteith's slander. Some time later, Heth again wrote: "With all the irons we have in the fire I think success must attend our endeavours, and think James R. will be sent for. Monteith did all he could to ruin James R. and I found it difficult to eradicate the unfavorable information created by the falsehoods he told. Monteith I find is pretty well known here; [he has a] reputation as a man who will bear close watching ... he has no standing in the Indian Office—his being kept so long at Lapwai has enabled him to do a world of mischief."[41] Regrettably, after the end of 1889, any evidence of a continuing conversation about Reubens and law school disappears from the public record.

The weight of evidence suggests, then, that Gay's image "They Donned War Bonnets" might be seen as documenting an occasion of celebration and of ceremonial exchange. James and Stephen Reubens had come to take their allotments and to request adjoining properties for their extended family in an area previously claimed by the Reubens family on lands among the most desirable on the reservation.[42] Grouping family claims in such proximity was contrary to at least one theory of allotment, which recommended Indian holdings be interspersed with white lands, checkerboard style, so Indians would be positively uplifted by the example of their white neighbors. Fletcher was questioned closely by the Board of Indian Commissioners on this point in January 1890, when she reported to them at the end of her first summer in Idaho. Her answer illuminates the logic by which she made the Reubens allotments. She told the board she grouped families together to simplify eventual probate and inheritance problems, continuing, "It has always been my aim to find out the vantage point on the reservation, the point most likely to be opened to settlement, and on and around that point I place my best Indians. I give the best land to the best Indians that I can find. I always help the progressive Indian first. . . . I am bound to give the Indian a chance, and some of these Indians and their descendants are going to secure and keep the chance which I have made for them."[43] James Reubens's allotment was surely such a "vantage point," located near a potential town site along the railroad that was planned across the reservation. It remains unclear whether Fletcher's initial queries about the Langford claim were pursued on behalf of the Presbyterian Church, as a way of clearing the ground for the Reubens claims, or both.[44]

Fletcher's work on the reservation thus did not begin with her arrival, nor with the miraculous cooperation of the Presbyterian Kamiah congregation. It was, rather, part and parcel of an ongoing Nez Perce history. It concerned land that had been in dispute since the first whites had arrived; it involved alliances and reunions that had been exacerbated by the War of 1877. It was shaped and formed not only by her considerable skills in negotiation and persuasion but also by an equally skillful set of Nimiipuu negotiators, whose concerns delayed her work, and who, when they decided those concerns had been redressed, permitted allotment to begin. To restore their point of view to the narration of the allotment is to return to them their property, in a sense, a story they helped to write and in which they play a significant part as active protagonists.

As with many historically based stories, not all the details of Fletcher's first weeks in Idaho conspire to form a tidy and satisfactory conclusion. About "They Donned War Bonnets," one question remains. Why were the Reubens brothers carrying war bonnets and an honor pole when they met Fletcher at Cold Spring? The record is suggestive, although not conclusive. While the occasion was Reubens's allotment, it is also likely that Fletcher and Reubens contin-

FIG. 10. Josiah Redwolf, 1970. Redwolf wears a headdress and rabbit fur cape from the collections of the Nez Perce National Historical Park, given him to wear when a staff member made this photograph. NEPE-HI-0148. Courtesy of National Park Service, NPNHP.

ued the ethnographic conversation they had begun in Kamiah the week before, when they had discussed many Nez Perce oral stories. Details of Gay's photograph and Fletcher's field diary suggest the men may have brought the war bonnets and pole to demonstrate a Nimiipuu ceremony for Fletcher, one held in the summer, perhaps even celebrated at that location. She later recounted it in her "Ethnologic Gleanings among the Nez Perces": "In early summer, 'when the grass is tall and everything is in full vigor,' the yearly gathering of the warriors of the tribe took place. All the people . . . came in their gala dress. At this time . . . the younger men held their dance and had a sham battle." On this occasion, honor poles, made by elder men, proven warriors, were ceremonially passed to two younger warriors who were "charged all with the obligations connected with" them for the next year.[45]

It is also possible that the image memorializes a symbolic occasion, the culmination of an agreement between these two powerful negotiators. The possessor of the honor pole, carried on this occasion by James Reubens, would be a battle leader, although unarmed.[46] The significance of the honor pole was discussed with an interviewer in 1965 by Josiah Redwolf, "the last surviving Nez Perce tribal member who participated in the Nez Perce War of 1877," portrayed in figure 10.[47] According to Redwolf, "If the Nez Perces were fleeing from their enemies they see the first place to fight from he pushed that in the ground and told his people turn back heres where we're going to lose or win. That's what that pole means."[48] Surely Redwolf's summary characterizes Reubens's part in the inception of allotment. Unarmed, except for his considerable wit and rhetorical skills, Reubens had staked a point of honor: Monteith would be replaced or allotment would not begin. Fletcher had agreed, aided in that goal, and now the two had become allies.

Part Two

Land

Introduction

Map and Territory, Space and Place

In January 1890 Commissioner of Indian Affairs Thomas Jefferson Morgan declared that "pupils" in federally supported Indian schools "should understand the significance of national holidays and be permitted to enjoy them."[1] He listed eight such occasions and gave specific instructions for how Indian students were to celebrate three of them: Washington's Birthday, Arbor Day, and Franchise Day, a new holiday memorializing the passage of the Dawes General Allotment Act, which was to be celebrated on 8 February as an occasion marking "the possible turning point in Indian history." To Morgan, celebrating Franchise Day and Washington's Birthday in quick succession should not be a cause for concern, for "no . . . opportunity should be lost by which Indian youth may be imbued with ideas distinctively national as distinguished from those that are tribal." He saw "a natural sequence in the exercises of the two days. The Indian heroes of the camp-fire need not be disparaged," he wrote, "but gradually and unobtrusively the heroes of American homes and history may be substituted as models and ideals."[2] The outcome of this program, however, was less an exact substitution than something more interactive, porous, and hybrid.

In attempting to prescribe the proper celebration of holidays Morgan was aware that on such occasions, cultural identity is performed and reinforced. *Performance*, according to theater historian Shannon

Jackson, "derives from a Greek root meaning 'to furnish forth,' 'to carry forward,' 'to bring into being.'"³ Holidays involve the ritualized and repetitive "furnish[ing] forth" of certain details: on Arbor Day, for example, we plant trees. He realized as well that holidays could be effective means of "bringing into being" certain substitutions based on selective forgetting. Celebrating George Washington's birthday, for example, rather than the anniversary of Chief Joseph's return to Idaho—hearing tales of "the hardships, dangers, and heroisms, by which the country of which [Indian students] are now to be a part has reached such a position" rather than the story of a local hero's principled resistance—would, Morgan hoped, cause students to forget "the fact that they are Indians."⁴

Remembering and forgetting, however, are selective and opportunely fickle processes, especially when they are tied to intercultural holiday observances such as those observed by training schools or celebrated in frontier communities. In such places, as Joseph Roach observes, ritual celebrations and performances can "illuminate the process of surrogation as it operated *between* the participating cultures. The key ... is to understand how ... societies ... have invented themselves by performing their pasts in the presence of others. They could not perform themselves, however, unless they also performed what and who they thought they were not."⁵ These instances of performance, surrogation, intercultural interaction, and selective forgetting are vividly apparent in accounts of how the Fourth of July was celebrated in Lewiston and at Fort Lapwai in 1889.

Although Commissioner Morgan included Independence Day in his list of federally sanctioned holidays, he did not issue precise instructions for its observance, presumably because the rituals of its celebration were so familiar. Since the early 1880s, on the Nez Perce Reservation, celebrants had participated in activities long associated with summer solstice gatherings—horse racing, dancing, drumming, and gaming—even as they had attended local patriotic celebrations featuring oratory, fireworks, and picnic feasts. In the neighboring town of Lewiston white territorial citizens frequently invited Native riders, drummers, and dancers to join their celebrations of their nation's birthday. The 1889 holiday may have seemed to be an especially significant "turning point" of the sort Morgan imagined, both for the citizens of Idaho Territory, poised on the cusp of statehood, and for the Nez Perces, who were considering the transformative consequences of the allotment. Yet as I demonstrate, the anticipated transformations—of frontier territory into modernizing state and of Nez Perce warriors into citizen-farmers—were divisive issues and proceeded in fits and starts. In the case of allotment the process was incompletely successful.

At the "Grand Celebration of the Anniversary of American Independence at Lewiston, I.T." in 1889, James Reubens had been invited to give the keynote patriotic address.[6] It might seem odd that the citizens of Lewiston would so honor a representative of the Nez Perces, with whom they had recently been at war. In fact, just twelve years earlier, as war threatened, rumors had circulated that Nez Perce warriors planned "to strike the defenseless settlers as they celebrated the Fourth."[7] Yet as Roach observes, ritualized public celebrations such as this often become occasions of "intercultural communication." And Lewiston's invitation seems to have signified that past hostilities could be erased in a "public [enactment] of forgetting."[8] In addition to asking Reubens to give a speech, Lewistonians invited "[t]he Nez Perce Indians . . . to take part in the exercises and they . . . accepted."[9] This celebration thus marked a mutual selective forgetting of the acrimonious past and produced a version of history that overlooked recent ruptures and discontinuities.

Lewiston's "Elaborate Programme" began with a "Ringing of Bells and Firing of Guns at Sunrise." Local residents had forgotten the fear these sounds might have evoked in wartime and now heard them as announcing a day of peaceful celebration. A "Grand Procession" that demonstrated the town's readiness to be part of a new state then set out from the courthouse. Led by the "Civic societies"—the "Brass Band," the "Fire Department," a "Naval Car," and assorted "Federal, Territorial, County and City Officials"—the parade also included more feminized and metaphorical embellishments. "A superbly decorated Liberty Car in which [Miss] Bessie Vollmer reigned as the beautiful goddess [of Liberty]" was followed by a "fairy car" prepared by the goddess's mother that "was trimmed and bedecked in fairy-like grace and delicacy and occupied by five as charming little fairies as ever returned to earth from the fabled landscapes of spiritual plains." Sponsored by the territory's leading entrepreneur, J. P. Vollmer, these "cars" established a figural connection between his capitalist ventures and the reign of liberty, between an imaginary rosy past and the area's continued fecundity. Next, down "an unbroken avenue of street decorations," came groups of citizens in carriages and on horseback and Nez Perce riders, who, it was promised, would be attired "in full war dress."[10] In its linear and hierarchical arrangement the parade thus displayed to white viewers an apparently natural progression from revolution in the name of liberty to incipient statehood, now possible because Indian warfare no longer threatened.

The Lewiston parade disbanded at the "Grove," a traditional place of community assembly.[11] The brass band played, the glee club sang, and to remind the assembled citizens of the drama of their origins, "Miss Sadie Poe gave an excellent reading of the declaration." (The strategic forgetting involved in this act, of course, was that more than a century after independence, women still did not possess the franchise.) The only disappointment was that "[t]he principal orator of the day . . . failed to arrive." This did not dampen the occasion, however, since several surrogates—local clergymen and J. P. Vollmer himself—made "volunteer speeches."[12] The day ended with a "Grand Pyrotechnic Display and Balloon Ascension at 9 P.M." and an elegant ball, which closed with the song "Home Sweet Home."[13] Throughout the festival the white community heard familiar music that sentimentally confirmed their unity and bellicose oratory prized not for its originality but for its recitation of mythicized beginnings and comforting platitudes.

In this frontier celebration the white citizens of Lewiston performed "what and who they thought they were not" for their Native guests (and even for their Native neighbors who did not attend). They were not intruders upon the land but its rightful owners; they were not backward frontiersmen but progressive entrepreneurs; and they were not at war, for the conflict of 1877 had ended Indian troubles in the region and statehood was imminent. Peace meant that

J. P. Vollmer, who had brought the first telegraph line into Lewiston and who operated the first private Bell Telephone line, could now promote the extension of the Northern Pacific Railroad across the Nez Perce Reservation and into Lewiston. His plans awaited only the so-called opening of the reservation, to be accomplished as soon as the newly arrived special allotting agent should carry forward the provisions of the Dawes Act, opening the desirable agricultural and mineral lands of the reservation to white exploitation.

This sunny picture depended, of course, on a strategic forgetting of the dismal economic conditions that had prevailed in the area, perhaps inadvertently made apparent in the *Lewiston Teller*'s report of the festivities: "There is no season of business depression which can restrain the patriotic ardor of the American people," the account observed. "The genius of liberty is an immortal inspiration which overpowers the force of adversity in peace as it does the strength of armies in time of war."[14] This was one of the few times an area newspaper, committed to the relentless promotion of local commerce, would admit, even by implication, that the economy of "this latest and best Oklahoma" was less than thriving.[15] The *Teller*'s note of realism in "Independence Day" suggests, as well, that the bravura patriotism of the holiday was produced not only for Nez Perce onlookers but also to reassure white citizens themselves—many of them on the brink of financial ruin—of Lewiston's bright economic and political prospects.

While Lewiston's citizens accepted the substitution of J. P. Vollmer for James Reubens as the day's featured speaker, the failure of "the leading Indian orator of America" to arrive for his speaking engagement had surely also reminded impatient developers of what they had hoped to forget—that tribal councils had thus far prevented allotment from beginning.[16] The delay in Reubens's return had also undoubtedly caused Alice Fletcher and Jane Gay to forgo the celebration. Partly to avoid the blandishments and pressures of anxious would-be sooners and partly because of the strategic noncooperation of the Nez Perces, they remained in the field, camped on the reservation's southwest boundary, ostensibly overseeing the resurvey of that line.

[99]

The Nez Perces who attended Lewiston's parade and celebration also found occasion for communal affirmation in traditional activities of games, singing, drumming, and dancing, whether as participants or as observers standing next to white onlookers who may have seen these same activities as pleasurably sensational entertainment. The procession of regalia-clad warriors, especially, would have confirmed their strong feelings of pride that a traditional way of life had persisted beyond the war and despite the internment. That pride may have also been tinged with resentment. As a Nez Perce onlooker told Jane Gay at the next year's celebration, "If the white people only knew how we feel . . . if they knew what these songs mean to us, there would be no more Tal-lik-lykts [war processions]" (C, 358–59). That is to say, at ritual occasions such as this, events are open to multiple and mutually exclusive interpretations.

East of Lewiston in the early weeks of July 1889, Nimiipuu gathered at their traditional place of assembly, the camp meeting ground on Lapwai Creek, to celebrate rituals marking their ancient and recent histories and to consider what the immediate future might hold. Here too a parade and oratory affirmed their cultural history and identity "in the presence of others," both white and Native. Missionary Kate McBeth, who had hoped the holiday would not involve the "heathen performances or racing," wrote in her diary of her shock at seeing "[s]o many in paint & blankets—many down the river Indians. [O]ne old one talked by Signs & his interpreter put it into Nez P. in the evening. . . . We heard the swift feet of ponies comeing & lo! the two naked riders came in sight, no saddle? no any thing! . . . Oh how I dread James R return from Washington."[17] Although to McBeth the gathering seemed barbaric, for the Nimiipuu who attended, the horse racing, drumming, games, storytelling, and war procession furnished forth a sense of belonging and cultural continuity.

This celebration included the firing of pistols and the ringing of bells to welcome James Reubens, who arrived on July 5 with news he could not yet fully make public. Too late to deliver the ceremonial oration at Lewiston, he instead addressed the Lapwai celebrants.

What he said can only be surmised from the *Teller*'s report, which summarized his speech, given "in the Indian language, which was heard by parties who understood the language and afterwards interpreted it to the whites." Unsurprisingly, the transmission admitted of some ambiguity. According to the newspaper, Reubens reported that the president had told him Monteith would remain as the agent at Lapwai "through his term of office," and "that he [Reubens] had better go home and tell his people to take up their lands in severalty and cheerfully submit hereafter to the orders of the government." The report concluded, "Reuben then told them that he, himself, had given up further opposition and advised all others to do the same."[18] The details here suggest the *Teller* reported a version of the speech its readers wanted to hear, while subsequent events demonstrated that those who supported Nimiipuu resistance heard something else. They understood that if Reubens no longer opposed allotment, Monteith's time as agent was, in fact, at an end. Thus the Lapwai celebration reaffirmed Nimiipuu sovereignty—both historically and in the current moment—for Reubens's speech signaled the outcome of a successful negotiation between sovereign governing bodies.

These two celebrations, each marked by repetition, surrogacy, and strategic forgetting, exemplify other situations of intercultural communication: treaty making, deeding land, and diplomatic negotiation, as well as ritual drama and storytelling, wherein a set of actions, words, and gestures are performed—furnished forth—within a context of former and future repetitions. Within this frame of understanding, parades, celebrations of annual events, and the exchange of stories become records of equal importance to the textual archive that supported allotment's imperatives, and they make apparent the exercise of Nimiipuu agency. They provide useful counterpoints to the top-down, univocal, and bureaucratized rationalization that seemed to promise the success of allotment. In the following chapters I pursue an extended analysis of how members of the allotting party performed their collective national past—as agents of an unbroken progress of westward expansion that brought excess lands under the plow—for the presumed enlightenment of the Nez Perces.

LAND

Forgetting that the Nimiipuu had long lived in this place, Fletcher and her workers endeavored to substitute maps, plats, deeds, and photographs of the reservation for embodied, traditional, place-based knowledge. I then compare those reductive attempts with two representations of that same territory furnished forth by Nimiipuu elders within a context of intercultural performance, both of whom acted as surrogates for generations of Nimiipuu whose history had been shaped by the place that was their homeland.

3. "The Square Idea"

The presence of Alice Fletcher, a lame, middle-aged white woman in smoked glasses and a flower-trimmed bonnet sitting under an umbrella in her wagon on the southwestern border of the Nez Perce Reservation, signaled that the federal expeditions undertaken to allot lands to Indians were of a quite different order than the great western surveying expeditions now more than twenty years past. Those earlier surveys had enabled territorial conquest by cataloguing resources in land, water, and minerals, foregrounding the unique physical features of specific western places. Allotment, on the other hand, aimed to transform the territories containing those resources into states united within a national grid of political administration and economic production. Thus the allotting enterprise conceptualized land as a space that could be rationalized, made visible upon maps that enabled its division into identically sized and shaped parcels, the boundaries of which could be described mathematically and which could be bought and sold by individual owners. The geographic attributes of the land—its topography, its climate, its amenability to cultivation—were less important than the rationalized description that would enable it to be owned, leased, bought, and sold.

To highlight the different ways of understanding a culture's relation to land, I use the relational distinctions between *space* and *place* as they are articulated by Arif Dirlik. For Dirlik, *place* is "[grounded] topography," and place-based thinking recognizes the interrelationship of the land and its inhabitants as they move over it, work within it, and celebrate rituals that connect them to it. "Groundedness," according to Dirlik, "calls for a definition of what is to be included in the place *from within the place*—some control over the conduct and organization of everyday life, in other words—rather than from above, from those placeless abstractions such as capital, the nation-state," or, in this case, in the United States Office of Indian Affairs. *Space*, by contrast, transforms specificity into abstraction for the purpose of establishing equivalent values.[1] A specific location, such as the Nez Perce Reservation, characterized by canyons, mountains, forests, rivers, and mineral deposits, may thus be spatialized—divided into rectilinear plots of equal size by procedures such as surveying and mapping. The resulting boundaries are marked on the land by fences and surveyors' corners, and the ownership of each segment is documented in a massive bureaucratic written record comprising plats and maps, birth and death records, deeds, and evidence of land transfers. In the resulting archive, maps and deeds substitute for lands and peoples and support the capitalist exploitations of new territory by establishing its ownership, its relative value, and its alienability.

The Bureaucratic Imaginary Encounters "the hard facts in the case"

Allotment was a policy of spatialization. Its cerebral and disembodied processes were to be carried out in lands already familiar and applied to people now pacified, and its implementation did not expose its agents to extremes of physical danger. Alice Fletcher, for example, traveled to and from Idaho Territory in a Union Pacific palace car and communicated with her employers by letter, telephone, and telegraph. She supervised the survey, documented the assignment of land, kept a written record of her work, and taught those who received allotments the basics of property ownership within a capitalist system. In sum, allotment entailed just the kinds of tasks at which women were thought to excel: establishing interpersonal relationships, benevolently supervising instruction, keeping track of the minutiae of names, dates, and family relationships, and managing a paper archive. These tasks could be done in offices, parlors, churches, and schoolrooms. Most important, because allotment was a means of establishing the dollar value of land, its agents must demonstrate the most unimpeachable honesty and spotless character—again, qualities more likely to be connected with women than with land-hungry white men who were settlers, developers, or adventurers. Yet as I demonstrate, Fletcher's work was necessarily both physical and cerebral, and the degree of her objectivity is a matter of some debate.

Near Lapwai lay most of the prime farming land of the reservation. Here Fletcher planned to begin her work, assigning tidy rectilinear plots to individual allottees.[2] The raw materials were at hand: a reservation with boundaries stipulated by prior treaty, and whereon allotment had already been partially implemented; a set of prior surveys and maps; a (rudimentary and incomplete) tribal census; and funding to provide rations, office supplies, and support personnel. Theoretically, Fletcher could ensconce herself in agency headquarters, whence, assisted by the local agent, she would register cooperative Nez Perces whom she would find "all in a row . . . , waiting . . . to be labeled in consecutive order and numbered upon the nicely photographed plats furnished by the department [of the Interior]" (C, 26). Figure 11 is an example of such highly abstracted plats.

Well-organized Native resistance and the considerable disarray in agency administration quickly forced Fletcher to change her plans and seek another location in which to begin her work. She left Lapwai, separating herself by sixty miles from the disorder. Her departure did not, however, diminish Nimiipuu resistance. Throughout her stay, with or without her knowledge, the theoretical presumptions of allotment that guided her work were challenged and modified by the people whose sovereign identity stemmed from their aboriginal relationship to the place in which they lived, a relationship Fletcher ultimately and necessarily learned to recognize, if not to respect. Upon her departure from Lapwai for Kamiah on 1 July 1889, Fletcher found the abstractions of allotment policy to be challenged by the Idaho terrain—its seasons, its climate, and its topography. She thus learned to modify her understanding of time and place, adopting a seasonal and migratory pattern resembling the one lived

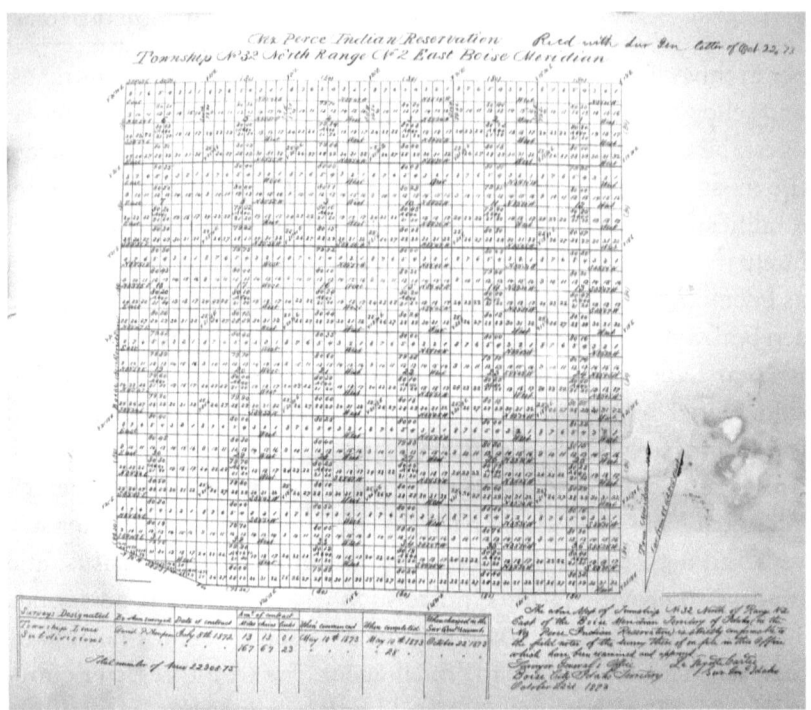

FIG. 11. Fletcher began her work using reservation surveys like David P. Thompson's cryptic abstractions for Township 32 North, Range 2 East, 22 October 1873. Survey Maps 1873–95, Fort Lapwai Indian Agency, RG 75, NARA Pacific Region (Seattle).

by her clients. The phrase "in the field" became more than a mere header to the letters and reports she sent to the Indian Office and to the Friends of the Indian assembled at Lake Mohonk. "In the field" was both geographically and philosophically precise, signifying her location away from the deliberatory *spaces* of a convention hall or legislative chamber, and locating Fletcher within a mountainous, arid, and topographically specific *place*. The phrase, and the place it stood for, grounded and gave weight to the modifications and amendments to the law she consequently proposed.

One of the first abstractions Fletcher revised was the idea that allotment could be accomplished in a predictable amount of time. When the *Lewiston Teller* reported her arrival on 30 May 1889, it confirmed "that she is of the opinion that the whole of this work can be accomplished and the allotments made, within the period of fifteen months." Her estimate fell short by ten months.[3] By October, after a long summer of moving very slowly across only a small portion of the reservation's lands, Fletcher wrote: "In a former report I stated that by October 1st, if all went well, I hoped to have one third of the tribe allotted. When I wrote that sentence I did not know the land I should have to travel over. Nor did the Surveyor realize the broken nature of the country. He says that in seventeen years experience, he never met so long a stretch of hard work. In running 3 miles one day, he was obliged to cross 3 cañons, each one nearly 2000 feet deep. Some of these gashes are absolutely impassable."[4] By December, when she left Lapwai to return to Washington DC at the end of the first allotting season, it was clear that Fletcher could give no exact prediction of the time the work would require, and by the beginning of the second season, she had learned to speak less specifically, informing the *Teller* upon her return, "The work of allotment will begin at once and [be] pushed with all possible energy."[5]

The matter of time also disturbed the fiction that lands could be made equivalent without regard to climate or season. Even as allotment was being conceptualized, Fletcher had argued to the Lake Mohonk reformers that "one hundred and sixty acres of land in one place is a very different thing from the same amount somewhere else."[6] In Idaho she found abundant support for her contention, and her early letters of report enjoin the bureaucrats in the Indian Office to consider "the hard facts in the case."[7] In the abstract world of the documents upon which Fletcher was to base her work, it was always spring, when green vegetation seemed to guarantee the land's fertility. In the field, by contrast, summer weather proved to be cruel and unpredictable. Within two weeks of her arrival Fletcher reported, "A hot windstorm last Tuesday burnt up all the grain upon these lands. . . . Irrigation is impossible, and no trees or vegetables can be raised, and even pasturage is uncertain during the summer months."[8] Without irrigation, spring was a brief illusion, and after a season of drought the land held less promise.

As Fletcher waited at the southwestern boundary of the reservation for James Reubens to return, she discovered challenges to the abstractions of allotment in the make-do methods of the very white settlers whose agricultural practices the potential Nez Perces allottees were supposed to emulate. Initially she did not make these observations a matter of official report. However, in a letter written "in camp" to her friend Isabel Barrows, Fletcher shared her growing concern:

> This is a much underestimated land to get your living in by farming. . . . It is quite interesting to me to . . . see how the men (white) manage. I find every man fencing in all his acres raising what ever he can on his land but turning all his stock upon the reservation which has here to fore been a free grazing ground. . . . By this method the settlers raise stock at little cost and can carry a large number of head & become moderately prosperous but if the reservation is cut off as a herding ground and the settler forced to maintain his cattle on his own land, the struggle for a livelihood becomes a serious matter. . . . You may think I am deeply interested in the white settlers & so I am for by them I can judge what can be accomplished in this country and so see what chance there may be for the Indians. This is my first experience in allotting mixed land, grazing & agricultural, & I see plainly that the amt. given an Indian for grazing land is too small for him to make a living off of. . . . [T]he outlook of the Nez Perce tribe is not as favorable as I might wish. I mean as to future business prosperity.[9]

I have quoted from this letter at length because it marks Fletcher's recognition that to accomplish a fair allotment, she would need to differentiate farming lands from grazing, increasing the amount of land deeded to those whose properties would not support agricultural pursuits. Knowing such apparent generosity would arouse the ire of would-be white settlers, she let it be known that she would personally oversee and attest to the correct grading of each allotment's potential for grazing or agricultural pursuits. This decision prolonged her location "in the field" and resulted in allotments with their equivalence measured not by size but by potential yield.

Additionally, the "hard facts" of prior histories on the land disturbed the fiction of a tidily bounded space comprising properties equally available for fair division and assignment. As she awaited Reubens's return, Fletcher concentrated her attention on the long-disputed borders of the reservation. Not surprisingly, the process of resurveying elicited anxious protest from white farmers, ranchers, and squatters whose properties bordered and sometimes encroached upon the reservation, and who depended on using its unfenced lands as pasture. Their tenuous economic arrangements thus threatened, these settlers were not inclined to yield their advantages without a fight. The local agent had already tried with little success to force white stockmen to remove their herds from reservation lands. For example, he had given notice to John Greer, who owned a mail station and ferry on the Clearwater River, "to remove yourself, family and property, including your stock, from the Reservation." Outraged, Greer wrote to the *Teller*, "I don't calculate to leave unless I am forced away. Is it possible that an Indian will be put here to handle the U.S. Mail sack. Will it be possible that a white man will feel safe in crossing this river at its highest pitch, and if it is not the case that an Indian will take charge of it, why can't I stay here as long as any white man, as long as I have paid my money for it?"[10] Greer's protest, racist and short-sighted as it appears to modern eyes, suggests that precedent would block federal attempts to establish permanent and honest boundaries. Local agents had traditionally overlooked the incursions of white entrepreneurs who had penetrated the invisible boundaries, invested time and money, claimed land, and increased its value with their improvements.

Concrete action buttressed written protests such as Greer's, since boundaries could not be literally and permanently inscribed upon the land. To be sure, former surveyors had strategically placed stones incised with section and township numbers, had piled boulders into cairns to mark the intersections of survey lines, had peeled back the bark of so-called bearing trees and incised or painted numerical identifiers on the exposed wood. In areas where there were neither boulders nor trees, they had dug pits at the appropriate locations. All these methods were impermanent and easily altered. Stones eroded and were scattered by weather and animals; trees burned, fell, or were cut down. Tree bark regrew and pits accumulated rubble and refuse. Frequently these processes were hurried along by human agents, both white and Native, who considered the survey to be an insubstantial and impermanent fiction that should yield to the requirements (real or imaginary) of those who lived in this place.

Thus Fletcher, who had originally planned to be an office worker, became a nomad, moving from camp to camp, following her surveyor, Edson Briggs, as he verified the outboundaries and graded the land. In her peregrinations she became intimately acquainted with how the terrain resisted attempts to rationalize it. In some places the amount of ore in the mountainous soil made Briggs's compass useless: "The mineral deposits in the mountains renders a needle worthless hereabouts, the solar instrument being in use exclusively. This instrument demands the sun and as there has been an average of 4 thunderstorms a day the delays are annoying when one wishes to get on with the work rapidly."[11] The delays intensified as forest fires began to rage, fueled by several years of drought. In August 1889 Fletcher reported, "[W]e are in a dense atmosphere of smoke from burning forest in the mts. East and North of us. The sun is invisible and we can see but a few rods distant. It is very trying to head and eyes. All this part of the country is the same way & the solar instrument is useless."[12] The smoke, heat, and dust forced the work crew to adopt slower and more labor-intensive means of surveying, pulling chains over mountains and through canyons.

Upon learning that James Reubens had returned and had advised his supporters to cooperate with the new policy, Fletcher proceeded to Kamiah, full of optimism. There her first act was to attempt to adjust the patterns of settlement in the valley to match the maps she carried with her in her hands and in her head. The existing allotments in the valleys of the Clearwater River, assigned under the provisions of the Treaty of 1863, had "enclosed plots of all sizes and shapes, quite oblivious to the points of the compass" (C, 129). Fletcher seems initially to have imagined she could relocate all inappropriately settled Nez Perces and justify the borders of their lands to match her plats.[13] This assumption depended on her strategically forgetting the place's prior history of occupancy and use. When Edson Briggs had finished verifying the existing survey lines, she wrote to the commissioner,

> I could see how the Indians have run their fences, roads, and laid out their fields, [and] it is clear that nearly every person must be more or less changed. It would be impossible to give them their land as they now occupy it and to discribe the tracts according to any subdivision in the legal survey. The fields cross the lines in every direction, frequently circling in and out of different lots. I have talked with a few of the more intelligent and they admit the necessity of "straightening out their land" but there will be bitter opposition from others. I have requested the Surveyor to measure the fields that are the most irregular in form that I may be able to make a fair and equitable exchange of land and adjustment. Fences must be moved and where the lay of the land will permit it the roads changed.[14]

Fletcher's choice of words here reveals the spatialized equivalences her theory embraced: People, not plats or laws, "must be more or less changed," in order that the process of allotment be "fair and equitable." Yet her phrasing also acknowledged place-based difficulties: while fences might be "moved," roads could be rerouted only with regard to "the lay of the land."

The earlier survey had been inaccurate and incomplete, to be sure. But the already existing patterns of cultivation recognized what Fletcher could not yet see: they followed the contours of land that could be plowed, planted, irrigated, and harvested. Her records from the earliest days in Kamiah show little awareness of the dislocations such procedures might cause to Nimiipuu landowners whose farms, fields, fences, and outbuildings did not match her overall plan. She notes, for example, that "the adjustment of the lines" entailed "sometimes . . . giving up plowed land to take unbroken land."[15] Nowhere in her correspondence, however, is there the glimmer of recognition that to prepare new lands for planting demanded backbreaking labor. For their part, Nimiipuu, who knew that earlier attempts to correct the boundaries had failed and who had suffered incursions on their lands for the past half-century or more, waited for her to come to her senses, asking ironically, "How is it?

LAND

The Government made my fence; you say it is all wrong. Are there two Governments? and which is right? We will keep the land as it is; by and by another Government will come along and pull up our fences again'" (C, 129–30). Eventually, by living on the land and among those who knew its history, Fletcher learned—at least partially—the wisdom of "keep[ing] the land as it [was]," a concept she acknowledged even if she did not always act upon it.

To a contemporary reader, Fletcher's textual descriptions, delimited with the precision of compass, square, and transit, fail to capture the violence entailed in her vision of how the Kamiah Valley, a place in which people had long lived and worked, might be transformed into a space that would meet the specifications of "the legal survey." Figure 12, Jane Gay's photograph of the Clearwater River at Kamiah, demonstrates more eloquently than any number of detailed written reports what Fletcher found in Kamiah. This image shows Fletcher and James Stuart amid a wide expanse of rocks along the Clearwater River. Fletcher sits on a large rock and faces away from the camera; Stuart stands facing the photographer, arms akimbo. Across the river, a farm is visible. The image shows what Fletcher's plats did not: the fertile bottom land had long been farmed by Nimiipuu, who had plowed and harvested, run fences, and built barns and permanent homes on their lands. Their properties did not exist in rectilinear 160-acre parcels, not because the owners were irrational and inexperienced farmers but because rocky river banks and steep foothills determined the boundaries of the fields.

Fletcher's response to these early challenges was strategic, if inaccurate. She noted that the process of adjusting and exchange would be lengthy, not because of the difficulties her abstract ideas had introduced into a functioning relationship of culture to place but because the Nez Perces showed an annoying propensity to maintain their traditional patterns of living—behaviors that policies such as allotment, education, and the celebration of Franchise Day were striving to erase. A month into the work at Kamiah, she reported, "This task of adjusting the fields to the Survey is not yet completed, owing to the exodus of the Indians to the Mountains to lay in their winter supply of dried fish and game."[16] Her explanation may have

FIG. 12. "Clearwater River at Kamiah," by E. Jane Gay, *Choup-nit-ki*, 100. ISHS 63-221.93, Idaho State Historical Society Library and Archives.

satisfied the commissioner, since both understood the extirpation of Native ways would not be immediate, but it also suggests Fletcher had not yet fully comprehended that the seasons dictated and delimited the behaviors of those who lived in this place.

In fact it was not until she was exposed to an early winter storm at the end of the first allotting season that Fletcher began to understand that the "exodus" in August was a practical decision, based on the residents' knowledge of local weather patterns. In mid-November, 1889, a local informant advised her to plan to leave Kamiah before winter storms could trap her party in the valley. Helping Fletcher prepare to cross the mountains to Lapwai, he told her "that the Kamians had to go to the mountains much earlier this year because the drought had burned their gardens and they had nothing to eat. They would all starve unless they killed much deer and caught much fish to dry for the winter's food." Fletcher and Gay received that information, Gay writes, in light of their own experience of camping on short rations and being caught in fragile tents in a violent storm. Now, "every Indian looked hungry in our eyes. It takes a bit of personal experience sometimes to correct the angle of vision" (C, 193, 194).

"everything ... done on the square": Allotment's Archival Record

Allotment not only required different types of labor; it yielded different kinds of records. The archive of the great western surveys was as heroic as the enterprises themselves. Much of the data collected by the Hayden, Powell, and King expeditions consisted of physical samples of rocks, ores, soils, and shales. These grounded the abstract maps and photographs of the western regions made by federally appointed and federally funded expedition workers whose task it was to document the land, its resources, and the heroic work of the scientist-explorers. Large-format photographs of the work, collected in folio volumes printed in limited editions, were presented to congressional sponsors and filed in federal archives.[17]

By contrast, Fletcher's work on the Nez Perce Reservation spawned a plethora of legal and documentary evidence as she sought to establish spatial equivalents. Early in the process, Gay wrote that white settlers were nonplussed by Fletcher's insistence that "'everything will have to be done on the square.' The introduction of the square idea has a depressing effect, for hitherto they have worked only in rings" (C, 14). The metaphor aptly contrasts the political chicanery of "rings," such as the infamous Tweed Ring of the prior decade, with the moral uprightness she attributed to Alice Fletcher. The allotting agent's objectivity was guaranteed by a paper archive of thousands of maps and plats that coordinated individual allottees with specific plots of land, their promise for yield graded mathematically, and with myriad written records interpreting those schematic representations. As an ethnologist conversant with theories of developmental anthropology, Fletcher sought to memorialize the practices and lifeways her allotting work would definitively foreclose. Thus allotment's artifactual archive comprised souvenirs, not samples. The documents and artifacts associated with allotment were housed in memory palaces—museums, libraries, and archives—where drawers, cabinets, and shelves held beaded saddles and bridles, headdresses, moccasins and regalia, baskets, weapons, stone pestles, digging sticks, miniature models of tipis and longhouses, and primitive foodstuffs. Their filing cabinets and acid-free boxes overflowed with written transcriptions of myths and traditional stories, lexicons and dictionaries of putatively defunct languages, records of physiological characteristics that supported the nascent sciences of anthropological classification, and, of course, the reports, maps, deeds, and other documents that would perfect allotment.

Fletcher endeavored to produce minute, particular, and specific written descriptions to serve both as legal evidence and antidote to the bureaucratic imaginary evident in the documents from which she was supposed to work. A series of representations related to her work in Township 32 North, part of the resurvey of the western and southwestern boundaries of the Nez Perce Reservation, illustrates the vexed issue of how three-dimensional land (place) might be transmuted into two-dimensional spatialized representations. Fletcher came to her work carrying plats that likely resembled those shown in figure 11, drawn by surveyor David P. Thompson in 1873. Made in support of the infamous "Thief Treaty" of 1863, such schematic representations documented the outer boundaries of the Nez Perce Reservation, aligned them with the Boise Meridian, and delineated equivalently sized plots of land, sequentially numbered, that could in future years be assigned to individual owners. These maps were not intended to document the specific terrain they enclosed, as Fletcher almost immediately discovered. Such abstracted documents were of little use to anyone who intended to inhabit, develop, or even simply traverse the reservation. Hence the allotting party produced compensatory and carefully detailed documentation that emphasized the difference between terrain and map, and thus between place and space. On 19 July 1889, for example, Fletcher wrote to the commissioner of Indian affairs describing in precise detail the topography of the segment of land Thompson had abstracted into a series of rectangles:

> Just here it seems proper to call your attention to the lack of topography in the field notes and consequently upon the plats . . . Mountains and Buttes and Cañons are not mentioned and the character of the soil not discriminated, but all of it called, "first rate." . . . Particular mention is made of Township 32. N. Range 2 E. which is claimed as "one

of the best townships of land in Idaho Terr'y." No mention is made of high buttes from 500 to 900 feet high, to alkali patches and hard soil which breaks and cracks....

I have respectfully called your attention to these misstatements in the field notes and the omissions concerning the broken, rocky, rugged nature of the land, because the official characterization of the land has continued to be eronious.[18]

In the next month Edson Briggs resurveyed Township 32 North, which was crossed by Cottonwood Creek and its tributaries, watercourses that were bordered by the "high buttes" Fletcher describes. Figure 13 and others of Briggs's maps carefully delineate the meandering stream beds. Closely spaced hachure lines suggest precipitous walls, and more widely spaced lines indicate a gentler slope. Their fanlike arrangement approximates the shapes of bluffs and buttes lining the canyon walls. He supplemented this hand-drawn record with voluminous survey notes in which he described and evaluated the land's potential. His records for Township 32 North repeat a common refrain: "Land hilly and broken. Soil rocky 2nd and 3rd rate. [G]ood grazing lands."[19]

On Briggs's carefully detailed topographical maps, blank space suggests level terrain but cannot begin to capture its forbidding nature. For these details Jane Gay's photographs more closely approximate the "hard facts," bearing out Fletcher's claim of "alkali patches and hard soil." Figure 14, Gay's photograph of "Squirrel Camp," shows a cabin that served as the allotting party's base of operations in Township 32. When Gay included it in *Choup-nit-ki* (fig. 15), she cropped it to a low rectangle, compressing the featureless sky and eliminating much of the foreground. This technique emphasizes the stone outcropping that cuts across the lower left corner of the image, a topographical feature too subtle to be represented on Briggs's maps but a significant impediment to a farmer intending to plow straight furrows paralleling the fences of his field. The treeless expanse, also exaggerated by the cropping, supports Fletcher's contention that the earlier optimistic classification of the land had been "eronious," as does the cabin's precarious balance atop piles of stones that bring it to the square against the slope of the hillside.

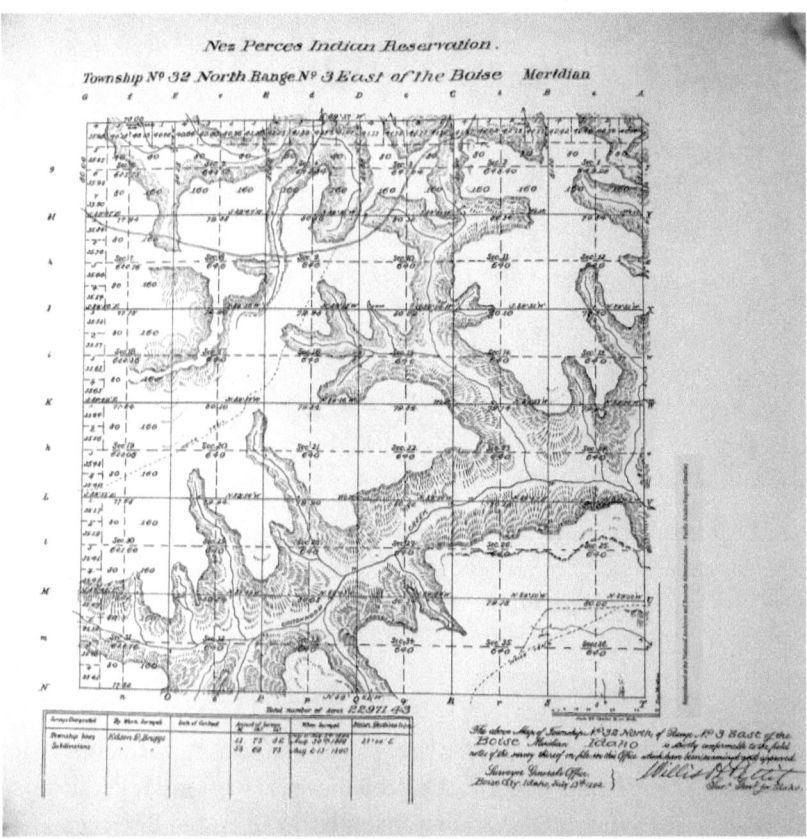

FIG. 13. Surveyor Edson D. Briggs added illuminating drainage detail for Township 32 North, Range 3 East, July–August 1890. Survey Maps 1873–95, Fort Lapwai Indian Agency, RG 75, NARA Pacific Region (Seattle).

Gay also included this image, uncropped, in her small private album titled "Where We Camped."[20] Here she wrote an accompanying narration: "We named it [Squirrel Camp] after the legions of grey rodents which honeycombed the ground, and destroyed all hope of a crop of anything which had to live on roots. . . . The settler who projected this cabin died before it was finished. After we had been on the ground a couple of weeks, we did not wonder that he died, we only wondered that he had expected to live, with such prospects. . . . [T]here was not in all our horizon a green leaf, only one yellow waste of stubble."[21] Gay's informal account confirms the

FIG. 14. "Squirrel Camp," 4–15 July 1889, by E. Jane Gay. Edson Briggs at left; Alice Fletcher in flowered hat stands with pail and broom at cabin door. Gay included the image at full size (as shown here) as figure 2 of "Where We Camped," SLHWA. ISHS 63-221.41, Idaho State Historical Society Library and Archives.

details noted by Briggs and Fletcher in their official reports, but in its focus on the specific site and the personal story of one failed homesteader, it is closer in tone to Fletcher's letter to Isabel Barrows. Under no obligation to support federal policy, Gay represented this location not as a potential and idealized space but as a place sited on visibly broken terrain and subject to invisible forces of time, season, extended drought, poor soil, and animal pests. Precisely because it is casual and private, her representation of "Squirrel Camp" makes apparent what the official record of maps and verbal descriptions could not admit, for details of how squatters had infiltrated the borders and failed to prosper had no part in the idealized forecast that Idaho was to be the next Oklahoma.

Gay's photographs, read in this context, demonstrate that the archive of allotment, although massive, was incomplete. Valuing the supposed objectivity of precision in representation, this bureaucratic record had no room for the "indiscriminate" details that cluttered the photographic image. According to Kelsey, "The condensation of significance delivered by the map, the table, and the report derived

FIG. 15. "Squirrel Camp," 4–15 July 1889, by E. Jane Gay. As included in *Choup-nit-ki*, 57. The Schlesinger Library, Radcliffe Institute, Harvard University.

in part from the capacity of these modes of presentation to eliminate much of what was, from the perspective of the scientific imagination, the irrelevant noise that routinely flooded the visual field."[22] In the formal documentary project of allotment, the photographs Gay produced did not function as a surrogate for the scientific precision of survey and map. Although the imperatives of allotment were feminized and domestic, the nature of science and bureaucratic discourse resolutely disallowed evidence such as personal accounts, informal snapshots, and letters to friends. Thus Gay's records of allotment comprise a different set of records, a counter-archive, as it were.

Gay had intended to publish some of her photographs as illustrations to popularly circulated accounts of western travel and adventure, as had her friend, Frank Hamilton Cushing.[23] She measured allotment's challenges and accomplishments in quite another register. As Gay's record makes clear, although allotting occasionally required extraordinary physical exertion, in its daily, repeated, and extended application it depended upon the skillful art of domestic persuasion tinctured with a stiff dose of moral superiority. Such endeavors were most efficaciously carried out in personal encounters; they were best documented on a smaller and personal scale, in images circulated individually, tucked into personal letters, collected in small albums, and, finally, archived in two capacious handwritten scrapbooks.[24] These records were produced not by a paid government agent but by a self-trained amateur photographer whose relation to the expedition was as an ad hoc domestic attaché. They did not become the property of a government archive. Rather, they remained in the family until 1951, when Jane Gay Dodge, Jane Gay's niece, donated them to the Schlesinger Library on the History of Women in America at Radcliffe University. These private records contain one of the most powerful critiques of the ideals of objectivity, precision, disembodied labor, and disinterested reform.

Gay was familiar with the conventions of representing western lands in words, numbers, and images as they had been established over the past thirty years by military men, anthropologists, explorers, and writers such as Frederick West Lander, Frank Hamilton Cushing, and John Wesley Powell, whose Washington DC social circles intersected with her own.[25] The conventions of landscape photography used by these early practitioners characterize Gay's initial approach to photographing the Idaho terrain. Yet the landscape images she made over the four summers she spent with Fletcher came to differ significantly from those of her precursors. Because Gay's work was not produced by federal mandate and because she made her photographs in the context of an endeavor of domestic settlement and cultivation, rather than one of exploration and conquest, they expose the imperatives of place as well as of space.

Gay's landscape photographs may thus be read in multiple registers.[26] Like Fletcher's genealogies, maps, and plats, they are two-dimensional instruments of rationalized and reductive commodification, for like maps, photographs frame views, flatten three-dimensional space, and establish equivalences and differences among them. Yet as with Commissioner Morgan's curricular plans to overwrite Native history with white, the results of such abstractive endeavors can be decidedly mixed. Gay's images temper the disciplinary potential of photography as an instrument by which landscape is spatialized—measured, valued, and framed—for she uses image making as a technology of critique, combining the evidentiary force of the image with her written records of the expedition. The collected letters and images in *Choup-nit-ki*, wherein Gay retrospectively documented the Idaho adventure, at times accomplish what map, report, survey, and photography taken alone cannot. These records attest to the specificity of the land as a place, characterized by topography, weather, and culture, and inhabited by specific, although not individualized, gendered and racialized bodies.

As did other expeditionary photographers, Gay presented the terrain of Nez Perce country as expansive, rich with potential resources of arable lands, minerals, timber, and water. Like theirs, many of her images seem to aspire to objectivity. They are uncluttered by irrelevant details and are generally unmarked by aesthetic pretension. Gay used the cliffs and buttes of the Nez Perce Reservation as vantage points from which to take the view from above so favorable to survey imagery.[27] Figure 16, for example, her photograph of Lewiston, Idaho, was probably made as she and Fletcher paused at the top of the Lewiston grade en route to Lapwai in May 1889. In *Choup-nit-ki* this image is translated into an ink sketch (fig. 17). Both iterations seem to defy time. The cloudless sky does not suggest a specific day, season, or atmospheric condition. In this detail it resembles the photographs made by Timothy S. O'Sullivan, whose practice of masking out clouds "was in keeping with the survey process; for topographers or geologists, cloud formations at any given moment were transient and incidental to the structure of a view. Masking out the sky could thus be understood as a way of eliminating a measure of photographic noise."[28] "Lewiston, Idaho" appears to be Gay's attempt to match the objectivity of the activities of survey and mapping carried out by Edson Briggs and his surveyors.

In other images Gay yielded, as did her peers, to the overwhelming beauty of the place, seeking ways to contain the seemingly limitless view within a rectangular frame. She experimented with panoramic views, suturing several wide-angle shots together, as in figure

FIG. 16. Lewiston, Idaho, probably 28 May 1889, by E. Jane Gay. ISHS 63-221.61, Idaho State Historical Society Library and Archives.

FIG. 17. "Lewiston," as included by E. Jane Gay in *Choup-nit-ki*, 7. The Schlesinger Library, Radcliffe Institute, Harvard University.

18, her composite image of Fort Lapwai. Such a photograph overtly proclaims its artifice, however, both by its visible center seam and in the resulting sense of flattened space. Gay was more successful at communicating the vastness of mountain wilderness, using devices of deep perspective such as the receding path of a river that draws the viewer's eye into the picture plane. In "North Fork of the Clearwater," figure 19, overlapping mountain ridges disappear into an indistinct background, indicating a terrain so vast that it defies a long focus. Were it printed at folio size, this image would match the work of classic survey photography in scope, luminosity, and depth of field.

Yet Gay's vision was constrained by the size of her glass-plate negatives. She made no prints larger than about 7½ by 4½ inches. Of the reductive nature of her medium Gay was surely aware, and in many of her photographs she strives to signal the disconnect between image and terrain. Only a few of her landscapes, for example, assume the superordinate view that characterizes "Fort Lapwai" and "Lewiston, Idaho." Many other views, taken from within the terrain, emphasize the difficulty of travel in the Idaho back country on foot, by wagon, or on horseback, exemplifying Dirlik's observation that place is both "product *and* work."[29] Such images show how transforming place into space demanded the "[s]teady work from day-light to dark" from the surveyor and his chainmen, "walking, climbing, on hands & knees up and down cañons" thick with "thorn bushes [that] sometimes induce[d] inflamation of the eyes."[30] In such images Gay has not intentionally masked out clouds to yield featureless skies; rather they show scenes blanketed in the dense smoke of summer forest fires. While the smoke sometimes beautifully delineated receding ridge lines, as is the case in figure 19, it as frequently blurred or totally obscured the far distance and the horizon line. When the smoke cleared, the harsh summer sunlight bleached out contrasts, producing flattened and two-dimensional images.

The arid land itself resisted the processes of wet-plate photography. Thus a number of Gay's images proclaim on their surfaces the labor involved in their making, bearing visible traces of wipe marks or unevenly applied fixative. In figure 20, "The Damp Thermopylae," the allotting agent's tent sits at an uncomfortable angle

FIG. 18. Fort Lapwai, by E. Jane Gay, *Choup-nit-ki*, 11. ISHS 63-221.62, Idaho State Historical Society Library and Archives.

FIG. 19. "North Fork of the Clearwater," by E. Jane Gay, *Choup-nit-ki*, 54. The Schlesinger Library, Radcliffe Institute, Harvard University.

on a rocky hillside. The sky is featureless, and the blazing noonday sun has erased any shadows that might lend an illusion of dimensionality to the image. No source of water is visible, and the resulting smears across the image's surface demonstrate Gay's claim that "[p]hotography in a semi-arid country is not a cheerful occupation" (C, 367).[31] Nor, by extension, is surveying, allotting, or farming.

Several of Gay's photographs, too full of distracting visual "noise" to serve as objective documents, skillfully illustrate the specificities of place Fletcher labored to communicate to the Indian Office as her migratory path familiarized her with the details of the Nez Perce Reservation: "The plats of this region and the field notes fail to give any picture of the reservation, for instance, on the north boundary of Sec. 3. T. 33. N. Range 3. East you descend suddenly over 2000 feet within one mile of horizontal measurement. Yet no mention is made of it."[32] Abstractions may have sped the bureaucratic processes, but in the field, as Fletcher repeatedly learned,

FIG. 20. "The Damp Thermopylae," ca. September 1890, by E. Jane Gay, *Choup-nit-ki*, 317. ISHS 63-221.209, titled "One of Alice Fletcher's Survey Camps (Camp Thirsty)," Idaho State Historical Society Library and Archives.

abstract thinking presented a real danger to man and beast, be they surveyor, farmer, pack horse, or grazing stock. When Briggs surveyed this same section in July 1891 he attempted to communicate its topographic facts in his map (fig. 21), again using density of hachure to indicate slope, but the conventions governing his representations did not allow him to indicate precise elevation. A private and informal image made by Gay best illustrates the problem. In figure 22 the treacherous angle of barren land is evident even without the accompanying support of a caption or descriptive prose. A hill bisects the picture plane at a forty-five-degree angle. The upper left triangle of the image is a featureless sky; the lower right-hand triangle is filled by a nearly barren hillside, punctuated by brush and bare branches. At the bottom of the hill stretches a wide swath of large, sharp rocks. Two trees silhouetted on a far background hill lend a sense of relative size and distance.

The image's caption, "Where Dick Fell," seems to mark it as a private, not a public document. Dick was a pack horse. In the letter accompanying this photograph Gay tells her correspondent a detailed story about how the "ponderous" animal, carrying a load of wood

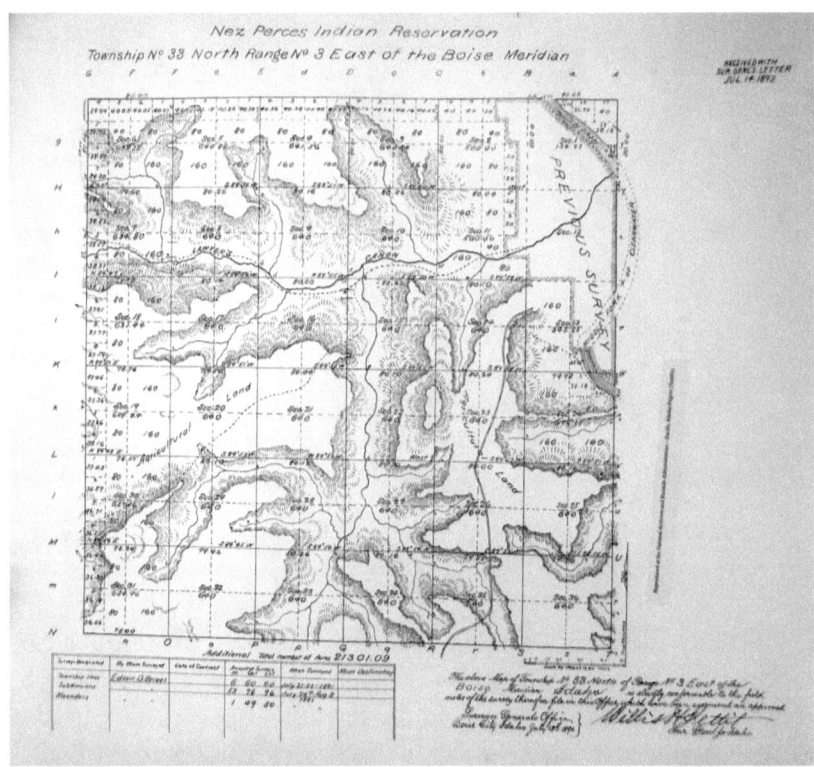

FIG. 21. Additional topographic features appear in Edson D. Briggs's survey of Township 33 North, Range 3 East, July–August 1891. Survey Maps 1873–95, Fort Lapwai Indian Agency, RG 75, NARA Pacific Region (Seattle).

and led by an inexperienced young boy, had "miss[ed] his foot hold [and] rolled over and over to the bottom" of this steep slope (C, 405). Such quotidian details as injuries to pack animals have no place in the heroic narrative of western conquest, where danger is often transmuted into heroic action or entertainment and is illustrated by images of intrepid male explorers scaling precipices or balanced nonchalantly at the edge of vertiginous cliffs. Hoxie and Mark omit this incident from their edition of Gay's letters. Since the loss of a pack animal would have presented a serious challenge to the success of allotment at a moment when Fletcher was frantically trying to finish the season's work, it is difficult to understand why they chose to delete the information.

[127]

FIG. 22. "Where Dick Fell," November 1891, by E. Jane Gay, *Choup-nit-ki*, 405. ISHS 63-221.69, Idaho State Historical Society Library and Archives.

These minutiae do, however, demonstrate how a photograph can represent both space and place. Uncaptioned, "Where Dick Fell" shows a representative slice of Idaho terrain, a space. I have used it as such to illustrate my point about Fletcher's attempt to give specificity to that terrain, to render it as a place. The written caption ties the photograph to a place, to work, and to an event now past but still embedded in Gay's and Fletcher's embodied perceptions of and encounters with a dangerous and resistant terrain. Gay's personal narration foregrounds the labor of moving supplies, managing recalcitrant animals, and attending to their needs. It illustrates, as well, the interdependence of people, even those engaged in cerebral work, with each other and with animals in surviving in a harsh terrain. The allotting agent performed largely invisible labor that transformed lands and peoples into abstract documentary statistics; yet early in the project she moved herself into the field to ensure the fairness of the allotment process. That guarantee depended on her engagement with the land over which she walked, drove, and rode. This same land demanded the muscular, bodily labors of surveyors, chainmen, and camp workers.

Yet if these workers formed an intricate and interdependent network, their relationship was not without its hierarchies of gender and race. The labor of James Stuart, the Nez Perce guide, translator, and Fletcher's chief assistant, was largely intellectual. Edson Briggs supervised the surveying crew, many of whom were Native men, by virtue of his race, his gender, and his specialized knowledge. Jane Gay worked as a cook, performing feminized and embodied labor; but when she wrote of her detached and cerebral functions as photographer, she referred to herself as "he." As a white woman she saw herself as an equal to Fletcher and Briggs, and superior to the Nez Perce men—surveyors, camp workers, and even Stuart—upon whom her safety and comfort so largely depended. These hierarchical codes of race, and especially of gender, were shared by those who received Gay's images and letters. Although her ad hoc records did not have evidentiary status to the federal Indian Office, they circulated to private networks of eastern correspondents who wielded immense ideological influence, and thus became a silent and unacknowledged part of how women involved in Indian reform saw the ongoing work of allotment.

As a case in point, I turn my attention to a specific group of landscape images, Gay's photographs of Fletcher's field camps. The two women sent individual prints of these photographs to various friends and correspondents; Gay also collected copies into small captioned albums measuring 5½ x 11 inches (see figs. 23 and 24). It would be easy to trivialize these albums, their every physical detail suggesting private intent. Gay hand-bound these books, sometimes with scalloped suede, and tied them with grosgrain ribbon. She embellished the covers with hand-lettered titles and line drawings. She seems to have given some of them as keepsakes to close friends such as Kate McBeth, who had shared the experience and/or who knew the principals intimately. Others she may have sent to her eastern correspondents. As well, she may have used them as trial versions—rough drafts, if you will—of *Choup-nit-ki*, the two privately published larger albums that document the entire allotment.

To dismiss these several small albums as merely private, however, is to miss their unmistakable ideological freight.[33] They mirror the larger public collections made by earlier expedition photographers, such as Timothy S. O'Sullivan, but their resemblance is mediated by

FIG. 23. "Where We Gathered Indian Songs," [by E. Jane Gay], cover, Acc. 632, Lawyer Collection. Used with permission of Douglas R. Nash, donor. Restricted access, NPNHPA.

FIG. 24. "Where We Gathered Indian Songs," [by E. Jane Gay], interior, Acc. 632, Lawyer Collection. Used with permission of Douglas R. Nash, donor. Restricted access, NPNHPA.

gender. As Kelsey observes, O'Sullivan's images served a dual purpose: they captured the beauty of western vistas and, at the same time, demonstrated the devotion of the members of the survey to their task, "show[ing them] engaged in work and oblivious to the visual appeal of their surroundings."[34] Gay's photographs likewise emphasize the daily challenges of camp life, especially within the context of her albums with their accompanying humorous and extended narration, but they do not embrace the fictions of masculine adventure and/or generic disinterestedness. The women who move within these frames engage physically and intellectually with the dry, smoky, hot, precipitous place in which they work, but they do not seem to be endangered by it.

An outsider's eye can distinguish these campsite images one from another primarily by attending to details of the terrain, for the other elements of the images remain virtually the same. One or more members of the allotting group stand in a cleared space amid the detritus of camp life—bedrolls, wagons, boxes of paperwork and provisions, axes, chains, and surveyors' equipment, a camp fire, and perhaps horses and tack off to the side. Several wagons and two or three tents frame the foreground view; Fletcher's tipi-shaped Sibley tent dominates the image. Within the albums the camps are distinguished one from another primarily by Gay's captions. Some, such as "Camp at Cold Spring," are named for location; others—"Camp Desolation" and "Camp Thirsty"—point to the foreboding terrain. Still others, such as "Checking for Rattlesnakes," strive to make the invisible apparent. To Gay and Fletcher the images served as a locus of memory echoed by their destination—a memory parlor, not a memory palace. Arranged chronologically in the album, the photographs are numbered sequentially and the captions function to evoke narrated memories. Fletcher, Gay, and Gay's niece, Emma Jane Gay, who received the letter containing the image "Camp Bearing Tree," would read the image by focusing on the tree at the center of figure 25, where Briggs had located an earlier surveyor's boundary mark by peeling the bark of the tree, much to the astonishment of those who watched (C, 173).

Those who received the small albums as keepsakes, especially

FIG. 25. "Camp Bearing Tree," by E. Jane Gay, *Choup-nit-ki*, 173. The Schlesinger Library, Radcliffe Institute, Harvard University.

those who lived in the East, who may have joined Fletcher and Gay to pore over the images at Fletcher's fireside in Washington DC, did not share the embodied memory of the Idaho terrain. They thus read the images differently, seeing in them the sum of Fletcher's work in carrying forth the ideals of education, uplift, and reform that united their work. To them the images bore potent if mute witness to the strength of two middle-aged white women, rough camping in a terrain that only a decade before had been a battleground. Even the format of these albums carries public meaning. The books, small enough to be held in one hand, confirm the intimacies of allotment and imply the manageability and containment promised by its attendant ideological claims.

Thus while the albums proclaim and fulfill their private intent, their public function is consistent with allotment's domestic imperatives. Many of the recipients of these images were women associated with reform groups such as the Washington Indian Association, as was Gay's close friend Henrietta Bradley, or were wives of prominent legislators and lobbyists (Jean Lander, Electa Dawes, Isabel Barrows, and Mrs. Thomas Jefferson Morgan). To these influential women the photographs offered tangible evidence that the work of allotment was domestic and could be carried out by other, similarly devoted women. For example, Gay's image of "Squirrel Camp" did not accompany Fletcher's report to the Indian Office. Yet it was surely known among the partisans who supported allotment. She included it in "Where We Camped," a small souvenir album she made for Susan and/or Kate McBeth, who owned other unmounted prints of the image as well. McBeth, for her part, often forwarded photographs to the Presbyterian Board of Foreign Missions with her periodic reports. A print of this image surely accompanied Gay's letter of 15 July 1889 to Henrietta Bradley, which contained a long description of the women's efforts to domesticate the cabin shown in the photograph, exemplified by Gay's managing to bake bread in an especially recalcitrant camp stove (C, 57–59).

In their wider circulation, Gay's letters and photographs were mediated by gender. She may have included a print of this image in the version of this letter she sent to Captain Richard H. Pratt, bringing the private challenges of the hard facts of allotment to the attention of a man centrally involved in Indian policy matters. He, in turn, published the letter in the *Red Man* (without an accompanying illustration), adding a title that emphasized the centrality of gender to the enterprise, "A Brave Woman Allotting Lands to Indians in Idaho." While the "brave woman" of the title is clearly Fletcher, Gay's letter makes a claim for her own equally important labor, veiled by her habitual use of the masculine pronoun when she wrote of herself as the photographer. For readers of the *Red Man*, who lacked the artifactual evidence of the photographic image, Gay detailed the circumstances of the photographer's work: "[O]ne . . . morning, so bright that your photographer takes an instantaneous view at five and a half A.M., and finds it overtimed, you rise while it is yet night. . . . The sun streams down. . . . Your photographer grumbles about the softening of his gelatine plates."[35] In these brief sentences Gay's second-person narration overtly invites readers to imagine themselves within the *place* of allotment, foregrounding the persistent physicality of an insufferably hot early summer morning. Within this forbidding terrain two "brave [women]" must pursue their duties.

The camp photographs rarely document any action that could be associated with the process of allotting. They do not show the surveyor and his team clambering into the canyons and scaling mountainsides. They capture moments of repose, when the work of allotment had paused. Yet the images, collected in albums and/or circulated singly, signify "Alice Fletcher and Jane Gay at work." Fletcher's Sibley tent, clearly labeled with her name and in form suggestive of Native tipis, links the domesticity of her camp sites to the promised domestication allotment was to enable. Standing by the tent flap, Alice Fletcher, corseted, wearing a dark dress or coat, shaded by her inevitable flowered bonnet, was indubitably a lady and, because she was "in camp," always incipiently at work. Based on these images, eastern supporters of the civilizing agendas of the Indian Office could continue to believe that taming the land was a matter of rationalizing it, that it could be accomplished by a diminutive middle-aged woman, and that the results of her work were able to be contained in diminutive hand-lettered albums.

4. Ethnographic Knowledge and Native Cartography

As she prepared to return to Idaho for her second summer's work in 1890, Fletcher was intent upon giving more attention to her ethnological investigations. Such work was, to her way of thinking, entirely congruent with her allotting duties. However, as I demonstrate, the two foci of her work—one cultural and historical, and the other political and progressive—were often at odds. At worst, Fletcher used her scientific work to escape the considerable annoyances of her bureaucratic responsibilities; at best, her scholarly investigations fed her growing realization that Nimiipuu culture and history were intimately tied to the land she had initially seen as a two-dimensional abstraction. Ultimately, local knowledge forced her to seek several important modifications to allotment policy.

F. W. Putnam, whose institution and work had benefited from Fletcher's earlier field work among the Omahas, encouraged her to gather information and artifacts from Nez Perce informants, as well. She assured him she had "already planned" to do so, "and as a beginning Miss Gay photographed the sunken places, the sites of the Ancient winter dwellings and also the old graveyard. Of these I will write you when I send you the photos. I have beside the articles I mentioned a memorial staff I took from a mound of stones—the only one I saw on the reservation—and I will send that to you with an account of the religious ceremony of which it is the memorial. I will do all I can to preserve materials for you."¹ Letters such as this make clear that as she went into the field with those who were to receive title to their lands, travel Gay praised as evidence of Fletcher's disinterested concern to ensure that each allottee received the maximum measure of land under the law, the allotting agent had other agendas in mind as well. Fletcher the anthropologist saw—and sometimes looted—ceremonial sites, encouraged her informants to furnish her with details about their uses, and purchased from them artifacts she could ship east to be stored in Putnam's memory palace until her future ministrations could transmute them from objects connected to a place and its culture into evidence in support of a narrative of evolutionary anthropology.

The tension between Fletcher's anthropological avocation and her professional duties as an allotting agent intensified in March 1890. En route to Idaho to begin her work she visited her friend the philanthropist Mary Thaw, who proposed, "that [Fletcher] resign from Ind[ian] work she to pay me an annuity of $1200 . . . to begin July 1st." Fletcher considered this offer to pose a "serious question for me to meet & answer."² Thaw's gift ultimately took the form of an endowment to Harvard, where the money funded a chair for Fletcher, the first to be held by a woman in that institution.³ Even before these arrangements were finalized, the prospect of the award allowed Fletcher to begin to think of herself as a professional scholar. The promise of a permanent annuity meant she could resign immediately from government employment and devote all her attention to her anthropological investigations. Even as she pondered the decision she intensified her efforts to gather ethnographic resources.

Arriving in Idaho in late April 1890 with her mind full of new possibilities and half-formed plans, Fletcher consulted with her friend Susan McBeth, who had pursued amateur ethnological investigations among her congregants and who had collaborated with several of her theological students to compile a Nez Perce–English lexicon that would further her missionary work. Aging and ill, McBeth agreed to share her work with Fletcher, who wrote to Putnam with great excitement:

I've struck a mine of great ethnological wealth here. Miss S. L. McBeth who has been nearly 20 yrs among this tribe as a missionary is . . . quite a scholar. . . . She is the lady who has prepared all the native preachers educating them entirely herself. She has made a very careful study of this people, their myths etc. & their language. She has a dictionary & grammar besides all this other material nearly ready to print. She offers to work with me & let me use any thing she has out of regard for what I have done, she of course to have the credit of her own work. She is now an invalid—partly paralized—& alone can never get her rich stores into shape. Shall I take her offer? Would you like to print the history & entire record of the Nez Perce & a dictionary & grammar of this language. It may cost too much, but if Mrs. Thaw lives I think she would help out of her great esteem for Miss McBeth's missionary work. *It is our ground.*[4]

This passage clearly demonstrates the overlapping interests impinging upon Fletcher's allotting work in this second season. By this account, Susan McBeth offered her data because she admired Fletcher's work (whether the anthropological pursuits or the allotment activities is unclear). Mary Thaw might fund the publication because of her regard for McBeth's missionary work, especially as it would have been narrated to her by Alice Fletcher. The Peabody Museum would win the intellectual laurels. Significantly, Fletcher summarizes the case in a metaphor—"It is our ground"—that lies very close, in fact, to the literal case. Civilization's success would be proved by allotment; allotment had enabled the collection of ethnographic data, the publication of which would be underwritten by Presbyterian labors and monies; that same denomination's missionary work had been instrumental in launching the allotment program in Kamiah.

Throughout the summer and early fall of 1890 Fletcher vacillated between pursuing her academic future and fulfilling her present responsibilities as allotting agent, which she hoped to complete by the coming winter. She chose to work in the Kamiah area, where people were more cooperative, where land titles were largely uncontested, and where several of her informants lived, including Billy Williams and Nancy Corbett, the grandmother of James Stuart. Not coincidentally, Susan McBeth lived nearby in Mt. Idaho. Fletcher wrote frequently to Putnam, mulling over the question of whether she could complete the allotment and, if she could not soon bring it to an end, whether to resign her position. She wrote,

> I am lingering here . . . to get a little more out of Miss McBeth's *Ms.* so that I can do more intelligent work among the Indians. . . . As soon as matters are settled, I think it would be best for me to write personally to Commiss Morgan, with whom I am on very friendly terms & tell him that I must close my work here early this season in order to return East & write. It has occurred to me that if you decide to have me work up Miss McBeths material I might get the Gov't to send me here to do the little that will remain in the field & so save expense in getting here & going about.[5]

Just a month later, however, she warned Putnam she would not be able to finish the allotment "this Fall." She proposed to tell Morgan, "I shall leave the Service, but will complete this allotment which it would be difficult for another to take up, but ask permission to return East at once & come back here for a few months next year to close up."[6] Her optimistic estimate marks the degree to which she had not yet fully comprehended the resistance of potential allottees in the Fort Lapwai area. To finish the work there required a good deal longer than "a few months." In 1891 she spent her longest field season in Idaho—from 18 April through 9 December. She returned again in 1892, working in the field from 7 May through 12 September; and when she departed, she had still not fully completed the allotment.

Even as she tried to imagine a way to fulfill both her obligations, Fletcher became further distracted by a letter from Commissioner Morgan asking her to send him "suggestions relative to an Indian Office exhibit in the World's Fair at Chicago." Drawing on her earlier experience in planning the Indian Office display at the 1885 New Orleans World's Industrial and Centennial Cotton Exposition, Fletcher wrote a long reply, recommending a developmentally based exhibit designed to "[show] a native culture set in varied conditions, transformed by civilizing agents so as to be received into our national life."[7] Already anxious to consult personally with Putnam about the details of the academic work she would accomplish under Thaw's funding, Fletcher took Morgan's letter as a catalyst and decided to abbreviate the second field season so she could work personally with both men. Consequently, the time it took her to finish the allotment was surely lengthened by her attention to her anthropological research, for she continued to use the next two field seasons to gather ethnographic data. Ultimately, those data would influence the way she allotted lands.

"Inside history": Local Knowledge

As she accompanied allottees into in the field and supervised the marking of each property's corners, Fletcher compiled a full genealogical record of each allottee, a process Jane Gay ironically described in this fashion: "Her Majesty sits all day long in her inquisitorial chair . . . solicitous of the uncles, aunts and cousins, tracing relationship through labyrinthian channels, searching after the suppositious head of the family who is to have 160 acres thrust upon him *nolens volens* when found" (C, 122). Brief entries in Fletcher's field diaries suggest that her "inquisit[ion]" of potential allottees yielded not only genealogical information but also ethnographic data. In these interactions Nimiipuu performed their past for her. In the discussion that follows I amplify the idea of performance to include Victor Turner's observation that the term "derives from Old French *parfournir*, 'to complete' or 'carry out thoroughly.'"[8] In this sense Nimiipuu performances bring the past forth, carrying out its full implications for the present. As Diana Taylor observes, performance of this sort also "functions as an epistemology." These intimate and interpersonal occasions echo larger public ritual performative instances such as the Fourth of July, occasions upon which the "transfer [of] . . . social knowledge, memory, and a sense of identity" occurs as stories and rituals are reanimated, genealogies recited, and the interconnection of lives, culture, and land is reaffirmed.[9]

Just before departing the reservation in December 1889, for example, Fletcher had interviewed Ou-na-ne-we-nan-ny (Celia Reubens, mother of James Reubens), presumably to finalize the details of her allotment. As part of the interchange the elder woman presented Fletcher with several gifts. Immediately upon her return to the capital, Fletcher wrote to Putnam:

> I have obtained some articles for the Museum. A basket having a hole in the bottom into which a stone is fitted & in which the Camas & other roots are pounded by a stone pestle. I have an old pestle made in the last century & in use up to the time I secured it & the basket from Kok-sot-pa-lo, an old woman who remembers Lewis & Clark.[10] I deemed the articles worth securing on account of this historical connection. I will write out the story to go with the basket which this aged woman made & the pestle which she has used all her life.[11]

The basket and pestle are still a part of the Peabody Museum collections. For Fletcher, the significance of these items was not that they were given in friendship, nor was it their work value in the past or present, nor even their antiquity. Rather, she decided the basket was "worth securing" because it established a connection with Lewis and Clark's arrival, an event Fletcher recognized as a legitimate history. Only later would other informants lead her to recognize more fully the long history antedating white contact and within which these items had been made and used.

In 1890 Fletcher's inspections of properties to be allotted in Kamiah took her to the locations of aboriginal villages and settlements such as Ah-kaht-tse 'ween, shown in figure 26. Here James Stuart reclines and Alice Fletcher stands "in housepit depressions . . . opposite present-day Kooskia, Idaho."[12] Across the river stand fences and buildings that Gay's caption identifies as "Nicodemus' Home" (C, 352).[13] The log cabin surrounded by tidy fences and trees does not signify the successful outcome of an allotment, however. The improvements visible here had been made before Fletcher's arrival in Kamiah and establish the connection of Wa sin me sa kart sa's home to those earlier dwellings for which evidence remains in the image's foreground. Thus the photograph links past and present in a record of continual occupation. According to Robert Lee Sappington and his co-researchers, Ah-kaht-tse 'ween had, in fact, been "occupied from ca. 2500 BP into the historic period."[14]

In *Choup-nit-ki* Gay presented this image on its own page, framed

FIG. 26. "Clearwater River—Nicodemus' Home on the Left," by E. Jane Gay, *Choup-nit-ki*, 352. The Schlesinger Library, Radcliffe Institute, Harvard University.

by hand-drawn lines. In the upper right-hand border of the frame she added a pen-and-ink sketch of the home, made from a different angle that that of the photograph. In the drawing the large tree that partially obscures the house is removed and the aspect of the house rotated. As a result the profile of the dwelling echoes the shape of the mountain in the background of the photograph immediately below, a figural similarity that aligns this home with the land on which it stands. Presumably this homestead fell within Fletcher's initial description of Kamiah farms, the contours of which did not conform to the square ideal. Yet, surely because of the clear evidence of the family's long tenure upon the site, she made a split allotment to Wa sin me sa kart sa, part of which included this decidedly nonrectangular plot. Briggs's plats, shown in figures 27 and 28, show the allotments. Figure 27 shows one part of Wa sin me sa kart sa's allotment, #1631, near the top left, nestled in a curve of the Middle Fork of the

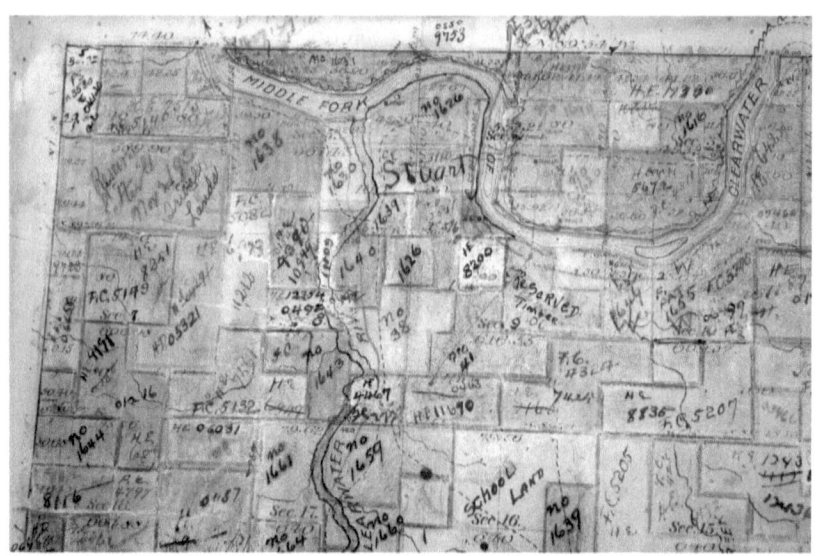

FIG. 27. Allotment detail for Township 32 North, Range 4 East, by Edson D. Briggs, September 1889. Survey Maps 1873–95, Fort Lapwai Indian Agency, RG 75, NARA Pacific Region (Seattle).

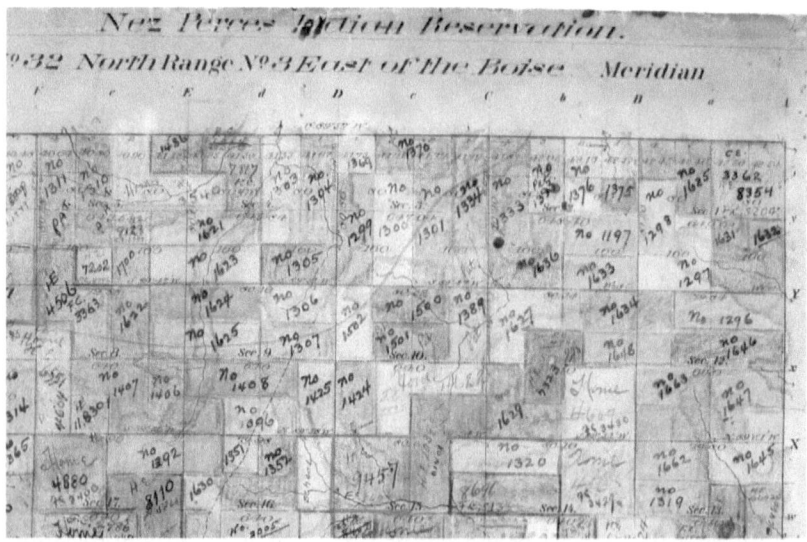

FIG. 28. Allotment detail for Township 32 North, Range 3 East, by Edson D. Briggs, September 1889. Survey Maps 1873–95, Fort Lapwai Indian Agency, RG 75, NARA Pacific Region (Seattle).

Clearwater River. In figure 28 another part of allotment #1631 is in the upper right.¹⁵ Part of the allotment of Kar yokts (Nancy Nicodemus), #1633, lies slightly to the left. Figures 29 and 30 reproduce the patent receipts for these two allottees.

Fletcher's ethnographic and allotting interests coalesced in an incident that yielded what was surely her most important piece of ethnohistorical data, a hand-drawn map that demonstrated to her the long connection of the land upon which she worked with the sovereign political structure of the Nimiipuu. One of the ethnographic studies she had hoped to complete during 1890 was to be based on a list of pre-contact villages she had extracted from Susan McBeth's work.¹⁶ She told Putnam she was planning "to send a paper to the [American Association for the Advancement of Science] on the villages & village sites of these people—but I fear I cant get it ready." Her research had stalled because she had not been able to correlate McBeth's list of villages with their locations and thus to discern their importance to Nimiipuu political organization. She wrote of her confusion: "This tribe is queer—I can't find any central organization. Their little villages had each its head men or chief—While certain localities were more prominant than others, it was from their situation as to the mountain or fishing sites on the river. . . . [T]there seems to be no myths of mygration."¹⁷

Fletcher found the key to this conundrum early in her third allotting season, in June 1891, when her Nimiipuu friend Jonathan/Billy Williams (Kew-kew'-lu-yah), collaborated with her to draw the map of Nimiipuu lands shown in figure 31.¹⁸ Kew-kew'-lu-yah, the father of Kamiah pastor Robert Williams, had begun to narrate Nimiipuu history to Fletcher when he took his allotment in the late summer of 1889, and over the next several months he "came often to talk . . . about Lewis and Clark and the exploits of his own grandfather" (C, 147). To Fletcher this map promised to bring coherence to much of the information she had already gathered—not only the list of Nez Perce village and place names she had obtained from Susan McBeth but also the items of material culture she had gathered, the stories she had heard about Lewis and Clark from Celia Reubens and from

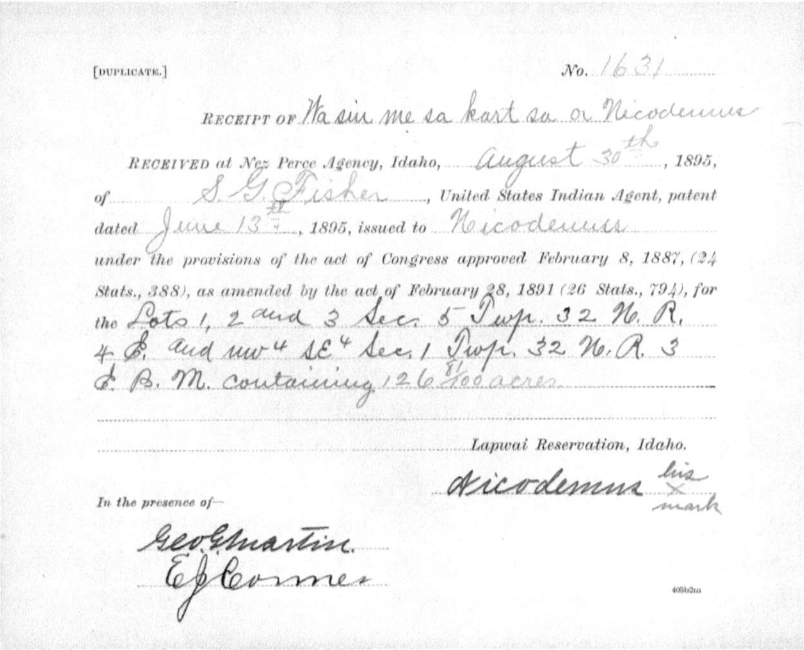

[DUPLICATE.] No. 1631

RECEIPT OF Wa sin me sa kart sa or Nicodemus

RECEIVED at Nez Perce Agency, Idaho, August 30th, 1895, of S. G. Fisher, United States Indian Agent, patent dated June 13th, 1895, issued to Nicodemus under the provisions of the act of Congress approved February 8, 1887, (24 Stats., 388), as amended by the act of February 28, 1891 (26 Stats., 794), for the Lots 1, 2 and 3 Sec. 5 Twp. 32 N. R. 4 E. and nw 4 SE 4 Sec. 1 Twp. 32 N. R. 3 E. B. M. containing 126 81/100 acres.

Lapwai Reservation, Idaho.

Nicodemus his x mark

In the presence of—

Geo. G. Martin.
E. J. Comer

405b2m

FIG. 29. Patent Receipt No. 1631, of Wa sin me sa kart sa, or Nicodemus. Patent Receipts (Nez Perce) 1895, Northern Idaho Agency, RG 75, NARA Pacific Region (Seattle).

Kew-kew'-lu-yah, and the missionary stories about the subsequent journey of four Nez Perce men to St. Louis in 1832.

The map was a major coup, for in its time, it was unique.[19] Fletcher wrote to Putnam:

> I've secured from one of the oldest and most remarkable men of the Nez Perce tribe a map on which he has drawn all the Nez Perce Country, and located all the villages of the tribe 77 or 78 of them (I forget which with out referring to my notes). I've the names of these villages & many curious items. . . . I want the map to go to the museum eventually. . . . This is the first time the villages etc. of this tribe have been gained & I've also the inside history of the four men who went to St. Louis for teachers in 1832, those whom Catlin painted. . . . *I don't want any one but the Museum to get it to keep.*[20]

Enshrined in the Peabody Museum of Archaeology and Ethnology,

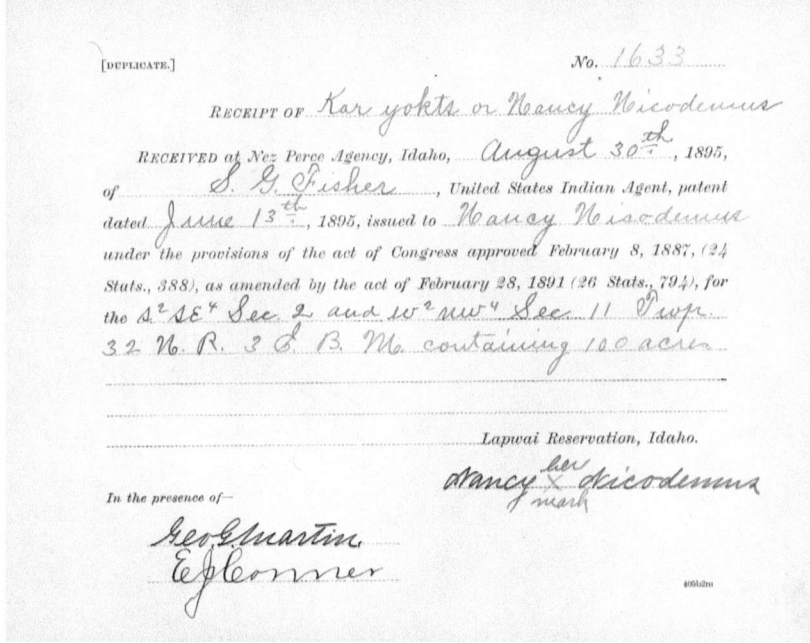

FIG. 30. Patent Receipt No. 1633, of Kar yokts, or Nancy Nicodemus. Patent Receipts (Nez Perce) 1895, Northern Idaho Agency, RG 75, NARA Pacific Region (Seattle).

Kew-kew'-lu-yah's map would stand as physical evidence of her worthiness to hold an endowed chair at Harvard.

Many of the details of Kew-kew'-lu-yah's map exemplify Native cartography, characterized by Mark Warhus as "pictures of experience . . . formed in the human interaction with the land and . . . a record of the events that give it meaning."[21] In its details such a map would seem to illustrate the embodied understanding of *place*. Yet Billy Williams, whom Fletcher considered to be a primitive thinker, performed a task emblematic of modernism and cognate to her own work, condensing masses of embodied and oral memory into an abstract, portable, and permanent form. The information represented by this map is highly mediated—by translation, by the guiding questions of Kew-kew'-lu-yah's interlocutors, by their incomplete note taking, and by their carefully structured retrospective accounts. For his part, Kew-kew'-lu-yah proffered his information for a purpose,

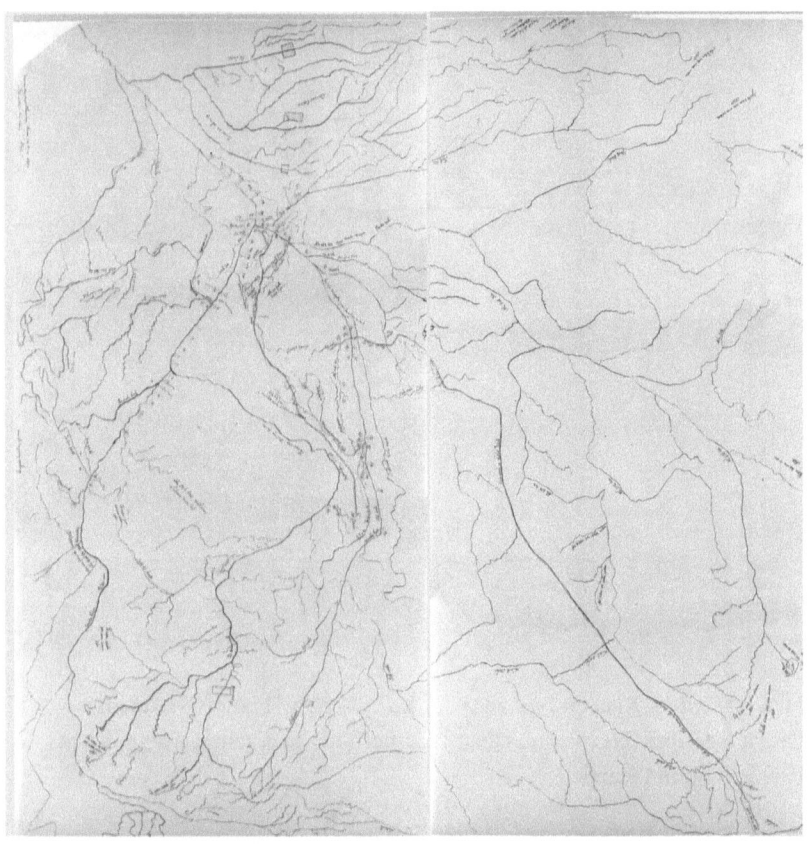

FIG. 31. "The Nez Perce Country," as drawn by Kew-kew'-lu-yah, July 1891. Ms. 4558 (58), Papers of Alice Cunningham Fletcher (1838–1923) and Francis La Flesche (1859–1923), National Anthropological Archives, Smithsonian Institution.

selectively forgetting, condensing, emphasizing, and arranging it to further his own ends. As a document the map thus occupies a middle ground between place and space, between embodied knowledge and intellectual property, between living history and museum artifact. It might most productively be read as Kew-kew'-lu-yah's performance of his past in the presence of others, an occasion upon which he demonstrated what he was and was not. As a surrogate for elder informants who had visited him in dreams, he was as surely a conduit of performed memory as were the mounted regalia-clad warriors riding in the annual Fourth of July war processions. Although his map answered Fletcher's questions, in the process of its making, he engaged her in a relation of exchange, demonstrated to her the historical and political claims of Nimiipuu to their territory, and implicitly enjoined her to acknowledge the land's history and the Native sovereignty deriving therefrom as she went about her allotting tasks. In his dealings with Fletcher Kew-kew'-lu-yah seems even to have anticipated the future uses of the information he furnished.

Although the resulting map and the ethnographic monograph that interpreted it appeared under Fletcher's name, the interview and the intellectual labor that produced them were collaborative. Fletcher seldom worked alone, and rarely directly acknowledged the work of her translators, informants, and editors.[22] To have done so would have marked her as less than professional. As Dana D. Nelson has established, the quintessential social scientific professional in late nineteenth-century America was a single white male researcher, whose superior mind would transmute the information he gathered from Native informants into verifiable knowledge. Fletcher conformed her work to this model. In this case she depended on several unacknowledged collaborators. James and/or Harriet Stuart likely translated the conversations, since neither informant nor interviewers spoke both languages. Jane Gay, whose photographic portrait of Kew-kew'-lu-yah is part of Fletcher's documentation, also served as the principal investigator on at least one of the three days of this event.[23] Kate McBeth, who had recently begun to realize the rich historical knowledge held by such elders as Kew-kew'-lu-yah, took her own set of notes. When the map was finished Fletcher invited several other Nimiipuu elders to "[test its] accuracy"; apparently they amended some of the locations.[24] Finally, the interview took place under the invisible but immensely influential gaze of absent interested parties: Fletcher's employers, mentors, and funders and a host of otherworldly informants, "old people" who visited Kew-kew'-lu-yah at night to refresh his memory and furnish him with information ("NPC," 187).

According to accounts of this occasion written by the white women who conducted the interview, Kew-kew'-lu-yah produced the map over a period of several days, drawing it in pencil on a large sheet of paper.[25] Fletcher writes that he "would sit as if lost in thought, then he would suddenly resume his pencil and proceed rapidly to trace rivers and streams and to mark village sites" ("NPC," 187). When the map grew too large for a single sheet, a second paper was attached, probably creating some distortion in the final product. Kew-kew'-lu-yah drew a representation of the territories traversed and occupied by the Nimiipuu at about the time of their first contact with Lewis and Clark. Like many other examples of Native cartography, his map is primarily one of routes of hunting, migration, and trade. The relative positions and directions of rivers and streams coordinate fairly closely with western maps. The map lacks symbolic representations of political boundaries; rather, the outer limits of Nimiipuu territory abut the edges of the paper, where route-lines take sharp right-angle bends or simply cease. Dots indicate the locations of seventy-eight villages that "were either in existence or their sites known at the beginning of the [nineteenth] century" ("NPC," 189).[26] At some point Kew-kew'-lu-yah also verified the names of villages Fletcher had already obtained from Susan McBeth and helped her locate them on his map. In the process he narrated a history of each.

In August 1891, after making a copy for herself, Fletcher sent the map to Putnam. The original has long been lost, as I discuss later in this chapter. We know from her notebooks, diaries, and letters that she almost immediately appropriated the map, adapting and amending it to support her own agendas. She added a compass orientation, probably to help her compare this map with others in her possession.[27] She numbered the villages, keyed them to her written interpretation, and indicated their locations with red dots. She added the Native names of these villages and may, as well, have added contemporary Anglicized place names, again likely as a means of facilitating comparison of this map with others. She may have made additional annotations to prompt her memory of salient facts as she later worked on her lengthy interpretation of the map.[28] In these activities of naming and grouping, which continued through the summer of 1891, she would have had substantial assistance from James Stuart and other Nimiipuu informants; in subsequent years, as she continued to study and write about the map, she corresponded with Kate McBeth, who helped her verify the spellings and translations of place names and to recall other details, often by consulting Kew-kew'-lu-yah and other elders.

With the map Fletcher sent Putnam a photograph of Kew-kew'-lu-yah made by Jane Gay, apparently to serve as an attestation of its authenticity. In her account of making the image, reproduced here as figure 32, Gay writes, "The Photographer has taken a snap at Billy as he sat resting at Miss Kate's door" (C, 381–82). The offhand sentence discounts the evident craft and the collaborative nature of this image's making. Gay arranged the pose, chose the framing and focal length, released the shutter, and made the print. In the resulting image, dodged edges produce the oval format characteristic of heroic portraiture. The light falls from above, illuminating Kew-kew'-lu-yah's forehead and eyes and suggesting a kind of halo. Turned in a three-quarter pose, he gazes into the distance. He wears a western-style frock coat and a white lace-trimmed cravat or scarf. In his left arm he holds a book, probably a Bible. This prop reminds us that Kate McBeth was a collaborator, hovering about, insisting that Kew-kew'-lu-yah hold the book.

When she reproduced the portrait in *Choup-nit-ki*, Gay continued to direct its interpretation, captioning it "Old Billy Williams." In her written commentary she added a salient detail: "[T]he coat Billy has on is one he cut and made himself *out of a blanket*" (C, 382; emphasis added). Although Kew-kew'-lu-yah did not read or write English, he appears to be a civilized and Christianized Indian, an interpretation demanded by his attire and by the book he holds. The resulting transformation of blanket into coat and savage into Christian is a trope that reappears in the title that Allen Conrad Morrill and Eleanor Dunlap Morrill gave to their biographical study of the McBeth sisters, *Out of the Blanket*, a phrase signaling the success of the missionaries' benevolent and transformational civilizing efforts.

Yet Kew-kew'-lu-yah's portrait escapes the frames and meanings adduced to it by his white interlocutors. The coat is still also a blanket. The book he holds constitutes what photographic theorist Roland Barthes terms a *punctum*, a detail in the image that "changes

FIG. 32. "Old Billy Williams," June 1891, by E. Jane Gay, *Choup-nit-ki*, 382. ISHS 63-221.101, Idaho State Historical Society Library and Archives.

my reading" by its mere presence. . . . I am looking at a new photograph, marked in my eyes with a higher value."[29] To white viewers whom Gay imagined as her audience for this portrait, the book adds a "higher value" to the image. Yet this punctum can also "change [our] reading" if we note that Kew-kew'-lu-yah does not hold or embrace the book. In fact, he likely was unable to read. Rather, it seems to be propped against his chest. The awkwardness of the pose suggests that he may have agreed to having this prop included in his portrait from complex motives of his own—surely to signify his strategic alliance with Presbyterian Christianity but also perhaps as a way of positioning his own embodied knowledge as primary, and book-knowledge as its supplement.

The interview that produced the map, while clearly a civil and productive informational exchange, nevertheless included a certain degree of negotiation among various parties, for, as Peter Nabokov has argued, map making may be "a mode for cross-cultural argument . . . a rhetorical device for staking out social or diplomatic positions," especially "in those charged circumstances when cultures are jockeying for the political or psychological upper hand."[30] Such is surely the case with this encounter. As Kew-kew'-lu-yah drew the map, Fletcher elicited its historical component by asking him questions that would contribute to the comparative study of past Native political structures she was then writing, in which one of her foundational assumptions was that the present could be severed from the past, for she was the agent of a law meant to erase Native polities and to transform Native subjects into American farmers. In Kew-kew'-lu-yah's narration, however, the past was closely tied to the present moment and to its future consequences. He framed his answers to emphasize the Nimiipuu connection to a territory he had seen steadily diminished over the span of his lifetime by explorers, fur traders, missionaries, and other agents of imperialism, all bent on inscribing their claims on the place he knew so intimately.

In point of fact, then, Kew-kew'-lu-yah stood to gain as much from those who interviewed him as they did from him. The benefits he anticipated were not immediate and personal, however. In June 1891 he was about seventy-six years old. He had already claimed his allotment and ensured that his family had received properties adjoining his own. He was confident the McBeth sisters would continue to support his family's claim to leadership among the Presbyterian Nimiipuu and understood his son Robert's position as pastor of the First Kamiah Presbyterian Church to be secure. Kew-kew'-lu-yah anticipated future benefits, intimately connected with his insistence that he spoke for otherworldly informants. These unseen collaborators had reminded him of the existence of long-abandoned village sites, and of the persistence of Nimiipuu identity over the duration of contact and intercultural exchange, an identity deriving from the terrain they occupied. Thus despite a biography that to Fletcher, McBeth, and Gay signified adaptation, acculturation, and even assimilation, he occupied a place in a chain of surrogations—as a mouthpiece for the departed elders and the old ways, and as a relay point for Nimiipuu survivance, the logic of which asserts that past estates cannot be severed from the present or the future.

The very form of the map demonstrated to Fletcher that Native wisdom, drawn from long experience upon the land, might furnish forth solutions to some of the problems that had plagued her. Kew-kew'-lu-yah's body was figuratively present in the map and in the portrait that accompanied it. Of Native mapping practices, Nabokov writes: "Before representing [land] . . . some native traditions expected you first to listen to its stories and learn its names, to follow it with your feet or to find a way to dream at its most propitious locations. Only after practicing a range of such knowledge-engendering practices *with* the landscape might you be able to truly depict it on a flat surface. This was often the reverse of the non-Indian process of appropriating space by first naming and drawing it, and only then by striding over or settling what was thereby already your own(ed) conception."[31] The map Kew-kew'-lu-yah drew represented the land he had traversed for nearly eighty years, the villages in which he had lived, and the location of sites related to his own biography. Based on these embodied experiences, he demonstrated to Fletcher an alternate mode of cartographic representation, one unlike that employed by the Indian Office, upon which linear distances were drawn to a standard scale. Such abstracted and equivalent representations were of little help to Fletcher, for they did not predict the difficulty of traversing the terrain. It mattered little if points A and B were separated by only three miles if the transit between them entailed climbing into and out of two or three canyons. These facts were well known to Kew-kew'-lu-yah, for as Fletcher wrote, "His knowledge of the country represented was gained by traveling over it, mostly by foot. On the map the rivers, trails, and canyons are all drawn alike, these to Billy were practically passage-ways in getting about the country" ("NPC," 188). As Sappington and his colleagues observe, his is a map of routes, wherein "variability of scale probably reflects travel time [and, I would emphasize, embodied experience] rather than actual distance" ("NPC," 180).

In the process of correcting the reservation's boundaries Fletcher had perforce learned that her idea of inscribing impermeable lines on the land was a cartographic fiction. Nimiipuu and whites attended each other's Fourth of July celebrations. Cattle and their owners, both Native and white, had long ranged in and out of the reservation; streams and rivers meandered across section lines; and railroad lines would soon transect the land. The boundaries of Kew-kew'-lu-yah's map, by contrast, were only the edges of the papers he drew upon. Within the territory it represented, Nimiipuu had intermingled with other indigenous northwesterners such as the Cayuses, Shoshones, Palouses, and Spokanes ("NPC," 190, 198, 199, 200–2). Villages were impermanently sited. For example, the people of Wah-na-we had "moved in a body to the Yakama tribe in Washington on account of the horse-stealing habits of the white men in their vicinity" ("NPC," 199). The major routes on which Kew-kew'-lu-yah had walked or ridden had also been used by fur traders, missionaries, explorers, and most recently by white settlers ("NPC," 196, 199, 201, 202, 204, 207).

Yet as Dirlik insists, "[P]orosity of boundaries is not the same as the abolition of boundaries."[32] As Fletcher involved herself in the map's interpretation, she wrote of the successive treaties that had mandated boundaries not visible on the map but omnipresent in her mind—lines drawn to enclose smaller and smaller territories. Her notes drive home the violence entailed in the acts of division and exclusion. She writes, for example, that "[t]he people of [Lum-ta'ma-po] refused to enter into the treaties of 1855 and 1863," and that "[t]he Treaty of 1863 . . . did not include any of the villages of [Group 2]" ("NPC," 207, 192; see also 193, 196, and 208). Did she reflect on her own implication in the ongoing process of marking these shrinking boundaries? Was she disturbed by how drastically allotment would further diminish those holdings? Because such qualms are not the stuff of scientific record, we cannot be sure, but it seems at least possible to imagine that in the process she, like her informant, encountered ghosts of the past.

By 1891, after two summers in the field, Fletcher had become convinced that in many cases a single 160-acre allotment would not support a family farm of the kind imagined by allotment's theorists. Kew-kew'-lu-yah's information confirmed the insight, for his stories demonstrated to her that the land had seen a variety of uses, adapted to its variations in terrain and resources. Nimiipuu had lived in valley villages during the winters, camped on the high prairies and dug kaus and other roots in the spring, fished in early summer, gathered camas in July, and hunted in the fall ("NPC," 190, 195). These seasonal uses meant they were migratory, not sedentary, and depended on common, not individually owned, lands and resources. They located their villages close to food, water, and materials for constructing dwellings, tools, and clothing; village groupings derived from subsistence patterns and from kinship relations. Fletcher writes, "As a rule the villages were situated on the banks of a stream, and the inhabitants [of a given village] considered themselves as kindred" ("NPC," 189). Understanding the past relation of kinship systems to the land confirmed Fletcher's inclination to allow at least the most promising of her clients to take their allotments contiguously, rather than to insist they "checkerboard" their claims with lands destined to be sold to white settlers. Such a family-based grouping echoed earlier village structures and, in the process, yielded a more generous use of land, allowing relatives to pool individual resources in a commons approach to grazing, plowing, and developing their respective allotments. Such groupings would also mitigate the fractionation of land in subsequent generations as original allottees died and their allotments were divided among their heirs in smaller and smaller segments.

Because Fletcher wished to maximize the success of these most promising allottees, she and her staff were puzzled by those who requested split properties, part of which may have been located in a fertile valley, and another segment on an arid bluff, a precipitous hillside, or in another inexplicable location that seemed to augur failure. Gay's accounts contain several anecdotes that show how Fletcher and her white assistants endeavored to teach, exemplify, and guide their wards into wise agrarian thinking. She writes:

> It is quite common, now, for the Indians to ask the Surveyor's advice about their allotments and that is a great step forward. Sometimes one will say, "I want *this* land." "Not if I can help it" says Briggs. "You'll starve to death on that land; sage brush wont grow on it."
>
> "This is my land," says another.
>
> "Do you want to set up a rattlesnake farm?" says Briggs.
>
> "It is all stones; not half an acre of plow land on it."
>
> ... And the Indians laugh and, in nine cases out of ten, take his advice. (C, 175–76)

For Gay and her readers, these anecdotes confirm what everyone wanted to believe: disinterestedly benevolent federal agents were giving the Nez Perces the raw materials for success. Yet it is also apparent that for every nine clients who made wise choices of land containing arable soil, sufficient water, and access to market routes, a tenth refused to take guidance, and for equally wise, if occulted, reasons. Such irrationality might be seen as strategic, as Kew-kew'-lu-yah's narration of past histories made clear. He told Fletcher, for example, of Il-law-kart-'part-poo (Villages 22 and 22a), located between high cliffs that trapped heat and light. These extreme conditions meant that "[t]he region hereabouts was barren. The Indians said: 'The white people do not like this place, as nothing will grow here.' Consequently the natives were not intruded upon. To this village those who were not in sympathy with the Christian element in the tribe resorted in the winter to hold their old-time practices, as they were here out of reach of the progressive Indians, the missionaries, and the teachers" ("NPC," 196). In telling these histories Kew-kew'-lu-yah demonstrated to Fletcher that land had value beyond the purely economic. The locations she and Briggs saw as lacking in agrarian resources nevertheless held ceremonial, ritual, and cultural value. Thus certain segments of allotments were taken strategically, some "because of some graves," as Kate McBeth put it, and others surely to preserve sites of religious and ceremonial significance.[33] These split allotments represented on the land the multiple loyalties of those who had embraced Presbyterianism or Catholicism and still followed traditional observances and of those who had no intention of becoming Christians.[34]

Kew-kew'-lu-yah's map and oral history, with their insistence upon the interconnection of land and Nimiipuu cultural identity, ceremony, and cosmology, guided the modifications Fletcher made to her allotting procedures and furnished her with data for her ethnographic investigations, for she seems finally to have "[gotten] at the tribal organization" of the Nimiipuu.[35] She learned, in short, that their political structures were place-based. In the most literal sense, topography had produced sociopolitical groups: "The *Lok-ka-mah-sam* (*Lok-ka*, pine tree, *mah-sam*, mountain), or Craig Mountain, seems to have divided the people into two grand divisions," she wrote ("NPC," 189). Topography even determined its inhabitants' bellicosity. Of the early inhabitants of the Kamiah Valley Fletcher notes, "The people of this group were not so warlike. . . . [O]wing to the character of the valley, no enemies could reach it except through the territory claimed by Group 11 [*Tsy-was-'poo*]" ("NPC," 203). In a more figurative sense, topography elicited statecraft. Of Tsy-was-'poo, the terrain of which included the area along the South Fork of the Clearwater, she wrote, "The positions of the villages had certain strategic advantages. They commanded the approaches from the east and the south. . . . [T]hey also commanded direct access to Camas Prairie, . . . which was a meeting ground for trade." She concludes, "[T]his seems to have been the controlling group of the entire tribe." Such "leader" villages, then, regulated the access of other groups to those resources ("NPC," 205, 192). How-pa-loo (Village 3) and Suck-ko'-ly-e-kin-ma (Village 31), for example, "directed the time of hunting" in their immediate vicinities (192, 200, 192). Well-'eyou-way-we (Village 18) extended permission to other groups to hunt meat in their territories (196). Pa-lote-pe (Village 69) directed the camas harvest, sending messages to all the villages of the group "[w]hen the time arrived for digging camas" ("NPC," 198). This inward-looking and outwardly affiliative arrangement allowed common resources to be equitably managed. In narrating these relationships, Kew-kew'-lu-yah demonstrated to his interviewers, and by extension, to the church and governmental agencies they represented, that so-called primitive peoples had arranged themselves in geographical and political groupings intimately related to terrain that minimized conflict over resources, making lands, water, game and fish, kaus, camas, and other foodstuffs equitably available.

This orderly system offered a striking contrast to the chaotic and decidedly uncivil machinations of local Idahoans who beset Fletcher upon her arrival and throughout her work. In the allotments Fletcher was overseeing in 1891, incivility seems to have been the dominant mode of interchange. Evidence from Kew-kew'-lu-yah's map would have been key to Fletcher's endeavors to resolve some of these hotly contested claims. From the moment of her arrival on the reservation in 1889 she had been aware that the land in the Lapwai area was hotly contested, especially the Spalding, Craig, and Langford claims, and that property in these townships could not be deeded to Nimiipuu claimants without legal challenge. Plots attractive to potential allottees were often the same valley and riverine lands upon which railroad developers planned to build. The letters Fletcher wrote during the summer of 1891 contain complex justifications for deeding land in these areas, buttressed by long historical disquisitions often extending as far back as Lewis and Clark. This is not a method of argument Fletcher commonly used; it seems, rather, to have been suggested to her by her increasing knowledge of the length of tenure of Native inhabitants in these places. Ironically, of course, she did not always use such knowledge to secure Nimiipuu claims. Just one month after obtaining Kew-kew'-lu-yah's map, she wrote one of the fullest explications of the history of the Langford claim in a letter designed to secure the Presbyterian church's title to lands in the Spalding area.[36]

"a chain of surrogations"

I have thus far demonstrated that in the performative moment of its making, Kew-kew'-lu-yah's map enabled Nimiipuu survivance by "furnish[ing] forth" to Fletcher the complex connections among culture, political organization, historical narration, and the specificities of place.[37] At least some of that wisdom seems to have guided her practice of allotting land; more of it surely informed her future ethnological investigations. But those future possibilities were limited by Fletcher's assumptions that the map was an artifact, like the other items of material culture she acquired—by means fair and devious—on the reservation. That is to say, she saw it only as indicative of a past. Its connection to the future was precisely what her efforts as an allotting agent and ethnologist sought to erase in overt acts of selective forgetting. The copy of the map Fletcher made for herself did not contain all the information Kew-kew'-lu-yah furnished. She omitted several villages established after 1855, because they "had no place in the old order as shown on the map" ("NPC," 189). For Fletcher the anthropologist, authentically (that is, ethnographically) interesting villages were only those that antedated white contact. Moreover, she sent the original of this document to F. W. Putnam for the Peabody Museum collections. Such a transmission, according to Roach, typifies processes of modernity, in which "environments of memory" (places) are replaced by "archives . . . [and] monuments," spaces wherein objects and documents are collected, inserted into a narrative encoded as definitively past.[38]

Yet Kew-kew'-lu-yah's map was a living document, shared with Fletcher in an intercultural performance that anticipated its reanimation. The subsequent histories of the map demonstrate two of its future uses, one foreclosed through the processes of acquisition, preservation, transfer, and preparation of artifacts in the curatorial process, and one that has reinserted the map's information into an ongoing conversation about the place of the present-day Nez Perce

Reservation. Apparently when the Peabody Museum received the map, it was put aside with the other items sent by Fletcher in anticipation of her future curatorial and research efforts. According to an 1894–95 Peabody Museum report, the items she had sent were "awaiting labelling and arrangement."[39] Indeed, Fletcher did oversee the "labelling and arrangement" of a group of Nez Perce items she intended to display at the World's Columbian Exposition, as I discuss more fully in part 3. Kew-kew'-lu-yah's map, however, seems not to have been among these items. It was — to use a word carefully avoided by the Peabody — lost. Fletcher continued to work from her copy of the map as she drafted "The Nez Perce Country," a project to which she periodically returned over the next several decades, although she did not publish the resulting study. After she died, "a dealer in second-hand books ... in Washington ... acquired [her] library and other effects," which may have included her notes and her copy of the map. This dealer "sold" some of the papers, and apparently "deposited" the rest with the Bureau of American Ethnology.[40] At this point Fletcher's copy of the map temporarily disappeared, and it was not until the mid-1960s that Deward E. Walker Jr. "located" it among the Fletcher papers in the National Anthropological Archives ("NPC," 179).

Had the original map entered the active Peabody collections, it might have continued to serve as evidence, as it had in 1891 for Fletcher, in ongoing legal disputes about land. In the mid-twentieth century, as the Indian Claims Commission sought to resolve a number of lawsuits brought by Native plaintiffs against the United States, researchers began to gather evidence necessary to establish "the nature of aboriginal use and occupancy of particular areas in order to determine [whether a plaintiff] were entitled to compensation for lands taken by the United States, either by treaty or otherwise, and just what lands were in question."[41] As part of the investigation C. Marc Miller, a principal of the Pacific Northwest Land Company in Seattle, who had been "employed by the Department of Justice to make a research of the Nez Perce Indian Reservation for the purpose of arriving at a fair value for the land ceded to the Government in the Nez Perce Indian Treaty of 1863," wrote to the

Peabody, asking if the map were still available and if it could be copied for his company's "inspection."[42] The museum was unable to furnish it to him. Regrettably, Kew-kew'-lu-yah's map did not figure into this important compensatory lawsuit.[43]

More recently the map — or, more precisely, a surrogate of Fletcher's copy, itself a surrogate for the lost original — has been rejuvenated. In a fully annotated facsimile publication, Robert Lee Sappington, Caroline D. Carley, Kenneth C. Reid, and James D. Gallison have made an edited version of Kew-kew'-lu-yah's map and Fletcher's monograph generally available for the first time.[44] Their work emphasizes the map's deep chronological dimension. They reanimate the knowledge of Kew-kew'-lu-yah and the elders who were his informants, make visible the work of Fletcher and her occulted research assistants, and engage them in a continuing conversation about the long ecological and anthropological histories of Nez Perce country. Kew-kew'-lu-yah's map has allowed Sappington and his colleagues to verify the location of several early villages. It documents important cultural locations in "the most densely populated area within traditional Nez Perce territory," many of which "have been impacted by Lower Granite Reservoir and by the construction of railroads, highways, and other developments" ("NPC," 200). If we understand "impacted" to signify "destroyed or occulted," we may again note the prescience and importance of this document's insistence on Nimiipuu presence and occupation of these now inaccessible places.

In a way, this contemporary publication of Fletcher's monograph recapitulates the multivocal and collaborative circumstances of the map's original making in early June 1891. Its pages contain a chorus of voices: Kew-kew'-lu-yah provides the foundational information and Fletcher the organization and framing of the data. A careful reader may also discern the contributions of the other collaborators: James Stuart quietly translating, perhaps offering questions of clarification and/or adding his own version of events; and Jane Gay's and Kate McBeth's eager questions. To the collaboration, the contemporary scholars have added their own interpretation of the original event. Assuming that the basic data are Kew-kew'-lu-yah's, they have placed what they understand to be Fletcher's clarifying comments in parentheses. To this foundational document, they have added, in brackets, their own and their colleagues' input to the conversation. At times the length of the added commentary from contemporary researchers exceeds that of the primary material. The ultimate effect is that of an anthropological collaboration across several hundred years.

Nor is Kew-kew'-lu-yah's map the last in this chain of surrogated representations of Nimiipuu territory made by Nimiipuu elders. In 1965 the supervisor of the Clearwater National Forest, Ralph Space, who was "interested in locating the campsites of Lewis and Clark [on] the Weippe Prairie," acquired another such map, reproduced here as figure 33.[45] As Space "rode over the roads on the Weippe Prairie," accompanied by Harry Wheeler and Corbett Lawyer, the two elder men showed him "the points of historical interest," and Lawyer, the grandson of Tlu-la-lal-quil-soot (Chief Lawyer), who was a signatory of the first treaty to diminish Nimiipuu lands in 1855, "drew a sketch of the Weippe Prairie as it was before white men took it over."[46] An annotation on the map identifies it as "Weippe Prairie in 1885 by Corbett Lawyer." Lawyer's map illustrated his and Wheeler's narration of the history of this place, which is summarized by Space in his brief typewritten commentary, "The Indians."

As did Kew-kew'-lu-yah's map, Lawyer's sketch testifies that long before whites intervened to divide and apportion lands, an effective political organization oversaw the equitable distribution of resources in food and timber. As Lawyer told Space, "[T]he Indians had divided camas digging rights to avoid conflict. Some communities were alloted areas but there was a commons where other Indians could dig unmolested." Lawyer's map also illustrates the connection of Nimiipuu culture to the land. According to the two elder men, "A short distance South of Weippe and near Fords Creek is a small area a little higher than the meadow. At one time this area had a fine grove of large ponderosa pine trees. They have all been cut or broken off except one. In the pioneer days Fourth of July celebrations were held here and before the coming of white men ... this was the Indian area for playing games. They raced their horses

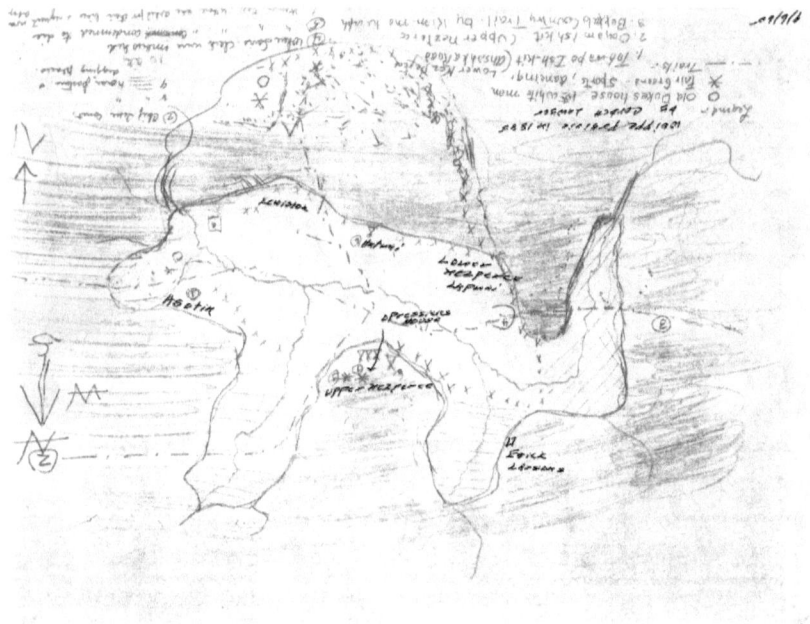

FIG. 33. "Weippe Prairie in 1885 by Corbett Lawyer," 6 September 1965. Ralph Space Papers. Reproduced by permission of Special Collections, University of Idaho.

around this knoll and played a number of games."[47] Lawyer then described the details of the games he had played at such festivities, establishing himself as a participant in an uninterrupted procession of summer celebrations.

Like Kew-kew'-lu-yah's, Lawyer's map is not drawn to an exact mathematical scale but shows relative distances, tracing the route of a trail through the prairie to buffalo country. As did Fletcher, Gay, and McBeth, Ralph Space found the map's value to be in its relation to Lewis and Clark and identified locations thereon that were related to the story of these explorers.[48] Subsequent historical investigators have continued to work with the map, as did Sappington and his colleagues with Kew-kew'-lu-yah's. Most recently Gene Eastman, a conservation officer with the Idaho Department of Fish and Game, has annotated Lawyer's sketch, overlaid Lawyer's information onto a modern map, and verified the location of the villages with aerial photographs (see fig. 34).[49]

[162]

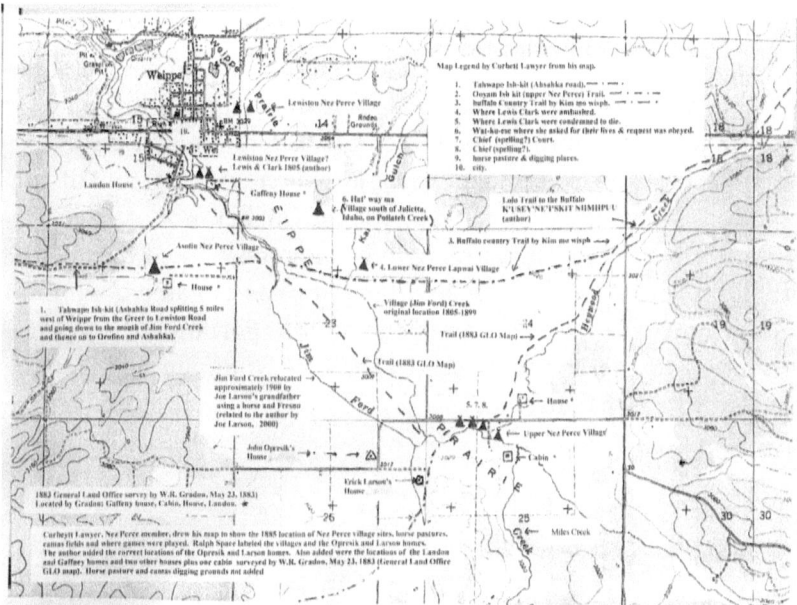

FIG. 34. Weippe Prairie Map (overlay by Gene Eastman of "Weippe Prairie in 1885 by Corbett Lawyer" onto a contemporary map). *Bitterroot Crossing*, vol. 2, 94. Reproduced with permission of Gene Eastman.

In its conception and application, allotment was intended to be a one-way process, administered from above by officials representing the rationalized and benevolent institutions of civilization, bringing its blessings to those who were unable to attain these benefits for themselves and who were thought to be unable to recognize the value of those changes. To be accomplished, allotment depended on an elaborate bureaucratic apparatus whereby lands and peoples were to be measured, counted, identified, and made equivalent. Yet despite the conception of its theorists, allotment was a two-way process. The peoples who were its objects demonstrated early and late that the imposition of these transformative practices would not proceed without their consent, and only after considerable negotiation. The record of their resistances lies in official state archives—in memory palaces—but is also evident in the acts of performance (parades, speeches, rituals, interviews, storytelling, and map making) whereby cultural memory is preserved and reanimated.

LAND

In this section I have placed these archives in a comparative relationship as a way of demonstrating their similarities, which include intersubjective performance, intercultural communication, and selective forgetting and remembering through ongoing acts of surrogation. I have done so to argue for the importance of giving attention to sources that generally have not constituted part of the official records but that, when attended to as ongoing communication rather than as silent artifacts, offer important corrective information and verify the unbroken chain of Nimiipuu claims to the place in which they live.

Part Three

Citizens

Introduction
E Pluribus Unum

In early July 1890 Idaho Territory stood poised to enter the union as the forty-third state. The process by which territories become states is intended to produce uniformity in the land and its inhabitants. The Ordinance of 1785 mandated that territorial possessions be surveyed and divided into a system of equivalent grids. To match this uniformity of space, the Northwest Ordinance of 1787 contained provisions intended, as Bethel Saler has written, to "[foster] a commonality between the people in the western territories and the rest of the nation . . . [by encouraging] shared customs and principles," among which were "federal rules of descent and conveyance of property . . . trial by jury, proportional representation . . . security of private property and public education."[1]

A century later, as western states with large indigenous populations entered the union, ensuring the uniformity among their potential citizens became a matter of increasing concern.[2] Idaho's potential citizens included not only white farmers, ranchers, and merchants but also their Native neighbors, each of whom would soon hold title to a parcel of land and each of whom, after a twenty-five year probationary period, was to receive the franchise. In order that potential voters would identify as a part of Idaho's polity, the provisions of allotment necessarily included "technologies of citizenship: discourses, program, and other tactics aimed at making individuals . . .

capable of self-government."³ Church and state united their efforts to instill in potential Native citizens the ideals of equality under the law, representative democracy, heteronormative nuclear families, modern agricultural techniques, the ability to read and write in English, and Christian morality.

In the minds of white reformers, democratic ideals of equivalent citizenship differed markedly from tribalism, a supposedly primitive social organization in which unenlightened groups of peoples remained unthinkingly subject to the whims of hereditary chiefs whose powers did not derive from the informed consent of the governed. Allotment thus depended upon a host of disciplinary tactics intended to transform communitarian tribesmen into individualized democratic subjects, each with the capacity for freedom and self-regulation. Among these free individuals, a healthy competition might arise, and those who were best suited to excel in the rough-and-tumble world of capitalist exchange would rise to the top. The contradictions entailed in this formulation have been aptly summarized by Rosemarie Garland Thomson as "democracy's paradox": "[T]he principle of equality implies sameness of condition, while the promise of freedom suggests the potential for uniqueness."⁴ In the discussion that follows I explore this paradox, showing how the contradictory aims of producing free individuals who were simultaneously democratically equivalent citizens framed Alice Fletcher's application of allotment policy on the Nez Perce Reservation.

Federal allotment policy was inconsistent from its beginning, plagued by the "messy, non-generalizable, and contingent practices, institutions, and discourses" that Barbara Cruikshank identifies as part of the process of producing "democratic subjects."⁵ These inconsistencies manifested themselves both in the legal provisions of the Dawes Act, which was continually modified, and in the confused motives and inconsistent behaviors of those who planned and administered it. At least part of the rationale upon which reformers had advocated for the Dawes Act was that because graft and political corruption had so thoroughly infiltrated the federal reservation program, Native peoples needed to be rescued from their federally appointed guardians. As the delegates to the fifth Lake Mohonk

Conference proclaimed, "The passage of the Dawes bill closes the 'century of dishonor.'"[6] Blatant cronyism infected the Indian Service: appointments as agents and administrators had become political plums, awarded to friends and supporters, and withdrawn as federal administrations changed from Republican to Democratic control and back again. So grievously had the ethical administration of federal Indian policy failed that in 1869 the Grant administration had transferred responsibility for its oversight to Quaker and Protestant missionary societies in an attempt to stem the graft. Under this program the Nez Perce Reservation was assigned to the Presbyterian Church.

Church men and women, however, proved to be barely less venal than their lay counterparts. Moreover, because Presbyterian missionaries and administrators linked church preferment to political tribal governance, they exacerbated divisions within Nimiipuu groups that had emerged early in the history of Indian-white affairs in the Washington and Idaho territories. Early territorial administrators and developers had adopted an opportunistically mistaken notion that the Nez Perces, a loosely affiliated group of bands who shared a common language and religion, constituted a unified political unit called a tribe. Concerned with establishing the rule of (white) law among his converts, in 1842 Presbyterian missionary Henry Spalding convinced federal agent Elijah White to name a single head chief, Inauzakamma (Ellis), with whom he would negotiate. In the Treaty of 1855 land-hungry white negotiators led by Isaac Stevens named Tlu-la-lal-quil-soot (Lawyer), a Presbyterian Nez Perce from the Kamiah group, as principal chief, although his appointment was not supported by Nimiipuu who lived in the Salmon and Wallowa valleys. In subsequent treaty negotiations Tlu-la-lal-quil-soot's supporters retained their land holdings, while others lost their homelands to white settlement. Consequent tensions over land and religious practice ultimately fueled the hostilities of 1877, in which blood relatives fought on different sides; after 1885 the political divisions persisted, as those who had supported Joseph returned with him to the Colville Reservation.

Presbyterian Indian agents and missionaries also produced

divisions between their followers and those who had converted to Catholicism. Although Catholic missionaries did not reside in the Lapwai area until 1875, Nimiipuu had converted to Catholicism beginning with contact with the French-sponsored Hudson's Bay company men, and these converts had kept in touch with area Catholics at Coeur d'Alene mission.[7] By most accounts, Presbyterian missionaries and Presbyterian agents vehemently opposed the expansion of Catholicism within their domains. In 1873, for example, Agent J. B. Monteith reportedly asked permission from the federal government to forbid Catholic observances on the reservation but was told it would exceed his authority.[8] He did, however, effectively oppose the construction of a Catholic church and school.[9] For his part, Henry Spalding preached vituperative sermons against Catholicism. These practices could, and did, sow discord. Perhaps because the Catholic church did not enjoy federal support, it did not interfere with affairs of state among its congregants. Unlike Spalding, who appointed chieftains like Inauzakamma who would support his agendas, Catholic missionaries left traditional political leaders in charge of daily life among Catholic Nez Perces.[10] Nor did they pursue the total assimilation that characterized Presbyterian efforts.

Beginning in the 1870s divisions among Presbyterian congregants on the Nez Perce Reservation were exacerbated by an unseemly feud between the two missionaries Susan and Kate McBeth. Susan, the elder sister, had arrived on the reservation in 1873. Several years later, after Kate had joined her in Kamiah, Susan increasingly came to believe her sister to be alienating the affections of her theological students. The two settled into a pattern of bickering and rivalry that came to involve their congregants, the local agent, the Office of Indian Affairs, and the Presbyterian Board of Foreign Missions. In 1885, attempting to effect their removal from the reservation, Agent Charles Monteith wrote in detail to Commissioner of Indian Affairs J. C. Atkins about Susan McBeth, blaming her for local tensions,

> [c]ommencing with the people of Kamiah and the Catholics between whome Miss S. L. McBeth succeeded in breaking down all friendly intercourse. She turned her attention to Lapwai and brot about the same

state of feeling between the people of Lapwai and Kamiah, so that friendly visits between the two sections were almost unknown. Not content with what she had accomplished she succeeded in dividing Kamiah itself into what is known as the Lawyer and Williams factions, so that the feeling which now exists is as bitter as can be found in any community made up of Protestants and Roman Catholics. It seems as tho her desire was to build up an aristocracy at Kamiah, and the only way to succeed was to bring about factional disturbances.

Miss S. L. McBeth has not been alone in this work. Her sister Miss Kate C. McBeth has proved a valuable assistant. Both have repeatedly interfered with reservation affairs thru the Indians....

They have caused a feeling of enmity to spring up and grow which cannot be eradicated for years to come, in fact — in my opinion — not till those who are at the head of the factions have passed away.

Concluding his letter, Monteith called the McBeth sisters "a disgrace to the cause they represent."[11]

Before Monteith could banish her, Susan McBeth left Kamiah for Mt. Idaho, just outside the reservation border. Here she established a seminary in which she trained a small group of Nez Perce men as Presbyterian ministers.[12] Kate was transferred from Kamiah to Lapwai, where she concentrated her efforts on overseeing the domestic instruction of Nez Perce women. Subsequently, tensions between the two women ebbed and flowed, but the dissension between them and their supporters frequently lay at the root of disputes that concerned both church and local politics. While Monteith could surely not be called an impartial witness, he was correct in attributing a great deal of the tension among Presbyterian congregants to the machinations of the two women. Susan McBeth had sponsored Robert Williams as the first ordained Nez Perce minister of the Kamiah Presbyterian Church, preferring him over others of her students, particularly the Lawyer brothers, whose claim to preferment stemmed from their father's status as the chief appointed in 1855. She distrusted Archie and James Lawyer, for they were distressingly independent thinkers who seemed to her always to be in danger of backsliding into "heathen" ways. The Lawyers, moreover, enjoyed longstanding political ties with the agency and, through the agency, with the tribal police and the Indian courts. Indignant at McBeth's favoritism, the Lawyer brothers and their supporters brought a series of legal cases against Williams in both civil and church courts, charging him with inappropriate conduct with women. In the winter of 1889–90 Robert Williams was censured by the Presbyterian Church and suspended for six months from his ministry in Kamiah.

During Alice Fletcher's second allotting season in the summer of 1890, these religio-political divisions were acute. She and Jane Gay had befriended both McBeth sisters and carefully ignored their acrimony, avoiding any mention of tension or rivalry in their correspondence and records. As did the McBeths, Fletcher and Gay blamed differences among the Nimiipuu on the Lawyer family's traditional alliances, claiming that they sought to retain political power and privilege by allying themselves with "the Agency Indians," a group who emblematized all the abuses of the corrupt reservation system and its practices of political preferment (C, 259). According to Gay, "The old chiefs . . . hate Robert [Williams . . . because he] was the first to take his land; and because he tells the people there are no more chiefs but all the people are equal, all citizens, and the chiefs are no better than the rest and have to obey the laws just the same." In her reductive summary, "Archie Lawyer . . . stands for the power of the old chiefs as Robert stands for simple right and justice and godliness" (C, 257, 258, 259).

As I demonstrate in the two chapters to follow, divisiveness within the tribe had multiple sources. Surely the McBeth squabble was a major factor, as was the involvement of the allotting party in refurbishing the Kamiah First Presbyterian Church.[13] But the technologies of education, competitive capitalism, and racialization also contributed mightily to the divisions among neighbors and even within families among the Nez Perces. Such indecorum and discord in the realms of policy, law, and administration among the churched interests charged with effecting peaceful and fair administration did not escape the notice of Commissioner Morgan. Introducing his *Annual Report* for 1891, he named "stability" as a desideratum in Indian affairs, declaring, "Having determined upon a policy, we should regard it as permanent until its work is accomplished. ... The day of experiment should be ended. Consistency in legislation, uniformity in administration, permanence of the tenure of office based upon intelligent comprehension of the work to be done ... would very materially hasten the successful accomplishment of the wise ends of the Government."[14] Although the government had failed—and would continue to fail—to produce consistency within its own house, under Morgan the Office of Indian Affairs made every legislative and educational effort to ensure that as a precondition to their new status as citizens, its Native wards would behave decorously and predictably. That commitment to consistent behaviors among the Nez Perces colors both Gay's and Fletcher's descriptions of how the Fourth of July was celebrated in 1890, for each regarded unity among these fractious groups as a measure of their advancement toward citizenship.

5. Technologies of Citizenship

On 3 July 1890, having demonstrated that its citizens could overcome their differences sufficiently to perform the functions of democratic self-rule, Idaho became a state. With duly elected representatives to stand for their interests in the legislative assemblies of the federal government, the state's citizens would defer to the laws enacted by those bodies, putting aside whatever political differences divided them. They celebrated at Fourth of July festivities across the new state, performing the usual recitations of democratic unity in difference despite the fact that resentments were still strong in Lewiston, once the territorial capital, that Boise had been chosen as the state capital.

Three different celebrations marked the holiday on the Nez Perce Reservation, one at Kamiah, about which Gay and Fletcher, who had returned in 1890 to the valley to conclude their work there, wrote in glowing terms. The two events at Lapwai were documented by Kate McBeth and—at a much later date—alluded to by Jane Gay. Discrepancies among these accounts suggest the degree to which discord prevailed among the celebrants and make apparent the considerable efforts of allotment's proponents to mask or contain the discord. Because the accounts of these events were published in various forms and at several different times, I here include a chart of the documents to which the following analysis refers (see fig. 35).

Fig. 35. Accounts of 4 July 1890

Kamiah Presbyterian celebration	Lapwai traditional celebration	Lapwai Presbyterian prayer meeting
Eyewitness accounts by ACF —Letter 22804 to CIA, 12 July 1890 —"Fourth of July among the Indians," *Christian Register*, 31 July 1890, 4 —Excerpts from letter 22804 included in ARCIA 1890: xix **Photographs of picnic** by EJG —ISHS 63-221.218 —ISHS 63-221.221 —Acc. 632, NPNHPA	**Eyewitness account** by Kate C. McBeth, Diary, 4 July 1890	
Retrospective eyewitness account (of the Kamiah celebration), paired with **hearsay** account (of the Lapwai traditional celebration) by EJG —Letter to "B." [Isabel Barrows], 10 July 1891 (later included in edited form in *Choup-nit-ki*; see below)		
	Hearsay account (of the Lapwai traditional celebration), a portion of EJG to Barrows as printed in "Life on the Reservation II," *Christian Register*, 10 March 1892, 173	

Retrospective eyewitness account (of the Kamiah celebration), paired with **hearsay** account (of the Lapwai traditional celebration) by EJG; illustrated
—Letter 22, *Choup-nit-ki* (1902), 355–67
   —Photograph captioned "Camp at Lapwai Tal-lik-lykt" made by EJG at Lapwai in 1892 (*Choup-nit-ki*, 358)
   —Pen and ink sketch titled "The Barbecue," adapted from photographs made by EJG at Kamiah in 1890 (*Choup-nit-ki*, 365).		

Abbreviations: ACF = Alice C. Fletcher, ARCIA = *Annual Report of the Commissioner of Indian Affairs*, CIA = Commissioner of Indian Affairs, EJG = E. Jane Gay, ISHS = Idaho State Historical Society, NPNHPA = Nez Perce National Historical Park Archives.

While the fact that Nez Perces celebrated in several ways at several different places is not in itself unusual, this year had been marked by exceptional discord. Moreover, scholars who have studied the allotment period presume that unity had prevailed at the Fourth of July until Jane Gay intervened in 1891, helping obtain a ban on racing and other traditional observances, an event I analyze more fully in this chapter. I contend that divisiveness among Nimiipuu groups had deep roots, persisted throughout the allotment period, and was exacerbated by divisive tactics used by the missionaries, by Gay, and by Fletcher.

"as happy & peaceful a day as I ever saw"

At Kamiah in 1890 Gay made several photographs of the salmon feast, and Alice Fletcher sent descriptions of the occasion in a letter to her friend Isabel Barrows, wife of the editor of the *Christian Register*, and in her weekly report to Commissioner Morgan. Barrows and Morgan each printed Fletcher's description nearly verbatim (as she surely knew they would) in publications that reached a wide audience of readers interested in the activities of allotment and Indian civilization. Fletcher's two accounts, as published, are nearly identical. Yet each emphasizes and omits certain details in anticipation of the reactions of those who would read it.

The *Christian Register*, a weekly Unitarian newspaper widely read by the reform community, published Fletcher's description under the title "Fourth of July among the Indians," in a department titled "The Home," where it adjoined features titled "Mother's Vacation," "Major Paddlefoot," and similarly lighthearted fare. In it Fletcher included sentimental details aimed at the *Register*'s feminine readership, such as this description of the dawn: "While this deep valley in one of the cañons of the Clearwater was yet in shadow, though the mountains were golden in sunlight, the songs of the morning service were heard, ushering in the Fourth." Published on 31 July 1890, Fletcher's letter was in print distribution within weeks of the event it reported. The short interval between event and report suggested that the celebration was newsworthy, an effect buttressed by details calculated to demonstrate the readiness of the Kamiah Nez

Perces for the responsibilities of citizenship and the early success of allotment in producing exemplary democratic subjects. Fletcher describes a stately procession of Nez Perces, "clad in citizens' dress," arranged according to age and sex, marching through the pine grove surrounding the Presbyterian Church, singing solemnly, "We'll stand, Fourth July." Several Native orators "commented upon the happiness of an orderly, Christian life as contrasted with the wild, roving habits of former times." Celebrants feasted on "beef, salmon, canned fruits[,] bread, cake, and wild potatoes" served "upon tablecloths spread on the grass, with china plates, cups, etc." After the evening fireworks, which "delight[ed] . . . the children," the celebrants reconvened for "a fervent service of prayer and song," a fit conclusion to "as happy and peaceful a day as I ever saw."[1] No hint of strife or discord mars Fletcher's report. Yet dissensus lurked, the direct result of Susan McBeth's preferential treatment of Robert Williams. Williams, pastor of the Kamiah Presbyterian Church, was apparently absent from the celebration, for he was still under suspension from his pulpit for alleged adultery.

Fletcher included most of these same observations in her weekly report to Morgan, who printed an excerpt from the letter in his introductory remarks to the 1890 *Report of the Commissioner of Indian Affairs*. There the letter concludes a section in which Morgan announced he had recently mailed to all field agents a circular recommending the appropriate celebration of holidays. In this context Fletcher's words illustrated that such holidays might become occasions of "training for . . . American citizenship." As published here her letter omits the description of the dawn and adds one brief but significant detail: "After dinner the business of adopting certain persons into the tribe was attended to."[2] Fletcher likely included this sentence because she and Morgan had earlier discussed whether and how those who did not have pure Nez Perce blood might claim allotments on the reservation.[3] To Morgan this additional information would have confirmed that Fletcher had followed his instructions to refer these matters to a tribal vote. Why, though, had the *Register*'s account omitted this detail? Likely, it introduced an unseemly cognitive dissonance: if tribal members were exercising their sovereign prerogative of determining tribal membership, the degree of their assimilation might seem to be less than Fletcher had claimed. Her carefully framed letters, then, confirmed to *Register* readers and congressional representatives alike that Native Christians, prepared for such observances by devoted missionaries, were adept at performing the behaviors appropriate to the nation's birthday.

Morgan omitted from his report a detail Fletcher had been careful to include in her letter: that the Kamiah celebration "was observed by a large *part* of the Indians *of this vicinity* . . . over 500 were present."[4] The emendation thus repeated the strategic assumptions of representative democracy used in earlier moments by Elijah White, Henry Spalding, Isaac Stevens, and other Presbyterian agents who had previously dealt with the Nimiipuu. In reporting the vote on adoption, Morgan allowed the assent of a part of the tribe to stand for the will of the whole; and the performance of voting was offered as proof of the government's goodwill in seeking the advice and consent of the Nez Perces.[5] The fact that such a vote was contingent on federal approval also remained unmentioned.

Gay's accounts of the Kamiah celebration have a more complex genealogy. She first sent a description of the occasion in a letter to Isabel Barrows on 10 July 1891, more than a year after the fact. Six months later Barrows published part of her letter in the *Register*. At an even longer remove, in 1902, Gay included the entire letter in *Choup-nit-ki*, illustrating it with two photographs of the people who attended and a line drawing of the salmon feast. To Fletcher's report of the "happy and peaceful" Kamiah festivities, Gay added several details to cement the illusion of the congregation's unity and citizenly behavior. She recounts that the "perfectly planned" "barbeque and . . . feast" were served to "[t]he people . . . by the elders and deacons of the church," transmuting the celebratory traditional fare into a sacrament. She continues, "Elder Felix selected a specially choice bit from the toasting salmon for Her Majesty and not until the last one of the great company had left the table, did he and his fellow servers submit to be waited upon" (C, 364, 365). This communion-like meal precedes the adoption vote. As a result of the vote, writes Gay, "several Indians who . . . had long lived with the tribe and had no other home" were welcomed. Finally,

> the old men were asked to listen to the reading of the list of allotments so far as it was finished and to approve the work. It was interesting to note the care with which each name was considered and the readiness to supply any omission, or correct an inadvertent error. If a child had been born since a family had been registered, there was solicitude to have it counted in, or, if there had been a death, the desire was unanimously expressed to have the allotment stand for the benefit of the next of kin. There was no dissension in the council on that 4th of July, for all the malcontents had gone to Lapwai. (C, 366)

In these carefully chosen details, Gay makes an implicit argument that the Kamiah Nez Perces were nearly completely assimilated. Elder men, leaders of the church, make the necessary decisions for the tribe; they respect Fletcher's work, and they offer corrections only to ensure its perfection. They are concerned that the details of allotment, with its assurance of individually held, heritable property, be precisely administered. Moreover, their accord is "unanimous."

Two other details in Gay's account disturb the illusion of tribal unity, however. She tells her correspondent that Alice Fletcher delivered a speech to the Kamiah celebrants, translated by James Stuart, in which she explained the holiday's meaning. Gay connects the details of the speech with the influence of Presbyterian missionaries, remarking that in "Her Majesty's" oration, "that pestilential Declaration of Independence came upon the scene again" (C, 365). Her phrasing here refers to her earlier account of Susan McBeth's exile from Kamiah: "She was charged with inciting the Nez Percés to insubordination [against the agent, Charles E. Monteith]. What she actually did was . . . teach her pupils something of the nature of the United States' government and laws, and, unfortunately, she began with the Declaration of Independence. From what we know of Miss Sue, we are confident that she did not . . . apprehend the pernicious nature of the document in question" (C, 62). Her allusion, however indirect, to the exiled Susan McBeth raised the specter of discord, for while Gay credits McBeth for the civic content of her school's curriculum, Monteith had charged her with exacerbating divisions among the Nimiipuu. These divisions Gay tries—unsuccessfully—to dismiss with her summative statement that unanimity had prevailed in Kamiah because anyone who disagreed with allotment or with the reign of Presbyterian piety "had gone to Lapwai" to celebrate, presumably joining the traditional celebration.

While Kamiah residents gathered under the approving eyes of Alice Fletcher and Jane Gay, sixty miles to the west, in Lapwai, celebrants attended either the traditional gathering or a Presbyterian camp meeting. Many likely did both. Noting the day in her diary, Kate McBeth fretted that the "heathen" group's celebration would overshadow the more sedate observances she had labored to introduce, and wrote: "the roving & tala klik heathen performance have both been given . . . but the Worship the Lords supper are not mixed with it this year thank God."[6] She did not elaborate, and her brief entry is the sole evidence that a Christian camp meeting was held at Lapwai in 1890. It was not mentioned by either of her friends, surely because they did not attend.

Not having witnessed the Lapwai festivities did not prevent Jane Gay from writing about the traditional celebration, however. At some point Kate McBeth must have recounted its details to Gay, who, like Fletcher, was not above manipulating information to support a moral point. Despite the fact that she had its details only on hearsay, Gay wrote a long account of the traditional celebration in her 1891 letter to Barrows. If Fletcher had emphasized the unity among the Kamiah celebrants, Gay framed her account as an epic struggle between recidivism and Christian progressivism at Lapwai. To Barrows, and to the *Register*'s readers, she offered a historical sketch of this summer holiday celebration, noting its congruence with "[a]n old ceremony of theirs [that] occurred at about this season, one of the leading features of which was a general exchange of wives. . . . [A]s the tribe took on civilization, horse-racing and gambling were added to the programme, together with the absorption of our national beverage; but the old leading feature was not expunged." In the face of this stubborn adherence to tradition, Gay continues, in 1890 a committee from "a few of the progressive Indians [at Lapwai had] appealed to the Agent to prevent the *Tal lik lykt* (war procession), the races, and the gambling, but to no effect." Instead, agency officials, several of whom reportedly enjoyed horse racing, allowed the traditional activities to continue without intervention. Gay accuses them of being "utter[ly ignorant] of the true nature of the Indian 'celebration,' . . . in which naked men ride and wailing women follow."[7]

Gay then contrasts the Presbyterian observance at Kamiah with the traditional celebration at Lapwai (and, notably, does not mention McBeth's camp meeting). Rather than open with a dignified parade of celebrants "in citizens' dress," the Lapwai celebration began with a war procession led by Chief Joseph, who, according to an untitled news item in the *Lewiston Teller*, was visiting the Idaho reservation on a sixty-day leave from the Colville Reservation.[8] This train of mounted warriors did not disband at the church but rode "right through the grounds of the [Fort Lapwai Industrial] school." At night, rather than enjoy fireworks, the Lapwai celebrants "raided" "the girls' dormitories . . . , and general license prevailed among the tents of the Indian camp just outside the school enclosure." The detail implies that the school's civilizing efforts were nearly undone by traditional celebrations, which "reviv[ed] . . . old-time scenes, and excit[ed] the Indians almost to frenzy,—as one man said, 'almost beyond his power to resist.'" These indulgences, she concludes—somewhat imaginatively, to be sure—caused "the blood" of its participants to "[dance] hotly through the Indians' veins, and their wild nature mounted to the top."[9] Her phrase invokes a connection between traditional activities and an inborn savagism carried through Indian blood, and it echoes a growing assumption that because appearances and behaviors of civilization could be taught, learned, and manifested—or forgotten—at will, blood was the undeniable signifier of racial identity and of racially determined behaviors.

Gay concluded her letter to Barrows with an account of the Kamiah celebration closely resembling Fletcher's. This portion of the letter did not, of course, appear in the *Register* because it repeated what Fletcher had published there about eighteen months before. A fuller version of the letter is included in *Choup-nit-ki*, which Gay compiled in 1902. Here she implies she had personally observed both the Kamiah and Lapwai celebrations in 1890, an illusion buttressed by three photographs and a pen-and-ink drawing, captioned "The Barbecue" (C, 365). Two of the photographs, both undated, are placed within the narration of this celebration. One is captioned "Leaving Camp. Kamiah, July 4th." The second, uncaptioned image shows a large group of Native people and is placed in the album in proximity to the observation that "the Photographer tried to get a picture of the people as they sat on the yellow grass" (C, 367). "The Barbecue" (see fig. 54) is a composite sketch based on two photographs Gay took in Kamiah in 1890, in which Natives wearing non-traditional attire cook fish over an outdoor fire (ISHS .218 and .221). The third photograph, reproduced here as figure 36, is strategically, if incompletely, captioned "Camp at Lapwai. Tlal-lik-lykl. July 4" (C, 358). Taken from afar, the image shows a procession of mounted riders. The parade, although visible, lacks sufficient detail to allow it to be associated with any specific celebration. It surely was not made on 4 July 1890, for Gay was at Kamiah. More than likely it was made in 1892, when Fletcher wrote in her field diary: "Fantastic procession. Miss Gay taken off by John McFarland who takes photographs with a stealth box."[10] Thus, in the context of *Choup-nit-ki*, an image made at a great distance, perhaps secretly, two years after the event it ostensibly documents, guarantees the veracity of Gay's description of an event she did not, in fact, attend.

These several accounts, when read resistantly and comparatively, and bearing in mind when, for whom, and by whom they were written, demonstrate a long-standing division among the celebrants of the Fourth of July on the Nez Perce Reservation. On the evidence of Fletcher's account alone, one might believe allotment and assimilation to be well entrenched. Adding Gay's later retellings to the record produces an impression of a more fractious occasion. The fullest available record suggests that on 4 July 1890, traditional and Christian Nimiipuu held, likely willingly, separate celebrations. Each group of revelers was aware of how the others were celebrating, and each group performed their identities—who they understood themselves to be and, by implication, who they were not—in the presence of some observers and in the virtual presence of others. In

FIG. 36. "Camp at Lapwai. Tal-lik-lykt. July 4," by E. Jane Gay, as reproduced in *Choup-nit-ki*, 358. The Schlesinger Library, Radcliffe Institute, Harvard University.

McBeth's, Fletcher's, and Gay's written descriptions, the meaning of the celebration thus emerged comparatively, as each contrasted the celebration she attended—sometimes overtly and sometimes subtly—with what was happening on the other side of the reservation. Taken together, these histories suggest that the day's festivities symbolized allegiances and behaviors that remained—and would likely long remain—incompatible.

"the means of tracing any family that I have allotted": Blood, Anthropometry, and Identity

Allotment depended on the fiction of democratic equality. The Nez Perce wards of the nation would yield yet another massive quantity of land that allotment would create as "excess," and in exchange, they would be given a gift of inestimable value: American citizenship. To prepare them for citizenly responsibilities, as Commissioner Morgan expressed it, they would need to "be imbued with ideas distinctively national as distinguished from those that are tribal."[11] Each individual citizen would own an equivalent amount of land; each citizen's vote would carry equivalent weight. This transformation would be produced by "technologies of citizenship" — laws, curricula, anthropometric data, and all manner of written records designed to produce discrete individual subjects. Of these, the most important was a written genealogical record of kinship that mapped the orderly patrilineal transfer of property.

Among allotting agents, Alice Fletcher had gained a reputation for her meticulous system of documenting kinship. Commissioner John H. Oberly had praised her as "the only special agent . . . that has done her work completely and entirely, and with complete intelligence concerning the subject" and requested that she instruct other agents in her methodology.[12] To the Board of Indian Commissioners in 1888, she described the system she had developed while allotting land to the Omaha and Winnebago tribes and that she would also use among the Nez Perces:

> To help the decision as to heirship at the end of twenty-five years I have made a . . . complete registry of the tribe, showing both lineal and collateral descent. . . . By the index of this registry I can trace a man's relations throughout the entire tribe. This registry affords a check against double enrollment and allotment, and it will give to courts in the future the means of tracing any family that I have allotted. By doing this work of registering, which the law did not require of me, but which my conscience required, I have tried to meet the difficulties relating to the Indian property which still await stronger laws to secure safety and justice.[13]

This sanguinary documentation signals a deep distrust of the Native clients it claims to benefit: no one so registered by Fletcher could claim more land than that to which the individual was entitled. Such a record enabled a precisely calculated blood quantum to ensure that land would not be given to those of non–Nez Perce descent. This obsessive documentation also produced a unique Native individual subject located within a linear and collateral family who could be matched with a plot of land similarly identifiable by mathematically precise coordinates of township, range, section, and lot.

Like similarly abstracted theoretical procedures, this apparently capacious set of procedures was flawed. Fletcher's "complete registry" had not been independently verified for completeness. Nor did she work with reference to a "complete" census on the Nez Perce Reservation.[14] Her system presumed a heteronormative couple, currently married only to each other, both of unmixed blood. Some Nimiipuu, however, practiced polygamy, and some were serially monogamous. Many had intermarried with spouses who were Scottish, Irish, Cayuse, Umatilla, Flathead, or whose lineage derived from other ethnic and tribal groups. None of these contingencies fell within Fletcher's tidy plan. For all her precision, in describing her procedures Fletcher carefully avoided using the term *marriage*, the federal definition of which was not codified until 1890, when the commissioner decreed an Indian "family" to be "persons living together as man and wife, according to their custom and manner of Indian life, at least one of the parents being of Indian blood."[15]

Fletcher presumed a tribe to be a discrete and self-evident entity, but a question soon arose: How were members of "the tribe" to be identified? In 1890 she wrote to the commissioner regarding "certain persons . . . whom it is doubtful . . . have any Nez Perce blood and therefore entitled to Allotment on Nez Perce lands. . . . [T]he tribe has demanded that I investigate all such cases. In thus doing I have discovered some individuals who have always lived with the tribe, knowing no other home, but who are not Nez Perce." In this case the person in question was the son of a Flathead woman who had been raised by a Nez Perce stepfather and who was married to an Umatilla. Thus "neither he [the son] or his wife [was] entitled by birth to an allotment on Nez Perce lands."[16] Morgan ruled, for the interim, that such cases "be closely scrutinized" and that tribal authorities could adopt such people, their decisions subject to approval "by the Department."[17] Such adoptions were surely among those considered by the Kamiah elders seven months later.

Over the next two decades, on the Nez Perce Reservation and elsewhere, the issues of blood, identity, and tribal affiliation continued to be hotly debated. These topics entered discussions of Indian policy at precisely the same moment *Plessy v. Ferguson*, the infamous case that launched an era of legalized racial segregation, established blood quantum as the means of making racial classifications. The manifest absurdity of identifying a person's racial identity by calculating the percentage of components of her/his blood has been widely critiqued by contemporary scholars and activists. M. Annette Jaimes calls such policies "usurpation[s] of indigenous sovereignty" and begins her essay on "Federal Indian Identification Policy" with two acerbic epigraphs challenging the connection of blood to identity: Ward Churchill suggests a fraction of bodily weight might yield an equally useful measure; Jimmie Durham muses, "I claim to be male, although only one of my parents was male."[18] Yet as Jaimes makes clear, and as a host of other studies have established, the assumption that blood carried racial qualities was foundational to late nineteenth-century racial and eugenic science. By 1917, as an increasing number of allottees reached the end of their twenty-five-year probationary period and were ready to receive their lands in fee patent, blood quantum had become increasingly important. In that year Commissioner of Indian Affairs Cato Sells determined "that fee patents would simply be issued to all allottees of less than one-half Indian ancestry, while competency determinations would still be required for those of one-half or more Indian blood."[19]

During the 1891 field season Fletcher became involved with another method of scientifically delineating individual racial identities. F. W. Putnam, who was preparing the anthropological exhibits for the upcoming World's Columbian Exposition, involved her in a massive undertaking of biometric classification, administered by his assistant Franz Boas, whom Putnam had appointed to head the Physical Anthropology Section. Boas wrote to colleagues working among Native populations across the Americas, Fletcher among them, asking them to furnish him with statistical data "[f]or the purpose of making a series of charts showing the physical characteristics of the various Native Peoples of the American Continent for the World's Columbian Exposition in Chicago." A printed circular outlined the procedures for gathering the data and included minute instructions to field agents. The project presumed that blood was a racial identifier and that racial identity was best traced matrilineally. Those furnishing data were told questions regarding the number of children applied "only . . . to women." "Do not exclude half-breeds," Putnam and Boas instructed, "but try to ascertain the amount of admixture of foreign blood." Their instructions include directions for measuring facial features and structure, provide a lexicon for describing color of skin, and ask that "[w]henever possible" agents "obtain a lock of hair, which must be sealed up in an envelope at once and marked with the number of the record of the individual and with the name of the tribe."[20] These directives accompanied "a set of instruments & a number of blanks" to be filled out and returned to the investigators.[21]

Although such methods should have appealed to Fletcher's scientific and bureaucratic leanings, she reacted with ill-disguised scorn, at least partly because she resented the fact that Putnam had appointed Boas, not her, to head the anthropological exhibits. She replied to Putnam (not to Boas), "I shall begin at once to coax Indians to be measured. It will be hard sometimes I fancy. Do you want *only* full bloods or shall I take some mixed bloods to show persistence of type. I recall a family of 4 or 5 brothers, it would be interesting to find the type, particularly as I can in this instance I think get the Mother, a full blood."[22] Her reply suggests she had not carefully read the instructions, the first paragraph of which had answered this question (or it shows her intentional disregard of those directives). It also signals her resistance to Boas's methods, which would yield a mathematical and statistical type that transcended individual cases. Such a display differed significantly from the one Fletcher had suggested, in which she wanted to display "a native culture set in varied conditions, transformed by civilizing agents so as to be received into our national life."[23] Although its self-aggrandizing dimensions are apparent, her response nevertheless trenchantly critiques institutionally based and abstractive science that lacked grounding in local details.

Fletcher assigned the time-consuming tasks of measuring and recording data for Boas to Jane Gay, who, as was her wont, produced several witty critiques of such disciplinary technologies, one textual, the others photographic (C, 368). As a lark, Gay filled out one of

Boas's forms with her own vital statistics. Indicating her age as sixteen, she identified her father's tribe as "Jeshuran" and her mother's as "Highlander."[24] For "mode of life," Boas's form required an answer conforming to the following categories: "[W]hether leading an agricultural life, whether hunter or fisherman, whether living on rations furnished by whites and whether the occupation requires sedentary life, life on horseback, in canoe, etc."[25] Gay answered that her mode of life was "migratory."[26] Such flippant responses exposed several of the inherent flaws in Boas's thinking. In the first place, his data depended on compliant and truthful responses. His questions presumed that Native subjects followed a clearly delineated and singular "mode of life," leaving no possibility for answers such as "all of the above" or "none of the above." Finally, the categories are racialized, as Gay's rejoinder makes clear: surely well-educated "migratory" white investigators, who spent their summers on horseback, in wagons, canoes, and railway trains were not the intended subjects of such intrusive questions.

Boas's questionnaire presumed a common and consistent tribal identity marked by premodern modes of life. Native informants who were being documented prior to receiving an allotment or who were measured for Boas's data were not expected to engage in complex performances of willful self-effacement. Some of the World's Columbian Exposition displays guaranteed the consistency of their subjects by using wax figures arranged in tableaux or habitat groups designed to capture a moment representative of typical lifeways or bygone cultural practices.[27] Figure 37 is a photograph of one such exhibit illustrating my point, "Women's Work in Savagery," a diorama exhibited in the Women's Building at the Chicago World's Fair. In a souvenir booklet sold at the fair this image is captioned: "Models of Typical Indian Squaws. Preparing the Hide of Buffalo."[28] The skills being shown here are presumptively outmoded, since by 1893 buffalo had disappeared from the plains. The barefoot women at work wear fringed and beaded buckskin dresses and use "primitive" tools to prepare a hide. They are positioned in a generic outdoor surround that does not distract viewers' attention from the implements, the garb, and the laborious process.[29]

FIG. 37. "Women's Work in Savagery," Women's Building, 1893 Columbian Exposition exhibit. Negative #12257, Record Unit 95, box 61, Smithsonian Institution Archives.

Modern white scientists and government agents, however, retained the privilege of multiple and opportunistically fictional identities. That sort of playfulness, as Gay's response to the questionnaire demonstrates, was a privilege of the white investigators who extracted the identifying data. In Gay's own writing, for example, she is (often simultaneously) the Author, the Photographer, the Cook, the friend, and/or simply "I." In a series of seven self-portraits made years after allotment was finished, Gay photographed these avatars.[30] Her face is visible and identifiable in only one of the images. It is unclear why Gay made the images so long after the events they purport to represent, but their staging suggests they engage a project similar to that of the anthropological habitat groups: they represent a mode of life now definitively past. Gay's photographs of herself as the Cook, for example, seem to mimic Boasian theory as it manifested itself in the habitat groups popular in the era's memory palaces — world's

FIG. 38. "Behold the Cook!" by E. Jane Gay, *Choup-nit-ki*, 227. The Schlesinger Library, Radcliffe Institute, Harvard University.

fairs and anthropological museums.[31] They furnish forth a wealth of meticulous and highly realistic details carefully arranged in representational tableaux. The caption "Behold the Cook!" echoes the collective and nonspecific titling of such exhibits, for the type, not the individual, is the focus of the display. As does the exhibition diorama, this photograph, figure 38, invites the viewer to corroborate a performance of typicality. Like the diorama, "Behold the Cook!" is simultaneously precise and generic. The beholder can count the sticks of firewood at the Cook's back, can recognize and enumerate the cookware, can even read the brand name on the can of baking powder that sits atop the barrel serving as a work surface. As do the Native women, the Cook works within a surround that stands for a larger concept—a wooden shed here suggests the series of camp kitchens in which Gay cooked while in the field.

In their contrast, the two images demonstrate how the idea of typicality produces and maintains the illusion of race. The diorama's demeaning title racializes its subjects, as does the darkened skin, the bending and kneeling poses, and the large bare feet of the waxen figures. The facial features likely followed Boasian statistics delimiting the typical Native woman's circumference of head, length and type of nose, position and shape of ears and brow, even texture and color of hair. In Gay's photograph, by contrast, race is naturalized and unmarked. Yet the visual codes gesture toward (white) typicality: the Cook stands erect.[32] Her legs and arms are clothed, and she presumably wears shoes. Although she works in rough surroundings, she uses cast-iron pots and commercially packaged commodities. Her face is coyly and modestly hidden behind a bonnet associated with pioneering white women, who covered their heads and hair to preserve their pale complexions, and just enough jawline is apparent to guarantee her identification as white.

The technologies of human sciences—anthropometry, blood quantum, photography, taxidermy, and museum display among them—seemed thus to offer a sufficiency of predictive knowledge. They precisely identified individual landholders and, based on their bodily configuration and blood, suggested their readiness to assume modern citizenly duties. Dioramas, numbers, and bureaucratic forms are static, however, and in the field, as Fletcher and Gay repeatedly learned, the human subjects whom these data sought to circumscribe behaved in decidedly unpredictable ways, selectively embraced Fletcher's teachings, and often manifested their understanding of their use and their limits at most inopportune times.

"the ethics of partnership": Producing Behavioral Individuation

As a reformer Fletcher assumed her responsibilities included equipping her clients with skills necessary to compete in the world of agricultural and mercantile activity. As she told the Board of Indian Commissioners, her "conscience" drove her to undertake these tasks that "the law did not require." The soulless bureaucratic work of dividing and assigning land could become meaning-laden uplift when it was done with an extraordinary and voluntary devotion; a surplus of virtue, if you will. Thus Fletcher traced not simply lineal descent but also collateral relations; she not only assigned individual subjects to individual plots of land—she also personally supervised their choice. She could not simply assume that Nimiipuu who had lived on this land for centuries would be wise enough to know how best to cultivate it; her "conscience required" they be instructed in technologies of farming and planting, of bottom-line accounting, market pricing, and competitive bargaining. The tenderly violent pedagogies she employed to accomplish these aims included intimate supervision, strategic infantilization, instruction by exhortation and example, and a large dollop of guilt.

The gifts of allotment and the franchise entailed a violent revision of traditional lifeways, as Gay describes. She begins "Camp Life Experiences" ("CLE"), a letter published by the *Red Man*, with a lengthy account of how Fletcher began the process of transforming Nimiipuu men and women into potential citizens and businessmen.[33] Gay writes, "The Special Agent set up a blackboard in the office. It is the blackboard used by the missionary, and over the ghostly substratum of gospel texts . . . [s]ections are drawn and quartered and driven like wedges into the Indian brain by the Interpreter." The incompletely erased blackboard invokes the work of the earlier federal bureaucrats, missionaries, and teachers who had attempted the forcible charitable reeducation of their wards. The missionary's "gospel texts," then, literally and metaphorically prefigure this moment. Gay likens education, whether in biblical ethics or "elementary surveying," to death by torture, the violent sundering of a human body. While Fletcher and her translator "draw and quarter" hypothetical sections of land on the blackboard, the surveyor performs the same operation on the land, as he "runs out the valley and makes straight the crooked ways of Paradise [Kamiah]." When not instructing clients, "Her Majesty sits . . . in her inquisitorial chair," straitening the crooked ways of kinship of the families and resolving conflicting claims. "The machine is set going," Gay summarizes ("CLE," 7). This metaphor exposes the processes of education as complicit with and supportive of the more impersonal and rationalized methods of metrics, survey, statistics, and rationalized mapping.[34]

To the Nez Perces most closely associated with her, Alice Fletcher attempted to teach skills she thought would prepare them to compete in market situations. Her chainmen, many of them "returned students" from Carlisle or Chemawa, were among those subject to her intimate disciplinary supervision.[35] As federal employees they seemed to their duty-obsessed supervisors to manifest a distressing lack of accountability. They had "not learned to measure by the clock," according to Gay, and did not voluntarily rise before daybreak to join the surveyor in the field. They were improvident, running out of "grub" "just as the surveyor [was] starting out on a new survey with his plans all made for a run of a couple of weeks." To restock with provisions from the nearest market would take at least two days. As private businessmen, these workers seemed not to understand competitive pricing. When they were not pulling chain for Briggs, some of them hauled freight to the gold mines in Orofino, charging "just the same to freight goods over a route four days long as over one they can make in a day. They estimate by the number of ponies it requires" ("CLE," 7). That is to say, they had not embraced the equivalency mantra of western capitalism: time is money.

Perturbed by these behaviors, Fletcher tries "to teach the chainmen the ethics of partnership in general, and the arithmetic of their special combination." She begins by forbidding them to share provisions. Before Fletcher's intervention, according to Gay, "[t]here had been no attempt at equalization. The sack of potatoes was a sack; so was the sack of bacon or of flour or of dried apples." To help her workers economize by making wise choices (presumably of more potatoes and less bacon) and, most important, to demonstrate to them a method of individual and individualized reckoning, Fletcher gives each man a "little blank [book]" in which to "keep accounts, each one of the money he expended for the general good." To begin fairly, she decrees that the "plan could not be retro-active" ("CLE," 7), a decision echoing her early ideas about how allotment should proceed in Kamiah, by "chang[ing]" "nearly every person ... more or less" without regard to their previous holdings or improvements.[36] To the chainmen she declared that an equitable sharing of expenses "had to start now, letting the dead past bury itself" ("CLE," 7). Upon taking "an account of stock," Fletcher discovers the appalling extent to which the one-sack method had brought such fripperies as "canned currant jelly" into the common larder (C, 128). Judging the men incompetent to choose their own food (or to choose food that was appropriately inexpensive), she then draws up a shopping "list of such things as was best for them" and sends one of them off to purchase supplies for which they will equally pay and from which they will equally be provisioned ("CLE," 7). Fletcher and Gay clearly considered the behaviors of time-clocked labor and individual written budgets and reports to be necessary to the transformation of Nez Perces into responsible citizens. Neither seemed to remember that the men to whom Fletcher thought she was teaching these skills had already done time in federal Indian boarding schools and were thus surely familiar with the discipline of clocks, bells, and written reports. If they did not rise before daybreak and shared food indiscriminately, they did so by choice.

Fletcher's policy of grouping families on adjacent claims, which I have already noted, also exemplifies the tender violence of individuating technologies. In the first place, while it may have benefitted those who received it, such grouping stemmed as much from unwise policy as from enlightened benevolence. As she reported to the Board of Indian Commissioners in 1889,

> [W]hen twenty-five years from now the fee of this land becomes simple there can not fail to be a shrinkage.... The people can not continue to hold all the land that has been allotted to them. No equal number of white people could pay the taxes on a similar amount of land and hold it.... [A] heavy percentage of allotted land ... will fall away from the Indians by sale[;] consequently I have thought it best to put the family estate in a single tract, so that in the future when selling off the land the Indians would receive the benefit from that portion which they were able to hold, and be able to stand by each other, as they could not if they were more isolated.[37]

This is a damning statement. It makes clear the fact that the designers of allotment policy knew full well that after allotment, when Indian citizens became liable for federal and state taxes on their allotments, they would be forced to sell their lands (and Fletcher's use of the passive voice here is strategic: she hides the violence of the fact of foreclosure in the figure "will fall away from the Indians by sale"). Moreover, Fletcher did not *always* group families. Rather, she withheld the privilege for those she deemed to be "progressive." Her method thus produced the identity of "best Indians." As these allottees gained, others were punished for their recalcitrance: "It has always been my aim to find out the vantage point on the reservation, the point most likely to be opened to settlement, and on and around that point I place my best Indians. I give the best land to the best Indians I can find.... It helps to break up the dead monotony of the tribe. It has had the effect to awaken the ambition of others. I put the best man where he will have the best chance.... There is nothing so important as helping those that are progressive." While her logic is sound—those who receive advantageous allotments are more likely to succeed—her practices of favoritism amount to a disciplinary practice. As she confessed to the commissioners, "I have always had to coerce a few, and I rather enjoy it."[38]

Thus as allotment progressed, compliant and forward-looking Nez Perces found themselves rewarded with valuable lands. The Williams, Reubens, and Corbett families, for example, received adjoining tracts in fertile locations.[39] James Stuart, a "returned student," Corbett relative, and unfailing supporter of Fletcher, who for four years worked as her translator and driver, received an allotment abutting the railroad route, whence he could easily transport his goods to market (see figure 27, where Stuart's allotment is shown, top center). In sum, Fletcher's methods ensured that her judgment would be correct. Those she saw as promisingly inclined to accept allotment and accede to procedures designed to assimilate them received advantageous allotments and hence a better chance at success.

6. Fictions of Coherence

While Alice Fletcher and Jane Gay expected the Nez Perces to be consistently predictable in their behaviors, Gay's accounts of the allotment expedition present herself and Fletcher in multiple guises. The Photographer, the Cook, the friend, and "I" keep company with Her Majesty, the Allotting Agent, Miss F., and "you." To Fletcher's personae, Gay might also have added the Scholar and the Reformer.[1] As is the case with the groups of Nimíipuu who celebrated the Fourth of July in Lapwai and Kamiah in 1890, these carefully crafted personae produce each other's meaning: the Photographer and Her Majesty are the agents of abstracted policy, while the Cook and the Allotting Agent are the embodied laborers who perform the quotidian work of realizing those designs. "You" and "I" open, for Gay's purposes, a conversation about allotment and are the means whereby she invites the readers of her letters to recognize their implicit involvement in the process. "Miss F." and "the friend" stand for the affiliative relationships upon which Fletcher's field work depended, and which I analyze in this chapter. These personal ties are barely apparent in the official records of the allotment, but to explore them demonstrates how inseparable were the worlds of public policy and private affiliation.

Scholars anxious to include women within the genealogies of nascent professions in the late nineteenth century find a fascinating example in Alice Fletcher. Her allegiances place her at the forefront of the professionalizing human sciences and as a leader in developing and applying federal Indian policy based on Christian-defined notions of domestication and charity. She typifies the unmarried, educated, and well-connected New Woman. She brought to her undertakings—academic, federal, charitable, and personal—a strong sense of duty, an unflinching honesty, and a spotless reputation, sterling qualities of character necessary to allotment's success. As Loring Benson Priest points out in his history of the policy, Henry Dawes wrote, "[I]f my land-in-severalty bill should become a law, it will depend entirely on the character of the government agents, who execute its provisions whether it is a success or a failure. If it be entrusted to men of unflinching honesty and broad views, the Indian will be secure in the possession of homes on the best lands of the reservations; but if it is entrusted to dishonest men, the Indians will be cheated out of their lands."[2]

Although Fletcher exemplified Dawes's ideal man, she was, nevertheless, enmeshed in a web of personal obligation, affiliation, and patronage. Her devotion to ensuring that the Nez Perces were treated fairly during the allotment was compromised at times by her longer-standing and self-interested devotion to Presbyterian charity and her urgent desire to distinguish herself as an anthropologist. Thus, as I demonstrate, she was at times less than objective. Likewise, her developing career as an academic anthropologist was thoroughly intertwined with a federal policy she had helped to write and with friendships that often resembled family ties. While living on a federal wage she pursued her researches and used the material she gathered to obtain lifelong financial support for her work as a scholar from her close friend Mary Copley Thaw. Fletcher exploited Thaw's patronage, as well, to ensure that the Presbyterian missionaries on the Nez Perce Reservation would be financially supported so that after she had completed the allotment, they could continue to furnish her with anthropological information. To follow any one of these connections is to touch them all.

In making these assertions, I offer an interpretation of Fletcher's 1890 field season differing significantly from that written by her biographer, Joan Mark, who treats Fletcher's receipt of Mary Thaw's bequest as a detail largely unrelated to the allotment. Mark does not consider how the news of a lifelong endowment affected her subject's attitude toward her work as a federal agent. Nor does she acknowledge the extent to which Fletcher was personally involved in the restoration of the First Presbyterian Church at Kamiah, a project underwritten by Thaw funds and carried forth in large part on government time by government workers. Rather, Mark blames Jane Gay for the resulting tensions among members of the Kamiah Presbyterian congregation and traditional groups of Nez Perces.[3] As I demonstrate, such an interpretation should be revised in light of the narrative that emerges when Fletcher's official reports are read in conjunction with her personal correspondence, her diary, and Gay's letters.

"I wish I dared tell you about affairs here": Parlor Networking

While she was in Idaho in the summers of 1889–92 Fletcher maintained a voluminous correspondence. For any given week her field diary contains long lists of letters she sent and received. To read these letters as a chronological group is nearly impossible, for they are now held in widely scattered archives in Washington, California, Nebraska, Idaho, Massachusetts, and Washington DC.[4] Within those geographic locales, these records are often held by separate institutions and, within those institutions, they are filed in separate collections. The dispersal of these primary records mirrors Fletcher's fragmented subjectivity. Based on the letters I have accessed, I mark the irony that a woman obsessed with eliciting uniformity of behavior from her clients herself manifested such plural and often inconsistent behaviors. At the same time, I trace how her alliances with academy, church, and government combined—sometimes uneasily—as she directed the work of allotment.[5]

While in the field Fletcher wrote to federal, institutional and charitable, academic, religious, and personal correspondents, all of whom had an active interest in the success of her work, and many of whom stood ready to lend her aid, whether of money, influence, or simple encouragement. In a voluminous correspondence with the Office of

Indian Affairs, she kept her employers apprised of details she deemed it appropriate they know about her work, but by no means did she reveal the full extent of her activities on the Nez Perce Reservation. Additionally, she wrote several semi-official letters for publications read by the partisans of Indian policy reform, including the *Christian Register*, edited by the husband of her friend Isabel Barrows; Hampton Institute's *Southern Workman*; and Pratt's *Red Man*. To close friends Fletcher wrote in a different vein, sometimes confiding to them her doubts, her personal (often negative) impressions, and her frustrations with allotment policy. The most important of these confidants was surely her close associate Francis La Flesche (Omaha), who remained in Washington DC. She could count on La Flesche, who had been closely involved in her advocacy for an allotment law to protect Omaha lands, to sympathize with the challenges she encountered in the field, as is suggested by the entries in her field diary for late June 1889. Confronted with recalcitrant Nez Perces who refused even to meet her to discuss the allotment until Charles Monteith was replaced as agent, she wrote a series of letters, including a "Report to Commis." and "a long letter telling of affairs here" to "Capt. P." (Pratt).[6] She also noted two letters to Francis: "Wrote F." on 25 June and, just two days later, "Wrote F. in full of difficulties."[7] These letters, in which she tells "F" of her difficulties—"in full"—are now missing, likely destroyed by La Flesche upon Fletcher's death or in 1907 by Fletcher herself.

This gap in Fletcher's personal correspondence is regrettable, for it seems unlikely that she was as open with any other correspondent. The tenor of her missing letters to La Flesche can be inferred, however, from her other personal letters. She often turned for support, advice, and encouragement to powerful men such as F. W. Putnam and Thomas Jefferson Morgan. Mark writes, in fact, "All her life Alice Fletcher looked to men for help, although the help she got often came from women. The women she tended to take for granted" (SNL, 14). Yet Fletcher's correspondence suggests that at least during the years of allotment, she did not take her women friends "for granted"; rather, she methodically and intentionally exploited what

I call parlor networks of women friends, several of whom (Electa Sanderson Dawes, Isabel Chapin Barrows, and Caroline S. Morgan, for example) were married to men who wielded significant federal influence. As Catherine Allgor has demonstrated in an essay subtitled "Women and Patronage in Early Washington City," in the early nineteenth century, women were "[central]" "to the business of patronage," which often "took place in women's spaces, like parlors and dining rooms, during social activities usually considered 'private,' like calling and visiting"—and, I would add, by letter writing and sharing photographs.[8] It seems apparent that Fletcher used her friendship with women to further her own ends, often depending on feminine confidantes as surrogates to convey information she could not say to the men who directly supervised her work.

For example, Fletcher wrote periodically to Electa Dawes, herself an Indian reformer, whose powerful husband was the architect of the General Allotment Act that bears his name. This "dear Friend" was one "of the first . . . to hear the news" of the Thaw Fellowship and to receive Fletcher's assurance that she did not intend to "resign [her] present position," an observation surely intended to be conveyed to Henry Dawes. In this same letter Fletcher included a photograph of herself, James Stuart, and Chief Joseph "made by Miss Gay" (see fig. 1). By the time she wrote this letter, Fletcher had been in the field for four months and thus might have chosen from any number of other photographs to represent her work—Gay's image of the Reubens brothers in ceremonial regalia, for example (see fig. 8). Knowing Electa Dawes would share the letter with her husband, who was among the Presbyterian partisans who had supported Joseph's return from incarceration, Fletcher chose an image clearly aligning her with his interests. While she characterized Joseph as "a hero in many ways," she also confided, "I doubt if he is ever able to go much further in progressive ideas."[9] The statement was a way of signaling what she had no doubt learned while conversing with the tribal leader: Joseph obdurately refused allotment, and no well-meaning reformer could induce him to change his mind.

In her letter to Electa Dawes, Fletcher also evaluated the personalities of those with whom she worked, characterizing a new schoolmaster as "a simpleton," but assuring her friend that "Commis Morgan . . . promptly . . . relieved" the employee in question "& appointed one of his own choosing, a man of character & experience." Through these casual confidences, she laid the foundation for what seems to be the letter's main thrust, delivered in its penultimate paragraph: "I hope the Amendment to the Severalty Act giving 80 acres to every man, woman & child, irrespective of age or relation, has passed. It will settle many difficulties & put the distribution of land on a safer & better basis and make little difference in the aggregate amount allotted."[10] This confidential opinion, conveyed from one friend and reformer in Idaho to another in Washington DC was sure also to be relayed by the latter to her husband.

Another of Fletcher's friends, Isabel Barrows, shared her interest in Indian affairs. While in Idaho, Fletcher confided to this "very dear Friend" information that appeared much later, and in less direct ways, in her official reports. Barrows was one of the first to learn of Fletcher's doubts about the success of allotment. To this friend, the newly arrived allotting agent wrote, "I see plainly that the amt. given an Indian for grazing land is too small for him to make a living off of 320 acres for himself & wife about 30 head of stock and perhaps a small garden of a few acres without an outlet for pasture the white men must fare badly on such contracted spaces." She concluded her letter, "These people deserve better of the govt than they have. I wish I dared tell you about affairs here but I must be silent."[11] She made such off-the-record observations with clear intent. "In the field," more than a thousand miles away from the halls in which an amendment to the Dawes Act would be debated, Fletcher implicitly invited her friend to be her surrogate, for Isabel Barrows was the official stenographer both for the Lake Mohonk Conference of the Friends of the Indian and for the Board of Indian Commissioners. While it is unclear how much input Barrows had to the official deliberations of these bodies, she was clearly an informed partisan, and could strategically, if unofficially, share such inside information, both in her own parlor and in the atria outside the rooms where delegates gathered to determine official policy.

While she was in the field, Fletcher also carried on an intricately choreographed personal correspondence with Thomas Jefferson Morgan and his wife Caroline Morgan. Fletcher appears to have used a kind of private code in her field diary to remind herself which type of letter she had sent. She indicated her official correspondence with the notations "Ind. Comm." or "Comm.," while she noted her private letters as being sent to "Mr. Morgan." Similarly, she signaled her intent in the salutations of her letters, beginning her official correspondence with the formulaic "Hon. Commis. of Indian Affairs. Sir:"; she opened private letters with "My dear Mr. Morgan" or "My dear Gen. Morgan." Unsurprisingly, in her private correspondence, she discussed allotment with less obfuscation than she did in the public record. For example, in an eleven-page letter addressed to "My dear Mr. Morgan" and sent early in the first field season, she set the tone for and established the terms of an ad hoc agreement that the two of them would carry on a parallel private discussion. The letter begins: "Ever since your kind invitation *by Mrs. Morgan's hand* asking me to tell you of matters here I have [??] to find the hours to reply because I so fully appreciate your wish to really do something to better the Indians and the opportunity of getting practical and trusty information. I have watched so many 'investigations' that I am led to wonder, not that so little, but so much in the way of truth ever reaches the high officer's seat." Acknowledging that she had "written at length," Fletcher nevertheless also claimed, "There are many things I have not touched upon.... I have not wanted to expose the nakedness of the official here."[12] This remarkably frank letter makes it clear that Morgan's policies as commissioner of Indian affairs depended on privately gathered information, solicited by his indirect "invitation," as much as on the official reports of his agents in the field.

Similar letters followed. Often addressed directly to Morgan, many of them marked PERSONAL, or CONFIDENTIAL, and bearing a salutation signaling their private intent, these letters contain details about the administration of affairs at Lapwai that Fletcher felt were inappropriate to include in her public reports. She concluded each with queries about the health of "Mrs. Morgan" or with greetings to her. At the same time she maintained a parallel correspondence with Caroline Morgan, who served as a relay point between her husband and his field agent. For example, on 13 June 1891, Caroline Morgan wrote to Fletcher (using Office of Indian Affairs stationery and enclosing the note "in Mr. Morgan's letter"), "Much of what you have written has been very encouraging to Mr. Morgan & your suggestions & advice have been of great practical value to him. You perhaps have learned that he has authorized a new building, as per floor plans."[13] On this same day Commissioner Morgan had sent to Fletcher the notice of his authorization for a new school building.[14]

The degree to which Fletcher felt it reasonable to use private correspondence to criticize and even defame those with whom she worked emerges in two such letters she sent in October 1889—one official and the other to "dear Mr. Morgan." In the first letter she clothes her critique in language appropriate to bureaucratic Washington, requesting more employees and an increased budget, because "of the difficulties of my work which are incident to the Agency troubles."[15] Two days later, in a letter marked "Confidential" and addressed to "My dear Mr. Morgan" Fletcher wrote:

> Since I have been so frank with you I may as well add a few words about Mr. Monteith who was an entire stranger to me when I arrived. I have never met so bad a man. It may be that the United States has had Agents who stole [??] sums of money but they have never had, I trust, a man who has so misused his power to injure the best men in the tribe, to crush out the noblest elements at work among the people, to tyrannize in a manner that it seems difficult to believe in the fear of the strongest Indians. Mr. Monteith has alied himself to those only who would serve him, and has done [?] things which are a disgrace to humanity, not to speak of the Government which he was supposed to serve.[16]

In this case, other correspondents had confirmed Fletcher's condemnation of Charles Monteith. At other times, however, she offered compromised and decidedly biased information to Morgan. As she grew increasingly unsure of the basis of her support in Lapwai in 1891, her letters became correspondingly paranoid. She reported to Morgan in a personal letter that her surveyor, Edson Briggs, who had been her mainstay and unfailing supporter, seemed to be "working to keep his pay going longer than need be." While she would not go so far as to accuse him of the actionable offense of "cheat[ing] in grading the land," she was sure he was intentionally retarding her work.[17]

"gifts from some ... benevolent lady"

Alice Fletcher's feminine networks included a number of Presbyterian philanthropists, missionaries, and church officials. These partisans had much to do with events in Idaho, for the Nez Perce Reservation had come under Presbyterian administration as a result of the Grant Peace Policy. Their involvement, however, exacerbated the tensions between traditional Nimiipuu and those who supported and were supported by church interests. Nowhere does this affiliative network make itself more apparent than in Alice Fletcher's sponsorship of the refurbishing of the Kamiah First Presbyterian Church in July and August 1890. Although allotment did not begin in Kamiah, the settlement was the site of a large number of Fletcher's early allotments, due in large part to the substantial support of Susan McBeth and her Presbyterian mission students. Fletcher made it privately clear to her friend Isabel Barrows how foundational the labors of this woman and her sister had been to her success. Unsurprisingly, Barrows subsequently printed portions of Fletcher's letter in the *Christian Register*, under the title "Missionary Work among the Indians." "The Misses McBeth have here done a wonderful work in the past sixteen years," Fletcher wrote, describing the colorfully garbed Christian Indians coming to "gather under the pine-trees that cluster about the little 'church-house'"; "the services" conducted "in the native tongue"; and "the songs [which] are translations of our familiar hymns." She concluded with an appeal: "How I wish some one would send simple story-books for a Sunday-school library for each church!"[18] This disingenuous "wish" surely reached a greater number of charitable givers than any number of individual letters Fletcher might have sent. The request was promptly fulfilled and was recorded by Jane Gay as she later described the Kamiah Church: "Elder Billy [Williams] kept ... the big Bible well wrapped in its mazarine blue cotton cover on its crimson plush cushion (gifts from some Eastern Sunday school or some benevolent lady who has heard of the Nez Perces)."[19]

Central to this network of Christian charity was Fletcher's friend Mary Copley Thaw, wife of Pennsylvania railroad and manufacturing baron William Thaw.[20] Both these staunch Presbyterians followed Fletcher's anthropological work with great interest, and she corresponded regularly with them from the field. It is virtually certain that Fletcher had told Mary Thaw in great detail of Susan McBeth's efforts to further allotment among the Nez Perce Presbyterians in Kamiah, larding her letters with the kinds of indirect solicitations at which she excelled. Her hints elicited significant and continuing financial gifts, large and small, from the Thaws, including monies meant to be spent on refurbishing the Kamiah Presbyterian Church. The remodeling project, according to Mark, was "a serious error," for it "had helped to split the Kamiah Presbyterians, a split that survives to this day." However, Mark traces the "error" solely to Jane Gay, and charges, "She had made Alice Fletcher vulnerable to the charge of misusing men on the government payroll. She had turned the rival pastor at Kamiah, Archie Lawyer, who might have become a powerful friend, into a vociferous opponent of allotment" (SNL, 187). The biographer does not trace Fletcher's part in the work, although the written record shows her to have been fully involved in the project.

Fletcher set the wheels in motion for refurbishing the church almost immediately following the meeting she held there to discuss allotment on 22 July 1889. On 29 August she noted in her diary, "Took measurements at church." On 31 August she wrote: "Letter Mrs. Thaw. Mr. Thaw died [August] 17 in Paris. Mrs. Thaw will give $150 for Kamiah church."[21] Gay gave a fuller explication of Mary Thaw's generosity to *Red Man* readers. She describes the decrepitude of the church—a rotting foundation, sun-baked "weatherboarding," leaking roof, and broken stove—but, she emphasizes, the church was nevertheless "neatly swept" and its holy contents were respectfully cared for.[22] In Gay's account Briggs is the first to note the condition of the building. "[I]t's a shame," he says. "Her Majesty" adds, "I'd like to do something for the people." The Cook then raises a problem:

"The Agent might put us off the reservation for interference, as he did the little missionary [Susan McBeth] who tried to arrest the destruction of the Indian."

"Times have changed," said Her Majesty, "the things that were possible once are possible no longer. We shall not be disturbed. Perhaps the Government may turn the Church over to the Indians."

Now there is a blessed lady in the land towards the East who helps save the world from destruction by fire and brimstone, one who has only to know of good to be done to put her hand into her pocket, and the wherewithal comes out.

This blessed woman heard of the little Kamiah Church, and of elder Billy and the struggling Christian flock with their native pastor, and so one day before we quitted the valley for the season, a letter came, which enclosed, a text for a little sermon which her Majesty preached this last Sunday.[23]

Thus before leaving Idaho in late November 1889 Fletcher had made it clear to the Kamiah Presbyterian Nez Perces, again speaking from the pulpit of their church, that the building would be refurbished. She advised them to spend the winter preparing for the project by cutting new shingles and doing what they could to prepare for the work.[24]

En route to Idaho the next spring, Fletcher paid a condolence call on Mary Thaw in Philadelphia, at which time the philanthropist offered her the "annuity" that was to become the Thaw Fellowship.[25] Fletcher then stopped in Milwaukee and used a part of Thaw's earlier donation to the church to buy supplies: "111 rolls of paper for Kamiah & Meadow Creek Churches. . . . $11.25 Curtains 1.00 carpet 5.75, Muslin 1.44, silver 11."[26] She spent May and part of June in Lapwai, once more embroiled in agency politics and local disputes. Here she attended the trial of Robert Williams, minister of the first Kamiah Presbyterian Church, for adultery.[27] By late June, Gay and Fletcher were again in Kamiah, where, immediately following the 1890 Fourth of July celebration about which they both wrote in glowing terms, they began to work on the church.

Fletcher did not share this news with her network of correspondents. Her reticence suggests the extent to which she knew the project violated the separation of personal from professional interests upon which her reputation as an objective federal agent depended. She seems to have written in detail to no one (except possibly Mary Thaw) about this project: not Isabel Barrows, who would certainly have been interested in such a marvelous triumph of Christian rectitude, nor Caroline Morgan, nor Richard Pratt, nor Thomas J. Morgan. Six months after the restoration was complete she wrote to the commissioner of Indian affairs to request that the church, which was technically government property although sited on allotted land, be "turn[ed] over to the Presbyterian Board of Foreign Missions" because the congregants feared that "the Government will take the church and shut the door." In this letter she admits she had let "friends interested in the Presbyterian Mission" know of the building's disrepair, "and they contributed $230 toward repairing the church." Two hundred dollars of that amount had come from Mary Thaw. How that repair came about is reported in strategically passive phraseology: "This work was done in the summer of 1890, the Indians contributing shingles, cedar logs, and other materials."[28]

The written source upon which all subsequent accounts of the church restoration depend is Jane Gay's long descriptive letter to Henrietta Bradley, dated 15 August 1890, just a week after Fletcher noted in her diary, "The church completed."[29] That letter was never published, either in the *Red Man* or in the *Christian Register*. It did not, in fact, become even quasi-public until 1904, when Gay completed *Choup-nit-ki*. The details of the renovation were closely held, likely because the task involved many members of Fletcher's field crew: her chainmen, her translator, her surveyor, and even Her Majesty herself. This was, of course, a serious ethical and fiduciary violation, and when Gay mentioned any of Fletcher's employees, she was careful to emphasize that their part in the restoration was accomplished very early in the morning, before the work day began, or was undertaken on cloudy or smoky days when Briggs could not use his solar instruments.

I do not mean to imply that Fletcher's employees devoted every moment of the weeks between July 3 and August 7 to rebuilding the Kamiah Presbyterian Church. Local Nimiipuu congregants contributed much of the sweated labor; Jane Gay, who was an expert cabinetmaker, did the finishing work. However, it is also clear from Fletcher's field diary that work on allotment alternated with work on the church. On Saturday, July 12, for example, she wrote, "Clear & cool. At work allotting in field. Completed on East side of Clearwater"; on Friday, July 18, she reported, "Very warm. No better than yesterday. At work at church painting windows etc. Mr. Briggs began on the ceiling." Apparently the church work did not always wait for cloudy or smoky days: on a clear, hot July day when Briggs could have been in the field, he was at work on the ceiling. These two entries are representative of many others wherein Fletcher noted the work on the church in passive voice, and it is difficult to tell who performed which tasks—whether Indian church members, Gay, members of the allotting team, or Fletcher herself.

Fletcher's official reports for July and August contain no mention of work at the church. In July and August she sent fewer letters than usual to Washington DC, and what she did send was vague and brief. For example, on 12 July, reporting the accomplishments of the month just past (when work had not yet begun on the church), she wrote, "I have made 56 allotments in whole or in part in the West side of the Valley."[30] On 26 July, when the repair project had been under way for two weeks, she reported that "some 24" allotments in the uplands had been "run out . . . as I had directed," explaining the shortfall this way:

> The surveying party have suffered severely for the lack of water & feed *had I not remained behind* they could not have done the work they did. The weather is extremely hot, over 100° every day, sometimes rising to 110° in the shade. The springs are going dry and there is not a blade of grass for feed. Every ounce of horse feed has to be transported. . . . Next week we shall start at Meadow Creek and work out from there so as to have water & possibly some little feed. *I shall have to keep my headquarters here to send out these Indians who take the residue of their land in that vicinity.*[31]

Nothing in this report is a blatant falsification. Evidence from the field diary and from Gay's letters confirms that late July and early August were "extremely hot." But Fletcher's decision not to go into the field may have had as much to do with the ongoing work at the Kamiah church (which proceeded despite the heat) as with her wish to conserve supplies of grain and water for the pack animals. The same logic explains her decision not to move to Meadow Creek. Instead, she remained in Kamiah to complete her work there, both of allotment and of church reconstruction.

I have traced these intricacies in Fletcher's involvement with the church project not to condemn her fallibility of character nor to impugn her good intentions. Rather, I wish to demonstrate that the very inconsistencies and conflicting loyalties she decried in her Nez Perce clients characterized her work as well. Her involvement in refurbishing the church, however, made apparent to those who did not support Susan McBeth and Robert Williams that Fletcher was a dangerous partisan. Soon after repairs on the church were completed, supporters of the increasingly disaffected Archie Lawyer decided to meet separately on the other side of the Clearwater River as the Kamiah Second Presbyterian Church.

By the end of July 1890 Fletcher was increasingly torn between her allotting duties and the tantalizing suggestion Mary Thaw had made that she resign her post and devote herself to scholarship. These conflicting possibilities affected the situations she found herself dealing with in Idaho, as she strove to remain loyal to both of the feuding McBeth sisters and chose to support Robert Williams and rebuild his church, all the while knowing such support would alienate a powerful and important group of Nimiipuu who supported the Lawyer family. Not only did these so-called traditionalists establish a second church; they also demonstrated their contempt for her methods by refusing to cooperate with allotment. As pressures mounted, Fletcher more frequently demanded that the Nez Perces manifest obedience and consistency in their behaviors, and her imperious persona as Her Majesty dominated her tone. The July report from which I have quoted above concludes, for example, "It is almost impossible to get the Indians to follow the Surveyor & see their corners. The heat, the labor of it is too great and as every man can't be run out at the same time no one is willing to wait. I will have all see their corners that it is possible to drive to do it but some will not. The allotment would take fully 5 summers did I wait to secure every mans ordinances."[32] It seems clear from these revealing words that Her Majesty was having some doubts about how long the allotment might take, especially when the delay would keep her from the anthropological research. Yet she herself had caused the slowdown by diverting her attention from her allotting work.

"inclined to control my whereabouts": The (Il)logical Results of Behavioral Technologies

Throughout the summer of 1890, as she supervised the church work, perhaps wielding the occasional paintbrush, and "drove" the allotment at Kamiah, Fletcher considered Mary Thaw's offer, which, like most charitable support, came with strings attached. She discussed some of the conditions with F. W. Putnam, informing him, "Mrs. Thaw still makes her offer to me, but she seems inclined to control my whereabouts etc.—suggesting that I live with 'a charming old maid' dau. or sis. of a Presbyterian minister. Now I am not inclined to old maids nor to the blue atmosphere & I fear I should find my self in theological troubles all anew. I want to devote my self to science, not to any doxy. As matters stand I shall try & keep Mrs. Thaw happy, but stick to my Gov't work for the present."[33] Fletcher seems quite unaware of the irony that while she was busy directing Nez Perces in matters of daily life—where to live, when to rise in the morning, what to eat, what to charge for their labor, whom they might marry, and what faith they should profess—she resisted Mary Thaw's similar charitable meddling in her own affairs. As did some of her Nimiipuu clients, Fletcher extracted herself from the worst implications of her friend's interest without appearing to do so. Putnam, negotiating on Fletcher's behalf and for Harvard, convinced Thaw to transform her annuity into an endowed chair, which would be Fletcher's for life. This benefited both Putnam, who was trying to establish a regular program of graduate study in anthropology at the university, and Fletcher, by affiliating her with a reputable institution. It also placed Harvard and Putnam as buffers between Fletcher and her meddling benefactress.

In much the same way Alice Fletcher discovered a way to accept

Mary Thaw's money without agreeing to live with "a charming [Presbyterian] old maid," the Natives of northwest Idaho exercised their own wisdom about how to deal with the changes being thrust upon them by the federal government. Agency and reciprocal obligation were central to Fletcher's concerns in the summer of 1890: How might charity be given and policy applied if the bestowal of money, property, and the franchise were contingent upon their recipients' making drastic and unwilling changes in their lives? Even before arriving on the reservation in the late spring of 1890, Fletcher had had serious indications that tactics of benevolent suasion, used in tandem with federal land policy, would not be successful. En route to Idaho she stopped to check on the Omahas and Winnebagos to whom she had allotted land three years before. Gay comments: "The Omahas held a surprise in store for Her Majesty. It is not often that one has a chance to see one's own ideas blossomed out in vivid coloring in other people's lives; ones theoretical teachings already in fruition. It startles one: we cannot always estimate rightly the nature of the soil and climate. We drop the seed . . . but expect no rapid germination, scarcely to see the upspringing blade, certainly not the full corn in the ear" (C, 217).[34] Perhaps more than anything else Gay wrote, this passage suggests that Fletcher, as a theorist of allotment, was unprepared for and unwilling to acknowledge the far-reaching consequences of her ideas. The Omahas and Winnebagos had never been in the infantile and helpless state she had imagined. Given time to work out their own political situations, they now refused to allow Fletcher to direct them further.

The specific case in point involved the use of $10,000, recently released to the tribe. Fletcher and Gay, "on the presumption that the wards of the nation could have no will of their own," had happily begun to arrange for the money to be used to build "small frame houses . . . for the 'most deserving'" members of the tribe. The tribal leaders, however, insisted, "It belongs to all" and began to debate the wisdom of "a per capita distribution." "[E]ven the old and shiftless resented this paternal interference," Gay concludes (C, 219). Despite the technologies designed to enforce individuation, Omaha leaders had chosen a path disturbingly reminiscent of tribalism's communal sharing of resources.

In Nebraska in 1890 Fletcher had discovered the stable and equivalent identities she was sure she had established there had begun to disintegrate, and "a sort of kaleidoscopic shifting of the wives and husbands and children" had taken place, "to the detriment of [Fletcher's much-vaunted] family grouping system of allotment" (C, 216). In Kamiah, too, a similar process was under way, less than a year after she had triumphantly assumed that once she had "[made] a fair and equitable exchange of land and adjustment," order would prevail.[35] She wrote in frustration to the commissioner, "The people jump claims like grasshoppers and cause much extra labor by their activity in this particular."[36] Fletcher may have been annoyed, but apparently did not compare the "extra labor" of her bureaucratic work to readjust claims, redraw boundary lines, and re-site corners with the significant labor she expected allottees to perform, moving their homes, outbuildings, and fences and plowing new lands so that the contours of their lands would conform to the survey.

If the assignment of lands were so demonstrably mutable, how much less stable were the behavioral changes she had assumed would result from allotment? In any number of ways, small and large, it was becoming apparent that the ultimate effects of allotment—agrarianism, individual property rights, and paternalistic supervision—were going to be transitory, limited, and only strategically embraced by those who were their recipients. In the first place, not all the Nez Perces took allotments upon which they permanently settled. Although Yellow Bull did come to the Nez Perce Reservation from Colville in 1890 to take an allotment, others of Joseph's group did not. Joseph himself refused an allotment, insisting that his lands in the Wallowa Valley be restored to him and his people. At the same time, he did not live as an exile, but traveled from Colville to Lapwai and Kamiah in June 1890, as well as on several other occasions during the allotment years, and frequently thereafter, leading Fourth of July processions, visiting with relatives and friends, and remaining in touch with those who lived on the Nez Perce Reservation. On one of these visits Gay made the photograph of Fletcher, Stuart, and Joseph sent by Fletcher to her friend Electa Dawes (fig. 1).

Despite the processes of land reassignment, the Nez Perces did not discard their accustomed patterns of living. In the summer they gathered camas and hauled garden produce to sell to the miners in the Orofino area; in the fall they departed the valleys to hunt in the mountains. Nor did even the most apparently committed Presbyterian Nimiipuu fully embrace Christian religious tenets. When Felix Corbett's wife died in September 1890, Fletcher and Gay helped the widower realize his wish to have her "buried as white people are" (C, 298). But, as Gay writes with great insight, the Native women who gathered to watch the funeral preparations did not seem comforted by the "poverty of resources" demonstrated in the Presbyterian service. "What, to them, was the significance of the coffin?" Gay asked. "Was not the new white blanket of their own custom better? Did the white people not know that the shut up box would hinder the spirit from going to its own place? And why the . . . silence? Would not their own old funeral song cheer the departing spirit more truly? Were the white people's ways better for the Indian than his own?" (C, 299). Here, as she so often does, Gay compellingly registers the gap between the veneer of civilized behaviors and the rich cultural traditions these behaviors intended to cover.

Even Fletcher's own employees showed how limited was her control over their assimilation. James Stuart, manifesting a worrisome tendency toward independent thought and action, left Kamiah in early August 1890 to visit his wife in Lapwai and returned several weeks later than he was expected. Perhaps he thought that since Fletcher's attention was more on the work of repairing the church than on the allotment, she could spare him to other demands. Other records show Stuart had gone to Lapwai to support his wife Harriet as she brought legal suit against the agency physician, Dr. Gibson, and his wife, whom she had reported to the commissioner of Indian affairs for incompetence and cruelty to their Indian employees.[37]

The same chainmen whom Fletcher did not trust to share their provisions equitably acted in their own financial best interest: they went on strike, demanded "higher wages," and found wide support for their actions among their friends. The workers, Fletcher reported, "have entered into a league not to work for less than $2.50 per day. I have so far been unable to fill their places with Indians. I shall take white men if I can get them. Hands are scarce at this harvest time and I may have to pay more than $1.75 per day. I shall replace the men as soon as possible & push the work thro. *My determination to close is well known and advantage taken of it.* I could have had good Indian workmen, but they are now all gone off hop-picking and harvesting."[38] James Reubens, whom Fletcher had planned to send to law school and on whose behalf she had written letters of support and solicited funds, also seems to have disappointed her, although the details of his shortfall are only hinted at. He wrote her in an undated letter, marked *Private*: "I say this. I know my many faults. I do not or will deny them and you know them. . . . I do not think necessary for me to say, that I intend to do right and life right, about smoking I will not smoke in the office or in presence of ladies and gentlemen, but may smoke all alone and away from anybody &c all other things that I have done, I will quit them now and all the time, and I must & I will[.]"[39]

It seems to have escaped Fletcher's understanding that the Nez Perces would choose strategically, adopt the new ways that fit their best interests, and reject others. Chainmen moved to more lucrative occupations; Reubens remained in Idaho and developed the family lands he had bargained for. Moreover, they would behave in ways that might not please Fletcher or the Office of Indian Affairs, particularly in cases where the consistency, fairness, and equality that were supposed to have characterized allotment failed to materialize. The repair of the First Kamiah Presbyterian church thus emblematizes the arguments I have been making here. In many ways it was a blatant demonstration of Fletcher's disregard for consistency in behavior. The work was undertaken on government time and used government-funded labor. It benefited only the members of the tribe who were congregants of Susan McBeth, not the Lapwai Presbyterian group, the followers of Lawyer in Kamiah, or the Catholic or non-Christian Nez Perces. During the reconstruction work a group of Nimiipuu who supported the Lawyers protested and refused to help with the work. The same group brought the lawsuit against Williams, which meant that when the remodeling was completed, a surrogate pastor had the honor of preaching the first sermon in the restored church. Ultimately this group split from the First Presbyterian Church and established the Kamiah Second Presbyterian Church across the Clearwater River. While their actions were indeed divisive, they were certainly undertaken with good cause and, it might be argued, demonstrated most clearly an ideal to which Fletcher paid lip service: the principle of peaceful resistance and conscientious objection, furnished forth in decisive action.

Perhaps the most decisive summary of the shortfall of allotment's disciplinary technologies to inscribe a permanent change on its subjects is recounted in a letter written by Levi Jonas, a supporter and friend of Alice Fletcher, to the former allotting agent as the time neared for the sale of reservation lands. As allotment closed, people began to discuss (as indeed they had from the beginning) the idea that the Nez Perces need no longer be subject to the disciplinary supervision of agents and missionaries. Jonas reported that James Reubens had been soliciting support for the sale of lands by explaining to reluctant Nez Perces that with citizenship came self-control: "James Reuben able man explained . . . self controll is no more to rule over you but to rule over yourself if desire to drunk whisky there will be no one able to stop you, if you desire to be no more christian there will no one to prevent you from. So many of them signed the [land sale agreement] treaty for race horse, for war dances, for whisky, for no more collecting the money as church members."[40] Despite tensions among reservation factions, the point remains: nascent citizenship fueled the idea of self-determination and cultural renaissance.

Part Four

Endings

Introduction

"If the Work Is Ever to Be Finished"

Having left the reservation early in October 1890 after abbreviating her second field season, Alice Fletcher returned to Idaho earlier than was her wont, in April 1891, hoping to complete the allotment so she could turn her full attention to the research she could pursue as the Thaw Fellow and to the various ethnographic exhibits being planned for the 1893 World's Columbian Exposition. Ahead of her lay the most challenging part of her work — allotting the Lapwai area, where multiple claimants had long occupied the most valuable lands on the reservation. The written records for this third season show Fletcher to be, by turns, impatient, vexed, frustrated, and imperious, all in reaction to the interruptions and resistances that retarded the work she had hoped to force to a speedy conclusion. At least some of the pressure she felt was due to her early departure the year before: the unresolved cases from that season had followed her to Washington DC, where the winter's sojourn had offered the women little respite from their work. Gay reports that the "tribulations" related to allotment had "rolled on after us over the thousands of miles which lay between." Even when they were not on the reservation, she and Fletcher had found themselves embroiled in disputes over land. "We did not do it of our own premeditated free will," Gay writes. "[I]t was the United States mail that was responsible; that, and the policy which had taught the Nez Percé the art of letter writing" (C, 326). The technologies of civilization, it seems, were available to Native as well as federal partisans, and allottees who hoped to buttress themselves against the worst abuses of the new law did not hesitate to use them.

In her third field season Fletcher planned to make allotments to more than a thousand Nez Perces on the west side of the reservation. Yet she found herself repeating old work, making visible the abstract lines and corners of properties she had assigned two years earlier. Unlike a plot with a shape described by metes and bounds, an allotment on the Nez Perce Reservation was enclosed by imaginary lines that remained invisible until fences traced them onto the land. Thus "again and again a man will come and say that he cannot find his corners," Gay complained. "[O]ver and over again he is shown them at the expenditure of much time, labor and patience. There has to be an end of this if the work is ever to be finished. I suspect that many will never have a true idea of the size and shape of their allotments unless Uncle Sam fences their possessions or a white man rents the land" (C, 350). Since 1863 Uncle Sam had promised to furnish supplies so allottees might enclose their fields, but the promise was as intangible as the lines on the land. Most allottees did not have liquid capital to invest in miles and miles of barbed wire. Seeking to fund such improvements, they began to demand the right to lease or rent their lands to white men who had more ready cash, an outcome that, under the fiction of allotment law, was not supposed to happen until the twenty-five-year period of citizenly apprenticeship had ended. This terminus also proved to be illusory as the demands of cash and circumstance drove allotment to an ambiguous conclusion.

The profile of the letters Gay collected in *Choup-nit-ki* in 1904 suggests the uneven pace and dissatisfying trajectory of the work in these last two seasons. After a long-delayed but ultimately optimistic beginning in Kamiah in July 1889, the story of Fletcher's work seemed destined to follow a plot of resistance overcome by womanly patience and logical persuasion. The story would end with the transformation of the Lapwai Nimiipuu into Christian landowners like their relatives in Kamiah. This was emphatically not the case.

The second half of allotment dragged on and on, involving Fletcher in more and more battles that she could not win. Finally she ceased her field work, and left Idaho, but continued to deal with the paperwork spawned by allotment for the next several years. Nineteen of the twenty-seven letters collected in *Choup-nit-ki* cover the work of the first two summers (about twelve months' time, most of it spent in Kamiah). Six letters cover the third and longest season, and two summarize the work of the fourth summer's attempts. As Gay wrote in her final letter from the field, "None of us have written many letters this year. The season now drawing to a close has not been prolific of pleasant themes and our endeavor has been to refrain from dwelling upon much that has been forced upon our observation. The silences are eloquent, could you but read them" (C, 432). The slowing momentum of correspondence might inaccurately suggest lethargy or a lessening of effort. In fact, Fletcher worked steadily, even feverishly. But her successes were few and she found herself vexed on all sides by issues—some of her own creation, and others admittedly exacerbated by her own partisan loyalties—that were not easily resolved. Thus Gay found she had less and less to report, for she was reluctant to write of the challenges Fletcher was unable to resolve.

When she departed the Nez Perce Reservation for the last time on 13 September 1892, Fletcher announced, "[T]he field work of allotting these Indians is completed. No one entitled to land here is omitted, who wishes to take his or her allotment on this reservation."[1] The claim was partly accurate: she would do no more field work. It was also fallacious, if not outright false, since several hundred Nimiipuu had not received allotments, and not all of those were covered by the phrase "who wishes." They included minor children, those with unresolved claims, those whose religious and/or political affiliations had displeased Fletcher, and those who had openly resisted her work. I do not mean to imply that the allotting agent was derelict in her duty or that she overtly and intentionally misrepresented what she had accomplished. I do wish, however, to emphasize that her language in announcing the end of field work was carefully precise and that her signal of completion was, perhaps, a necessary fiction.

As I argue in this chapter, the sense of an ending is a narrative convention. Endings, like beginnings, bring structure to disorderly and discordant experiences, suggest causality, enable storytellers and story hearers to arrange vast quantities of information into meaningful patterns, and allow them to predict or anticipate outcomes and effects based on similar stories. Allotment was not concluded when Fletcher left Lapwai, nor was it finished when she submitted the final set of deeds and plats to the secretary of the interior two years later. Nor did the sale of surplus lands that "opened" the reservation in November 1895 mark the end of allotment's effects. The idea that allotment on the Nez Perce Reservation had a conclusion obscures the messy, unfinished, and massively disruptive outcomes of a policy that, from the moment of its inception, had been repeatedly revised by its architects, continued to be revised until it was finally rescinded in 1934, and, throughout the decades of its application, was challenged and resisted by those whose lives it attempted to reconfigure. As I complete these chapters, yet another inconclusive conclusion has offered itself, as the federal government has announced its intention to resolve *Cobell v. Salazar*, the latest attempt to bring closure to the abuses set into play by allotment. The case has been in litigation for thirteen years, and definitive resolution awaits congressional approval. It should be no surprise that, as legal scholar Robert Clinton has noted, "the settlement alone would not resolve the trust problem because many of the heirs who own tiny interests in [fractionated] parcels may not be willing to sell them."[2]

7. Irresolutions and Incompletions

Were the accounts written by Jane Gay to be taken as fully accurate representations of events on the Nez Perce Reservation, Independence Day in Lapwai in 1891 might be seen as the end of traditional celebrations of that occasion. Wishing to emphasize the emergence of a strong Christian Native leadership in this more traditional area of the reservation, Gay recounts the effects of a petition written with her aid (in the guise of the Cook) by a committee of Nez Perce Presbyterian elders determined to see the "prohibit[ion of] the old fashion" of "horse races and circling warhoop procession" at the upcoming celebration.[1] Within a week the commissioner of Indian affairs sent telegrams to officials at Lapwai, directing them to "[a]llow no racing, gambling or other immoral practices anywhere in vicinity of school," to the great consternation of both the agent and the group of Lapwai Nimiipuu who had begun to plan the celebration.[2] These angry partisans, according to Gay, blamed the missionary Kate McBeth for interrupting their plans, and "the guilty Cook escaped... the consequences of her rash deeds" (C, 361). While this account is not incorrect, it is riddled with eloquent silences.

This was the last account of a Fourth of July celebration Gay wrote and published.[3] She framed it as an ending brought about by the Presbyterian elders at Lapwai. "[A] great step has been taken in the right direction," she writes. "Hence forth there will be two parties in the tribe and a spirited fight will go on" (C, 362). At its base, the statement is false: there had been at least "two parties" — if not more — among the Nimiipuu from the advent of white missionaries and settlers, and despite an interim agreement made in 1887 to hold a "joint [Fourth of July] celebration," subsequent festivities had been held both in Kamiah and in Lapwai.[4] Moreover, at Lapwai the observances had often featured both camp meeting activities and more traditional observances. In 1891 there was indeed "no war procession." But this omission did not signal the complete triumph of Christian rectitude, nor the end of traditional activities. Rather, as Gay admits, at that celebration "a race track was marked out on the uplands and for a whole week the ponies galloped and the blankets were staked and lost and won, and just outside the school fence the camp was pitched" (C, 361).

What happened on that occasion might more correctly be read as a pause than as a conclusion. By the next year the prohibitions had been forgotten. Although Gay and Fletcher attended the 1892 celebration, neither wrote of it to any extent. Fletcher noted briefly in her field diary: "Fantastic procession / Miss Gay taken off by John McFarland who takes photographs with a stealth box."[5] Other records establish that any threat to the children at the Fort Lapwai Industrial School posed by "immoral practices," real or imaginary, seems to have evaporated, at least in part because in July 1892, according to Superintendent Edward McConville's report to the commissioner of Indian affairs, "The entire school was invited to spend the 4th of July in Lewiston, Idaho, and to assist in the exercises of the day, while the band furnished the music for the occasion. The band, followed by the school boys in uniform marching, and the girls riding, and carrying banners of the different States of the Union, made a display of which I was very proud."[6] Meanwhile, in Lapwai, "James Reuben, the leading Indian orator of America, was the principal speaker."[7] Darwin James, a Presbyterian church official visiting the area for the Board of Indian Commissioners, offers the most revealing evidence that the prim rectitude of the 1891 camp meeting was a momentary aberration. Shortly after observing the Lapwai celebration in 1892 he reported to the commissioner of Indian affairs, "The debauchery on July 4th was shocking, the Indians gave themselves up to revelry & low practices."[8] In short, in every respect the festivities in 1892 resembled those held for at least the past fifteen years. They included the war procession and they elicited the customary outraged Presbyterian response.

In another sense, Gay's account of the pivotal import of the 1891 petition and the resultant contretemps was correct: missionary and Presbyterian interests were at the heart of the problem. The concerns of Kate McBeth and Alice Fletcher, who pursued secretive and complex negotiations on behalf of Presbyterian interests, form an important — but heretofore overlooked — part of the discussions about an appropriate holiday celebration. Gay may have helped the Nez Perce elders draft their petition to the commissioner on 8 June 1891, but Fletcher's involvement spurred the Indian Office's response. Two days before the elders mailed their petition, Fletcher had sent Thomas Jefferson Morgan a personal letter about the matter. That letter is missing from the archive, but its content can be inferred from Morgan's reply of 15 June, which begins: "Your recent letters have been received and read with care and interest. I am especially obliged for the one (June 6th.) that came this morning, and have telegraphed both agent and Supt. not to allow the dances, and the latter to go on with the fence."[9] The Presbyterian elders had not mentioned dancing as part the activities they wished the commissioner to ban, nor did his telegraph of reply specifically prohibit dancing, although he may have assumed it to be covered by his general proscription of "other immoral practices." Morgan's specific mention of the detail in his letter to Fletcher suggests dancing was a matter of private discussion, among others, between the two.

The conversation between Fletcher and Morgan about how the Fourth of July would be celebrated was an incidental detail in a much more complex set of negotiations by which Fletcher eventually obtained lands for the Presbyterian mission on the grounds of the Fort Lapwai Indian School. The byzantine details of those arrangements may be summarized thus: in order to obtain lands for Presbyterian mission headquarters, a church, and missionary cottages, Fletcher supported several initiatives designed to consolidate the administrative and political power of School Superintendent Edward McConville, who was at that time competing with the agent, Warren Robbins, for control of the government schools on the reservation. Fletcher, no friend of Robbins, supported McConville's plans to build a new dormitory at Fort Lapwai, to consolidate and fence the school property, and to force Robbins to close his competing school at the agency in Spalding, just to the north. Ultimately McConville wanted to become independent of agency supervision.[10] In return, he agreed to cede twenty acres of school land at the old Fort Lapwai military reservation for a Presbyterian mission.

Underlying these negotiations was Kate McBeth's pathological fear of the "heathen" forces that seemed to her to surface at holiday celebrations, tempting her congregants to engage in recidivist behaviors. The war parade the Presbyterian elders sought to ban would have passed directly in front of her door, and the horse races would be held in the immediate vicinity, just at the south boundary of school lands, for in 1891 McBeth lived in a "root cellar" at Fort Lapwai.[11] Fletcher brokered an exchange of land that allowed the agent to relocate the parts of the celebration that could not be forbidden outright. The land swap allowed McConville to trade a plot of semi-arid grazing land on the uplands, originally a part of the federal Hay Reservation, for arable tribal lands immediately adjoining his school. Thus he could consolidate school/federal holdings and fence this additional valuable land for cultivation. At the same time, Fletcher argued, the exchange would "giv[e] the Hay reservation to the Indians," which "would be an advantage to allottees whose lines over-lap and encroach upon it."[12] Not coincidentally, the blufftop lands of the Hay Reservation became the place where the Nimiipuu who were so inclined could hold their traditional horse races, several miles away from the newly expanded school grounds and the missionary's house. Fletcher's correspondence with Washington regarding this exchange had included the personal letter of 6 June in which she had asked Morgan to ban traditional observances, including the war parade and traditional dancing.

Even as Fletcher was bargaining with McConville over the lands at Fort Lapwai for the Presbyterian mission, she was engaged in an even more secretive set of negotiations to obtain land on which a permanent home for Kate McBeth might be built. (The site of this dwelling is indicated in figure 39 as "Crawford House." Originally this home was named Thaw Cottage, for the donor whose funds allowed it to be constructed. Mazie Crawford, Kate McBeth's niece, lived with the missionary during the last years of her life.) On 15 August 1891 Jane Gay informed a correspondent that Mary Thaw had donated money to build a home for McBeth and that Fletcher was "already at work, planning how to cut the miles of red tape she knows will tie up that site. . . . [for i]f anything good is to be done here, it must be conceived and brought forth in profound secrecy, just as, in the outside world, deeds of darkness are" (C, 384–85).[13] This house was to be McBeth's alone, not to be yielded to a more important male missionary, not to be shared, and not to revert to Presbyterian control or possession during the missionary's lifetime. Fletcher and McBeth had hoped to locate all the Presbyterian mission buildings on the Langford claim, just south of the original Spalding homesite. Those lands, however, had long been claimed by Nez Perces who had farmed and developed them without interruption for the past half-century. A plot large enough to meet the church's needs could not easily be found in that location. However, a small plot could be reserved for McBeth's home, locating her in close proximity to the Spalding site.[14]

Fletcher sought to ensure that McBeth would not have undesirable (non-Presbyterian) Nez Perce neighbors. At immediate issue was James Moses, who had lived for sixteen years on properties closest to the Spalding site.[15] Unthinkably, Moses had appropriated the original Spalding home "to keep his horses in" (C, 400). A partisan of traditional interests in Lapwai, Moses was what Jane Gay called "an Agency Indian" and was one of Fletcher's most aggressive, outspoken, and successful opponents (C, 399). He had long cultivated ties with agency administrators, especially Charles Monteith, with whom he had business dealings. Figure 40 shows Moses's allotment claim, an especially lucrative one because the proposed rail line ran directly through it. It also contained "the Boom," a site along the Clearwater River long used by local Nimiipuu as a

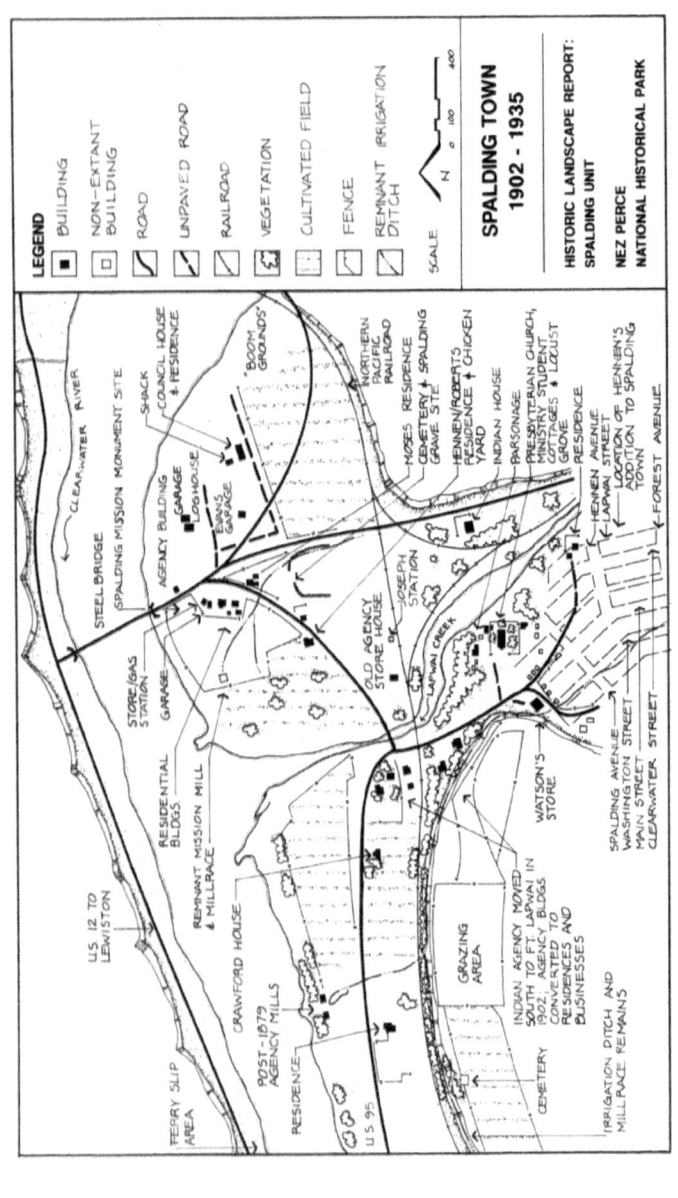

FIG. 39. "Spalding Town 1902–1935" (Gilbert, Luxenberg, and Tolon, *Historic Landscape Report: Spalding*, 60). On this map the site of Thaw Cottage is indicated as "Crawford House," just south of U.S. Highway 95. Mazie Crawford was Kate McBeth's niece and lived with the missionary during the last years of her life. Courtesy of National Park Service, Nez Perce National Historical Park.

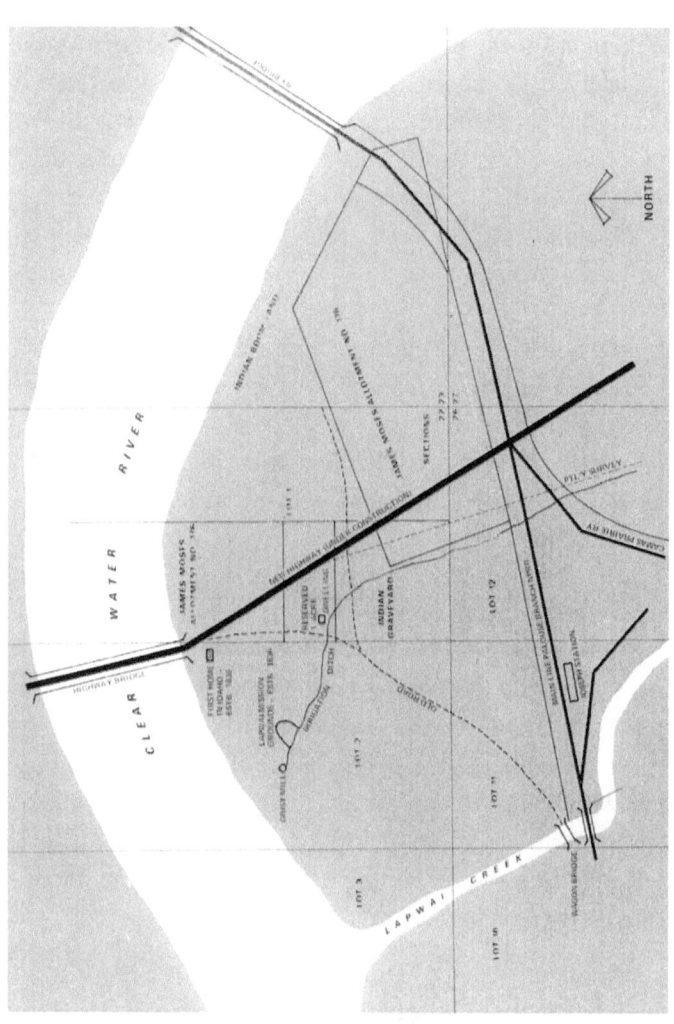

FIG. 40. Map of Spalding, Idaho, ca. 1900. From an "undated plat of Spalding" filed in the National Archives, Cartographic Branch [GPO 941-977]) and dated "ca. 1900" (Thompson, *Historic Resource Study, Spalding*, Map 7). Courtesy of National Park Service, Nez Perce National Historical Park.

commons from which they gathered driftwood logs from the Clearwater River.[16] Early in her work, probably when she arrived and began investigating the Langford claim and making initial allotments in the Lapwai area, Fletcher had become aware that this was an important site. She queried the commissioner of Indian affairs about the Boom and received a decision that it should not be allotted but should be designated as common tribal property.[17] By 1891, however, Moses had erected fences to enclose his allotment (as Fletcher wanted all her allottees to do, it should be noted), and in so doing had closed off the road leading to the Boom. Fletcher took this to be a direct challenge to her earlier directive that the site be considered tribal property.

The disposition of the Moses claim resurrected a number of earlier rivalries: between Lapwai-area Nez Perces whom Fletcher understood to be recidivists because they wished to retain their power as agency affiliates; and between Fletcher and Charles Monteith, who had lost his appointment as agent in 1889 at least partly because he lacked Fletcher's support. Moses's great threat to Fletcher was his strategic nonalignment. He was at ease with Christian and traditional Nimiipuu alike. In late June 1891, as tensions over the celebration of the Fourth of July continued to build, Fletcher wrote one of the most partisan letters of her career. The energy of the letter is proportionate to her knowledge that she was in the wrong. In it, she advised the commissioner of Indian affairs "not to grant [Moses's] allotment, which is likely to be a continual source of trouble to Indians who must get their wood at 'the boom.'" I quote at length from this letter, in which she recounted details that can only be described as vituperative and incendiary:

> James Moses during the year 1889 was the leader of the opposition to allotment. He was "Judge" in the Indian Court of Offenses. He is the leading Indian politician, a man of some ability, considerable tact, who has lived not by the labor of his hands but by his wits. He seems to have been able to ingratiate himself with Agents, secure a controlling influence and to stand between the Agent and the people. He speaks some English, is always well dressed, and has quite the air of a man of af-

fairs. He is nominally a Christian and equally a follower of the old "Tewats" or conjurers, he attends service in the morning and calls on the conjurors in the afternoon. He is thoroughly unscrupulous and is and has been a drawback to the people. It was his threats that made it impossible for me to get a man to work with the Surveyor during 1889. He threatened the life of my interpreter James Stuart and during all the season of 1889 sent messages by the Indian Police and other persons to such Indians as took allotments telling them they should suffer for their compliance. He and his followers have cost the government money in delaying my work here several months. In November 1889 he and his party defied me in open council, making statements to the people that I had forced the Kamiah Indians at the point of the pistol to take allotments and he would show me that the Lapwai Indians would not be so weak etc. I was forced to brand him publicly as a liar and when after doing all he could to move the Indians against me he failed, he came to me saying I "was hard upon him for he had to talk first on one side and then on the other." He and his clique have controlled matters with a high hand and the influence of this man is far more than that of the so called "wild Indians" of the tribe. Spl. Agent Gordon who at first thought I was severe upon James Moses, not knowing the man as I did, told me in Washington in the winter of 1889–90 that he had told the present Agent that this tribe could not advance until James Moses was deprived of position and influence at the Agency....

I have gone thus into detail because Jas. Moses represents a class of men that should not seem to be endorsed by the Government.[18]

The terms of Fletcher's condemnation of Moses mark the precise limits of her much-vaunted objectivity: she damns Moses for his facility at communicating with the various parties to the allotment debate, for his bilingual abilities, for his business acumen, for being "well dressed"—in short, for manifesting the very qualities of civilized behavior her allotment program sought to inscribe upon its Nez Perce subjects. But Moses had used skills that Fletcher would otherwise praise to delay her work and had resisted her attempts to force reluctant Nimiipuu to accept allotments. Worst, and unstated here, the lands comprising his allotment included and/or abutted the

ENDINGS

very site on which Henry Spalding's original home, mill, and mission lay, a location central to the Presbyterian version of area history.[19] It was at the point of pressuring reluctant allottees that James Moses and Alice Fletcher metaphorically faced off.

The record does not show that the two ever discussed the matter in person, but the series of increasingly venomous lawsuits, investigations, allegations, and complaints that dogged Fletcher after July 1891 stemmed from her unwise decision to challenge Moses's claim and to force a conclusion to the allotment at Lapwai. Moses responded to Fletcher's accusations in a measured and rational way: he made complaints in every possible venue. For example, the Inspection Report filed by Agent Miller on 26 December 1891 notes the "complaint of Jas Moses of his treatment by the allotting agent" and notes as well that "an injustice seems to have been done in this case."[20] Ultimately Fletcher did not succeed in denying Moses his allotment; rather, the property was divided into two pieces to maintain access to the Boom grounds for all area residents (see fig. 40).[21]

Involved in this series of complex negotiations about land (and in others of equal complexity as well), trying to finish several monographs for publication, and hoping to be personally involved in preparing displays for the World's Columbian Exposition, Fletcher was increasingly impatient with anything that threatened to keep her from finishing the allotment with maximum efficiency. She interpreted the hesitations of Lapwai-area Nimiipuu to take allotments as willful resistance that received unacceptable support from the agency and from "Agency Indians" such as Moses. Hence, in addition to her other requests of the commissioner in late June 1891, she asked that any Nez Perce who had not yet taken an allotment be prevented from leaving the reservation and be forbidden to go hunting in the late summer. The commissioner immediately telegraphed Agent Warren D. Robbins: "Allow no Indians to absent themselves from reservation to go hunting or elsewhere until they have reported to Miss Fletcher and selected their allotments."[22] Coming at almost the same time as the directives regarding forbidding traditional celebrations of the Fourth, the order was not well received and was widely flouted.

The prohibition was a serious misstep on Fletcher's part, for it amounted to her attempt to enforce compliance by starvation, since the fall hunt provided necessary food for winter survival.[23] Most Nimiipuu found it difficult to comply with Fletcher's demand for immediate action. A potential client would have to travel to find her in the field, and then wait for her to locate the land that he wished to claim, to verify the surveyed boundaries of the claim, to compare the titles, and to prepare the extensive kinship documentation Fletcher deemed to be a necessary part of the transaction. The process, by her own admission, "often require[d] a weeks sojourn, consequently a man must bring a pack horse & camp and wait, all of which takes trouble and forethought."[24] Had a large number of potential allottees decided to report for their land assignments so that they could leave for the hunt, the wait would have been even longer. In retaliation for these unpopular interferences, those at Lapwai who did not welcome the allotment involved Fletcher in a series of legal difficulties that threatened to remove her from her job and that ultimately resulted in the incarceration of one of her chainmen, Tim Ryan, who was prosecuted for selling liquor on the reservation.[25] Responding to the allegations against Ryan took Fletcher's time away from allotment work, and in early November she wrote a personal letter to Morgan to admit she would not be able to finish the allotment during the 1891 season as she had planned. She attributed the problem to "the intangible difficulties with which I have been contesting" that had "been increasing ever since your order against the war procession and horse-racing" and "your telegram . . . request[ing] that Indians should attend to their allotments before going on the hunt."[26] Fletcher carefully framed the case, neglecting to mention that these orders had not originated in Washington DC but were given in response to her direct promptings. Nor did the commissioner's telegrams amount to "requests." They were direct, terse, and unambiguous orders.

In sum, in Fletcher's plan, 1891 was to have been the year in which she completed her work in Idaho. The celebration of the Fourth of July of that year was to have exemplified the end of traditional celebrations and the beginning of occasions upon which Christian and patriotic observances would predominate. During the long season of 1891 she made every effort to force these conclusions, but because of her complex and often dissonant allegiances, not only did she fail to complete the field work, but she also created or exacerbated several allotment-related disputes that remained unresolved long after she departed. In fact, the 1891 season was characterized by irresolution and incompletion. Likely because of her conflicting allegiances, many of the projects for which Fletcher held her highest hopes did not materialize. In some cases it is difficult to determine why a promising idea suddenly dropped out of view. Key letters and other records seem to be missing, perhaps destroyed by Fletcher during 1893, when she suffered a long bout of depression, or in 1907, when she again burned much of her correspondence.[27] But this much is clear: Fletcher had left her most difficult work for last, and her ability to pursue it according to her high ideals was compromised by her conflicting obligations to the Peabody, to Mary Thaw, to the Presbyterian Church, and to the upcoming World's Columbian Exposition. She succeeded at few or none of these undertakings; many of them, despite beginnings that had seemed so promising, were never brought to completion. They remain open stories, and their irresolution makes them uncomfortable insertions into the narrative of Fletcher's work. In the balance of this chapter I trace several such entanglements that demanded Fletcher's attention during these final field seasons, showing how their pursuit impacted the project of allotment and how their completion depended on support from Nimiipuu workers, informants, and collaborators whose resistance may very well have short-circuited their realization.

Unseen Displays: Nimiipuu at the World's Columbian Exposition

During the 1891 field season Alice Fletcher devoted a great deal of time to thinking about two of the major institutional displays featuring Native subjects at the upcoming World's Columbian Exposition in Chicago. Commissioner Morgan had invited her to help plan the exhibit sponsored by the Bureau of Indian Affairs, and she expected to serve F. W. Putnam, who headed the exposition's Department of Ethnology and Archaeology, in a similar advisory role.

Based on her experience at the World's Industrial and Centennial Cotton Exposition in 1885, Fletcher could reasonably have expected to take a major role in planning and executing both displays and to place her Nez Perce accomplishments at the center of those exhibits, as she had with the Omahas in New Orleans a decade earlier. Like that earlier exhibit, a World's Columbian Exposition display might show a transformation from savagery to civilization, this time effected by the Dawes General Allotment Act. Despite Fletcher's plans and preparations, this did not happen.

Nor, in hindsight, should it be surprising that Fletcher's participation in either display was minimal, for neither was calculated to match her accomplishments. Although Commissioner Morgan invited her to take the lead in planning the government exhibit, she was seeking to disengage herself from federal responsibilities so she could assume her academic post. For his part, F. W. Putnam disappointed her by naming Franz Boas as his chief assistant. Although Putnam was a great supporter of women in anthropological study, he had complex motives in making this decision. Boas's research was scientific, quantitative, and cutting-edge, and the scope of his comparative vision was global. Fletcher's work, by contrast, had necessarily been personal, interpretative, and based in local USAmerican cultures. Moreover, the aging Putnam was likely thinking about who would carry on his work following the exposition, which Boas did, taking charge of the anthropological collections exhibited at the fair that then formed the basis of Chicago's new Field Museum.

Native cultures were exhibited at the 1893 Chicago world's fair in multiple and contradictory ways, but they conformed to the general progressive theme of the occasion, one that derived from an artificial but most generative declaration of closure.[28] The theme was most clearly articulated in Frederick Jackson Turner's address to the American Historical Association's gathering in Chicago in 1893. Turner began his paper, "The Significance of the Frontier in American History," by noting that, according to the 1890 federal census, a "frontier line" no longer existed. "This brief official statement," according to Turner, "mark[ed] the *closing* of a great historic movement."[29] The means by which that closure had been accomplished

[237]

were demonstrated in exhibits such as Buffalo Bill Cody's Wild West Show, the most sensational and profitable enterprise of the entire fair, although not an official part of the event. Located just outside the fairgrounds, Cody's performers presented daily reenactments of battles of the recent Plains Indian wars. Publicity brochures for the shows emphasized that the sham battles featured many of the original combatants, who "repeat[ed] the heroic parts that they [had] played in actual life."[30] Visitors to the entertainment zone, the Midway Plaisance, could view Sitting Bull's cabin, which, in the words of a souvenir program, had been transported to Chicago "[l]og by log and piece by piece" and "restored exactly as it stood in December, 1890, when the soldiers broke in and killed the celebrated plotter of the Messiah conspiracy and eternal foe of the Caucasian."[31] The Midway also displayed habitat groups from "Java, the South Sea Islands, Dahomey, the Soudan, Lapland, Arabia, Turkey and Algeria" to exemplify the customs of cultures understood to be exotic and backward.[32] Yet, as recent scholars have pointed out, the residents of these displays retained a seemly control over an exploitative situation and observed the crowds on the Midway with as much insight as they were observed.[33]

Within the fair proper, exhibits of Native cultures differed in size, intent, and sponsorship. Individual collectors and dealers displayed and sold Indian artifacts. State-sponsored exhibits often included items of Native manufacture, as did the Idaho building, which featured "needlework by the ladies of Albion, St. Charles, Soda Springs, and Fort Lapwai."[34] The several displays featuring Carlisle Indian School masked a significant disagreement among those who saw themselves as responsible for Indian civilizing efforts. Captain Richard Henry Pratt was determined to demonstrate the success of his eastern boarding school's programs at "break[ing] down tribal cohesion" while dissociating the school from both ethnological study and federally sponsored reform.[35] He vehemently objected to Commissioner Morgan's proposal that the Carlisle brass band march in the fair's opening procession in May 1893. Morgan had suggested the parade be "headed by 20 or more Indians, mounted, dressed in their native costumes of blankets, leggins, feathers, paint, moccasins, etc." as a way of "represent[ing] the inhabitants of America when Columbus discovered it." The Carlisle brass band would follow, "with their instruments and uniforms and completely civilized appearance," thus presenting a "contrast [that] would be striking and noteworthy." Trennert observes, "Nothing could have been better calculated to anger Pratt than to force his students to follow a group of 'savages.'" Refusing Morgan's suggestion, Pratt instead arranged for the Carlisle band to march in the October 1892 Columbus Day parade, seven months prior to the official opening of the fair. "Divided into ten divisions, each representing a craft taught at the school, the marching battalions and band received considerable praise."[36] Moreover, rather than participate in the model Indian school exhibit Morgan had planned, Pratt exhibited samples of his students' school work in the Liberal Arts Building.

The narrative of progressivism and the closed frontier structured the displays of the three major exhibitors of Native culture. Two of these came under federal sponsorship. The first, headed by Major John Wesley Powell, featured items from the collections of the Smithsonian Institution, the Bureau of Ethnology, and the United States National Museum; the display's contributions were summarized on a "linguistic map of North American Indian tribes" that highlighted the exhibit.[37] For the second federal exhibit, under Morgan's direction, Fletcher had suggested an elaborate comparative display, resembling, unsurprisingly, what she had put forward in New Orleans, "each section [of which was] to be devoted to an exhibit of the products of Indian labor, farming or other avocations, contrasted with specimens of primitive native work; these exhibits to be limited to articles (past and present) which are characteristic of the geographical peculiarities of that portion of our country which the section illustrates."[38] Morgan narrowed the focus of the exhibit to education, an enterprise he had made central to his administration. The Bureau of Indian Affairs offered a model Indian school occupied by different groups of Native students drawn from various federally sponsored reservation programs. The school was meant to show that federal educational programs under Morgan's direction were successfully imbuing the wards of the nation with the skills and behaviors consonant with advanced civilization.

The third, largest, and most notable display featuring Native cultural items was that of the Department of Ethnology (Department M), directed by F. W. Putnam, assisted by Franz Boas. The department's exhibits comprised ethnology, archaeology, history, cartography, the Latin American Bureau, and related disciplines in what Putnam had planned as an "open" exhibit.[39] That is, rather than draw the items to be displayed from the Peabody's collections, Putnam invited contributions from "every state board, and many historical and scientific societies, as well as owners of private collections," blending them—not entirely successfully—to construct a narrative "of the present status of American archaeology and ethnology."[40] Many of these contributions were later absorbed into the Peabody's collections. Thus Department M exhibits focused not on the present but on Native cultures as they had been "before they were influenced by the whites." Putnam solicited exhibits aimed to "show native industries entirely unaffected by our civilization."[41] Visitors to Department M could view several Native habitat groups "along the banks of South Pond" near the exhibit building.[42] They included Natives from British Columbia and participants representing the Iroquois, "Eskimo, Cree, Chippewayan, Winnebago, Navajo, and the Arawak of British Guiana"—but not the Nez Perces.[43] Such habitat groups claimed to present "a living picture of the typical native peoples of different parts of America; each family to be living in its native habitation; the people to be dressed in native costume, surrounded by characteristic household utensils, implements and weapons and engaged in their native occupations and manufactures."[44] The crowded Department of Anthropology building held Boas's laboratory of physical anthropology, wherein were displayed "charts and tables illustrating the physical characteristics of the native peoples of America" derived "[f]rom the data . . . obtained" from "thousands of measurements and special observations . . . taken of members of various tribes."[45] Thousands of smaller exhibits were furnished by individual and institutional collectors, both amateur and professional.[46] Here a small collection of Nez Perce foodstuffs and tools assembled by James Stuart was likely exhibited, possibly by Alice Fletcher, who was listed as an individual exhibitor in the *Official Catalogue*.[47] Alternatively that display may have been arranged by the Peabody Museum, which garnered an award for its "Eth. Coll. from Nez Percé Indians."[48]

Fletcher unsuccessfully attempted to mediate the philosophical disagreements of Morgan and Putnam and to find a place where her contributions might be taken seriously. Initially both men intended to involve her in their plans. In January 1892 Morgan had appointed Fletcher as his "Confidential Clerk . . . to assist [him] in preparing the Indian Exhibit at the World's Columbian Exposition."[49] On 4 January 1892 Fletcher wrote in her diary, "On Feb. 1 to take position at $1000 & be detailed for Chicago . . . [at a reimbursement of] $3 per day when about & handling expenses." Although the written record is incomplete, it seems likely that a combination of factors prevented her involvement in planning and overseeing either institution's display. The most significant of these factors was Morgan's disdain for "both . . . ethnology and ethnologists," whom he considered to be "the most insidious and active enemies" of federal educational policies.[50] While Fletcher clearly did not share Morgan's attitude, he was nevertheless her immediate supervisor, and until she could assume her endowed chair at Harvard, he represented her financial security.

Initially Morgan and Putnam held a two-day meeting, attended by Fletcher. Here they agreed to follow in both their exhibits a teleological arrangement based on current evolutionary anthropological theories. Such an arrangement necessarily also flattered Thomas Jefferson Morgan as the agent of progressive reform. Morgan stipulated that all Native North Americans exhibited by Putnam would be "the Indian Office Indians but they belong to the scientific exhibit," and that the arrangement of the exhibits should "put forth the school in its best light." Putnam agreed: "That could be very easily done by the arrangement of the grounds. We should start with the further end of the grounds with Tierra Del Fuegoans, and work up to the school, and right where the Indians of the United States come in, just at the culmination of that group, you would have your

[241]

school-house."⁵¹ Notably, Morgan wished to present a school rather than a farm as the apex of Indian civilization. The distinction suggests he recognized that the tactic of promoting agrarianism as allotment's centerpiece was losing force. The "[crisis] of expectation" within agrarianism plagued the sponsors of the Columbian Exposition as a whole, as Philip J. Deloria has noted. He writes that the fair attempted to mediate "anxieties [such as those] surrounding the impending failure of the agrarian ideal, as the western ranch economy went corporate and farmers joined the Populist Party to protest their losing position in the national economy" (*IUP*, 61). To have promoted allotment's commitment to the 160-acre family farm within such a context would have been a misrepresentation of which even the Indian Office seems to have been incapable.

The minutes of the discussions between Putnam and Morgan record very little participation by Fletcher. Following the second meeting, she wrote in her diary, "Decide[d] not to take appointment of comm. / Prof Putnam to see if he can pay me $50 per mo / very tired / nervous chill at night."⁵² Most of the details of her subsequent unsuccessful negotiations with the two men are missing. For weeks during the early spring of 1892, as Morgan, Putnam, and Boas actively planned their exhibits, Fletcher lay confined to her sickbed. Morgan found Congress to be adamantly resistant to funding his school exhibit and had to content himself with a much less elaborate display than he had imagined. From her sickroom Fletcher sporadically but unsuccessfully tried to interest Putnam in sending her to the Southwest to collect items for the fair. But time passed, and Fletcher still needed to complete the allotment, and thus she was not included in the plans of either Putnam or Morgan.

By mid-April 1892 she had left for Idaho to conclude the allotment. Over the months that followed she sat in ad hoc legal disputes in Idaho courtrooms, camped in the field, and worked intensively to complete her series of monographs on Omaha culture for the *Century*. After she left Idaho in mid-September she did not take a layover in Chicago, where the fair was about to open, although the city was a major stop on her route to Washington. During the winter months of 1892–93, when she might have been in Chicago busily involved in overseeing the construction and staffing of the (now more modest) model school or arranging the displays of Department M, she languished in bed in her new home in Washington DC, suffering a severe illness brought on by exhaustion and nervousness. Much of her diary for the entire year of 1893 is blank, offering little clue about how she extricated herself—or was extricated—from the business of displaying Indians at the World's Columbian Exposition.

Surely Fletcher's contradictory allegiances limited the degree to which Nez Perces might have been represented at the fair. The federally sponsored schools at the Nez Perce Reservation could in no way be considered to represent the ideals of Indian education for Morgan's exhibit, since the feud between the agent and the superintendent over who would administer the schools at Lapwai and Spalding had been exacerbated by Fletcher's partisanship. Nor did Putnam's focus on pre-contact culture match Fletcher's commitments to inculcating civilized behaviors among her allottees. Nez Perces had interacted closely with multiple cultural groups for more than a century, and evidences of their aboriginal purity were scarce. The progressive narratives structuring both men's exhibits were premised on closure: the purpose of Morgan's curriculum was to erase traditional culture, and Putnam wished only to show an imaginary moment of cultural purity that had predated white contact. Neither imagined the possibility of Native survivance. Neither wished to recognize that Native peoples had embraced modern behaviors and technologies without denying their cultural past. It is possible—even likely—that Nimiipuu informants and cultural producers chose not to participate in the fair's master story of inevitable white conquest and the closure of the frontier, for their lives continued beyond that artificial ending and they lived now with the consequences of that narrative. This alternative explanation provides a suggestive perspective on Fletcher's efforts to organize displays of Nez Perce culture for the exposition.

Although she ultimately was not involved in executing the Indian Office's model school or in the exhibits of Department M, Fletcher did spend a good deal of time between October 1890 and December 1891 thinking about how she might include Nez Perces in the fair. She pursued a number of possibilities but was able to complete none of them. She and Putnam discussed exhibiting Billy Williams's map, a plan that seems not to have materialized.[53] She considered taking one or more Nez Perces with her to Chicago. She and Susan McBeth had, in fact, planned that Robert Williams would accompany Fletcher.[54] In December 1891 McBeth placed an order for a dozen photos of Williams, remarking "I will doubtless need . . . many more."[55] Perhaps she anticipated that Williams would sell these images of himself at the fair, as did Geronimo and other Natives who became involved in similar enterprises. The next month McBeth warned her sister Kate not to discuss the possibility of Williams's going to Chicago, for "if they [his enemies in the Second Presbyterian Church] know of his being chosen by for the Exposition it will make them work the harder to kill him — i.e. get him out of the way faster."[56] Yet Robert Williams remained in Kamiah.

Fletcher also hoped to prepare a study of Nez Perce music, to be written in collaboration with John Comfort Fillmore, who, funded by the Peabody or by Mary Thaw, was to come to Idaho "in August [1892] . . . to take down Nez Perce music for a week or so with phonograph."[57] Yet Fillmore stayed away. In late July 1892 Fletcher wrote to Putnam: "[A]s to Prof. Fillmore, no word yet as to funds and the time is at hand when he could do field work. The weather is so intensely hot that I fear he could not endure the climate." Since the Nimiipuu were preparing to depart to the mountains for their annual hunt, she admitted she could not pursue the project.[58]

As part of his contribution to the fair, Franz Boas planned to edit a *Handbook of Native American Mythology* and invited Fletcher to contribute a chapter on Nez Perce myths.[59] Despite Putnam's advice not to hurry to comply with Boas's invitation, she continued to think about the possibility of such a collection, for she had been gathering Nez Perce oral narratives from the first moments of her arrival in Idaho.[60] Yet she apparently did not send them to Boas. Moreover, Boas seems to have abandoned the project, likely because he found himself deluged with his official responsibilities to Department M. Fletcher explored other avenues for the project, telling Putnam that "James Reuben (a full blood Nez Perce) is writing out the myths of the Nez Perce, and wants to have the volume published & sell it at Chicago in the Exposition. What steps should he take, or can I take for him? I think James R. will make a readable book."[61] These brief sentences, the sole mention of Reubens's potential project, suggest several possibilities. Perhaps Fletcher had tried to assign to Reubens the task of preparing Nez Perce stories for Boas, a tactic she had often used in her relationship with Francis La Flesche, who was central to much of Fletcher's work on the Omahas.[62] Or Fletcher and Reubens may have intended to collaborate, seeing such a collection as an extension of their conversations in 1889 about Nimiipuu stories and planning to market it as a supplement to the other Nez Perce materials Fletcher hoped to send to Chicago. It is equally likely, however, that Reubens refused to collaborate, seeing the project as a work better pursued independently of Boas and Fletcher, one that could be published under his own name and for his own profit. The details are unclear, although each case seems plausible. Reubens did not complete the collection. Fletcher, however, eventually did draft a full monograph about Nimiipuu origin tales and stories. In the study she does not mention James Reubens, although Celia Reubens, his mother, was one of Fletcher's primary informants and although Fletcher surely drew upon information James Reubens had given her. The resulting monograph, "Ethnologic Gleanings among the Nez Perces," remained unpublished in Fletcher's lifetime.[63]

Thus Nez Perces took a very small part in the elaborate displays of Native cultures within the World's Columbian Exposition. The fair featured full-size models of cliff dwellings, longhouses, earth lodges, and tipis; habitat groups in which people performed daily domestic and ceremonial activities; and massive collections of artifacts arranged to signify the progress of Native cultures from savagery through barbarism and into civilization. Fletcher had neither the time nor the resources to arrange for a group of Nez Perces to inhabit a full scale longhouse on the fairgrounds, even had she been able to locate Nimiipuu willing to participate in such a display. Her contributions were comparatively modest.

[245]

In 1891, before it became apparent she would not be a part of Putnam's team, Fletcher promised him she would obtain "the old long mat house" from the Nez Perces for him to exhibit at the fair.[64] Putnam's response to her signals that even at this relatively early date, he had the outlines of his exhibit clearly in mind, and he wished to warn Fletcher that although he welcomed her help, he did not intend to let her control what he would do. He replied with a detailed list of items she might try to collect, including "a complete outfit . . . a dwelling . . . such as the people lived in before contact with the whites; and all the utensils belonging to the house, as well as the implements, weapons, ornaments and dress of the people." However, he added, "If I cannot get a dwelling of full size . . . I would like to have a large model made, if you can find any Indian to do it. . . . Would not Miss Gay take this matter in hand as a special work and relieve you of all thought of the matter?"[65] Putnam seems to have had a clearer sense of what it would be possible for Fletcher to furnish than did the anthropologist herself. Eventually she did assign Jane Gay and/or a group of Nez Perces under the supervision of James Stuart to construct a model of a longhouse.[66] Fletcher hoped Stuart would also furnish for the exhibit "a model of an *alsoetas*, the place where the young unmarried women stayed during the winter camps."[67] She seems to have encountered some difficulty obtaining from the Nez Perces "a complete outfit" of the kind Putnam had requested. It is hard to discern precisely why, for Fletcher was never entirely forthcoming about any direct resistance she encountered. In this case she attributed the shortfall between what she had promised and what she furnished to the fact that her potential informants could not be trusted to meet deadlines nor to understand the full importance of the exhibit. Ultimately what Fletcher displayed at the fair was minimal. Boas's anthropometric exhibits included the "90 odd measurements" Gay and Stuart had made of local boarding school students.[68] Fletcher contributed items she had received as personal gifts in connection with the ethnographic interviews she conducted as she made allotments. For example, the display included the pestle and basket she had obtained from Ou-na-ne-we-nan-ny (Celia Reubens). Yet it should be noted that a fuller display of Nez Perce

FIG. 41. "Nez Perce Wallets etc. Henry Fair, Lewiston, Idaho." Courtesy of the Peabody Museum of Archaeology and Ethnology, Harvard University, 2004.29.6395.2, Digital file #98820034.

cultural production was well within the realm of possibility, as a photograph of a private collection of Nez Perce baskets, cradleboards, bags, weaving, and beadwork from the period suggests. Figure 41 shows the collection of Henry Fair, who worked in Lewiston, Idaho, "from about 1899 to 1910," according to Richard Storch. Fair had an "Art Store" in Lewiston that marketed "Photographic Supplies, Picture Frames, Artists' Materials, Nez Perce Indian Curios, Lewiston Views and Indian Photos."[69]

Just before leaving the reservation at the conclusion of her field work in 1892, Fletcher reported to Putnam: "The Exhibit, of a model of the old-time house, the foods of the people, roots . . . , dried fish, dried meats, weapons, . . . and costumes is in the hands of James Stuart. Many of the articles are ready, made by the Indians and he will work hard to have everything ready in the early winter. As soon as it is ready he will ship it to Chicago. I should be glad if he could go on & set it up."[70] Two days later she wrote to the commissioner of Indian affairs, "The Surveyor has left. I retain James Stuart until the 23 instant to obtain certain information & send it to me. Rather than take two long journeys myself & so delay my departure & *final completion* of my work."[71] The phrase I have emphasized marks Fletcher's realization that any terminus to her work was not yet within sight, but more to the point for this discussion, her careful phrasing ("certain information") suggests that she wished to keep Stuart on her payroll until he could oversee the final details of shipping to Chicago the items he had gathered. Later, to Putnam, Fletcher revealed a doubt about what might actually be sent, writing on 3 October 1892, "I hope that the Nez Perce Indians will not fail me."[72]

Stuart did send to Putnam most of the items Fletcher had listed, but he did not go to Chicago "to set it up." In fact, as far as I can reliably determine, no Nez Perces attended the fair as Fletcher's guests or as exhibitors under her sponsorship.[73] Yet these unrealized and incomplete plans should not be construed to suggest the Nez Perces had "failed" Fletcher in any sense of the word. Rather, the reticence, partial responses, or outright refusal of those who might have been involved with the enterprise seem only wise and logical. Had any Nez Perce informants been chosen to go to Chicago, whether to live in the model dwelling, to sell goods and merchandise, or to exemplify Christian rectitude, they would have been poorly paid for their time or, more likely, asked to participate at their own expense. Moreover, choosing participants to attend the exposition would have precipitated no end of furor at home. Had Robert Williams accompanied Fletcher to the fair, members of the Kamiah Second Presbyterian Church, as well as non-Presbyterian Nimiipuu, would correctly have understood it to be another instance of Fletcher's alliance with the McBeth sisters. So rather than a full-scale representation of pre-contact culture, the Nez Perce display in Department M was minimal: foodstuffs (camas bread, berry cakes, and dried elk meat) and basic implements (a pestle, an elk horn wedge, arrows, and a stone knife). A model of the longhouse was also likely exhibited; I have been unable to determine who made it, how large it was, or in what context it might have been shown. Yet upon reflection, the exhibit was rife with significance, for the foods (*not* the product of agrarian methods) and implements were intimately related to the place of their origin and still centrally important to Nimiipuu claims to political and cultural sovereignty.

The modest size and place-based emphasis of Fletcher's exhibit might in fact signal that the Nez Perces retained a strict control over the circumstances of their own representation. Knowing that items they would contribute to an exhibit would subsequently be diverted directly into the collections of the Peabody, as were the foodstuffs, models, and implements gathered by James Stuart and exhibited under Alice Fletcher's name, they may have refused to furnish irreplaceable cultural items. Already aware of the voracious and irresponsible methods of white merchants and collectors, Nimiipuu craftspersons surely also realized that any objective representation of the aesthetic, religious, or cultural significance of a piece of work would be impossible to achieve within the cluttered and disorderly mass of items displayed in the buildings, shelves, vitrines, and cabinets of Department M. That is to say, Putnam's exhibits, although thorough, were not subtle, and had no room for nuanced explanations of the complex cultural significance of these items.

Comparing the list of items exhibited in Fletcher's name with other displays of Indian culture furnished forth for the consumption, titillation, entertainment, and satisfaction of those visiting Chicago suggests that James Stuart furnished to her only a minimum number of items to satisfy her acquisitional instincts. No life groups of Nez Perces performed savagery for fairground visitors; no Nez Perce students from the Fort Lapwai Industrial School brass band marched in the parades or pretended to study in Morgan's model school; no wax mannequins dressed as primitive Nez Perces in buckskins and beads wielded the hide scraper and pestle to represent "Women's Work in Savagery." According to Fletcher's handwritten inventory, a single item of regalia was exhibited, a "Warrior headdress." Like the war parade that had preceded Fletcher's 1891 intervention and that has been a major part of Fourth of July celebrations since, it held varying meanings to those who viewed it. To those intent on seeing it as a relic of savagery now denatured by Joseph's promise to "fight no more, forever," it signified conquest. To those who may just have come from viewing the Wild West sham battle across the street, it may have been a reminder of the bravery of white settlers in conquering the Pacific Northwest. But to Stuart, to the maker, and to the Nimiipuu who rode in the war processions, it told a different story. Fletcher's handwritten draft of the shelf list of her display indicates that Stuart told her of this item: "The white beads represent hail, which comes to . . . scatter the surrounding enemy—the blue sky after the storm is represented by the blue bead."[74] To the Nimiipuu, engaged in a current struggle—less bloody, perhaps, but no less violent—for possession of their land and their stories, the battle remained open and inconclusive, although Alice C. Fletcher, a major leader of the aggression, had recently departed the field.

8. The Ends of Nez Perce Allotment

The complexity of such deceptively simple terms as *end* and *allotment* becomes apparent as one seeks to establish the event or events that might be taken as the conclusion of Fletcher's work. Endings, a convention of storytelling, are not always apparent within the mass of records related to a given event or policy. Such was surely the case with allotment. As early as June 1891, anxious to conclude her duties as allotting agent so she might devote her full energies to anthropological research, Fletcher had begun to anticipate her work's end, writing to Morgan that she had "allotted nearly all of the better class" of Nez Perces.[1] Consequently she took much less care to ensure that those whom she did not deem to be of "the better class" would receive the lands they had requested. For example, several months later Fletcher wrote Morgan, "There is one man who wishes land run out for his young son and an old Aunt ... that will require over one week's worth of the surveying party. The land is worthless except for grazing.... The labor and cost of running out these two allotments seems to me too great to be undertaken." Not incidentally, the land was being requested by "KipKapalikan, formerly one of the Judges and living at Kamiah," a man who had caused Fletcher several petty annoyances earlier in the allotment, largely because he had been an associate of Charles Monteith.[2]

In June 1891, of course, Fletcher could not have foreseen the difficulty she would encounter in the season ahead. Six months later she and Gay celebrated Thanksgiving with Kate McBeth rather than with their friends in Washington DC, but even though she remained at Fort Lapwai into the winter months Fletcher could not close the work. She returned to Idaho in early May 1892. Even then she encountered such serious delays that a white man, John C. Beelle, complained that the "work [had] been in progress for the last 4 years and to all present appearances it is liable to continue for the next 4 years."[3] Fletcher could not ignore the increasing discontent. In mid-August she admitted in a letter to Morgan, "[T]the allotment here *should have closed* early in July, and but for unforeseen difficulties . . . I should have been free before the close of July."[4] In a second letter written that same day she detailed a number of the "difficulties" holding her in place. They included "errors and complications caused by the old survey," the refusal of allottees to remain on the lands they had been assigned, and "the persecution of my best field hand Timothy Ryan, whom the agent has arrested upon false evidence for selling or giving liquor to Indians."[5] These were the "difficulties" she publicly admitted; undoubtedly others plagued her as well. "[E]ven the Indians complain and are becoming restless under this unnecessary delay," Beelle asserted. "I have talked with competent engineers . . . invariably they say that they would not ask for more than 2 years to have completed this work." Beelle's most damning sentences, however, were those concluding his letter: "We charge the parties in charge of said allotment dilatory and unnecessary delay of said work and we believe in misappropriation of funds and labor in rebuilding repairing the Kamia Indian Church, and that at a time when the men should have been in the field on alotment work. I do not [say] this because a lady is in charge of this work. From my youth up I have always been what is called a woman's rights man in addition all Indians who know me know me as their friend."[6]

Beelle spoke for many others. Even the Indian Office, shielded by distance and bureaucratic obfuscation from the local clamor, grew impatient. In late July 1892 Morgan sent the briefest of official letters to Fletcher, copying the secretary of the interior: "Madam: I desire your opinion as to whether it is desirable to commence negotiations now with the Nez Perce Indians for the cession of their surplus lands, and if not, at what time you think such negotiations might be undertaken, and your reasons for your opinion."[7] If the terse query were not a direct enough signal that even her close friend felt allotment should be concluded, Fletcher then learned that funding would cease as of 1 September and thus "all field work must close" by that date.[8]

The close of field work was less an ending than a beginning. "[N]egotiations" for the "surplus lands" commenced when Fletcher answered Morgan's query in these words: "It is my opinion that negotiations had better begin as soon as possible. The more intelligent portion of the tribe know that cession is inevitable, and while many of the tribe are absent from the reservation during the Fall, still a delay until the spring would be detrimental to the best interests of the tribe. The sooner these Indians are merged into the people of the State the better it will be for them."[9] Not only did the reply lend Fletcher's endorsement to federal impatience, it also resuscitated the timeworn tactic of taking the opinion of the most tractable members of the body politic ("[t]he more intelligent portion of the tribe") to be the opinion of the whole. In this case those most likely to oppose the speedy sale of land would be conveniently absent from the area for most of the fall hunting season, and negotiations could be well under way before they returned.

Once Fletcher understood that her funding would cease, she began to adopt extreme measures. She solved the problem of dealing with allottees who refused to claim their lands by assigning them properties without consulting them, simply matching their names with unclaimed plots. She had anticipated using this procedure as early as the previous September, when she had warned Morgan, "If this work is to be closed, it will become imperative that I allot those persons who will not attend to business, and show the location of the allotments to some Indian who will note the same and show the land to the allottee when he will take sufficient interest to make the trip."[10] This method approximates the procedure many people had expected Fletcher to use to accomplish allotment in the first place, since she could as easily have matched individual Nez Perces with plots of land without consulting their will in the matter. Her early insistence on showing allottees their corners resulted from her idealism, her wish to be fair, and her propensity to overachieve and micromanage. In her final letter to the commissioner from the field she indicates that in her final weeks on the reservation, she may have done even less, for she does not report showing corners to all allottees, nor even to their surrogates. She wrote: "I have taken every means in my power to secure every rightful claimant & to have every allottee see his corners. This has often been impossible owing to personal disinclination on the part of the allottee."[11] That is to say, she had matched each name on her census list to a blank plot on her map. These hasty measures suggest that closure is a mutable concept. Fletcher needed to be finished. It is at least debatable whether those who had not consulted with her about allotments, who had had their lands "thrust upon [them] *nolens volens*," to use Gay's apt words (C, 122), or who had never agreed to take allotments at all might have agreed that the process was at an end.

Thus on 13 September 1892 Fletcher claimed she had completed the field work related to allotment.[12] By her own judgment, nothing remained for her to do that she could not attend to from her office in Washington DC, even continuing to assign names to plots without consulting the allottees. But the exact point at which everyone who was entitled to an allotment on the reservation had received land — that is, a definitive end to the field work of allotment — remained maddeningly elusive. As Fletcher departed Idaho, she lacked the surveyor's field notes that would verify the locations of the last 209 allotments she had made.[13] Six months later the number of unverified assignments had increased to 250, many of them involving Catholics who lived in the Lapwai area, who were "not yet scheduled" because Fletcher was awaiting plats and Briggs's completed field notes.[14] Two years later J. A. Stephan, director of the Bureau of Catholic Indian Missions, penned a formal protest to President Grover Cleveland, claiming that "on account of their religion . . . alone . . . 200 Nez Perce Indians . . . have received no allotments of land and no provision has been made for lands for them." (Whether this number were in addition to the 250 that Fletcher acknowledged is unclear.) Stephan attributed this omission to "a disposition to punish certain members of the tribe for presuming to exercise the right of religious freedom." The most damning evidence he cited to support his claim of religious favoritism came from the 1891 *Annual Report of the Board of Indian Commissioners*, which he quoted at length and which contained the following charge: "Miss Alice Fletcher ... has been instrumental in securing valuable allotments of land for two or three of the most important [Presbyterian] churches and is still using her influence for the permanent establishment of the Lapwai Church in a more available situation."[15] These were the words of the very Presbyterians whose best interests Fletcher had served, and their transplant from the bureaucratic surround of the *Annual Report* into a letter written by a Catholic official alleging favoritism highlights the partisan nature of a procedure that Fletcher had taken great care to characterize as fair and objective.

Even after reservation lands had been put up for sale in November 1895, allegations of incomplete work persisted. On 11 December of that year, Its-ah-ha-yam (known as Captain Pierce), a member of the Joseph band, presented affidavits in support of his request for an allotment on the Nez Perce Reservation, which Commissioner of Indian Affairs D. M. Browning forwarded to the secretary of the interior for his decision.[16] As late as 1898 errors, modifications, and exceptions to the allotment were still a matter of official record. In his report to the commissioner, Agent S. G. Fisher noted that of the "1,997 trust patents sent to these people, over 100 ... have since been canceled." Some were duplicate allotments; others were erroneous. He continued, "Owing to the strong opposition of about one-third of the tribe to accept land in severalty, and *their refusal to give the allotting agent the number and names of their families*, much confusion and unavoidable mistakes were made during allotment which has since required hundreds of investigations and affidavits to adjust, quite a large number of which are yet unsettled. Some eighty-odd allotments have been made here since the allotting agent left the field, and there are a dozen or more applicants whose cases are still pending."[17] Apparently as a follow-up to this report, on 29 December 1899 Agent C. T. Stranahan sent a list of eleven unallotted claimants to the commissioner.[18] As these cases and others suggest, the end of allotment was largely a legal fiction. While lands had been assigned and lands had been claimed, bought, leased, and sold, a number of Nimiipuu had managed to elude the reaches of this law and remained apart from the structures of civilization, individuation, and enfranchisement that allotment sought to effect.

Other markers of the putative end of allotment were equally vague. As should be clear from the mass of paperwork that occupied Fletcher's attention long after she departed Idaho, allotment comprised far more than field work. She remained on the federal payroll as an allotting agent for some time after September 1892, returning to an office in Washington DC, where she transferred information from her field notes to official registers and plats and compiled her final report. Over the next decade and beyond she fielded queries and appeals from Nez Perce clients who wrote directly to her, whose concerns were forwarded to her by Kate McBeth, or who wrote directly to the commissioner of Indian affairs. On the reservation the survey lines Fletcher had labored to readjust were subjected to independent verification, especially in border areas where white settlers stood to gain property should Briggs's resurvey prove to be incorrect. The borders of the Nez Perce Reservation and the boundaries of individual allotments continued to be corrected well into the twentieth century. In his follow-up evaluation of Fletcher's work, Inspector William W. Junkin concluded, "Miss Fletcher's allotments were very unsatisfactory; could not find an Indian who had a certificate of his allotment" although, according to Junkin, Fletcher "thinks she has, no doubt, done her work faithfully."[19] Even had these necessary records—the surveys and surveyor's field notes, Fletcher's kinship records, deeds, and plats—been absolutely complete, their legal efficacy awaited the final approval of the Department of the Interior and, ultimately, of the Congress.

From its inception, allotment and its allied legal apparatuses were under continual revision, a process that began before Fletcher had completed her first field season and continued well beyond the 1934 Indian Rights Act, which repudiated the policies and results of allotment. Even before Fletcher's final field season, various Nimiipuu delegates had begun to visit Washington DC to bring their concerns before a greater power, one they hoped would be less partisan than Fletcher, and to press for modifications to the Dawes Act.[20] One such delegation of four Nimiipuu delivered a formal protest "to the cession of surplus lands" then under discussion with Commissioners Robert Schleicher, James F. Allen, and Cyrus Beede. It is highly likely that some or all of these Nimiipuu men had been absent from the reservation on the winter hunt when the end of allotment was announced. Even before George Moses, William Wheeler, Utsin Mellikin, and Kip Kip Pellicin had arrived in the capital, the three white commissioners wrote to warn the Indian Office that the delegation would try to present themselves as "speak[ing] for the whole tribe, regardless of the wishes of the majority."[21] Moreover, several Nez Perces who had supported the land sale, including Archie Lawyer, James Reubens, and Edward Conner, sent a telegram charging that the four "represent[ed] the non-progressive minority of our tribe."[22] I mention these details to emphasize the irony inherent in the negotiations: when it served the interests of the federal government, the opinion of a part of the tribe could stand for the whole, but when the matter at hand was not favorable to federal interests, a strict numerical plurality was invoked.

As I have established, allotment comprised not just the division and assignment of land but also a set of behavioral and legal provisions—technologies of citizenship—designed to further the assimilation of Native subjects. These processes—most especially the so-called probationary period wherein allottees could not alienate their land holdings—were being dismantled or strategically forgotten even before the winter snows of 1893 covered Fletcher's departing footprints. Although allottees could not yet sell their lands, they were permitted almost immediately to lease them. The cabals of white entrepreneurs who sought these leases, sometimes partnered with Nez Perce allottees, had heretofore simply appropriated to themselves the rights to graze their cattle on the reservation, so allowing allottees to lease their properties had some merit. Yet most of these early leasing agreements were patently illicit. The first such case was the most egregious, although surely predictable. In

January 1892, before Fletcher had even begun her final field season, Charles E. Monteith, acting on behalf of "certain residents of Idaho County . . . owners of and living upon lands adjacent to the south line of the Nez Perce Indian Reservation," and endorsed by Agent Robbins, requested permission "to lease a tract of land lying directly north of" those lands and within the reservation boundaries. The land, according to Monteith, was "not occupied by the Indians under the allotment act, and although at certain seasons of the year the Indians graze their stock upon this tract, the parties desiring to lease the same would not object to said stock grazing *as in former years*, jointly with their own."²³ Here I have emphasized certain of Monteith's words, the irony of which seems to have escaped the commissioner. The petition is Monteith's de facto (albeit post hoc) admission that his own cattle had in the past grazed—illegally—on reservation lands. The commissioner replied with what should have been an obvious refusal to endorse the proposition: "As none of the Indians of the Nez Perce Reservation hold trust patents for their lands, and none of the allotments made on the reservation have yet been approved by the Secretary of the Interior they cannot lease their *allotted* lands for any purpose." He reminded Robbins and the would-be lessees that it would "probably be more than a year before any of the allotments are approved."²⁴ Monteith, as was his wont, had opportunely misconstrued the facts. Technically, the lands he and his partners wished to lease *were* unallotted (since, as the commissioner had noted, the deeds had not yet been approved). Yet they had already been assigned to individual Nez Perces, who understood them to be their own properties.

Fletcher thus gave much of her attention during the first weeks of May 1892 to dealing with the local reaction to Monteith's brazen request. She had seen his letter while she was in Washington; when she arrived in Idaho, local partisans hastened to consult her about this affront to allotment's putative guarantees. Fletcher wrote several accounts of the matter to Indian Department officials, for at the time Thomas Jefferson Morgan was on administrative leave and R. V. Belt, an interim appointee who was not Fletcher's personal friend, occupied the post of acting commissioner. In an official letter reporting her arrival in Lapwai for the final field season, she wrote vaguely of the matter, declaring, "I met a large number of the tribe in the church at the Agency, the Agent being present. I made my announcements and told the Indians as this was probably the last time I should meet them in Council, if there were any questions or explanations concerning my work which they desired to ask they had better take this opportunity. . . . This session was peculiar and unpleasant, matters were brought forward concerning which the Indians and the Agent were at variance and I was forced to be a listener."[25] She wrote a longer and much more detailed version of this letter, likely as an early draft and possibly intended for Morgan. A letterpress copy of that document exists in Fletcher's personal records. Here she wrote: "[Monteith's] proposal had been presented to the tribe in Council a few days before my arrival and the Indians insisted on recounting to me the proceedings of the Council and their determination to protect their land from horses and cattle. They asked me if I did not know that there were 65 allotments in this tract, and that there were houses, fields, orchards, etc., where they had had their houses long before the Joseph war."[26]

Monteith's attempt to reinsert himself and his business within the boundaries of the reservation failed for the moment, largely because it was so egregiously premature. Yet it was a harbinger of what would happen as soon as the signal should be given that allotment had ceased, as Fletcher herself realized. In a personal letter to Morgan, then on leave, she observed, "Perhaps I ought to tell you that Mr. Monteiths letter which I saw in Washington proposing to lease 8 by 4 miles in the S.E. corner of reservation—has excited unanimous opposition . . . no land can be leased for cattle purposes by the honest consent of the tribe. Jas. Grant, the Agency Judge says he & a few Indians will sign with the Agent leases & then the tribe will be powerless to prevent the cattle men."[27] Very soon such leases-by-proxy would become business as usual.[28]

To this point, I have focused on the difficulties presented by recalcitrant or resistant Nimiipuu to Fletcher's efforts to conclude her work. The most significant barriers to a tidy, fair, and conclusive allotment, however, were presented by white landowners and entrepreneurs who had long lived on the reservation, used its lands for their own enrichment, and, sometimes in partnership with Nimiipuu friends, business associates, or relatives, considered themselves and their land holdings to be exempt from the petty details of federal Indian policy. Thus, even should Fletcher have been able to convince unwilling allottees to accept lands, she could not have closed the allotment, for any number of cases awaited the resolution of labyrinthine legal appeals. These cases involved tenacious and stubborn claims made by white men to valuable lands they would lose were allotment to be fairly and precisely concluded.

Several white men, for example, had enjoyed contracts to provide ferry services or to operate mail stations on the Nez Perce Reservation. The privileges associated with such licenses gave them the right to cultivate surrounding lands and to graze their cattle on the reservation. Early in 1890 Fletcher initiated an effort to close two mail stations, Caldwell's and White's, arguing they were no longer necessary and their owners had appropriated to themselves "amount[s] of land . . . great[ly in] excess of the requirements of the business on the account of 'public convenience.'"[29] Of course, to disestablish a white man, his family, and his possessions, including a cabin, fences, barns, and livestock, from these desirable lands presented nearly insurmountable difficulties.

Correspondence related to these mail stations flew back and forth over the four years of Fletcher's field work, and the cases were resolved only after she had departed.[30] For example, the dispute over White's station, the subject of three years or more of appeals, was finally decided in October 1892, when the commissioner of Indian affairs ordered Agent Warren Robbins to "revoke or withdraw the license" held by the current station operator, D. S. Fountain, calling Fountain "a trespasser." Robbins was directed to "appoint a suitable and competent member of the Nez Perces tribe and license him accordingly."[31] Fletcher had recommended the license be awarded to Jane Silcott, a Nez Perce woman married to a white man, who would be able to purchase White's "improvements."[32] In this case, unusually, the decision seems to have produced a final resolution. Silcott purchased the property, where she and her family established a ferry service.[33]

Each case was made more complicated by the connections among the white men threatened with expulsion, who often were also in league with the agent. William Caldwell supported White's efforts to keep his station, and vice versa. For his part, Caldwell had been a longtime business associate of former agent Charles E. Monteith in a highly profitable cattle business involving grazing their herds on reservation lands. Caldwell ferociously defended his right to lands enclosed within the Craig claim, an area settled by white men that fell within the boundaries of the reservation as they had been established in 1863. Lands on the Craig claim were finally allotted to Nimiipuu owners, among them the Phinney family, who immediately leased grazing and residential rights to Caldwell.[34]

Because the many interested parties supported one another in these disputes, the appeals process dragged on. To put the matter in terms of this chapter's theme, some cases did not have a definitive end. A decision handed down by a special agent or an interim commissioner, or even by one who held a more permanent position, could be unilaterally and capriciously reversed, depending on the judgment of the official assigned to review the case.[35] A case decided by one court could be appealed and the prior decision reversed. The records of allotment bear witness to this irresolution. Record Group 75 (Records of the Bureau of Indian Affairs) of the National Archives files contains a number of subcategories called "special cases," collections of interrelated letters that have at some point in the past been removed from the usual labyrinthine chronological filing system and grouped for ease of consultation by BIA investigators.[36]

Not surprisingly, the ongoing dispute related to the Langford claim has its own such classification as Special Case 37. One of the last tasks Fletcher sought to accomplish before leaving Idaho was to finalize allotments within this claim, where a number of Nimiipuu had declared their wish to be assigned. Lands here were fertile and close to major transportation routes and thus were among the most valuable properties on the reservation. Originally part of land set aside for mission properties under the Organic Act that had established Oregon Territory in 1848, the area was now home to the Lapwai Agency. Title to this land, claimed by private white clients, Nez Perces, the Presbyterian Church, and the federal government, had not yet been fully resolved despite a series of legal battles that began in 1872 and that by 1891 had reached Dickensian proportions.[37] Finally, on 31 August 1892, the acting commissioner of Indian affairs informed Fletcher she could "proceed to allot the ... lands."[38] Fletcher, however, did not carry out the commissioner's directive, replying by telegram, "Allotment of Langford Claim impossible until injunction is removed."[39] While this was surely the case, it is also highly likely that by early September, when she received the commissioner's go-ahead letter, Fletcher had determined to leave the Langford case for others to solve. That solution came three years later, in a most unfair and unsatisfactory arrangement, whereby as a part of the "Agreement with the Nez Perce Indians in Idaho" finalizing the sale of surplus lands following allotment, the federal government agreed to purchase the Langford properties for the sum of $20,000. Erwin N. Thompson has summarized the transaction most aptly: "[T]he real victims of this half-century old dispute were the Nez Perces. To pay the Langford estate, the federal government simply took $20,000 from the money appropriated to pay the Indians for their ceded lands. The Nez Perces, who had not been directly involved in the dispute, were much embittered."[40]

One of the largest groupings of files within Record Group 75 is Special Case 147, records related to legal difficulties associated with allotment. Some of the documents in Special Case 147 pertain to roads on the Nez Perce Reservation; some to specific allotments, such as the federal Hay Reservation; some to classes of negotiations (such as mission claims); and some to individual disputes. Probably the most notorious and surely among the most persistently unresolved of these individual problems is the Cox case. Correspondence related to this claim occupies a significant amount of file space within Special Case 147. Dozens more miscellaneous letters containing only brief paragraphs, small queries, and occa-

THE ENDS OF NEZ PERCE ALLOTMENT

sional updates related to the case have escaped that classification.[41] One of the first cases Fletcher engaged with, it continued unresolved for several years after she left Idaho. The allotting agent's struggles over this case offer an apt summary of the argument I have sought to construct throughout this book, and I use it as an appropriate, if inconclusive, end to this chapter. So central was this dispute in the last years of the allotment that the usually dour Fletcher collaborated with Jane Gay and posed for a series of four ironic photographic images (clearly made years after the fact) that, in their conception, resemble a Thomas Nast political cartoon. Gay included them in *Choup-nit-ki* to illustrate what she called the "Box case." I reproduce three of them here, in figures 42 and 43. They show a bonneted and corseted Fletcher who seems unable to escape the blandishments of a menacing figure constructed of documents and boxes and bearing the label "Box Case." In the first image of the series, Fletcher regards the case doubtfully, looking back at it over her right shoulder. This photograph humorously recalls Gay's assertion that the allotting agent had reason to regret her support for an educational policy that "had taught the Nez Percé the art of letter writing" (C, 326). The Cox case followed Fletcher tenaciously throughout four years and continued to occupy her time well after she had left the field. In the third image Fletcher fully confronts the case, as she had in the third year of allotment, driving home a point of law with the emphasis of pointing finger and threatening posture. But the final image in this series offers a conclusion that Gay very well knew was illusory. It shows Fletcher standing triumphant over a dismantled and collapsed set of documents. The agent still holds papers labeled "Box" under her arm, suggesting she had not yet effected a conclusion to the case.

Divisions among the various interest groups on the Nez Perce Reservation had placed the Cox case largely beyond her control, for try as she might to insist the case be resolved fairly and through prescribed legal means, she could not close it. The skill with which the claimants pursued their arguments challenged Fletcher's most closely held beliefs. One of her first official letters upon arriving in Lapwai in 1889 was addressed to Mrs. Julia Cox, informing her that the

FIG. 42. Box [Cox] Case, first of four images by E. Jane Gay, *Choup-nit-ki*, 340. The Schlesinger Library, Radcliffe Institute, Harvard University.

property upon which she had settled and begun to make improvements had already been claimed by Mrs. Lily Viles. Julia Cox was a Native woman who had been one of two wives of William Taylor Cox, a white man whose interests were closely supported by agency officials, both white and Nez Perce. But by common understanding, Julia Cox was not Nez Perce, either by blood or by residence. Fletcher advised her that before she could claim any land on the reservation, her identity "as a Nez Perce Indian entitled to land [had] to be proved."[42] This detail, however, did not cause Cox and her husband to leave the land where they had squatted in 1889. There they remained throughout more than five years of wrangling.

In the process of dealing with this case Fletcher solicited oral testimony from dozens of witnesses, arranged for at least three tribal council votes (each of which declared Cox not to be Nez Perce and declined to adopt her as a tribal member), and gathered reams of paper evidence, which she sent to Washington DC. But in each event, Julia Cox and her supporters resisted Fletcher's considerable federal and legal arsenal. According to Cox the witnesses who would

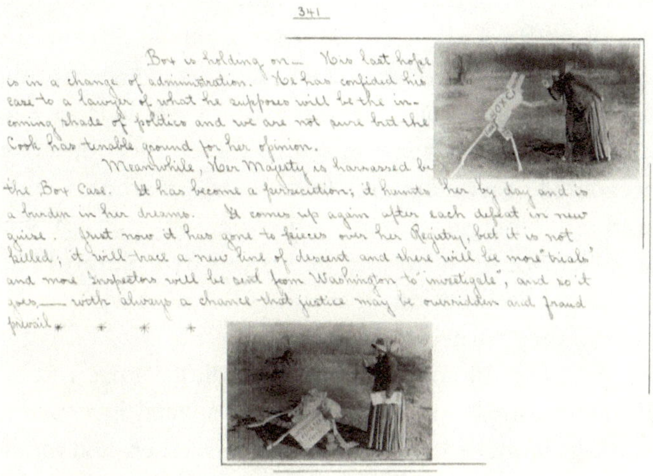
341

Box is holding on— His last hope is in a change of administration. He has confided his case to a lawyer of what he supposes will be the incoming shade of politics and we are not sure but the Cook has tenable ground for her opinion.

Meanwhile, Her Majesty is harrassed by the Box Case. It has become a persecution; it haunts her by day and is a burden in her dreams. It comes up again after each defeat in new guise. Just now it has gone to pieces over her Registry, but it is not killed; it will trace a new line of descent and there will be more "trials" and more "inspectors will be sent from Washington to "investigate", and so it goes,— with always a chance that justice may be overridden and fraud prevail. * * * *

FIG. 43. Box [Cox] Case, third and fourth of four images by E. Jane Gay, *Choup-nit-ki*, 341. The Schlesinger Library, Radcliffe Institute, Harvard University.

support her claim to tribal identity through blood lineage could not testify on her behalf because the hearings were held and votes were taken at times when these supporters were in the mountains on the fall hunt. (I pause to note this detail, for the presence or absence of key Nimiipuu voters seems to be central in a number of allotment-related issues, and Fletcher herself knew that introducing or taking votes on divisive issues might be strategically timed around the fall hunt.) Julia Cox, her husband, their seven children, and the children's assorted spouses, who claimed land amounting to nearly two entire sections of "the richest land on the reservation," deployed a number of other tactics that demonstrated their adept command of the discourses of civilizing reform. The families erected houses on the lands they claimed. They plowed, planted, and harvested crops.[43] And they fenced their lands with "wire . . . furnished her by the Agent," if Fletcher's allegation is taken to be true.[44] In other words, they behaved as civilized allottees, improving the land by adding to its value with their embodied labor. Knowing that Fletcher would depart at the end of each field season, and eventually would leave altogether, they simply outwaited her, refused to vacate their improvements, and threatened other claimants (who were armed only with deeds, plats, and other imaginary documentation) with physical violence.[45]

Most efficaciously, however, the various Cox plaintiffs exploited the politics of the situation. Knowing allotment was a volatile political issue, they turned to Idaho Representative Willis Sweet for support, ignoring the commissioner of Indian affairs and the secretary of the interior.[46] At Sweet's behest a special investigation into the claim was launched, unbeknownst to Fletcher, and the resultant legal proceedings demanded so much of her time in the late summer of 1891 that she was unable to attend to her other duties. The special hearing did not favor the Coxes, but even after Fletcher had boarded the ferry to leave Idaho for the last time, a representative of the family's interests came on board the boat to ask her to reconsider the case. She refused. The Coxes were instructed to vacate their claim. Here the record becomes confused. According to one source, they removed as many of their possessions as possible but were prevented from leaving entirely by foul winter weather.[47] Unsurprisingly, the next year they were back. With Fletcher securely in Washington and never to return, the agent proffered false testimony on Cox's behalf, denying he had ever received an order to vacate the properties. His perjury later cost him his appointment.[48]

During the period covered by this study and beyond, the Cox case remained open. The latest record I have found regarding it, dated 14 December 1893, bears out Jane Gay's ironic observation: "Kings are always arising . . . whose idea of dealing justly is often met in the simple reversal of the acts of their predecessors; who have no time to investigate and whose inclination is always to favor partisan adjustment" (C, 340).[49] In October 1893 yet another special agent, John Lane, was assigned to review the Cox claim. Once again Julia Cox "informed [Lane] that owing to the fact that the greater portion of the Indians were off the reservation in the Mountains she was unable to obtain her best witnesses and requested more time."

The trial was delayed for several weeks. Those who eventually testified at the hearing represented the divisive partisanship among the on-reservation Nez Perces, a dissensus allotment had done nothing to assuage. Testifying in favor of Cox were Fletcher's old nemeses Abraham Brooks and James Moses, among others. Jane Silcott, whom Fletcher had earlier befriended, also testified for Cox. Arguments against the Cox claim, unsurprisingly, were proffered by a group of Fletcher supporters, including Eddie Conner and James Hines (who had been her chainmen), James Reubens, and (by affidavit) James Stuart.[50]

The testimony eventually convinced Agent Lane that establishing a reliable lineage in support of a land claim was "no easy task . . . even where the conditions are the most favorable." Citing the testimony of Cox relatives as convincing him of the merit of her claim, Lane wrote, "I am of the opinion that Mrs. Cox is part Nez Perce and is therefore entitled to an allotment of land on the Nez Perce reservation."[51] Was this the end? Likely not, since Lane's decision did not address the issue Fletcher had always claimed would negate the dispute entirely: the land had already been allotted to Lily Viles, and previous allotments could not be rescinded.[52]

Another long chapter might be written about allotment's aftermath, tracing the checkered history of disputes occurring between the time Fletcher left the reservation in September 1893 and the firing of the gun that opened the lands to public sale in November 1895. Another long book might—and should—be written about the outfall of allotment and about the subsequent histories of the lands and the allottees. My purpose here has not been to write those histories, nor to chronicle each strand of this most complex event. Rather, I have examined the mode of its telling, and the records on which that (hi)story depends. These records have led to a story in which the plot form is intricately intertwined with dominant modes of narrative ideology. To conclude this study, however, I demonstrate that the records held in state-sponsored archives have supported historical narratives that further the illusion of completion, and I investigate how records that have escaped those usual archival containments might trouble those tidy narrative closures.

Part Five

Afterward

Introduction

"Double Pictures Have Met Us All along the Way"

In early July 1903, Independence Day was observed in Kamiah, Lapwai, and Nespelem as it had been for decades past. The celebration in Kamiah seemed to exemplify the success of the recently completed allotment. Here about a thousand celebrants gathered for camp meeting festivities lasting nearly two weeks and observed by several hundred white onlookers.[1] On the day of the Fourth a parade organized by James and Harriet Stuart (fig. 44) circled the campground, led by a small Indian marching band that "play[ed] patriotic airs." The band was followed by a procession of "100 little Indian boys, marching in ranks" and "a liberty car ... draped in national colors" carrying "50 little Indian girls dressed in white and waving flags." Stuart, now a civil engineer and founder of a recently established town that bore his name, was the afternoon's "principal speaker."[2] The words of those who delivered "addresses in English ... were translated into Nez Perce by Rev. Silas Whitman of Kamiah church No. 1," shown in figure 45.[3]

Six months later, in January 1904, when James Stuart traveled to Washington DC as "President of the Board of Trade of the Town of Stuart," he visited Alice Fletcher and Jane Gay at their home (C, 448). He very likely told them about the celebration he and his wife had sponsored in Kamiah, for the trio certainly would have discussed the changes allotment had brought to the reservation. Gay

[271]

FIG. 44. James Stuart and Harriet Mary Stuart. Stephen Shawley Collection, Historical Photograph Collection, University of Idaho Special Collections and Archives, Moscow ID, 38-0838.

FIG. 45. Silas Whitman standing by a tipi. Stephen Shawley Collection, Historical Photograph Collection, University of Idaho Special Collections and Archives, Moscow ID, 38-0268.

had been thinking about those changes that January as she wrote the concluding words to the scrapbook that would become *Choupnit-ki*. Yet in the "Writer's Note" closing the album, Gay memorialized not the Kamiah celebration but the Lapwai gathering. She effused, "Where the Indians at Lapwai camped at their Tal-lik-lykt [war procession] festival, they hold now, at the Fourth of July, a gospel meeting, and from the tents . . . , instead of war songs, hymns of prayer and praise echo through the valley." She illustrated her point with a photograph, reproduced here as figure 46, captioned "Camp Meeting at Lapwai, July 4," but did not specify the year in which the image was made (C, 448, 449). In fact, the terrain shown in the photograph establishes that the image was made in Kamiah, not in Lapwai.[4]

Gay likely received the details about the celebration at Lapwai included in her "Writer's Note" from Kate McBeth, with whom she and Fletcher had exchanged letters since departing Idaho some ten years earlier. Like Gay, McBeth was busy writing a book: hers, *The Nez Perces since Lewis and Clark*, contained a chapter titled "Fourth of July Camp-Meetings Past and Present." Here the

FIG. 46. "Camp Meeting at Lapwai, July 4," by E. Jane Gay, *Choup-nit-ki*, 449. This image is incorrectly captioned; the location is in the Kamiah area. The Schlesinger Library, Radcliffe Institute, Harvard University.

missionary chronicled her lifelong struggle against traditional observances associated with the "much-dreaded Fourth of July."[5] McBeth based parts of this chapter on accounts she had written in her diary, on letters in which she had described the celebrations to the readers of church missionary periodicals, and on newspaper clippings she had collected over the years, some of which she sent to Fletcher and Gay, and some of which she pasted into scrapbooks. One of her albums contains the three newspaper accounts of the 1903 Kamiah and Lapwai celebrations upon which my account here depends.[6]

One of these clippings, the *Lewiston Morning Tribune*'s account of the Lapwai celebration, suggests that Gay's "Writer's Note" was selective, at best. "Will Dance Again" makes it clear that in 1903 in Lapwai, as at Kamiah, the celebrations were attended by enthusiastic local observers, including "[m]any . . . ladies among the visitors [who] were perceptibly moved by the strange solemnity" of the war dance, as Gay, Fletcher, and McBeth had been in years past.[7] From Washington, distanced by space and time, Gay surely recalled these details but used them only as a point of contrast to the more sedate camp meeting observances of which she wrote, implying that the war parade, singing, dancing, gaming, and racing, once central to the celebration, were now a thing of the past.

Gay's "Writer's Note" uses comparisons as the basis of retrospective meaning-making. She begins: "As we have reviewed in these pages, there have walked beside us, hand in hand with the ghosts of the past, the actualities of the present, and double pictures have met us all along the way" (C, 445). In this final brief essay she juxtaposes a series of past and present scenes, liberally illustrated with photographs, all of which exemplify the success of allotment. Steamboats, grist mills, Native-owned ferries, locomotives, iron bridges, and tidy missionary cottages now characterize the Nez Perce Reservation, evidence of "influence[s]" that have "made the Nez Percé tribe so signal an example of progress in civilization." James Stuart's "business with the Government" offers Gay another point of comparison, for she writes that the Nez Perces who now visit Washington "do not seek audience of the 'Great Father,' to orate upon their fallen estate and beg for redress of real or fancied wrongs.... They go straight to the Capitol and call upon the Idaho Senators: they are American citizens and their rights are guaranteed by their votes" (C, 448, 449). Yet as her metaphor of "double[d] pictures" suggests, the present moment does not entirely efface the past.

The newspaper account published as "Will Dance Again" describes with evident relish the spectacle awaiting white observers of the Lapwai celebration, which had been sparked by "a revival of interest in ... traditional observances." The reporter observes, "[T]he *spirit of the old war council has been enthused into the younger blood* that will perform the wierd contortions ... tomorrow.... The war dance given by the Nez Perce is considered the best of any tribe in the United States."[8] These details, omitted by Gay, make it clear that the "traditional observances" had continued uninterrupted and were being carried forth by a new generation of Nimiipuu. In the newspaper account the awkward construction "the younger blood

FIG. 47. Tepees at Nespelem, July 4 celebration, with white visitors, ca. 1900–1905, by Edward H. Latham. University of Washington Libraries, Special Collections, PH Coll 409.63.

FIG. 48. Native American women riding horses (double exposure), ca. 1900–1905, by Edward H. Latham. University of Washington Libraries, Special Collections, PH Coll 409.4928.

that will perform" interprets cultural persistence as atavism stemming from inborn racial qualities carried in the blood. These ritual performances, however, are examples of survivance, intentionally taught to the younger people by the generation who were, in the fantasy of allotment, to have been the last to follow such practices.

At Nespelem, Washington, in 1903, the year before Joseph's death, he likely led the war parade at the Fourth of July celebration.[9] "[S]ome two hundred riders" assembled in a parade and were observed by white visitors, five couples of whom posed for their photographs in front of the tipis at the encampment, shown in figure 47.[10] This image and others were made by the Colville Agency physician, Edward Latham, an amateur photographer, in the early 1900s.[11] Another of Latham's photographs, figure 48, captioned "Spirit Land," shows a part of the annual ceremonial parade.[12] This image is likely an accidental double exposure, or perhaps an experiment, for Latham made no other such photographs. It presents a fortuitous example of the metaphor Jane Gay used in her "Writer's Note." She intended her "double pictures"—illustrated before-and-after narratives similar to those Fletcher used at the New Orleans Fair—to demonstrate progressive contrast.

Latham's double picture, on the other hand, shows cultural preservation and persistence. Here the members of the women's division of a Fourth of July parade ride with their ghostly counterparts, the haunting quality of the image enhanced by blowing dust. The double exposure emphasizes the fact that here at Nespelem, as at Lapwai, these parades furnished forth evidence of a cultural past neither lost nor forgotten. Indeed, at these summer celebrations, the ceremonies, observances, dances, and songs central to Nimiipuu heritage were "restored," taught, and transmitted to younger generations.[13]

9. After-Words

In the early twentieth century Nez Perces supplemented their performances with the technology of voice recording as a way of preserving their histories and transmitting the old ways to generations to follow. At the Fourth of July celebration in Lapwai in 1911, for example, Sam Morris (shown in fig. 49) was a featured speaker, as well as a participant in the singing. Using a wax-cylinder recorder, or graphophone, Morris recorded himself and a group of singers performing "Serenade Song, *K'ilowawia*," likely in connection with the traditional war parade, for *Qillóowawya* are departure songs, part of the "send-off for warriors."[1] Morris eventually recorded a total of sixty-nine wax cylinders, sixty-one of which have now been digitally remastered as a part of the Nez Perce Music Archive compiled by Loran Olsen. While it is not clear how Morris acquired his graphophone, his use of it recalls Alice Fletcher's earlier ethnographic work on the reservation. In 1890, as she began gathering linguistic data from Susan McBeth, she had planned to support her investigations with wax-cylinder recordings of verbal performances. She wrote in great excitement to F. W. Putnam that she had "found from the language that the people know of the tides of the ocean, also that they had a word for the earth quake—I am trying . . . to get at some hints as to their mygration. I told Miss McB. I must have skulls, etc. . . . I have two of the songs-words from Miss McB. &

FIG. 49. *Left to right*: Sam Morris (Sik-Um-Chets-Kun-In), Paul Eneas, and Billy Carter, Nez Perce Indians in blanket leggings and beaded moccasins, by Bowman Studio, Pendleton OR. Stephen Shawley Collection, Historical Photograph Collection, University of Idaho Special Collections and Archives, Moscow ID, 38-0428.

shall try & get the music. I am going to try & get a graphophone to use here."[2] This letter is an early indication of the anthropologist's intent to pursue ethnomusicological studies among the Nez Perces, another project she left unfinished when she departed the reservation in 1892.[3] Fletcher's records yield no indication that she succeeded in bringing a graphophone to the reservation, although she and Jane Gay had experimented with one in Washington DC.[4]

In 1897, however, when Chief Joseph visited Washington accompanied by Levi Jonas, James Hayes, Harry Hayes, and others, Fletcher entertained the delegation at her home and on two occasions recorded these men singing *Qillóowawya*.[5] Upon their departure she "[g]ave Levi Jonas 12 graphophone rolls with music requested on them for concert work at Nez Perce Res."[6] The next year Fletcher wrote to Kate McBeth and inquired, "Where is Jas. Hayes? Did you ever hear what became of the graphophone cylinders I gave Levi Jonas & those on which he obtained records for me?"[7] Like so many of the other stories associated with Fletcher's relations with the Nez Perces following her departure from the reservation, this one has no resolution. No evidence exists to suggest that Jonas returned the cylinders to Fletcher.

"every Nez Perce Indian, if the chance was given him, would register his complaint": John McConville

In July 1911, at the same celebration at which Sam Morris recorded "Serenade Song" using the graphophone to preserve an aural record of Nimiipuu culture and survivance, another archival activity was also under way (see fig. 63 for a photograph likely taken at the 1911 gathering). At this celebration Starr J. Maxwell (fig. 50), a Nimiipuu attorney and notary public, assisted by tribal council member Silas D. Whitman (fig. 45), gathered, translated, and transcribed sworn testimony from more than one hundred Nimiipuu about the difficulties allotment had brought into their lives.[8] Several of these respondents testified that everyone would register a complaint if given the chance.[9] Like Morris's recordings, Maxwell's interviews, collected in a document titled *Memorial of the Nez Perce Indians Residing in the State of Idaho to the Congress of the United States*, exemplified the spirit of the occasion. And like the singing, the testimonies in the *Memorial* (M) preserved the people's histories as "a strong and powerful tribe" (Stot-Ka-i, *M*, 111). As I have demonstrated throughout this book, the Fourth was an occasion upon which citizens of the United States celebrated their constitutionally guaranteed rights. In 1911 this holiday might have been an occasion upon which Nez Perces, trained in holiday observances mandated by the commissioner of Indian affairs in 1890, would celebrate their citizenly rights as well. Indeed, the document Maxwell and Whitman produced is a compelling and articulate performance of citizenship by those gathered at Lapwai. Rather than extol their rights, however, those who testified to Maxwell furnished an honest and damning indictment of allotment.

The *Memorial* presents a powerful contrast—a "double picture"—to Gay's optimistic "Writer's Note." To her carefully structured first-person accounts of allotment, which has furnished scholars and historians with the basis for understanding allotment's aims, procedures, and accomplishments, the *Memorial* stands as a counterarchive. Like *Choup-nit-ki*, it is a primary source document about allotment. Unlike Gay's record, it is a multivocal testament, beginning not in 1889 but in the early nineteenth century, and lacking the closure of a comparative "Writer's Note." The *Memorial* stems from the present messy realities of progressive policy gone awry, and unlike *Choup-nit-ki*, it emphasizes the need for the federal authorities to provide redress for the consequences of their neglect, bad policy, bad faith, and corrupt administration.

Those whose testimonies make up the *Memorial of the Nez Perce Indians* spoke in the presence of legally recognized witnesses; their words were transformed by Starr Maxwell from a collection of individual oral complaints that could be dismissed as "beg[ging] for redress of real or fancied wrongs"—as Gay dismissively described such efforts (C, 448)—into depositions holding legal weight. Depositions, according to *Black's Law Dictionary*, are "testimony . . . taken upon oral question or written interrogatories, not in open court, . . . and reduced to writing and duly authenticated, and

FIG. 50. Starr J. Maxwell (*seated*), James Maxwell, his brother (*standing*), Edna Maxwell (Starr Maxwell's first wife), and children. Courtesy of National Park Service, Nez Perce National Historical Park.

intended to be used in preparation and upon the trial of a civil action or criminal prosecution."[10] By asking careful questions of his deponents and then arranging their testimonies into a multivocal but coherent single document, Maxwell both honored individual cases and demonstrated the collective identification of those who testified. Thus the *Memorial* exemplifies the principle of *e pluribus unum*, an ideal centrally important to Fourth of July observances. These speakers—men and women who represented a range of opinions and religions, who demonstrated varying degrees of mastery of spoken and written English, and who ranged in age from twenty to ninety-four, testified in chorus that allotment had failed.

In their total, the testimonies presented in this document reprise post-contact Nimiipuu history as told by those who lived it. The very names of the deponents exemplify that history, for they include those with Nimiipuu names (Ew-yin, Wo-win-we-non-my, and others), with English versions of Nimiipuu names (Little Red Duck, Pile of Clouds), and with Anglicized surnames that invoke the history of white incursion: missionaries (Whitman, Spalding, and Lindsley), educators and soldiers (McConville), and Fletcher's assistants and opponents in allotment (Reubens, Corbett, Connor, Lott, and Moses). Tribal elders, some of whom were young men at the time of the earliest treaties with white invaders, narrate pre-contact conditions, attest to the relentless legally enabled reduction of Nimiipuu lands, and present compelling counter-narratives of watershed events such as the 1877 war. Younger speakers exemplify the result of these incursions. They had been forcibly educated and at times abused at boarding schools; they had been classified as "incompetent" to manage their affairs despite being of legal age and well educated; they had seen their rights usurped by corrupt agents, and they had lost land due to fractionated inheritances. Many of these affronts were the direct consequence of Alice Fletcher's partisanship during allotment and represented the shortsightedness of the theorists of allotment policy.

A memorial, according to *Black's*, is a "document presented to a legislative body, or to the executive, by one or more individuals, containing a petition or a representation of the facts. . . . In English law, that which contains the particulars of a deed . . . as in the case of an annuity which must be registered."[11] The form, then, relates to matters of deed and title to land. The *Memorial of the Nez Perce Indians* was presented to Idaho Senator William Edgar Borah on 14 August 1911, just a month after the testimonies were taken. Maxwell and Whitman may have chosen Borah to receive the document because he had publicly expressed support for the civil rights of individual citizens. In a 1911 speech, for example, the senator had asserted, "A government which will not protect me in my rights, though I stand alone and against all my neighbors, is a despotic government."[12] Those who proffered the *Memorial* requested exactly what Borah had promised his constituents: protection of their rights against "despotic" local and federal governments. They had, in point of fact, requested such protection earlier in 1911, when Silas Whitman, a duly elected tribal representative, delivered a petition to Washington DC requesting a federal investigation of local administrators. According to Whitman, before he left Lapwai in March, "Supervisor Lipps . . . refused to allow many of our people to withdraw some of their deposits, stating to them that he was afraid they would use some of the money to defray my expenses. He has not only not listened to our complaints, but has done what he could to prevent us from making our troubles known." Once he was in Washington, Whitman was roundly ignored, and after spending the better part of four months seeking redress, he returned home frustrated. Then, "because we were refused by the Indian Office and Interior Department our request to have an inspector sent here to do this work," Whitman states, "[w]e conceived the idea of taking testimony ourselves" (*M*, 43). In other words, Nez Perce representatives planned to do what the government would not: gather testimony from many of those who had been adversely affected by allotment.

This chorus of voices offers ample proof of allotment's failure on all fronts. It had not secured Nimiipuu lands, for by 1917, according to Dolores Janiewski, "Corbett Lawyer reported that only 967 allotments remained in Nez Perce hands out of the 2,009 issued by Alice Fletcher thirty years earlier."[13] Six years later, in 1923, according to Elizabeth James, the reviled Oscar Lipps reported that "the

Nez Perce held 100,000 acres of allotted and tribal lands, but Anglo settlers owned 650,000 acres. Almost every Nez Perce under the age of 27 owned land only through heirship, and often a dozen or more heirs received a tract of 80 acres to divide up among them. The only practicable solution, Lipps argued, consisted of selling the land and distributing the profit. Under existing conditions, the heirs could not even begin their own farms if they wanted to because all the productive land was gone."[14] Nor had allotment taught citizenship through white example, as had been its original intent. During the period of apprentice citizenship, the federal guardians who were to stand as examples continued to display the venal, corrupt, and incompetent behaviors that had characterized agency administration since the mid-nineteenth century. In the discussion that follows, I expand on each of these points with reference to the individual testimonies given, concluding that in addition to failing to secure land and grant privileges of citizenship, allotment had failed in more salutary ways as well: it had not assimilated the Nez Perces into the body politic, and it had failed to erase their cultural heritage.

"there is no land left to us": Philip McFarland

Most of the affidavits gathered by Maxwell yield incontrovertible evidence that allotment had not secured lands to individual Nez Perces and that subsequent amendments to the Dawes Act had deprived allottees of the right to make decisions about their property. As the time neared when allottees would own their titles in fee simple, supplementary legislation increased the supervisory powers of federal agents and superintendents. In May 1900, for example, a legal provision (31 Stat. L., 229) stipulated that if "by reason of age, disability, or inability any allottee of Indian lands can not personally and with benefit to himself occupy or improve his allotment or any part thereof, the same may be leased."[15] Yet the language of the provision also allowed the local agent to offer land for lease without consulting its owner, as Annie Mox Mox testified: "The Indian agent in charge has rented this land or heirship allotment of ours without our consent. We are the sole heirs and have a right to say, rent, sell, or do anything with the allotment" (M, 139). Six years later the

Burke Act hastened the depletion of allotted lands by allowing "competent" owners to sell their holdings. The following year the commissioner of Indian affairs was given "power to sell the allotment of an Indian in trust status." Thus "all allotted lands were potentially available for purchase if the government issued a fee patent or if the agent deemed such a purchase to be in an allottee's interest."[16]

Nor did the incompletely theorized heirship provisions of allotment policy benefit the Nez Perces. Alice Fletcher's meticulous kinship documentation had not, as she had hoped "saved" "the property . . . in some way to the proper descendant" following the death of the original allottee.[17] In deposition after deposition, complainants narrated cases in which, upon the death of a relative, the allotted lands had reverted to public sale and the remaining relatives lost their inheritances. They testified to Maxwell of allotments not received and of allotments made to minor children that had subsequently been canceled or disallowed. Nor had ample provision been made for the needs of future Nez Perces to have lands of their own and to become self-sufficient adults. Philip McFarland testified, "We have about 400 children born since the allotments were made, some young and some about 18 years of age or more that have no allotments, and there is no land left to us that we can allot them except our timber reserve, and unless the Government . . . fulfills its . . . obligations to us many of these children will have nothing with which to begin life when they are old enough to depend upon themselves for support" (*M*, 47). It is difficult to imagine, in the face of such evidence, that allotment's theorists had given enough consideration to providing for the future; nor had they anticipated that the number of Native citizens would increase.

The *Memorial* makes it clear that Fletcher's hasty departure had produced lingering problems. The allotments she had left unfinished, many of them within lands making up the disputed Langford claim, were not included in the land sale of 1895 and were eventually canceled, but the profits from their sale were not given to the Nez Perces. This unsatisfactory resolution was a major topic in the petition Whitman had carried to Washington. Harrison Red Wolf put the matter succinctly: "We believe that the allotments — something over 110—that have been canceled should revert to the tribe, or that the true value thereof should be paid to the people in the amount of $3 per acre which we received for the surplus land" (*M*, 58; see also the testimony of Noah Bredell, chair of the tribal council, *M*, 115–16). This was a modest demand, since the Langford lands were the most fertile on the reservation and worth considerably more than three dollars an acre.

Those who gave testimony to Maxwell and Whitman rehearsed other problems antedating allotment, issues Fletcher had grappled with and had failed to solve. They protested that white settlers continued to intrude upon their lands, exercising the age-old techniques of squatter sovereignty. Paul Jackson, for example, testified: "A white man named Charles Roller has taken possession of the allotments of Phillip Ellenwood, now deceased; he has not only taken possession of this allotment and deprived the lawful owners the use thereof, but he has intruded upon the rights of my mother, by claiming a portion of my allotment, also claiming a portion of two or three other allotments adjoining these places." According to Jackson, although Roller had confronted with a gun those who tried to protest his takeover, the agent, the sheriff, and the superintendent "did nothing" (*M*, 102). Other deponents complained of having no fencing materials, a crucial resource for marking the boundaries of their claims, as the allotting agent had noted when she arrived in Idaho twenty-two years earlier.

Nor had Fletcher's multiple queries about the disposition of resources tied to land—in water, minerals, and timber—produced a coherent policy. Many of Maxwell's deponents protested that their rights to resources of timber, game, and fish, although guaranteed by the treaties of 1855, 1863, and 1868, had begun to disappear. Jim Matt (Kol-Kol-Chaw-hin) recalled, "The thing that finally reconciled the people and made them feel inclined to sign the treaty [of 1855] was the fact that we reserved the game and fish rights, camping, and the use of the timber, and the rights to use the passes and highways, the use of the springs, streams, and fountains on the ceded land" (*M*, 87). Allotment, of course, had substantively diminished these treaty rights by assigning to individual owners lands rich in these resources, formerly understood to be available for common use. White men who purchased lands on the reservation after 1895, or who subsequently leased or purchased allotments from their Nez Perce owners, did not consider themselves to be subject to the treaty guarantees and loudly protested what they considered to be incursions on their properties. These problems, too, had only been exacerbated by Fletcher's premature withdrawal from her field responsibility, for her departure was a de facto admission of her inability to solve them.

"I am a free citizen of the United States . . . [a] voter in this State, and I desire equal rights with other citizens": Charley Half Moon

By submitting these testimonies to Borah, it might be argued, the Nez Perces were exercising their rights to representative government in precisely the way the Dawes Act had foreseen. But that would be an oversimplification. Maxwell and Whitman prepared the *Memorial* and sent it to Congress because the usual means through which citizens might seek redress had failed. Thus its litany of complaints about the usurpation of rights takes on an added urgency and vehemence, an effect magnified by the sheer number of complainants. Unlike a single representative or a small delegation engaged in face-to-face negotiation, this legal document contains the individual testimony of more than a hundred citizens, each with a specific complaint. Their stories, taken together, comprise a narrative of federal and local malfeasance that should not have been ignored. The *Memorial* represents individual cases, to be sure, but it also documents the abuses suffered by a specific group of deponents and by the Nimiipuu body politic, for, as Whitman put it, "If time was given, every Nez Perce Indian would sign a sworn statement registering his complaints" (*M*, 43). In the aggregate, the complaints show that the rights specifically guaranteed to U.S. citizens—the right to petition, the right to democratic representation, the right to due process of law, and most important, the right to freedom from unreasonable seizure of property—had been egregiously withheld. The *Memorial* demanded these rights be honored.

Citizens' rights to "petition the Government for a redress of grievances," guaranteed by the First Amendment to the Constitution of the United States, had been violated when Oscar H. Lipps attempted to prevent Whitman from traveling to Washington. Although Whitman persisted, the outcome of his effort exposed a shortcoming of that guarantee, for the First Amendment does not stipulate that a citizen's petition will be received, acknowledged, or acted upon. By ignoring Whitman and those he represented, the federal government had failed doubly. Not only had it ignored citizens' petitions; it had also refused, as it had so many times in the past, to acknowledge and to fulfill its legally incurred treaty obligations. The *Memorial* proffers evidence of that second failure by reprinting the texts of the Treaties of 1855, 1863, and 1867, and the 1895 land sale "Agreement" in its first pages. In the face of such a dismal record, the Nez Perces had taken action on their own behalf, demonstrating their competence to understand, to claim, and to enact their citizenly rights and responsibilities. On every page this document proclaims its intent not only to represent those whose voices are included but to expose the broader implications of their testimonies. Of the 128 depositions, at least twelve do not present specific personal cases but were given to support those who had borne the brunt of federal indifference. In the words of Pile of Clouds (shown in fig. 51), "I have no personal grievances, but I am in position to see the mistreatment of my people" (*M*, 126). Some of these deponents were members of the tribal council, as was Pile of Clouds, and thus exemplified the proper function of representative government. Their official and personal concern was echoed by a number of younger speakers who presented testimony on behalf of elder relatives whose lives and livelihoods were threatened by repressive policies.

Many of the complaints registered by those who spoke to Maxwell might be classified as violations of the due process clauses of the Fifth and Fourteenth Amendments, which "[protect] persons from state actions" and protect "property from unfair governmental interference or taking."[18] Some deponents, for example, complained that segments of their lands had been appropriated for the construction of roads, and that they had not been justly compensated for the seizure; many others asserted that their funds had been summarily

FIG. 51. Pile of Clouds (*left*) and Tah'mawiinúnmy, about 1910. Dickson-Cloud Family Photograph Collection. Used by permission of Nakia Williamson-Cloud.

appropriated by the agent. A major theme uniting all these testimonies is their protest against the competency commissions established by the Burke Act, nine-member review boards charged with the responsibility of "classify[ing] the Nez Perce Tribe of Indians according to their intelligence and ability to transact their own business affairs" (M, 117).[19] While the competency provisions were ostensibly designed to protect Native landholders from unscrupulous exploitation by outsiders, those who were scrutinized by the commissions and ranked as less than competent surely thought otherwise. Their fitness to represent their own concerns was measured by their answers to questions such as these: "Is [the applicant] addicted to the use of intoxicants?" "If the applicant is a married woman, what is the reputation of her husband? Is he a man who would be likely to get possession of his wife's property and then desert her?" "What practical business experience has [the applicant] had?"[20] The questions and their answers depended on subjective judgment, rather than verifiable facts, and are tainted by racial prejudice, for no white landholder had had his right to own property diminished by his use of alcohol, his reliability as a spouse, or his degree of business expertise.

The adjudication of competency might, of course, result in a positive, if intrusive, evaluation such as this: "After carefully weighing the applicants qualifications, and in view of the fact that, though he does not read or write, yet speaks good English, is industrious, sober and reliable and is thought well of by his white neighbors, I believe he has the necessary business qualifications to enable him to manage his own affairs."[21] Other applicants, however, especially those who did not have the good fortune to be "thought well of by [their] white neighbors," might receive evaluations such as this: "[T]he allottee is an habitual drunkard and gambler, and is wholly incompetent to take care of his property, his application is denied, and the trust patent and accompanying papers are herewith returned."[22] It is clear that if disinterested parties did not oversee this process, an allottee might indeed become the object of "unfair governmental interference or taking." And disinterested parties, whether local or federal, were a rarity.

Thus many of Maxwell's deponents sought to make the procedures by which members were appointed to the competency commissions into a more representative process, asking that they be duly elected, rather than appointed. Thomas Lindsley, who was "classed as No. 2 grade," summarized the problem in terms of representative governance: "[T]hese nine men were not the choice of the people, were not voted for by the people, and were selected with prejudice to the people." He continued, "We have the right to vote . . . for county officers, State officers, and the President of the United States, and we should have the right to vote more especially when it comes to interests of . . . our own and in which no other persons are interested (M, 91, 91–92). The membership of these commissions was manifestly not representative. Indeed, the process by which commissioners were appointed mirrored the divisive and religiously inflected policies Fletcher had followed in allotment, favoring those who were Christian and Presbyterian. The petition Whitman carried to Washington delineated the potential abuses of such appointments, alleging that the commission was not a representative body, that the members had "allowed their personal friendship and enmity toward many members of the tribe to predominate in making the said classifications," and that "a majority of the nine men . . . were either ministers of the gospel or elders in the church, and for that reason discriminated unfairly toward members of the church as against Indians who were not members of the church" (M, 117).[23] Not surprisingly, such partisanship yielded highly prejudicial outcomes. Solomon Hoona told Maxwell that he had not received monies due him upon the sale of the estate of his deceased wife because "the superintendent disputed my claim that I was legally married . . . , claiming that the minister, Robert Williams, was not ordained, and therefore the marriage was not legal. At the hearing I was unable to prove or produce the records to show that Robert Williams was ordained. . . . The persons contesting my rights to this allotment claim that I was married to another woman by a Catholic priest" (M, 82). Hoona's case had revived an internecine dispute that had arisen more than twenty years earlier, during the interregnum of Alice Fletcher and her missionary friend Susan McBeth.

After an applicant had submitted a request for a patent in fee, the competency commission and the federal officials involved in making these determinations deliberated behind closed doors. Such a procedure surely violated the principles of due process of law establishing "the right of the person affected thereby to be present before the tribunal which pronounces judgment upon the question . . . and to have the right of controverting . . . every material fact which bears on" the matter.[24] Maxwell's deponents found it to be difficult, if not impossible, to exercise directly "the right of controverting" the ratings they had received. In the *Memorial* they performed that right. For example, He-yume-toke-te-nikt (Mabel Halfmoon), a young woman who had been "educated at Chemawa," had received a letter informing her that her fee patent had been denied because her "qualifications to care for [her] own affairs are not clearly shown" (*M*, 75). The evidence upon which this determination was based was not disclosed, nor did the letter He-yume-toke-te-nikt received offer her the opportunity to refute the decision.

Those allottees who were deemed incapable of managing their own monies were subjected to other ostensibly benevolent procedures designed to protect them from the fraudulent and predatory schemes of their white neighbors. These measures amounted to a de facto seizure of property. A landowner who sold, leased, or rented his or her lands did not always directly receive the money. Rather, the agent or superintendent took control of the funds because it was assumed that the newly rich allottees would squander their money. The monthly pittance doled out by the agent caused great hardship to those so classified. As We-yah-la-hom ironically observes, "I understand the superintendent claims the reason he withholds most of the moneys of our people is to keep them from gambling it away or spending it for whisky. If anything would induce them to gamble it would be the small amounts paid to them monthly" (*M*, 110). Dozens of Maxwell's deponents protested such unreasonable seizures of property. Annie Seth offered the most specific condemnation of this supposedly benevolent interference. Seth had recently inherited an allotment, which she sold for $3,500. As she testified, her money then was deposited with the superintendent. Since this money has been paid in I have only received two payments of $25 each. If I should receive $25 a month for every month hereafter it would take 11 years and 6 months for me to get all of this money. With that much money to my credit, notices are posted that my credit is not good, and that people should not sell me anything on time; if they do, they do it with their own risk. *I consider this an imposition and libelous* and that a great wrong has been done to me. I demand the full amount of money that is due to me, *to invest as I choose.* (M, 80; emphasis added)

Seth's claim demonstrates that the attempts of federal agents to exercise paternal supervision produced the very conditions they intended to mitigate.

Other depositions expose the incompetence not of naive Nimiipuu allottees but of those charged with managing their affairs. Advised by the agent to deposit monies from the 1895 land sale in local banks, at least a dozen deponents testified that bank failures in the nearby towns of Moscow and Juliaetta had left them destitute. As He-yum-ka-yon-mi testified, "In 1895 I was induced to make a deposit . . . in the Moscow National Bank. . . . This bank failed and I lost my money. . . . I was persuaded through Indian Agent Fisher and through his interpreters to make the deposit . . . and this is what induced many others of the Nez Perces to make deposits there" (*M*, 107). The local bankers presumably exemplified the qualities of character demanded of "competent" allottees: they were men of "good character and reputation," "industrious and self-supporting," and, above all, possessed of "practical business experience."[25] If these bankers could not manage the monies entrusted to them, how, the deponents wondered, could they themselves be seen as incompetent to manage their funds? Could they do any worse than utterly fail and lose 90 percent of their cash? In light of such spectacular incompetence, Charley Half Moon's demands seem measured and logical: "I desire the free use and control of my money and property, as I understand that I am a free citizen of the United States in the State of Idaho, and voter in this State, and I desire equal rights with other citizens" (*M*, 72).

AFTERWARD

"We were then a strong and powerful tribe of Indians": Stot-Ka-i, Henry E-nah-la-lamkt, Three Eagles, and Im-nee-wo-ton-my

The *Memorial* addresses not only present abuses but also earlier claims that had gone unresolved for a half century. Despite the considerable efforts of James Reubens, Nez Perce scouts who had supported federal troops in 1877 remained uncompensated. Nor had the Oklahoma internees received reparations. Children attending government boarding schools still suffered harsh discipline and lived in unsanitary dormitories. Local agents and superintendents continued to take advantage of their positions to line their own pockets. The recitation of these past but unforgotten defaults highlights a second important function of a memorial: whether a monument, an obelisk, or a document, a memorial exists to prompt public recollection of a person or an event. Maxwell's document thus served as an antidote to federal amnesia by refusing to allow the Indian Office's neglect and stubborn refusal to honor its treaty promises to be forgotten.

The *Memorial* constitutes a remarkable archive within which Nimiipuu voices narrate Nimiipuu histories that redress the amnesia of majoritarian accounts. Maxwell led the elders who testified (among them one elder woman) through a recitation of their personal connection to the series of treaties with which the *Memorial* begins. Several had witnessed the occasions of theft and federal default on the treaty promises, had survived the disastrous seizure of the Wallowa Valley and consequent hostilities, and with the closing of allotment, had seen the Nimiipuu land base even more radically diminished. Their versions of these events extend the history of the people beyond the end of the 1877 war. Their voices establish them as the forebears of subsequent generations who will continue to claim their rights in the face of aggressive and intentional forgettings and premature closures.

These elder testimonies, strategically interspersed throughout the document, share several notable characteristics. Only infrequently do these deponents advance personal claims. They speak historically, as leaders and members of a sovereign nation. Those who attest to having attended the negotiations of 1855 assert and reassert, "We were then a strong and powerful tribe of Indians and were much respected by the other tribes of the United States on account of our numbers and strength" (Stot-Ka-i, *M*, 111; see also Three Eagles, *M*, 114–15). They declare that Nimiipuu "territory . . . covered a vast area of the country and . . . [t]here was no time that our people ever wanted for meat or fish" (Henry E-nah-la-lamkt, *M*, 113). Im-nee-wo-ton-my poignantly recalls, "I remember quite distinctly the condition of our people before the signing of the treaty of 1863. Our people were much better contented than they are now. They had more freedom; could go and come when they pleased . . . and we were not hampered and molested as we are now" (*M*, 129). These recitations demonstrate that federal default had diminished common resources and, as a result, had forced the Nez Perces to depend upon an unreliable and incompetent partner. All these wise elders urge that the diminution cease.

These testimonies supplement and challenge standard histories with the words of those present at other watershed moments, particularly the Joseph War. As both Stot-Ka-i and Three Eagles insist, the war began because white settlers intruded upon Native property. Stot-Ka-i declares, "As far as I know, the cause of the war was the murder of one of the leading Nez Perce Indians who had a ranch fenced and some fruit trees and land in cultivation, and a white man came and intruded on the Indian's land, taking a part of his improvements, and dispute arose from this and the white man killed the Nez Perce in cold blood. The Indian was unarmed and unable to defend himself. The Indians made complaint, but the white man went unpunished" (*M*, 112). This narration challenges several standard historical accounts by making it clear that Nez Perces in Wallowa practiced agriculture and improved their properties well in advance of allotment. Moreover, he locates the onset of the Joseph War in an unredressed seizure of property and the murder of a Nez Perce man. Charley Wa-to-lina was even more outspoken: "I feel that Joseph and his band were imposed upon and forced him to this war. I and many of my people believe that this trouble was brought about to take Wallowa Valley and other territories away from us" (*M*, 54). Every deponent who testified about this war emphasized its unfinished nature. Reparations remained unpaid for properties lost as people moved from the Wallowa area to the reservation in 1877 and for other properties—in land, improvements, livestock, and personal possessions—they were forced to leave behind when they returned from Indian Territory to the Northwest in 1883 and 1885. Most seriously, the Wallowa country had not yet been restored to its rightful owners. Seven years after Joseph's death, as these witnesses make clear, his passing had not ended the matter. Others had not forgotten his quest. They joined their voices in a chorus memorializing the war, the unjust seizure of lands, and the unfulfilled treaty promises. Based on this memorial, subsequent generations, possessed of a Nimiipuu account of the issues, would carry on his work.

The *Memorial* was printed as a congressional document under Borah's sponsorship, but it is not apparent that it elicited significant federal response. Concerns about seizure of property, personal assets, competency evaluations, and heirship continued to be sent to Washington, and Congress has yet to resolve completely the settlement of land claims comprising *Cobell v. Salazar*.[26] Nonetheless, the *Memorial* stands as a marker at the tomb of allotment, attesting to its failure either to secure Nimiipuu lands to Nimiipuu peoples or to extend "manhood," the franchise, and citizens' rights to Nez Perce allottees.

10. After-Images

Although federal officials made little or no response to the *Memorial of the Nez Perce Indians . . . to the Congress of the United States*, it has since become a cornerstone of Nimiipuu cultural history. Copies of the document were printed under Borah's sponsorship and sold for ten cents each. Many of the original deponents and other interested tribal members owned personal copies, for the document served as a kind of local archive that contained both the words of treaty agreements between the Nez Perces and the federal government and the words of those who had been affected by those agreements.[1] Within the homes of these local owners, print copies of the *Memorial* may have joined other records—physical, textual, and photographic—in private collections. Wary of appropriation and misuse of these items, many Nimiipuu historians, collectors, archivists, and elders have assembled such private collections—of baskets, weavings, bags, and beadwork made by themselves or by family members—and of paper records—newspaper clippings, letters, photographs, scrapbooks, and other memorabilia—that function as counter-archives to those held in official, state- and university-sponsored memory palaces.

Those who have constructed these archives might well be described using the words of cultural historian Michel de Certeau as "unrecognized producers, poets of their own acts." In his book *The Practice of Everyday Life*, this scholar considers the "dispersed, tactical, and makeshift creativity of groups or individuals . . . caught in the nets of 'discipline.'" For de Certeau, capitalism is one such "discipline," and he posits that consumers might in fact also be cultural producers who demonstrate their agency by the uses they make of the goods they purchase. Such repurposing, he asserts, comprises "an antidiscipline."[2] My focus here is not on capitalist consumption but on other forms of discipline—the technologies of allotment—that can also be resisted through antidisciplinary tactics of mirroring and repurposing. As I have demonstrated, the academic discipline of anthropology, supported by archives of illicitly appropriated cultural items, posited a theory of progressive development used in the 1870s and 1880s to justify a federal policy of Native assimilation and extinction. In this concluding chapter I show that collecting and archiving can be mimicked, that the archival impulse might be turned upon itself—in this case by Native cultural producers who have reclaimed, re-collected, curated, and preserved materials that support stories told from within, place-based narratives of survivance.

Starr Maxwell's *Memorial* might be seen as an antidisciplinary act wherein the oral testimony of "poets of their own acts," transcribed by Maxwell and Whitman, spoke back to the written words of the treaty agreements introducing the document and to the federal officials who refused to grant them a hearing. The juxtaposition of the two kinds of evidence corrects the incapacity of official archives to account for oral and experiential memory. A number of those who gave oral testimony to Maxwell were also, in fact, private archivists. They pointedly referred to documentary evidence in their possession, asserting that they could support their claims by producing the written public forms recognized by state courts and tribunals. For example, the several deponents who testified about fractionated heirships supplemented their testimony with copies of letters they had received from distinctly unhelpful federal officials, as did He-yume-toke-te-nikt, who had applied to sell her allotment. In the preceding chapter I quote from the dismissive response she received. Harrison Red Wolf asserted that he "h[e]ld copies of letters to my father . . . which show the trust imposed in my father" (*M*, 57). James Grant, the tribal record keeper since 1892, based his testimony on written records of births and deaths in his possession—an internal census demonstrating that hundreds of children born since Fletcher's departure had not yet received lands (*M*, 40). The collection of voices of more than a hundred Nimiipuu and, by implicit reference, the evidence of their own privately held archives, thus were joined in the *Memorial*, which stood as a summative reference point for how matters stood between the Nez Perces and the federal government in 1911.

By the late twentieth century, many of these issues were still unresolved, but few copies of the *Memorial* remained, yellowed, torn, and "battered" but held as "priceless heirlooms," according to Dennis Baird.[3] Thus in 2000 the Northwest Historical Manuscripts Series republished the *Memorial* with an introduction written by Diane Mallickan. This series might be described as an attempt to establish a place-based public archive, a mirror of larger libraries and collections, located in the place of Nimiipuu culture, its principles of organization honoring histories told from within that place. In large public archives, letters written by Nimiipuu or transcriptions of their oral testimonies are conventionally filed with the papers of white heroes or bureaucrats. For example, several letters written in the early 1880s by James Reubens to Oliver O. Howard, for whom he had served as scout and translator during the Nez Perce War, are held in the archives of the Bowdoin College Library in Brunswick, Maine. There they are filed with other letters related to the "western command period" of Howard's career.[4] Others of Reubens's letters are boxed with Alice C. Fletcher's incoming correspondence at the National Anthropological Archives in Washington DC. Thus documents produced in one place that refer to local history or to figures of local note may be held in severalty, thousands of miles away from the place to which they refer, accessible only to interested parties who possess the means and credentials to seek them out. As a place-based archive, the Northwest Historical Manuscripts Series re-collects such sources, often pairing them with local records such as newspaper accounts, and with oral testimony from local elders and other informants, publishing them in thematic volumes, the logic of which more closely honors Native epistemologies. These records are readily available to those whose history they represent. This publishing initiative has gathered thousands of archival sources and transcriptions of oral testimony in such volumes as *The Nez Perce Nation Divided: Reports on the Aftermath of the 1863 Treaty* and *A Collection of Primary Sources on the Nez Perce Exile in Canada, the Indian Territory, and Their Return to the Northwest: 1877–1886*. Similar initiatives are under way.[5] These books document the existence of a coherent Nez Perce cultural heritage preserved by strategic uses of memory, oral transmission and argumentation, law, diplomacy, and written testimony.

This is not to gainsay the great importance of large public archives that gather documents in central locations for general use. Still, protocols of preserving, sorting, filing, and presenting archival holdings to the public follow dominant epistemologies. Even the physical form of documents determines their archival destinations and uses. For example, individual flat paper documents—letters and manuscripts—more easily conform to archival epistemologies than do hybrid, three-dimensional media such as newspapers and scrapbooks. Although scrapbooks are a common part of the holdings of public archives, they present "complex preservation problems," according to scholars who study the form.[6] Their pages may be made of cheap paper that degrades quickly; they may contain materials such as newspaper clippings that become brittle and discolored or stain other items that touch them. Photographs and memorabilia once firmly affixed to scrapbook pages may work free as the glue dries and ceases to bond artifact to page. Because albums are impermanently bound, often having interchangeable pages, their leaves may tear loose and become separated or disordered. Moreover, the content and logic of these hybrid forms challenge archival classification: Is a scrapbook a digest of news? A family history? A memoir? A historical document? Scrapbooks often have a complex provenance and lack contextual information to support their credentials. Thus archivists try to identify the author or authors of the collection, whose identity helps them to evaluate the scrapbook's content and to decide how it should be inserted into the existing historical narrative and the standard categories of knowledge.[7] These challenges suggest the counter-archival potential of scrapbooks. As private history-making initiatives they are exquisitely and specifically place-based. Because they collect, document, and preserve evidence of the past, scrapbooks mirror in small the functions of state-sponsored museums and archives. But their form and logic often resist the means by which public knowledge is made. Their interpretation depends in large part on external information—on the biography of the album maker, for example, or on specific cultural and communal knowledge—to be fully legible. Within a place-specific context, however, they can be the basis of antidisciplinary knowledge.

Scrapbooks take many forms. Some hold a single medium or genre; others, such as family albums and baby books, may mix photographs, clippings, and letters with memorabilia such as ribbons, flowers, and locks of hair. Here I focus on two types of scrapbooks: collections of newspaper clippings and family photograph albums. As Ellen Gruber Garvey has established, scrapbook collections of items clipped from newspapers were common in the nineteenth and early twentieth centuries and constitute "an elaborate circuit of recirculation, . . . a reflection of personal identity made from mass-produced and distributed publication."[8] Clippings scrapbooks are common among the albums held in northwestern Idaho archives. Some of these collections are pasted or taped into simple and inexpensive spiral-bound notebooks, and other are bound in more elegant and durable forms. In assembling these books, scrapbook makers follow sometimes idiosyncratic but always suggestive logics. Although they frequently do not provide the standard archival documentation of date and source, these amateur historians arrange the items they have saved in meaningful ways. Often an album maker groups thematically related items, for example, as did Kate McBeth when she collected newspaper accounts of Fourth of July celebrations. Album makers may add information to what they have clipped, underlining significant passages and/or annotating them in written sidebar comments, thus linking public and newsworthy events to private concerns.

Because this public information is presumptively available elsewhere, "[s]ome archivists," according to the editors of *The Scrap-*

book in American Life, "are particularly averse to clippings scrapbooks."⁹ That "elsewhere," in archives and research libraries, is often an unindexed cabinet containing microfilm copies of major newspapers or a chronologically arranged vertical file—a series of folders containing newspaper clippings of local interest, sometimes loosely categorized by subject, that comprise a digest of items culled by a librarian from local newspapers. Privately made scrapbooks of newspaper clippings mirror and add focus to these public archives, gathering, arranging, and preserving on their pages items meaningful to the scrapbook maker. These private assemblages of news items present a challenge to the official archive's attempts to encompass all worthy knowledge. They expose its propensity to overlook the local or to attempt to cover items of local interest by maintaining a vertical file. Privately collected and assembled albums of news clippings, then, can proffer usable and difficult-to-find information, and can serve as the basis for alternatively emplotted local histories.

Unlike the microfilmed files of major newspapers, which challenge even the most seasoned researcher with the sheer number of pages to be combed through, and unlike the vertical files of smaller state or local historical societies, where the logic by which the clippings were taken and filed is often obscure, privately made scrapbooks—thematic digests of news significant to a particular individual, family, or community—may document the close connection of federal policy with family and community, as do many Nimiipuu albums. In one such scrapbook held by the Nez Perce National Historical Park, for example, the album maker has clipped, arranged, and pasted into a notebook a series of newspaper accounts covering legal decisions related to allotment in the early twentieth century, interspersing them with notices of local events that had meaning to his own family—celebrations, high school football games, and beauty contests.¹⁰ These clippings come from small local newspapers that may not have been preserved or microfilmed, that are not generally available or easily searched, and that add an important local dimension to a scholar's understanding of how large national policies touched individual lives in specific places, far from the spaces in which those abstract policies were conceived. More im-

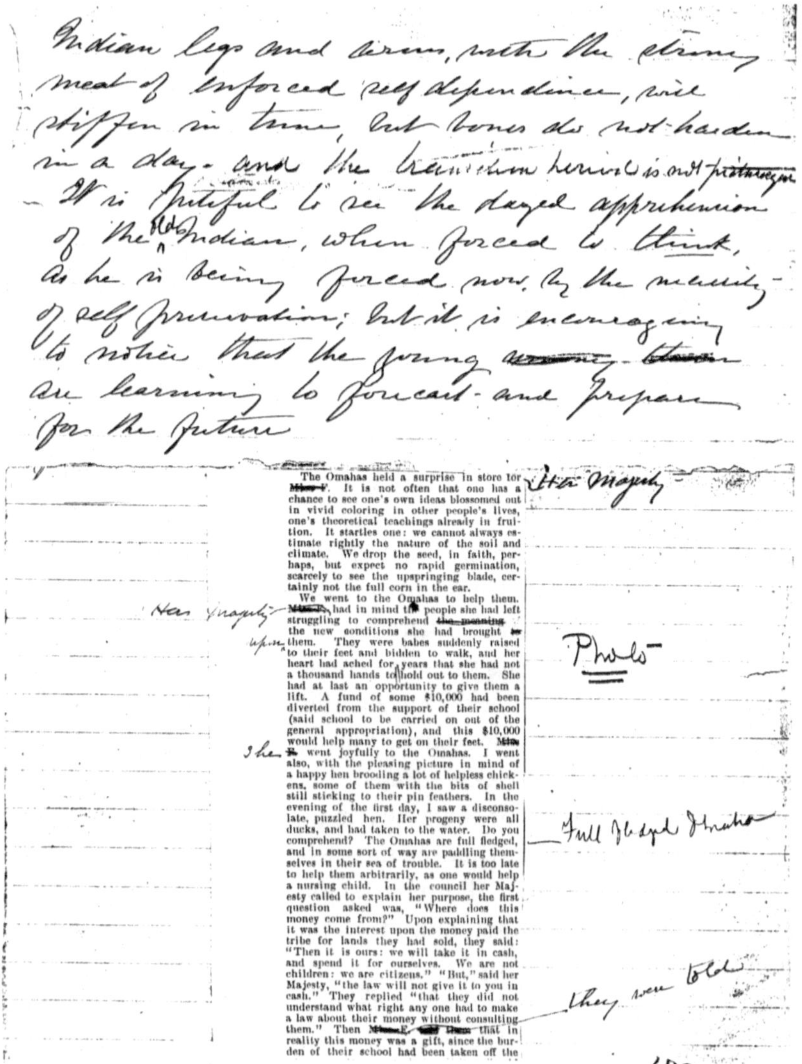

Indian legs and arms, with the strong meat of enforced self dependence, will stiffen in time, but bones do not harden in a day. And the transition period is not picturesque — It is pitiful to see the dazed apprehension of the old Indian, when forced to think, as he is being forced now, by the necessity of self preservation; but it is encouraging to notice that the young ~~women~~ ~~them~~ are learning to forecast and prepare for the future

Her Majesty —

I he

Her Majesty —

Photo —

Full fledged Omaha

they were told

172

The Omahas held a surprise in store for ~~Miss F.~~ It is not often that one has a chance to see one's own ideas blossomed out in vivid coloring in other people's lives, one's theoretical teachings already in fruition. It startles one: we cannot always estimate rightly the nature of the soil and climate. We drop the seed, in faith, perhaps, but expect no rapid germination, scarcely to see the upspringing blade, certainly not the full corn in the ear.

We went to the Omahas to help them. ~~Miss F.~~ had in mind the people she had left struggling to comprehend ~~the meaning~~ the new conditions she had brought ~~to~~ upon them. They were babes suddenly raised to their feet and bidden to walk, and her heart had ached for years that she had not a thousand hands to hold out to them. She had at last an opportunity to give them a lift. A fund of some $10,000 had been diverted from the support of their school (said school to be carried on out of the general appropriation), and this $10,000 would help many to get on their feet. ~~Miss~~ went joyfully to the Omahas. I went also, with the pleasing picture in mind of a happy hen brooding a lot of helpless chickens, some of them with the bits of shell still sticking to their pin feathers. In the evening of the first day, I saw a disconsolate, puzzled hen. Her progeny were all ducks, and had taken to the water. Do you comprehend? The Omahas are full fledged, and in some sort of way are paddling themselves in their sea of trouble. It is too late to help them arbitrarily, as one would help a nursing child. In the council her Majesty called to explain her purpose, the first question asked was, "Where does this money come from?" Upon explaining that it was the interest upon the money paid the tribe for lands they had sold, they said: "Then it is ours: we will take it in cash, and spend it for ourselves. We are not children: we are citizens." "But," said her Majesty, "the law will not give it to you in cash." They replied "that they did not understand what right any one had to make a law about their money without consulting them." Then ~~Miss F. said~~ that in reality this money was a gift, since the burden of their school had been taken off the

FIG. 52. E. Jane Gay, Letter 14, draft manuscript of *Choup-nit-ki*, page 172, ca. 1901–1904. Idaho State Historical Society State Archives and Research Center.

portant, in choosing, arranging, underlining, and annotating such an album, its maker has produced a working draft of a particular family and local history.

Other more hybrid Native scrapbooks and albums resemble those made by E. Jane Gay, now a major source for those who study the history of allotment. Gay assembled the working draft of *Choup-nit-ki*, from which her niece, Emma J. Gay, copied the handwritten pages of the final albums, in much the same fashion as one would make a clippings scrapbook (see, for example, fig. 52).[11] For large segments of *Choup-nit-ki* Gay used clippings of the newspaper versions of letters she had sent to the *Red Man* and the *Christian Register*, striking out, annotating, arranging, interlineating, and revising those early accounts to match her present purpose and indicating with numbers where she planned to include photographs as illustrations.

Choup-nit-ki includes not only transcriptions of Gay's newspaper columns but also letters, sketches, drawings, and photographs, addenda that increase its value as a historic source. Photographs make visible evocative details barely hinted at in Gay's prose, such as the regalia worn by the Reubens brothers at Cold Spring in August 1889 (fig. 8). While Gay framed this encounter as an informal entertainment staged for the amusement of the stranded women, the photograph suggests that the men who posed for her saw it as a ceremony finalizing their allotments. Conversely, Gay often tried to expand a photograph's potential meaning with visual reinterpretation and explanatory text. In *Choup-nit-ki*, for example, she chose not to use any of the several photos she made of the salmon feast in Kamiah in July 1890.[12] (I reproduce one of them here, as fig. 53.) Instead she included a simplified sketch that reduces the number of figures and foregrounds the details of the cooking arrangements (fig. 54). In support of this image Gay added a narrative emphasizing the sacramental overtones of the feast.

Emma J. Gay's meticulous drawings ornamenting the pages of *Choup-nit-ki* link the experience of Fletcher and Gay to a larger body of ethnographic knowledge. Emma based some of her illustrations, such as those ornamenting the List of Photographs in the album (fig. 55), on museum holdings, anthropological sources, and souve-

FIG. 53. "Salmon Feast," July 1890, by E. Jane Gay. ISHS 63-221.218, Idaho State Historical Society Library and Archives.

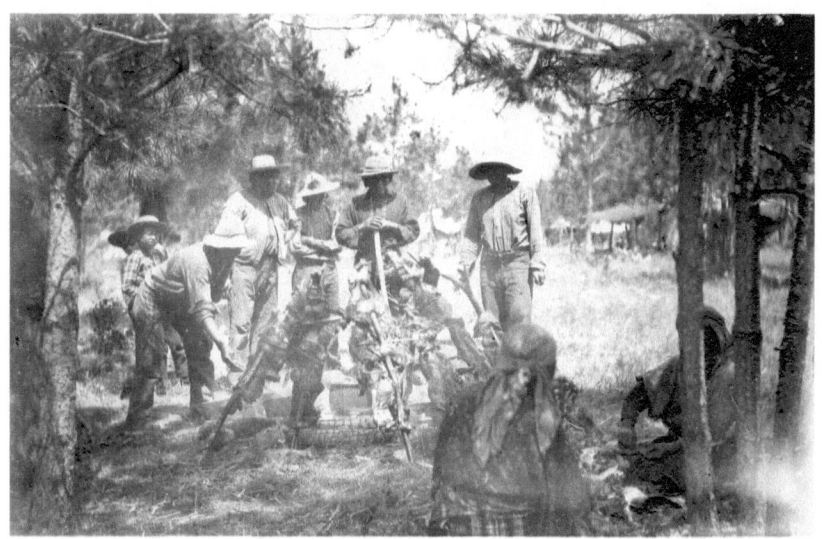

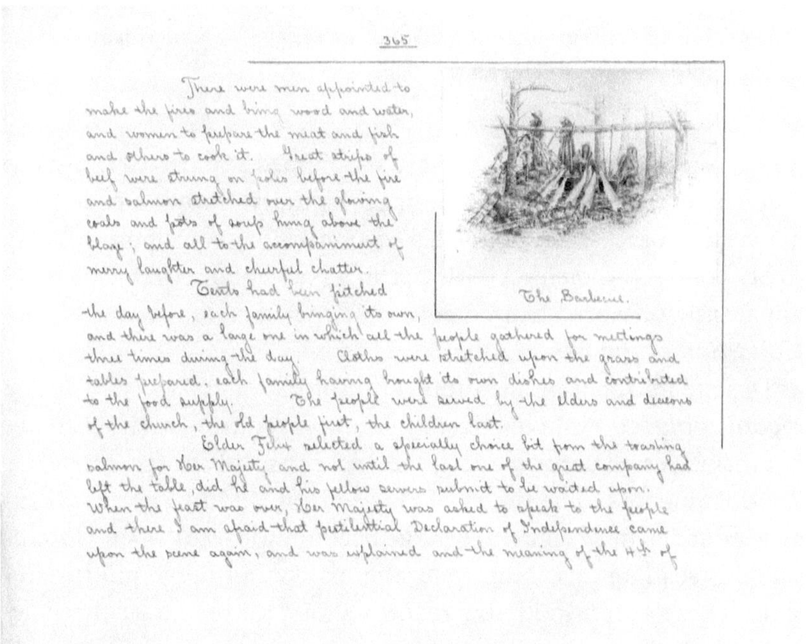

365

There were men appointed to make the fires and bring wood and water, and women to prepare the meat and fish and others to cook it. Great strips of beef were strung on poles before the fire and salmon stretched over the glowing coals and pots of soup hung above the blaze; and all to the accompaniment of merry laughter and cheerful chatter.

The Barbecue.

Tents had been pitched the day before, each family bringing its own, and there was a large one in which all the people gathered for meetings three times during the day. Cloths were stretched upon the grass and tables prepared, each family having brought its own dishes and contributed to the food supply. The people were served by the Elders and deacons of the church, the old people first, the children last.

Elder Felix selected a specially choice bit from the roasting salmon for Her Majesty and not until the last one of the great company had left the table, did he and his fellow servers submit to be waited upon. When the feast was over, Her Majesty was asked to speak to the people and there I am afraid that pestilential Declaration of Independence came upon the scene again, and was explained and the meaning of the 4th of

FIG. 54. "The Barbecue," *Choup-nit-ki,* 365. The Schlesinger Library, Radcliffe Institute, Harvard University.

FIG. 55. List of Photographs from *Choup-nit-ki*, xi. The Schlesinger Library, Radcliffe Institute, Harvard University.

nirs Gay had collected. In one case she clipped and pasted drawings made by others onto the album page. Figure 56 shows a page from her version of Kew-kew'-lu-yah's account of the Nimiipuu embassy to St. Louis, ornamented with Catlin's sketches of two of the men, apparently scissored from a copy of *The Manners, Customs, and Condition of the North American Indians*.[13]

Despite its apparent plenitude of information, *Choup-nit-ki* is a record compiled by an outsider to Nimiipuu culture, a detached but not disinterested participant in the application of the federal policy she documented. The limits of Gay's vision and of Fletcher's efficacy as an agent of cultural change become apparent when *Choup-nit-ki* is read against Nimiipuu albums containing similar materials. These antidisciplinary records show, for example, that Gay refused to document certain topics, while others remained invisible to her. To cite only the most obvious example, she seems never to have made an image of a Nimiipuu man or woman wearing rega-

[308]

FIG. 56. *Choup-nit-ki*, page 396. The Schlesinger Library, Radcliffe Institute, Harvard University.

lia at a Fourth of July celebration. Nevertheless, Gay's photographs have become commonplace illustrations in a wide range of secondary sources, where they are usually presented without a discussion of their limits as documentary and evidentiary sources.

Gay's images are part of the myriad photographs of Nez Perces made before, during, and since the allotment period, many of them since collected in libraries and archives, where they provide students of Nez Perce history with illustrative materials. Despite the size of this photographic archive, the range of images that appear in encyclopedias, general histories, and specialized studies seems surprisingly limited. Chief Joseph, for example, repeatedly stands for Nez Perces in the aggregate, past and present. The propensity seems to be to use photographic images simply as illustrations, not as documents worthy of analysis, and to disregard the wealth of images of modern Nez Perces made since the late nineteenth century. This lack of variety suggests the persistence of an ethnographically based ver-

[309]

sion of Nez Perce history that reaches its putative conclusion at the end of the Nez Perce War.

To this public photographic archive might be counterposed the photographs collected in private Nez Perce family albums.[14] Such sources stand outside the structure of official, capitalist, and imperial epistemologies and constitute for their makers and preservers a source of cultural continuity and reaffirmation. The photographs in these albums were made by Nimiipuu with cameras, or were commissioned by Nimiipuu from commercial photographers, their content and poses resulting from the negotiation between conventional studio portraiture and the sitters' wishes. In figure 57, for example, Katherine Cloud stands in front of a commercial backdrop and baby Bert's cradleboard rests in a Victorian wicker chair belonging to Hanson's Studio. Her personal adornments, the cradleboard, the woven throw, and wallet are family possessions, likely made by Katherine Cloud or by other family members. Portraits such as this can offer a potent counterpoint to the standard repertoire of images—here I am thinking of "Women's Work in Savagery," a representation made just twelve years earlier. These portraits—made at the behest of the sitter and held within place-based personal archives—resituate the narration of Nimiipuu history from the memory palace and history book to the family, tribe, and homeland.

Family albums, as those who study scrapbooks and ephemera have established, exist within the cultural surround of modern forms such as photographic technology, newspapers, postcards, magazines, and other inexpensive print media.[15] They signal their makers' command of "reading, visual literacy, and consumption of mass-produced goods."[16] In other words, such albums exemplify Philip J. Deloria's claim "that a significant cohort of Native people engaged the same forces of modernization that were making non-Indians reevaluate their own expectations of themselves and their society" (*IUP*, 6). Their makers showed the same facility with these technologies as did other citizens who consumed and used these forms. Still, I would argue, Native family albums should also be seen as cultural bulwarks against the exoticizing, documentary, and sometimes demeaning uses of photographs, written reports, newspapers, the prac-

FIG. 57. Katherine Cloud and Bert Cloud, by Hanson's Studio, Genesee ID, ca. 1905. Dickson-Cloud Family Photograph Collection. Used by permission of Nakia Williamson-Cloud.

FIG. 58. Funeral of James Stuart, 1929. Used by permission of Diane Mallickan.

tices of ethnographic study and collection, and the archival complex.

These family albums, often bound between elaborately ornamented padded covers that characterize mass-produced scrapbooks, hold letters, photographs, clippings, and other ephemera. The photographs memorialize family events—births, weddings, christenings, deaths, and family reunions. Figure 58, for example, comes from the photograph collection of descendants of James Stuart and shows family members gathered for his funeral. Other images, such as figure 59, may bespeak the "consumption of mass-produced goods," showing people posing on the steps of wood-frame houses, holding cameras, or standing by the side of cars and pickups. Yet not every apparent signifier of consumer consumption is what it seems to be. Figure 60, for example, shows the home James Stuart, a skilled builder, constructed for his younger sister Nancy in Kooskia (formerly Stuart) Idaho. The home indeed bespeaks a blend of consumer goods and local materials brought together by the vision, labor, and skill of a local craftsman.

These Native family albums may contain postcards purchased during vacations taken by family members or friends, sometimes to sites of Native significance, such as "Navajoland."[17] They place the

FIG. 59. The Dickson-Cloud family, Dickson Ranch, ca. 1915. *Left to right, back row*: Ruth Cloud, Katherine Cloud, Elsie Cloud, Ermath Cloud; *front row*: Ellory Cloud, unnamed woman holding camera, Clayton Dickson, Lilyan Cloud. Dickson-Cloud Family Photograph Collection. Used by permission of Nakia Williamson-Cloud.

FIG. 60. Home built by James Stuart for his sister Nancy in Kooskia, Idaho. Used by permission of Diane Mallickan.

family within their local community in snapshots of social gatherings, sports teams, school groups, beauty contests, and parades and holiday celebrations. They connect the local to the national and international community over the course of several twentieth-century wars as well, showing, for example, portraits of uniformed family members (see fig. 66). Informal snapshots made by Nez Perces with cameras challenge the facticity of the posed and even of the supposedly candid images made by white photographers of the allotment era. Jane Gay's images of Nez Perces in or near tipis were made as anthropological documentation, wherein traditionally attired Nez Perces stand stiffly in front of a supposedly primitive mode of shelter, or were taken in the field, where the Nez Perce chainmen as well as other members of the allotting team slept and worked in tipis (see fig. 25, "Camp Bearing Tree"). Gay wrote nostalgically of these camp shelters in her concluding "Writer's Note": "We could not to-day pitch our tent here, there and everywhere upon the Indian land, and lie down to sleep with perfect confidence in the protecting power of the three tape fastenings of our door flap, . . . for

FIG. 61. "Remember this? It was fun wasn't it?" Historical Photograph Collection, University of Idaho Special Collections and Archives, Moscow ID, PG100-173.

the white man has entered the land, with pick-axe and plough and pistols" (C, 445). Her comment is one of closure, signaling that with the opening of the reservation and the advent of private property had come potential violence.

Family album images such as figure 61 both refract against Gay's field shots and capture within a single frame the kind of "double picture" I discussed earlier. In this snapshot several people stand next to a tipi, while others work to erect tent poles for a second. A pickup truck apparently used to transport the building materials stands at the left. Visible in the background are the unmistakable signifiers of civilization — a fence and a frame house. The difference between Gay's two photos of tipis and the recollections they evoke lies in the brief comment written on the obverse of this image: "Remember this? It was fun wasn't it?" That comment places the snapshot firmly within a social context of mutual pleasure, of a shared history nostalgic in tone but lacking the foreboding sense of finality and closure that Gay's conclusion proffers.

In another instance two pages of a private album hold a set of six

FIG. 62. Pages from Dickson-Cloud family album.

Used by permission of Nakia Williamson-Cloud.

snapshots of members of the Dickson-Cloud family on the fall deer hunt in 1915 (fig. 62). These photographs do not function as ethnographic documentation of a disappearing way of life. Rather, they are pictures taken from within, by one or more family members who rode with others along the river bank, slept next to them in the tipis, and perhaps posed for a family group snapshot. Such informal images stand as evidence that in the early twentieth century, Nez Perces continued to exercise their rights to the hunting and fishing grounds they had claimed in the earliest treaties, claims they reasserted in documents such as the *Memorial*. And although twenty-first-century digital photographs made on similar occasions might show hunters wearing insulated boots, carrying high-powered rifles, and driving pickup trucks, the annual fall hunt continues to be a meaningful part of their lives.

Unsurprisingly, many family albums contain photographs made at Fourth of July celebrations. Often in their composition they echo the more polished commercial images made by photographers such as Lee Moorhouse or Edward Latham, as does figure 63, identified on its obverse as "Indians when they had their 4 of July last year. 1911." At other times, however, these snapshots effectually re-turn the photographic gaze, making *participation* in the celebration, not watching it, the subject of the image and inviting the viewer to share an insider's perspective. Figure 64 was included in an album made by a Nimiipuu woman in the first part of the twentieth century. Like most of the other images she collected, the photograph is uncaptioned and offers no information about the identities of the men who are pictured.[18] On the obverse, however, someone has written "at Spalding / July sure hot." These five words locate this image of two men in regalia standing in front of a tipi in a specific place—Spalding—at an exact if not specific time: July. The men surely are participating in an annual summer celebration. Some viewers—outsiders—guided by captions like "sure hot" will thus be prompted to add to the image information that might have been obscured by the photograph's arrest of a single moment—the vivid physical sensations of heat and dust, and the odors of sweat, horses, and riders. Other viewers—family members sharing the album—may have

FIG. 63. "Indians when they had their 4 of July last year. 1911." Historical Photograph Collection, University of Idaho Special Collections and Archives, Moscow ID, PG100-029.

made the tipi, sewed the regalia, or constructed the drum. Still others — friends, relatives, community members — may add their own information, as has photographer/artist Nakia Williamson-Cloud, who has identified these men. All these community members, past and present, join the two men in the photograph as part of a ritual that bound the Nez Perces together long before Alice Fletcher arrived in Idaho and that has continued for more than a century.

Such family albums were not intended to be part of a large documentary public collection, nor to be sent to donors and patrons as evidence of the success of a charitable enterprise, nor to be donated to an archive as the result of a collector's avarice or a researcher's project. They comprise a potent resistance to the knowledge-making activities of ethnography and census that underwrote allotment's efforts to produce propertied individualized citizens. Their subjects remain anonymous in the large sense but are recognizable to those who see them with a knowing eye. Few of the people in these scrapbooks are identified by name. The album form may provide a partial explanation for this omission: it is difficult to write on black pages. Many early twentieth-century commercial album pages were pre-

 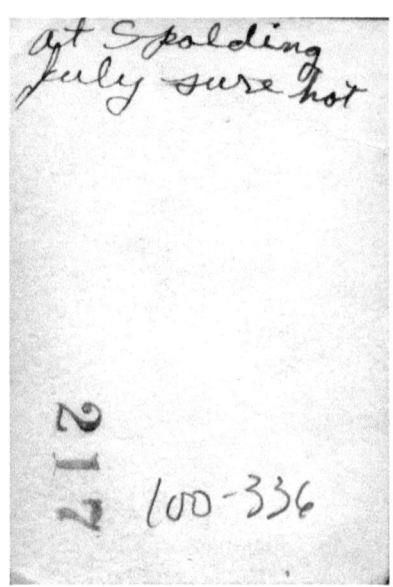

FIG. 64. "At Spalding / July sure hot." John Miller and Gene Ellinwood, tentative identification by Nakia Williamson-Cloud. Historical Photograph Collection, University of Idaho Special Collections and Archives, Moscow ID, PG100-336.

cut with corner slots. This design made it easier to mount photographs in the book, but left little room for captioning. A photograph that could easily be inserted could also easily fall loose, becoming intermixed with other loose images, and would therefore not remain tidily affixed next to an identifying caption or in its assigned position on a page. Nor do many of these photographs have identifications written on the obverse. The tasks of identifying, ordering, sorting, and preserving a number of snapshots may be put aside in the press of other activities. Thus a custodian of family history, one with a knowing eye, becomes the key to reading these images. One who can identify the people in a photograph may also be able to tell stories of the situation in which the photo was made or other stories about the subjects. As photo historian Richard Storch observes, "in the case of Native people, the information embedded in the image was an extension of the oral tradition."[19] History is not missing from these albums. It resides in other epistemological places—not in chronologically ordered and tidily numbered pages, nor in careful documentary captioning, but in memory, in the oral, narrative, storytelling skill of those who know the meanings of these images, and in invisible bonds of inherited knowledge they are able to share.

Snapshots of family gatherings often show multiple generations of a single family, but that family is defined by its own internal logic and does not always follow the patterns Alice Fletcher tried to establish as the standard for orderly inheritance of land. Frequently such photographs show extended family groups, a network of elders, aunties, uncles, and cousins. Within a given album the people comprising such groups may vary over time. Babies become teens, teens become parents, elders disappear and are replaced by their offspring—but the poses remain largely the same. Parents and elders sit in the center of the group; older children stand behind them or at their sides; members of the youngest generation perch cross-legged in the front or on the laps of their grandparents. Occasionally babies in beautifully beaded cradleboards lie on the ground or are propped against an elder's knee. The Dickson-Cloud family album contains a number of photographs made in the same setting—at the side of a frame house, between a window and door. I have included two of them here—both made on the same occasion—as figures 59 and 65. The unchanging nature of this surround both resembles and differs from the use of standard studio backdrops. The professional photographer's canvas backdrop of a landscape or garden, and the studio props of chairs, settees, desks, and columns serve as a kind of trademark that allows contemporary scholars to identify now-defunct studios that did not otherwise mark their images. So, too, do the same house, door, and window serve to identify a particular family group. Additionally, however, the unchanging nature of the house and yard lifts these photographs from the quotidian to the enduring, for the people who pose there return again and again to this spot to celebrate their family's continuance. Posing in just this way in this precise location establishes their presence together, in their home and on their land.

In these private family albums amateur snapshots may often occupy the same page as more formal and aesthetically standard-

FIG. 65. Katherine Cloud, Elsie Cloud, Ruth Cloud, Ellory Cloud, Ben Cloud (*with camera*), Clayton Dickson, Evie Cloud, Ermath Cloud, Lilyan Cloud. At the Dickson Ranch, ca. 1915. Dickson-Cloud Family Photograph Collection. Used by permission of Nakia Williamson-Cloud.

ized studio shots. In the years immediately following the 1895 land sale, photographic studios sprang up in nearly every small northwest Idaho town, eager to profit from the ready cash of allottees.[20] According to Storch, "there were at least a dozen photographers working on or near the Nez Perce Reservation [and] it was fairly common for local Native people to frequent the studios for individual or family portraits."[21] Many of these professionally made images marked an important occasion—a christening, engagement, or marriage, a son or daughter leaving for or returning from military service—events of such moment that they called for a professionally made formal portrait that was sure to turn out well. In figure 66, for example, a young family poses before a studio backdrop. A man dressed in a World War I navy uniform sits on a bench, holding a baby. Next to him on the bench stands a small boy, dressed

FIG. 66. "Nez Percé Indian Family—World War I." Josephine Klason-Haight Photograph Collection. Acc. 478, box 1, folder 72, cat. #35659. Courtesy of National Park Service, Nez Perce National Historical Park.

FIG. 67. Harriet Stuart (*left*) and Annie Parnell Little, by E. Jane Gay. ISHS 63-221.83d. Idaho State Historical Society State Archives and Research Center.

in a miniature version of the same uniform. Standing to the man's right, with her hand on the baby's shoulder, is a woman who wears a long ornamented dress. These and other studio portraits assert a proud Native identity displayed through choice of attire, pose, and accessory.[22] Here, just a decade after Jane Gay made images such as figure 67, a portrait of Harriet Stuart and her sister, Annie Parnell Little, dressed in western attire that seemed to guarantee their assimilation, are Nimiipuu men and women who have placed themselves before the camera's eye, surrounded by baskets, beaded bags, and cradleboards, wearing necklaces, sashes, war bonnets, hairpipe breast plates, and beaded moccasins (see fig. 68; see also figs. 49 and 51). The apparent ease and the joy and pride evident on the faces of many of the sitters suggest that these images occupy a distinctively different category than many similar ethnographic studio shots, in

FIG. 68. Unidentified Nez Perce women. Josephine Klason-Haight Photograph Collection. Acc. 478, box 1, folder 66, cat. #35659. Courtesy of National Park Service, Nez Perce National Historical Park.

FIG. 69. "'Reubens Bro's' Nesperce Tribe," by Major Lee Moorhouse. Stephen Shawley Collection, Historical Photograph Collection, University of Idaho Special Collections and Archives, Moscow ID, 38-0453.

which regalia was donned at the behest of the photographer, whose intent was to profit from a manufactured display of Native exoticism and in which the poses are stiff and subjects unwilling.[23] Contrast, for example, Moorhouse's portrait of the Reubens brothers (fig. 69), with Gay's "They Donned War Bonnets" (fig. 8), which seems, within this continuum, to occupy a middle ground between photographs in which the sitters are willing and one in which they are coerced.

Many Native family albums include portraits such as figures 70 and 71 of family members who attended federal boarding schools such as Carlisle, Chilocco, or Chemawa. These portraits may be accompanied by images of sports teams dressed in baseball, football, or track uniforms, such as figure 72, of Clayton Dickson with the Chilocco Indian Agricultural School baseball team. Such images were likely made by the school's official photographer. At Richard Pratt's Carlisle Indian School, John N. Choate, the school's photographer, also produced before-and-after shots documenting the schools' ostensible success at transforming Native children into the image of white propriety. The school offered such paired photographs as premiums to entice white patrons to subscribe to one of the several periodicals produced by the "Carlisle Indian printer boys." In every issue produced in the late nineteenth century, the *Indian Helper* made this "Standing Offer": "For TEN [new subscribers to the paper], Two PHOTOGRAPHS, one showing a group of Pueblos as they arrived in wild dress, and another of the same pupils three years later, or, for the same number of names we give two photographs showing still more marked contrast between a Navajoe as he arrived in native dress, and as he now looks, worth 20 cents a piece."[24] The disciplinary uses of such images have been carefully and sensitively analyzed by scholars such as Laura Wexler, who argues that such "photographs were a central resource" of "noncorporeal, affect-based models of discipline."[25] Carlisle shamelessly used these double pictures to attract financial support, advertised them as having a monetary value (twenty cents), and sold them as souvenirs to subscribers in exchange for their support of Carlisle's programs of assimilation.

The concept of "doubled pictures," however, may also signal the

FIG. 70. Harriet Mary, Nez Perces, student at the Carlisle Indian School, by John N. Choate. Cumberland County Historical Society, Carlisle PA. PA-CHI-13b. Another photograph in the CCHS collection says Harriet Mary was from Bald Head's Camp, Oakland (Agency).

FIG. 71. James Dickson at Carlisle Indian School. Dickson-Cloud Family Photograph Collection. Used by permission of Nakia Williamson-Cloud.

FIG. 72. Clayton Dickson (*middle row, far left*) with the Chilocco Indian Agricultural School baseball team. Dickson-Cloud Family Photograph Collection. Used by permission of Nakia Williamson-Cloud.

different destinations and different interpretations copies of a given photograph may elicit. Such an image, placed in a family scrapbook, for example, can assume a very different meaning. A formal school portrait might satisfy a white "friend of the Indian," whose reform sensibilities were bolstered by visual evidence, that the Indian education programs were fostering progress toward assimilation. A copy of the same portrait might be an object cherished by family members separated from their child by miles and years. Within the album, parents could reclaim a distant child as part of an intact Nimiipuu family (see fig. 73). Because many such collections span a family's history through several generations, the same album may contain Kodachrome 1960s-era public school pictures of the Carlisle student's children or grandchildren, the succession of portraits suggesting a continuity of family pride in intellectual accomplishment.

Archivists and researchers question the value of family albums "as primary source material" because "they usually arrive [at the archive] devoid of context, with no attribution, provenance, history, or biographical information."[26] In other words, they cannot easily be

FIG. 73. Clayton Dickson at Chilocco Indian Agricultural School. Dickson-Cloud Family Photograph Collection. Used by permission of Nakia Williamson-Cloud.

FIG. 74. Horse procession. Dickson-Cloud Family Photograph Collection. Used by permission of Nakia Williamson-Cloud.

connected to the larger abstract narratives supported and produced by state-sponsored archives. The standard interpretive frames of heroic biography, the sweep of emplotted (white-dominated) history, the consolidation of "national" property, and the provenance—the legal documentation of a transfer of property—are absent. Yet these albums offer an antidisciplinary corrective and demand new interpretative frames to account for the counterintuitive but crucial information they represent.

As I write these final words, *Cobell v. Salazar* awaits congressional approval. Regardless of its outcome, related lawsuits surely will continue to seek a more complete accounting for tribal funds. Thus I have written of these family albums as a conclusion, for they proffer a silent but weighty opposition to assumptions that Native claims such as these should be put aside and that Native peoples should take their places as part of multicultural America. In the specific case I have written about here, these records, with their "doubled pictures," insist that assimilation was never as complete or as successful as its proponents claimed it would be.

Figure 74, an uncaptioned photograph, is taken from the point of view of a rider joining a line of horses. The rider sees the procession from a position within it, a point of view dominated by the back of the horse's head. Ahead, in the deep background, a line of horses and riders weave through the trees, ascending the hill in single file. Here the photographer is a participant-observer, as Gay was of Fletcher, involved in as well as detached from the photograph. Unlike the outside viewer, this image maker and those who share the album containing the snapshot know where the procession is going, who the other riders are, and the purpose of the trip. The vantage point from inside, within Native culture and Native epistemology, establishes that despite the technologies of modernization deployed against tribal members in the name of benevolent progress, those who made and transmitted these albums and their descendants continue to look forward, having maintained a proud, vibrant, and sovereign Native identity.

Notes

Abbreviations

ACF	Alice Cunningham Fletcher
ARCIA	*Annual Report of the Commissioner of Indian Affairs*
C	E. Jane Gay, *Choup-nit-ki: With the Nez Perces*
CIA	Commissioner of Indian Affairs
"CLE"	E. Jane Gay, "Camp Life Experiences," *Red Man* 11, no. 5 (April/May 1891).
FLF	Francis La Flesche
FWP	Frederick W. Putnam
ISHS	Idaho State Historical Society
ISPARL	Idaho State Public Archives and Research Library
IUP	Philip J. Deloria, *Indians in Unexpected Places*
LC	Library of Congress
M	Starr J. Maxwell, comp., *Memorial of the Nez Perce Indians Residing in the State of Idaho to the Congress of the United States*
NAA	National Anthropological Archives
NAB	National Archives Building, Washington DC
NACP	National Archives and Records Administration, College Park MD
NARA	Pacific Alaska Region (Seattle) National Archives and Records Administration, Pacific Alaska Region, Seattle WA
NPIT	J. Diane Pearson, *The Nez Perces in the Indian Territory: Nimiipuu Survival*
NPNHP	Nez Perce National Historical Park

NPNHPA Nez Perce National Historical Park Archives
PACF   Papers of Alice Cunningham Fletcher (1838–1923) and Francis La Flesche (1859–1923). Ms. 4558, National Anthropological Archives.
PMAE   Peabody Museum of Archaeology and Ethnology
RBIC   *Annual Report of the Board of Indian Commissioners*
RG   Record Group (from Records of the Bureau of Indian Affairs)
SLHWA   Schlesinger Library on the History of Women in America, Radcliffe Institute, Harvard University. All the records related to Jane Gay, which comprise a large part of the Jane Gay Dodge Papers, 1861–1951, are available in electronic facsimile as part of the Harvard Open Collections Program.
SNL   Joan Mark, *A Stranger in Her Native Land: Alice Fletcher and the American Indians*
TJM   Thomas Jefferson Morgan

Unless otherwise indicated, citations to documents contained in Record Group 75, Records of the Bureau of Indian Affairs, refer to the collections of the National Archives of the United States, Washington DC (NAB), Records of the Office of the Commissioner of Indian Affairs, Series 4, Letters received, 1881–1907.

Nez Perce Reservation surveys and land patents illustrated in figures 11, 13, 21, and 27–30 are all in Record Group 75, National Archives and Records Administration, Pacific Alaska Region (Seattle): Survey Maps, compiled 1873–1895, Maps and Charts from the Department of the Interior, Office of Indian Affairs, Fort Lapwai Indian Agency; and Patent Receipts (Nez Perce), 1895, No. 1617-1995, Patent Receipts, Fort Lapwai Agency, 1895, Northern Idaho Agency, Bureau of Indian Affairs.

All citations from the National Anthropological Archives (NAA) are from Ms. 4558, the Papers of Alice Cunningham Fletcher (1838–1923) and Francis La Flesche (1859–1923), unless otherwise noted.

Preface

1. *Cherokee Nation v. Georgia*, 30 U.S. 5 Pet. 1 1 (1831).
2. "Leave No Tribe," 2.
3. "Leave No Tribe," 3, 4.
4. "Leave No Tribe," 1.

Introduction

1. James Stuart's name is also spelled Stewart in the documentary record. Here I follow the spelling he used on his business letterhead.

2. See, for example, Gulick, *Chief Joseph Country*, 286, where the cropped image shows only Joseph and Fletcher, and Josephy, *Nez Perce Country*, 147. Slickpoo's *Noon Nee-Me-Poo* reproduces the full image but erroneously identifies Fletcher as Kate McBeth, the Presbyterian missionary (197). In Josephy's *500 Nations*, the cropped photo shows only Joseph (417).

3. Josephy, *Nez Perce Indians*, 630.

4. In this book I use Nimiipuu to signify a perspective from within this culture, and Nez Perce, the name given these peoples by white interests, to signal an outside, modern, or sometimes colonialist, point of view.

5. For another account of the end of the Joseph War, see McWhorter, *Yellow Wolf*, 220–37. Yellow Wolf emphatically declares: "We were not captured. It was a draw battle.... Had we known [that we would be sent to Eeikish Pah] we never would have surrendered" (225). He asserts that Nimiipuu combatants understood the battle to have ended by mutual agreement (224).

6. ACF to Electa Sanderson Dawes, 2 Oct. 1890, box 10, Henry L. Dawes Papers, 1833–1933, Library of Congress (hereafter cited as LC).

7. Philip J. Deloria examines the efficacy of such "marker[s]," violent events that historians use as termini, or turning points that signal the end of armed resistance and the beginning of intercultural relations premised on "Indian containment and pacification" (*Indians in Unexpected Places*, 16, 51, 15–51; hereafter cited as *IUP*, with page numbers).

8. Gay, *Choup-nit-ki*, 37. I have taken all quotations from *Choup-nit-ki*, Gay's two-volume scrapbook history of the allotment, from the facsimile version in the Jane Gay Dodge Papers posted electronically by the Harvard University Library as part of their Open Collections Program (hereafter cited as C, with page numbers). In the occasional instances when I quote from other print versions of this material, I indicate doing so.

9. "Grand endeavors" echoes the title of Fleming and Luskey's collection of images of Native peoples made by nineteenth-century photographers. Here I refer both to the image makers whose work is documented in that book and to other similar collections of images of Native peoples.

10. I use the term *landscape* intentionally, to signal that Gay's images frame the terrain as an artistically composed view. Or, as Jackson puts it in *Landscape in Sight*, "[L]andscape is not a natural feature of the environment but a *synthetic* space, a [hu]man-made system of spaces super-

imposed on the face of the land, functioning ... to serve a community" (305). Jackson's emphasis on space and its functions anticipates my arguments in part 2.

11. ACF to Electa Sanderson Dawes, 2 Oct. 1890, box 10, Henry L. Dawes Papers, 1833–1933, LC.

12. I take the term *manifest domesticity* from Kaplan's widely cited essay of the same title, reprinted in *The Anarchy of Empire*. This essay has been the impetus for many subsequent studies of women's involvement in colonial ventures. Here I wish to extend the range of Kaplan's inquiry by giving attention to the peoples who were the object of feminized efforts of education and domestication and to how they adapted to and resisted these civilizing efforts.

13. Pearson's *The Nez Perces in the Indian Territory* is one of a number of recent studies that document how Native sovereignty has persisted despite the sequence of federal policies designed to assimilate, reorganize, terminate, and reconstitute Native nations (hereafter cited as NPIT, with page numbers). Leibhardt's "Allotment Policy" traces the effects of allotment law among the members of the Yakima Nation. See also, among others, Fowler, *Arapahoe Politics*, an ethnographically based study arguing that "[Arapahoe] ... history" be taken as a template for contemporary "decisions and relationships" (xvii); Rosier, whose *Rebirth of the Blackfeet Nation* focuses on the period between "the Indian New Deal and the termination eras" in that nation's history (2); and Biolsi, *Organizing the Lakota*, a book that focuses on the New Deal era. See also Beck, *The Struggle for Self-Determination*, a study that shows "[h]ow ... the Menominee survive[d]" this series of legal onslaughts (ix); and Lambert, *Choctaw Nation*, a work that documents the "exercise" of "tribal sovereignty" (15). Within this group, my work most closely resembles that of scholars who seek to establish Native texts and performances as key historical counter-narratives. See, for example, Ridington, whose "Omaha Survival" reads Fletcher and La Flesche's account of the Omaha Sacred Pole and its associated ceremonial observances as "Omaha ... tribal history" (39); Iverson, "*For Our Navajo People*," a collection of Diné documents, speeches, and photographs that demonstrate "the Navajo commitment to place and their determination to exercise control over their lives and lands" (1); Hoxie, whose *Parading through History* establishes ceremonial celebrations as the thread of continuity in Crow Nation history; and McMillen's *Making Indian Law*, a study combining legal history, archival research, and historical narrative to demonstrate the interconnections of ethnohistory and Native land claims cases.

14. Vine Deloria Jr., "Revision and Reversion," 86. The multiple failures of allotment law have been widely documented. See, among others, Otis, *Dawes Act*, an early history that concludes that "the government failed utterly at the crucial point of the program's administration" (80); Hoxie, *Final Promise*, a study detailing the Dawes Act's multiple amendments and pointing to tribal "revivals" in the present moment (187, 241–43); Priest, who in *Uncle Sam's Stepchildren* locates the policy's failure in the "misapplication by administrators rather than the evil intent of legislators" (252); McDonnell, *Dispossession*, a book that blames "flawed" federal policy, weak local administration, and "unscrupulous, land-hungry whites" (5); Gates, "Indian Allotments," 141–42; Leibhardt, "Allotment Policy," 84; and Fixico, "Federal and State Policies," 391. Other useful overviews of allotment include Carlson's *Indians, Bureaucrats, and Land*, a study of the agrarian intent of the act; Kinney's *Continent Lost*, a broad historical survey, and Prucha's *Americanizing the American Indians*, a useful collection of writings by white "Friends of the Indian."

15. *Annual Report of the Board of Indian Commissioners*, 1885, 46 (hereafter cited as RBIC, *with year*). The assumption that Indians need not be consulted about allotment was general among those who drafted policy in Washington DC and was echoed locally. Nez Perce agent Charles E. Monteith, for example, wrote to the secretary of the Board of Indian Commissioners, "As regards [the Nez Perces'] desire for allotments and patents their wish has never been consulted. . . . I believe it to be the duty of the Gov't to *push* the Indians on to civilization, not lead and expect them to follow" (9 Dec. 1885).

16. I adapt my term *memory palaces* from cultural historian Pierre Nora's "Between Memory and History." In this essay he writes of "places of memory (*lieux de mémoire*)," in which "moments of history" are enshrined, "like shells on the shore when the sea of living memory has receded" (12). By transmuting "place" into "palace" I wish to allude to the configuration of many such edifices as palatial cabinets of curiosities, or as trophy cases containing artifacts of national conquest. I also intend to invoke the rhetorical principle of association, whereby tangible objects and specific places serve as technologies of memory.

17. *Annual Report of the Commissioner of Indian Affairs*, 1873, 4 (hereafter cited as ARCIA, *with year*).

18. According to Priest, "The coincidence of pressure for railroad legislation with passage of the Dawes Act inevitably arouses suspicion that the measure was passed to secure more land for railroads" (*Uncle Sam's Stepchildren*, 223). See also Hoxie, *Final Promise*, 46–49. Senator Henry

Dawes, for whom the bill was named, enthusiastically supported legislation that would open western lands to tourism and settlement. The law also had the powerful support of the Northern Pacific Railroad.

19. Priest, *Uncle Sam's Stepchildren*, 217.

20. Walker, *Conflict and Schism*, 77.

21. According to Hoxie, allotment was accomplished in two phases. First, land was apportioned and attention given to "transforming Indians into 'civilized' citizens"; "[i]n the second phase, Americans altered much of that . . . program. . . . [T]hey no longer sought to transform the Indians or to guarantee their equality" (*Final Promise*, xviii). Although Hoxie's trajectory is precise, I wish to challenge the intentionality and foresight implied by the idea of "phases."

22. For a history of the debates preceding the enactment of the Dawes General Allotment Act, see Priest, *Uncle Sam's Stepchildren*.

23. For summaries of the complex series of amendments to the Dawes Act, see McLaughlin, "Dawes Act," Royster, "Legacy of Allotment," and Kinney, *Continent Lost*, among others.

24. A. C. Belt to ACF, 5 July 1889, Letters Sent, vol. 93, Records of the Office of the CIA, NAB.

25. Hagan, "United States Indian Policies," 57.

26. For a long list of amendments to Dawes that affected leasing and alienation of land, see Price and Clinton, *Law and the American Indian*, 80.

27. Olund, "From Savage Space," 129.

28. See, for example, Kaplan, who asserts that "by taking as foundational the confrontation between white settlers and Native Americans, [we overlook] how intimately the issues of slavery and emancipation and relations between Blacks and whites were intertwined with each stage of U.S. imperial expansion." Kaplan therefore emphasizes "a North/South axis" to her study (*Anarchy of Empire*, 18). See also Curiel et al., for a similar argument: "The assumption that American history moves from east to west remains deeply ingrained in cultural imagination. In such national narratives Chicanos and Asian Americans remain perpetual latecomers, cast in the role of 'recent' immigrants and foreign nationals" (*Post-Nationalist American Studies*, 4). Only recently have scholars begun to resist the tendency of post-nationalist American Studies to overlook the importance of white-Native histories. For exemplary studies, see Huhndorf, "Picture Revolution"; Huhndorf, *Mapping the Americas*; Elliott, "Indians, Incorporated"; Pfister, *Individuality Incorporated*; and Philip J. Deloria, *IUP*.

29. Elliott, "Indians, Incorporated," 159n1.

30. Kaplan, *Anarchy of Empire*, 18.

31. The September 2005 issue of *American Quarterly*, titled "Legal Borderlands: Law and the Construction of American Borders," offers a case in point. The announced purpose of this special issue is to establish the importance of discourses of law, sovereignty, citizenship, and USAmerican identity within a contemporary frame of global American Studies. The editors of this special issue proclaim, "the border cannot contain sovereignty" (Dudziak and Volpp, Introduction, 593); the essays in this issue demonstrate how imperial USAmerica has advanced its claims at home (on immigrant, queer, and racialized bodies) or abroad (in the Philippines). Yet none of these studies refers to Native sovereignty, either present or past. For example, Dudziak and Volpp claim, "American history is marked by episodes that can be simultaneously conceptualized as violations of the law and as actions sanctioned by law" (Introduction, 596). For centuries the application of law in violation of the law has characterized U.S. relations with Native nations. For centuries, discourses of manifest destiny, citizenship, and sovereignty have been perfected upon the bodies of Native Americans and then employed extra-nationally. No essay in this collection makes more than a passing mention of these facts.

32. Appadurai, "Heart of Whiteness," 796.

33. Although the topic lies outside the scope of this study, I want to mention the scholars who have begun to study colonialism's effects on indigenous nations in a global context. See the essays collected by Ballantyne and Burton in *Bodies in Contact*; Perry's *On the Edge of Empire*, a study of British colonialist attempts to domesticate Natives in British Columbia; Reynolds's work on *Aboriginal Sovereignty*; and Rafael's *White Love*, an insightful reading of U.S. colonial interventions in Philippine history, among others.

34. Kaplan, *Anarchy of Empire*, 25. Similarly, in *Tender Violence*, Wexler has examined the means by which nineteenth-century white women reformers effected and documented their benevolently violent policies of pacification. For the encounters between white women photographers and Natives, see Bernardin et al., *Trading Gazes*. See also Simonsen's *Making Home Work*, an investigation into the intertwined labors of white and Native women reformers to establish domesticity in the U.S. West. For foundational studies of the interrelationship of domesticity and global colonial conquest, see Stoler, *Carnal Knowledge*; Stoler, "Tense and Tender Ties"; and McClintock, *Imperial Leather*.

35. Rand, "Primary Sources," 138–39.

36. Henry Dawes felt that the success of the allotment program would "depend entirely on the character of the Government agents who execute its provisions, whether it is a success or a failure" (qtd. in *Friends' Intelligencer and Journal*, 4 June 1887, 367).

37. Mark, *Stranger in Her Native Land*, 43 (hereafter cited as SNL, with page numbers).

38. See Mark, SNL, 168, for an account of this portrait's making.

39. In a letter to her friend Electa Sanderson Dawes, Fletcher confessed that Senator Henry M. Rice had called her "a dreadful bulldozer" (25 Jan. 1883; Henry L. Dawes Papers, 1833–1933, LC).

40. Under duress, and only many years after she had begun to collaborate with and depend upon Francis La Flesche, Fletcher shared authorial credit with him for her Omaha ethnographic work. *The Omaha Tribe* bears both their names. In her Nez Perce ethnographic manuscripts Fletcher named some but surely not all her Native informants, but because she did not publish these studies in her lifetime, it is debatable whether she would have shared the authorial credit.

41. I have expanded on the structure of the gendered personae used by Gay in my "Lost in the General Wreckage," 45–67.

42. In many ways, then, the people and events I work with here fall within the purview of those Philip J. Deloria has studied, answering, in part, his question, "[H]ow might we think of the unexpected nature of Indian lives lived in dialogue with . . . the shifting histories of non-Indian expectations?" (*IUP*, 226).

43. John W. Noble to CIA, 17 Apr. 1889, RG 48, NAB.

44. Senier, *Voices*, 62.

45. The specific details of Fletcher's early life remain vague, for in April 1907, realizing that that her life would be a matter of interest to biographers and scholars, she destroyed many personal records (ACF, Diary, 4–19 April 1907, Papers of Alice Cunningham Fletcher; hereafter cited as PACF). I thank Joanna Scherer for providing this information. Fletcher kept a daily diary for most of her adult life. These small books are collected in series 10, box 12A, PACF.

46. Early in his career Putnam, too, had frequently delivered public lectures on ethnology, anthropology, and archaeology. For a list of Putnam's lecture topics in 1886 see Browman, "Peabody Museum," 517n3.

47. See Sekula, "Body and the Archive," for an exploration of how composite photography enabled projects of scientific racism.

48. ACF to Frederick W. Putnam (hereafter FWP), 29 April 1886, Acc.

87-6, UAV 677.38, box 7, Pusey Library. Courtesy of the Harvard University Archives.

49. I make this assertion based on several undated snapshots of Francis La Flesche and Jane Gay together in the garden of the Washington DC home they shared with Fletcher. One of these photographs shows Fletcher, clad in a long white summer dress, standing in the garden with her hands on a small tripod-mounted box camera (series 28, box 33, PACF). Because these photos appear to have been taken on the same occasion, and because some of them include Fletcher, while others do not, I assume she may have been operating that camera.

50. Mark's intent is to trace Fletcher's intellectual biography and to establish her as a pioneer woman scientist. In her preface the biographer recounts her changing perceptions of Fletcher, which developed from identification and idealization to critique and repulsion and finally to tenuous objectivity (SNL, xviii).

51. The details of Fletcher's religious life remain obscure. I have found one letter that suggests she struggled to maintain a distance from theological disputes. She wrote to F. W. Putnam that should she allow Mary Thaw to control the circumstances of her life, "I fear I should find my self in theological troubles *all new*. I want to devote my self to science, not to any doxy" (emphasis added; 18 June 1890, FWP Director's Records, Acc. 92-1, Peabody Museum of Archaeology and Ethnology, Harvard University).

52. Untitled note, *Red Man* 9, no. 11 (Nov. 1889): 1. Mark's treatment of Jane Gay is compromised by her decision to use Gay as a foil to Fletcher. She writes, for example, "On the face of it Jane Gay had all the advantages . . . [b]ut what she did not have was Alice Fletcher's driving will. . . . Jane Gay was a character, talented and funny . . . [b]ut Alice Fletcher had character in the old-fashioned sense of that word: moral strength, self-discipline, and fortitude" (SNL, 192). I do not share this interpretation and do not find that the documentary record supports it.

53. For a treatment of the relationship between Fletcher and Gay as an example of queer domesticity, see Simonsen, *Making Home Work*, 118–32.

54. I am indebted to Elizabeth Jacox for this information. According to Jane Gay Dodge's reminiscences, "Miss Gay tutored President Johnson's grandchildren . . . at the White House" ("Brief Biography," 1, Jane Gay Dodge Papers, Schlesinger Library on the History of Women in America; hereafter cited as SLHWA). This claim has not been substantiated.

55. Catherine Melville to Connally Trigg, 1 Feb. 1862, Andrew Johnson Papers, LC.

56. Dodge, "Sketch," 2, SLHWA.

57. Dodge, "Brief Biography," 1, SLHWA.

58. According to Mark, Gay and Fletcher had been classmates at Brooklyn Female Academy and had become reacquainted "at a public lecture" (SNL, 166). Mark bases these claims on two typescript recollections written in 1939 and 1951 by Gay's niece, Jane Gay Dodge, and held in her personal papers by the Schlesinger Library.

Accounts of how Gay became Fletcher's companion in Idaho also depend upon Dodge's recollections. They are unsupported by any other documentary evidence prior to the first mention of "Miss Gay" in Fletcher's diary on 3 Dec. 1887, PACF.

59. Fletcher's 1888 diary notes a series of correspondence she sent to and received from Gay. I have not been able to locate these letters and assume they are among the records Fletcher destroyed in 1907.

60. ACF, Diary, 22 Feb. 1889 and 19 Apr. 1889, PACF. Gay's earliest field photographs include many that appear to be intended as anthropological illustrations. Most were taken outdoors and show lodgings and ceremonial structures. Another small group includes studio shots, several of them hand-colored, of regalia-clad Natives posing in front of scenic backdrops. Gay also took photographs of Winnebago people dressed in everyday attire. She seems to have made few images in Nebraska that were intended to represent the land.

The Winnebago images are scattered. The Nebraska State Historical Society holds the most complete collection. The Peabody Museum and the Idaho State Historical Society also own a few of these images. Gay seems not to have made small albums of the Winnebago images, as she did with some of her Idaho photographs. Rather, she interspersed the Nebraska photographs throughout *Choup-nit-ki*, infrequently differentiating them from those of Nez Perce subjects. A number of Gay's Omaha and Winnebago photographs also served (uncredited) as the basis for the engraved illustrations in Fletcher's *Century* series on the Omahas and in her coauthored two-volume ethnography, *The Omaha Tribe*.

61. See Kelsey, "Viewing the Archive," for a brief history of congressional funding for photographic endeavors associated with federal western initiatives (712).

I have found no documentary evidence to support a widespread assumption, probably deriving from Jane Gay Dodge's reminiscences, that E. Jane Gay was, or wished to be, a federal appointee. Dodge wrote that her aunt "was to go along [with Fletcher to Idaho] as official photogra-

[344]

pher, her expenses to be part of the Government project; (not the camera outfit! *She* paid for that.)" ("Brief Biography," 5, SLHWA). Yet Gay does not appear on Fletcher's monthly reports as a salaried employee; the documents appointing Fletcher to her post and outlining her responsibilities in the field do not mention a photographer. Fletcher did not file expense claims for a portable darkroom and supplies, glass plates and developing chemicals, or for a wagon and team to haul these supplies around the reservation. Nor do Fletcher's field diaries, where the anthropologist kept a close tally of her personal expenses, suggest that she privately reimbursed Gay. Fletcher does not mention Gay in any of her official correspondence with the Bureau of Indian Affairs, nor did she use Gay's photographs as evidential support for her official allotting work.

62. In her old age, after she moved to England in 1906, Gay became a much more active feminist. See ACF to FLF, 16 Sept. 1910, series 4, box 5, PACF.

63. I thank Diane Mallickan for this insight.

64. Philip J. Deloria, *IUP*, 6.

65. In focusing on these four men, I do not mean to imply that Nimiipuu women were not also important forces for intercultural communication and for tribal activism. Harriet Mary Stuart, for example, was interned in Indian Territory, attended Carlisle, and for the rest of her adult life regularly wrote to the Department of Indian Affairs to document and protest abuses (especially against women employees) at the Nez Perce Agency. She also recruited students for and accompanied Nez Perce students to Carlisle. Yet the allotment-related archive from which I have worked in writing this study is dominated by the four men I mention, all of whom interacted with and challenged Fletcher.

A number of exemplary works have studied "educated Indians who both frustrate and facilitate interactions between Anglos and Indians and gain positions of leadership" (McMillen, *Making Indian Law*, 196n2). They include Pfister's *Individuality Incorporated*, a study of boarding school education of Native students; DeMallie's *Sixth Grandfather*, a careful delineation of Black Elk's position between the worlds of complex Sioux tradition and the pressures of modernity; Hoxie's account of Crow advocate Robert Yellowtail, a "cattleman, Baptist, self-taught attorney, Republican, federal employee and advocate of 'real democracy' in Montana and elsewhere" (*Parading through History*, 168); and McMillen's study of Fred Mahone (Hualapai), through whose biography he tells the "story of Indian activism and the residue of colonial law in the 1920s and beyond" (xvii). For a valuable list of similar studies, see McMillen, 196n2.

66. See, for example, Joseph's "An Indian's View of Indian Affairs," published in *North American Review* in 1879, during his internment in Indian Territory. See also Gidley, *Kopet*, 35–39, for a timeline of Joseph's public appearances between 1885, when he returned to the Northwest, and 1904, when he died.

67. James Reubens's name is also spelled Reuben, Ruben, or Rubens. In this book I use Reubens, the form he most frequently used in his correspondence.

68. Undated newspaper clipping, Kate C. McBeth scrapbook, Acc. 632, Lawyer Collection, Nez Perce National Historical Park Archives (hereafter cited as NPNHPA).

Such language as "representative of the higher type of Indians" has given way in modern parlance to equally unreflective terminologies such as "progressive" and "traditional" as classificatory labels. I avoid such categorization here because it seems more accurate to recognize the motivations of Reubens and Stuart and many others like them as complex and mutable, often changing opportunely, or modifying with the passage of time. See Hoxie, "Exploring"; Szasz, *Between Indian and White Worlds*; and David Rich Lewis, "Reservation Leadership."

69. "Jas. Reuben, Indian," unsourced newspaper clipping, series 1, box 1, PACF. Kate McBeth probably sent it to Fletcher sometime after 1891.

70. Thompson, *Historic Resource Study, Spalding*, 149.

71. Untitled news notes, *Arkansas City (KS) Traveler*, 3 Aug. 1881 and 2 Aug. 1882.

72. Slickpoo, *Noon Nee-Me-Poo*, 256.

73. In 1981 Carlson noted, "A number of historians have chosen to end their tribal histories with the allotment of the reservation or just before its allotment, leaving examination of the allotment era to persons concerned with the problems of assimilation and cultural change in the modern era" (*Indians, Bureaucrats, and Land*, 20). Five years later, Vine Deloria Jr. echoed his observation, writing that tribal histories had, to date, "seem[ed] to neglect the history of Indians over the thirty-year period following the General Allotment Act and give to this statute a power and effect that it certainly did not have at the time it was passed" ("Revision and Reversion," 86). Since then many studies have extended their scope into the present moment to document the persistence of tribal groups as sovereign entities. I have earlier listed a number of exemplary books. Still, taken as a whole, this group of works focuses on issues after 1934, and few consider allotment as it was applied in specific tribal instances.

74. Josephy, *Nez Perce Indians*, 633.

75. Josephy, *Nez Perce Indians*, 643, 644. Similarly, Haines devotes two pages of his concluding four-page chapter, "Lands in Severalty," to allotment and two pages to tribal history since 1895. Scholars wishing to follow tribal history after 1877 have depended upon Walker's *Conflict and Schism*, a compressed and anthropologically informed account of the Nez Perce transition into modernism; Riley's MA thesis, "Nez Perce Struggle," a brief but highly useful overview of tribal governing bodies; and Slickpoo's *Noon Nee-Me-Poo*, the official tribal history. The last third of Slickpoo's volume furnishes the most complete account of the modern Nez Perce peoples. Still, the account is largely summative, and the book's final chapters anticipate a projected second volume that would more fully document the "movement towards self-determination" (284). McCoy's *Chief Joseph* has established how historical studies of the Joseph period written by white historians have served to consolidate white USAmerican identity.

Some part of this historical foreclosure may be due to the apparent paucity of sources. According to Riley, "much source material pertaining to various phases of tribal history since 1900 has been lost or destroyed" (3).

76. See also Trafzer, *Northwest Tribes*.

77. A footnote to the republication of this document reads, "All of the spelling and punctuation are copied as in the documents removed from the cornerstone" ("Documents," 363).

78. Reubens, "Nez Perces Indians," 361–63.

79. Vizenor, *Manifest Manners*, vi; emphasis added.

80. Burton, "Introduction," 11.

81. I am indebted to Dennis Baird, Lynn N. Baird, and Robert Applegate for several conversations about the difficulties of managing and retaining records in archival collections.

82. Not all of the images in *Choup-nit-ki* were made by Gay in Idaho. The book includes photographs of Omaha peoples and places. As well, it contains several images made long after Gay left Idaho in 1892, probably by Kate McBeth or by her niece, Mazie Crawford, also a photographer.

83. According to Elizabeth Jacox, when Emma Gay died, her companion, Edith Emerson, inherited parts of her estate. The inheritance included a number of boxes of heavy glass plate negatives (presumably some of them made by Jane Gay), which were discarded (e-mail to author, 12 May 2011). I mention this detail because Mark asserts, with no documentary basis, "Jane Gay did not continue her photography after she and Fletcher returned to Washington. The career that had at first seemed so promising

eventually came to nothing, like the others she had tried" (SNL, 192). Yet the Papers of Alice Cunningham Fletcher include photographs Gay made long after 1892, even some prints she made after she moved to England, which she sent to Fletcher (series 10, box 12, PACF).

84. Steedman, *Dust*, 57.

85. Aldama, *Disrupting Savagism*, 72.

86. I have adapted the concept of counter-memory from the work of Roach, who explains that cultural performances often expose "the disparities between history as it is discursively transmitted and memory as it is publicly enacted by the bodies that bear its consequences" (*Cities*, 26).

87. As Dirlik makes clear, the "temporalities of a Eurocentric conceptualization of the world" presume themselves to be "the yardstick for determining stagnation in history as well as exclusion from it" ("History," 249).

88. Lennard J. Davis, *Resisting Novels*, 201.

89. See Lowe, who argues, "The bildungsroman emerged as the primary form for narrating the development of the individual from youthful innocence to civilized maturity, the telos of which is the reconciliation of the individual with the social order . . . [and] identification with an idealized 'national' form of subjectivity" (*Immigrant Acts*, 98).

90. Dirlik, "History," 254.

91. Dirlik, "History," 278–79.

92. To my knowledge, no one has yet attempted to trace the layered ownership of specific plots and claims. The overwhelming number of geographically dispersed records that would need to be located and sorted makes such a project a daunting challenge.

Part 1. Introduction

1. Deffenbaugh, "Report of Missionary," ARCIA, 1885, 73; emphasis added. The numbers vary for internees who were "received" into Lapwai-area congregations. The Session Records of the Lapwai Presbyterian Church record: "The object of the meeting was to receive the persons who had recently returned from the Indian Territory where they were members of the Nez Perce Presbyterian Church. They were received and given the right hand of fellowship as their names were called from the roll by their former pastor Rev. A. B. Lawyer. . . . The names of these thirty persons were ordered on the Roll of the Lapwai Church" (qtd. in Sugden, *Seventy-Five Years*, 5). The discrepancy may indicate that the other fifty returnees were received by other churches on the reservation; it may also suggest that Deffenbaugh inflated the number.

2. Hoxie and Mark, Introduction, xxxii.

3. Slickpoo, *Noon Nee-Me-Poo*, 210.

4. This brief summary does not fully represent the complexity of allegiances on the Nez Perce Reservation. Nor does it recognize that despite their nominal conversion many Nimiipuu honored traditional beliefs and ceremonies and that many strategically changed their religious affiliations.

5. See Pearson for a discussion of the several religions practiced by the internees (NPIT, 238–50).

6. Roach, *Cities*, 27, 13, 28.

7. Morrill and Morrill, "J. P. Vollmer," 5.

8. For an image of the two together, probably taken in Indian Territory, see "Chief Joseph Photos," www.American-Tribes.com. (http://amertribes.proboards.com/index.cgi?board=plateau&action=display&thread=858). I thank Phil Cash Cash for sharing this link with me.

9. For accounts of the evolving relationship between Joseph and Reubens, see Nerburn, *Chief Joseph*, 360–72, and Pearson, NPIT, especially 135, and 264–65.

10. My distinction between Joseph's and Reubens's methods of argumentation is necessarily simplified and should not obscure the fact that Joseph himself often based his arguments upon the sympathy of those in power to effect the release of his people. See, for example, a newspaper account of an interview with the leader in which "he pointed to the graves [in Indian Territory] and said, with sadness: 'Keep this in your heart. Tell it to the Great Father in Washington, that maybe his heart will be touched and he will take pity upon this suffering people'" ("The Unhappy Nez Perces," *New York Times*, 29 Oct. 1883).

11. Reubens to A. B. Meacham, 10 Mar. 1880 (O'Neal and Baird, *Collection*, 145).

12. Price, ARCIA, 1882, lxiv–lxv.

13. The RBIC of 1887 characterizes the first areas chosen for allotment under the Dawes Act as "smaller reservations where the Indians are somewhat advanced in education and habits of industry" (7).

14. "The Return of Joseph and His People," *Lewiston Teller*, 12 Apr. 1883.

15. Senator Henry Dawes's address to the Board of Indian Commissioners in 1887 makes clear the sense of urgency with which these reformers pressed for the Allotment Act: "President Cleveland said that he did not intend, when he signed this bill, to apply it to more than one reservation at first . . . [b]ut you see he has been led to apply it to half a dozen. . . . [T]he greed of the land-grabber is such as to press the application of this bill to

the utmost." Later in this same address Dawes repeated himself, declaring, "Something stronger than the Mohonk conference has dissolved the reservation system. The greed of these people for the land has made it utterly impossible to preserve it for the Indian" (RBIC 1887, 88, 89).

16. Pearson's record of the journey taken by this initial party is the most dependable secondary account (NPIT, 270–73).

17. Charles E. Monteith specifically mentions "the husband of James Reuben's cousin," as being among the group, recommending that if "he was one of the more active hostiles . . . it would not be advisable for him to return" (to CIA, 16 Oct. 1882; Lapwai Agency Files, Idaho State Public Archives and Research Library; hereafter cited as ISPARL). Pearson is the only scholar to note that this group included Reubens's "friends and relatives" as well as "several of the poorest widows and orphans" (NPIT, 271).

18. Sources disagree on the number comprising this group. Lewellyn E. Woodin, the Quapaw agent, reported that twenty-nine internees had accompanied Reubens (ARCIA 1883, 79); Monteith reported that the Lapwai congregation had approved the return of thirty-one persons; and Slickpoo writes that Reubens "was granted permission to take thirty-three . . . women and children back to Idaho" (*Noon Nee-Me-Poo*, 200). See also Pearson, NPIT, 271 and 348n19.

19. Monteith to CIA, 16 Oct. 1882, Lapwai Agency Files, ISPARL.

20. Kate McBeth's account places the arrival of the group on a Thursday evening, likely 5 July (Kate McBeth booklet, Acc. 632, Lawyer Collection, NPNHPA); Pearson says they arrived on 7 July (NPIT, 272). On 5 July 1883, the *Lewiston Teller* reprinted a news item from the *Idaho Democrat* (dated 27 June) reporting that several of the women from this band had been seen shopping locally.

21. McBeth, "Letter from Miss McBeth," Acc. 632, Lawyer Collection, NPNHPA.

22. McBeth, *Nez Perces*, 100.

23. Pearson, NPIT, 272.

24. Pearson, NPIT, 189.

25. As Pearson observes, among the internees, "Christian women wore western-style dresses they made from calico, checkered government-issue cloth, or wool" (NPIT, 189).

26. Pearson, NPIT, 272.

27. Slickpoo, *Noon Nee-Me-Poo*, 200.

28. Many of the records relating to the release and transport of these

internees are filed in RG 393, Pt. 1, E715, Department of the Columbia, NAB, as well as in RG75. Thanks to Dennis Baird for this information and for copies of these letters.

29. *ARCIA*, 1886, 71. Deffenbaugh puts the number at 116 ("Return," 72); Dozier counts 118 ("1885," 24); Haines places it at 188, but this is likely a typographical or proofreading error (*The Nez Percés*, 333).

30. Pearson, NPIT, 291.

31. Ruby and Brown, *Half-Sun*, 220–21.

32. *ARCIA*, 1885, lvii.

33. McWhorter, *Yellow Wolf*, 289–90.

34. Deffenbaugh, "Report of Missionary," *ARCIA*, 1885, 73. Although accounts vary, there seems to be general agreement that those who had professed or converted to Presbyterianism during their internment were returned to the Idaho reservation rather than being sent to Colville with those who remained "under indictment" (Slickpoo, *Noon Nee-Me-Poo*, 200). Kate McBeth's retrospectively written account says, "[T]he Christian portion of them [were] allowed to return to the reserve" (*Nez Perces*, 149). Her niece, Mazie Crawford, later wrote, "[T]he return of these captives [was] based on the acceptance or rejection of Christianity. . . . Those who professed a belief in Christianity were allowed to remain here" ("Nez Perces in Indian Territory," Ts., Acc. 632, Lawyer Collection, NPNHPA). Finally, according to the 1884 *RBIC*, "The proposed return of Chief Joseph's band . . . still occupies attention. In the judgment of some of their best friends it would be expedient for them to settle in some other neighborhood, rather than on the Nez Percé Reserve. . . . [T]he lady missionary who has been longest on the reserve [Susan McBeth] fully concurs. The Nez Percés, both in Idaho Territory and in the Indian Territory, have no warmer friends than these; and few, if any, are so well acquainted with all that pertains to their welfare" (36). Mylie Lawyer, the great-granddaughter of Chief Lawyer, was more direct. Speaking of the involvement of the McBeth sisters in the disposition of the returnees, she paraphrases them as saying, "We don't want these people here. Their hands are bloody with white man's blood. We don't want them" (interview by Robert Chenoweth, 27 Sept. 1999. Nimiipuu (Nez Perce) Lewis & Clark Oral History Interviews, Grant #FY-83 231, NPNHP).

35. Deffenbaugh, "Return," 71.

36. Deffenbaugh, "Return," 72.

37. 9 Apr. 1885; qtd. in Dozier, "1885," 24.

38. Qtd. in Dozier, "1885," 25.

39. Kate McBeth, Diary, 3 July 1885, "Kate McBeth's Papers," *Kate and Sue McBeth*, University of Idaho website.

40. Morrill and Morrill, *Out*, 302.

1. A False Beginning

1. "Open the Reservation," *Nez Perce News*, 15 June 1882. For similar editorial sentiments, see "County Division," *Nez Perce News*, 28 Dec. 1882, and "The Agency System," *Grangeville (ID) Free Press*, 17 Dec. 1886, among many others.

2. "The Coming Boom!" *Grangeville (ID) Free Press*, 8 Apr. 1887. See these similar editorial pronouncements: "The Indian Severalty Law," *Lewiston Teller*, 14 July 1887, and "Open the Reservation," *Grangeville (ID) Free Press*, 9 Dec. 1887. Of these same Camas Prairie lands, Alice Fletcher wrote two years later, "When the white men first came ... the bunch grass waved over [Camas Prairie] and made it beautiful in spring and early summer. That has now disappeared, turned into white man's beef long ago and is to-day replaced by dry, rustling weeds. The slopes facing the west and south are rocky and sterile, ... the side toward east or north would be capable of raising grain, while the slope opposite would hardly afford pickings for a goat" ("Among the Nez Perces").

3. Welch, "Alice Cunningham Fletcher," 142.

4. "Reservation Matters," *Grangeville (ID) Free Press*, 13 Jan. 1888.

5. "The Reservation," *Grangeville (ID) Free Press*, 3 Feb. 1888.

6. See, for example, the speech of Isaac Stevens at the treaty negotiations of 1855: "What shall we do at this council? We want you and ourselves to agree upon tracts of land where you will live; in these tracts of land we want each man who will work to have his own land, his own horses, his own cattle, and his own home for himself and his children" ("Proceedings at the Council. 29 May 1855," "Treaties, Laws, and Executive Orders," Government Documents, *Kate and Sue McBeth*, University of Idaho website). See also Article 3 of the 1863 "Treaty with the Nez Perces" (Baird, Mallickan, and Swagerty, *Nez Perce Nation*, 426).

7. In the opinion of Charles E. Monteith, the twenty-acre allotment "clause in the treaty [of 1863] has not been observed on account of the absurdity thereof. A great majority of the Indians have inclosed and are cultivating lands ranging from 30 acres to 80 acres" (to E. Whittlesey, 9 Dec. 1885, NAB).

8. Stuart to CIA, 20 Nov. 1886, 385, NAB.

9. Norris to CIA, 2 Feb. 1887, 5026, NAB. In his report to the commissioner of Indian affairs for 1888, Norris reemphasized the Nez Perces' awareness of the new legislation: "The Indians have become anxious about the matter of allotments under the act of February 8, 1887, and seem troubled by the cloud of uncertainty with which the subject is enveloped. They understand that a survey of the reservation for the purpose of allotment was authorized in July, 1887, and no visible steps having been taken, nor the survey entered upon, those ready for allotment, and wishing to take their land according to the surveys, are embarrassed by the delay. I trust it will not be long postponed. I should regret any unnecessary delay that might discourage those who are in the line of progress" (ARCIA, 1888, 87).

10. ACF to CIA, 26 Aug. 1889, 25370, NAB.

11. An inspection report filed by T. D. Marcum dated 13 June 1889 found Charles Monteith had "neglected to enforce the law with respect to citizens stock intruding on the reservation, and that he also failed and neglected to execute the orders of the Hon. Commr. of Indian Affairs with respect to the removal of intruding stock from the reservation by adopting a policy of delay. . . . The fact is patent that delays were inaugurated by Agent Monteith to protect the interest of stockmen whose herds were grazing on the reservation and to the prejudice of the Indians" (19592, RG 48E682, M 10707, roll 30, Inspections, NAB).

12. *Lewiston Teller*, 23 May 1889.

13. "Stock from Indian Lands," *Lewiston Teller*, 20 June 1889.

14. ACF to CIA, 26 Aug. 1889, 25370, NAB.

15. ACF to Isabel Barrows, 10 Sept. 1889, Samuel J. and Isabel Barrows Papers, bMS Am 1807.1 (175) folder 1, Widener Library, Harvard University.

16. Publicus, "Change of Indian Agents," *Nez Perce News*, 9 Mar. 1882.

17. 11 March 1886, Interior Department Appointment Papers: Idaho, 1862–1907, microcopy 693, roll 16, Nez Perce Indian Agency, A–M, 1868–1902, NAB. Presbyterian Church interests hastened to assure the Indian Agency that Monteith should be reappointed, as he was.

18. "Agent Monteith Again," *Grangeville (ID) Free Press*, 16 July 1886.

19. Although local whites realized Monteith's unfitness to be agent, at least one area editor nevertheless urged his readers not to oppose the appointment because Monteith supported allotment ("Indian Agent Monteith," *Grangeville [ID] Free Press*, 12 Apr. 1889).

20. "The Work of Allotment," *Lewiston Teller*, 11 July 1889.

21. Inspector T. D. Marcum's Report dated 15 June 1889 begins, "The condition of affairs at the [Nez Perce] Agency is by no means complimen-

tary to the service." It then details the succession of agents, who, when they were relieved or removed, "carried away [their] cash and property papers." It summarizes the disputes between the school matrons, one of whom had been "arrested [and] tried . . . for committing an assault upon the wife of the Agency Physician." Marcum opined, "The main cause of all the recent disgraceful rows at this Agency is due to the fact that a strong minded, vindictive woman with a rule or ruin disposition, was the power behind the throne" (19594, RG 48E682, M 10707, roll 30, Inspections, NAB). Surely this was not an auspicious condition under which another strong minded woman would try to begin her work.

22. J. W. Page to Secretary of the Interior, 20 May 1889, 13619, NAB.

23. Council Proceedings, 19 Mar. 1887, 9895, RG 95, NAB.

24. Henry Heth to CIA, 22 May 1889, 14369, NAB. Inspector T. D. Marcum was of the opinion that "there is no testimony showing any connection or business relations existing between Agent Monteith and W. A. Caldwell, yet the opinion prevails with many about Lewiston that their interest in some way is mutual, and Mr. Monteith's conduct, while Agent, shows, at least more than an ordinary concern in Caldwell's business interest" (13 June 1889, 19593, RG 48E682, M 10707, roll 30, Inspections, NAB).

25. See, for example, J. W. Page's assertion, "Mrs. Eaves [the wife of the schoolmaster] entered my house & assaulted my wife. Had a warrant issued for her. Was put of[f] reservation by Heth [the Agent], who is drunk half the time" (to Secretary of the Interior, 20 May 1889, 13619, NAB). News of these events was even noted in the *Washington Post*. See "Trouble at the Nez Perce Reservation," 21 May 1889.

26. CIA to ACF, 4 May 1889, 184, NAB.

27. ACF, Diary, 27 May 1889–30 May 1889, PACF.

28. ACF to CIA, 8 June 1889, 15976, NAB.

29. ACF to CIA, 20 June 1889, 17003, NAB.

30. Monteith's self-reported response to this demand was characteristically authoritarian: "I have replied . . . that the 'severalty act' is a law and must be obeyed; that they must not procrastinate, but act quickly" (*ARCIA*, 1889, 182).

31. In 1887, addressing the Board of Indian Commissioners, President Grover Cleveland observed, "Half the woes I have had to do with in the Indian Territory come from the white men that go in there, marry Indian girls, become Indians, get property, and become, to a great extent, the governing class down there" (*RBIC*, 1887, 135). While the geographic lo-

cation is not the same, the process of white men marrying Indian women and thereby becoming eligible for land seems to have been widespread.

32. ACF, Diary, 5 June 1889, PACF.

33. Untitled news note, *Lewiston Teller*, 17 Mar. 1887.

34. Kate C. McBeth, Journal, "History of Mission Work and Workers," *Kate and Sue McBeth*, University of Idaho website.

35. ACF to CIA, 15 July 1889, 20118, NAB.

36. ACF to J. C. Lowrie, 15 June 1889, Letterbook 1, PACF.

37. ACF to E. O'Neill, 15 July 1889, Letterbook 1, PACF.

38. CIA to ACF, 24 Aug. 1889, 20118, NAB.

39. ACF to F. F. Ellinwood, 19 July 1889, Letterbook 1, PACF.

40. Thompson, *Historic Resource Study, Spalding*, 156.

41. E. J. G. [Gay], "Woman Allotting Lands," 5.

42. To Captain Richard H. Pratt, Gay wrote, "They have quietly protested in three petitions" and held "a secret council where money was raised and a messenger despatched to Washington to plead their cause," but she implies that the main source of discussion at these councils was the issue of Monteith's appointment (C, 41), adding only that Reubens was also enjoined to "find out whether Her Majesty [Fletcher] really represented the Government, and if what she says is true, that the Indians must take their lands in severalty" (C, 45).

43. ACF, Diary, 8 and 10 June 1889, PACF.

44. [Gay], "Brave Woman Allotting," 2.

45. "Synopsis of Proceedings of a Council held by Inspector W. W. Junkin with the Nez Perce Indians, December 29th, 1892," RG 48E682, M 10707, roll 30, Inspections, NAB.

46. ACF to CIA, 18 June 1889, 16979, NAB, and 19 June 1889, 16980, NAB.

47. ACF to CIA, 11 June 1889, 15536, NAB, and 20 June 1889, 17002, NAB. The field notes, the commissioner answered, had been sent to the agency two years earlier (CIA to ACF, 12 June 1889, Letters Sent, vol. 93, Records of the Office of the CIA, NAB). Fletcher replied, using the strategic passive voice, "I have found the field notes, their presence not being known" (15 June 1889, 16607, NAB).

48. E. J. G. [Gay], "Woman Allotting Lands," 5.

49. ACF to CIA, 8 June 1889, 15976, NAB. See also Gay, who wrote that the local cattlemen "seem to be utterly ignorant of the intent of the Severalty Act" (C, 13–14). Elsewhere she reported, "We were waited upon by white settlers, and committees of white settlers and presidents of Cattlemen's associations. They all seemed to think that the Special Agent had

been sent out to establish their claims to free grazing on the Indian land. They were very gracious and all wanted to do something, or give us something—a cow would add to our comfort and ponies were handy, but after a while they charged us two cents a pound for hay more than it was worth" ("Where We Camped," 6–7, SLHWA).

50. "Opening of the Nez Perce Reservation in the Near Future," *Lewiston Teller*, 20 June 1889.

51. The *Lewiston Teller* published the full text of the Dawes General Allotment Act on 9 Feb. 1887, 7 July 1887, and 13 July 1889.

52. ACF to CIA, 8 June 1889, 15976, NAB. Depending on her audience and purposes, Fletcher's presentation of the degree of Nez Perce understanding of allotment varied. In her end-of-year report to the commissioner she wrote that James Stuart "had written to the Indian Commissioner on the passage of the Severalty Act and obtained a copy of the law, had studied it and was ready to brave persecution in carrying out its provisions" (ACF to CIA, 26 Dec. 1889, 1262, NAB). To the Board of Indian Commissioners, she declared: "When I arrived there [was] only one man on the reservation—*I except the officials*—of the entire tribe only one man had read the severalty law" (RBIC, 1889, 150; emphasis added). To Captain Richard Pratt of Carlisle Indian School, she claimed: "When I convened the people to talk of Severalty I found that not only were the Indians uninformed as to the law but they fully believed all that the white people here about were saying. Not a person did I meet, white or Indian, but one or two returned students who had read the law. Even Mr Monteith did not know its provisions" (25 June 1889, Letterbook 1, PACF). As I will establish below, Fletcher's claims to Pratt, especially about Monteith, were exaggerated to emphasize Monteith's unsuitability for the position of agent. Gay, too, attributes ignorance of the Dawes Act to the Nez Perces, reporting that even after Fletcher had read the law to them and "explain[ed] its provisions . . . the rows of old red sandstone sphinxes make no sign. . . . They never heard of the 'Dawes' Bill'; they cannot take it in" (C, 36).

53. [Gay], "Brave Woman Allotting," 2.

54. Hoxie and Mark's edition of Gay's letters omits the sentence about the man who noticed the image's reversal. Without that observation, it is easy to read this incident as evidence of Native naiveté about photography and its powers.

55. ACF to CIA, 25 July 1889, 21213, NAB.

56. [Gay], "Brave Women in the Field," 2.

57. ACF to CIA, 25 July 1889, 21213, NAB.

2. Another Beginning

1. The obscured background in "They Donned War Bonnets" is caused by smoke from area forest fires. In "Where We Camped," Gay captioned this image "The Nez Pérce War Pole" (No. 6, SLWHA). She also made at least one photograph of the men "charging," an unsuccessful image, since her shutter could not capture the movement (ACF, Diary, 10 Aug. 1889, PACF; see C, 58). A third shot shows the group apparently bidding farewell to Alice Fletcher, who stands at the lower left. It is variously titled "They Formed in Line" (C, 141), "Good Night at Cold Spring" (Idaho State Historical Society 63-221.12; hereafter cited as ISHS), or "Good Bye" ("Where We Camped," No. 29, SLHWA).

2. Like the image of Fletcher and Chief Joseph, "They Donned War Bonnets" has been widely reproduced but with little attention given to the circumstances it represents. See, for example, Haines, where it is captioned "Warrior carrying Nez Percé War Pole" and where it faces the chapter titled "War" (*Nez Percés*, 254). In Trafzer's *Nez Perce* the caption discusses Nez Perce skills in horse trading (22).

3. This photograph is likely Gay's "Camp at Cold Spring" (C, 143, and ISHS 63-221.20).

4. Morrill and Morrill, "J. P. Vollmer," 12, 13.

5. Stranahan, *Pioneer Stories*, 47. Little documentation supports the claim that Reubens and Vollmer were close friends. Morrill and Morrill's essay presents the biographies of these men as having suggestive parallels but provides no substantive evidence of their friendship. They base their major contentions on Stranahan's history, which is undocumented and anecdotal.

6. Monteith to CIA, 15 July 1889, 19757, NAB. Thanks to Dennis Baird for sharing this letter with me.

7. ACF, Diary, 10 June 1889, PACF.

8. ACF to CIA, 11 June 1889, 16063, NAB.

9. ACF, Diary, 11 June 1889, PACF.

10. Acting CIA H. V. Belt to ACF, 4 May 1889, Letters Sent, vol. 92, Records of the Office of the CIA, NAB.

11. ACF, Diary, 13 June 1889, PACF.

12. Reubens to ACF, 27 June 1889, Incoming correspondence, PACF.

13. ACF to Richard Henry Pratt, 25 June 1889, Letterbook 1, PACF. This letter has likely been overlooked in earlier histories and biographies because of its damaged condition. In the letterpress copy held by the National Anthropological Archives, the ms. is so damaged by water that large portions of it are illegible.

14. ACF to CIA, 26 June 1889, 17736, NAB.

15. Noble to CIA, 22 June 1889, 16606, NAB.

16. Reubens to ACF, 27 June 1889, Incoming correspondence, PACF. On 23 June, the *Washington Post* briefly noted Reubens's meeting with Commissioner Belt and Secretary of the Interior Noble ("Indians Object to their Agent").

17. The back pay for these scouts was not remitted until 1899, and even then incompletely. See Maxwell, *Memorial*, 59. The issue was a bargaining point in 1892, when sale of the "surplus" reservation lands was under debate; the 1893 treaty "specifically promised an immediate investigation and settlement of all of the 53 scout claims" (Stranahan, *Pioneer Stories*, 43).

18. Reubens to CIA, 28 June 1889, 17116, NAB.

19. Reubens wrote to his friend Archie Lawyer almost immediately after he returned from Washington DC regarding reparations for stock sold by two members of Joseph's band before leaving Indian Territory "who were entitled to some money, *now in the hands of the Indian Agent at Fort Colville Agency*" (8 July 1889, Letters, 1864–1904, MG 5066, University of Idaho Special Collections; emphasis added). The letter suggests that either the commissioner had immediately complied, wiring money to the Colville agent, or, as is more likely, that he had informed Reubens that such money was available.

20. "Indian Reuben," *Lewiston Teller*, 27 June 1889.

21. ACF to Richard Henry Pratt, 25 June 1889, Letterbook 1, PACF; emphasis added.

22. Later, as Fletcher understood her situation more clearly and knew who her allies were, she more frequently adopted this tone of moral indignation and personal condemnation.

23. ACF to CIA, 26 June 1889, 17736, NAB.

24. I have not found a document to establish when Fletcher learned that Monteith would be replaced and thus decided it was time to move on to Kamiah. Reubens had written to her on 27 June; she would have received the letter more than a week later, about the time he returned on or about July 5. But Reubens also had access to the telegraph and may have informed her much earlier when he felt he had succeeded.

25. Morrill and Morrill, "J. P. Vollmer," 15.

26. "The Work of Allotment," *Lewiston Teller*, 11 July 1889. See also "Indian Reuben," *Lewiston Teller*, 27 June 1889; and "The Allotment," *Lewiston Teller*, 4 July 1889.

27. ACF, Diary, 16 July 1889, PACF.

28. "Indian Agency," *Lewiston Teller*, 25 July 1889.

29. CIA to Monteith, 13 Sept. 1889, 25911, NAB; see also 13 Sept. 1889, 30135, NAB and CIA to W. D. Robbins, 13 Sept. 1889, 25909, NAB.

30. ACF, Diary, 28 July 1889; 4 Aug. 1889; 9 Aug. 1889.

31. James [Reuben] to CIA, 7 May 1875, Special Case 37 [Langford Claim], NAB.

32. Josephy, *Nez Perce Indians*, 397.

33. "Progress of the Allotment," *Lewiston Teller*, 15 Aug. 1889.

34. ACF, Diary, 29 July 1889, PACF.

35. ACF to FWP, 2 Aug. 1889, UAV 677.38, box 9, Pusey Library. Courtesy of the Harvard University Archives.

36. ACF to Henry Heth, 28 Aug. 1889, Incoming correspondence, PACF. As an anonymous reader of this ms. for the University of Nebraska Press has pointed out, Francis La Flesche also attended Columbian Law School.

37. Heth to ACF, 5 Oct. 1889, Incoming correspondence, PACF.

38. ACF, Diary, 31 Aug. 1889, PACF.

39. ACF to John Wesley Powell, 7 Sept. 1889, Records of the Bureau of American Ethnology, NAA.

40. Heth to ACF, 5 Oct. 1889, Incoming correspondence, NAA. Monteith's allegations would have been supported by the Presbyterian Church, who had assumed responsibility for the Nez Perce Reservation under Grant's Peace Policy.

41. Heth to ACF, 17 Oct. 1889, Incoming correspondence, NAA.

42. The allotment numbers of Celia Reubens, their mother, as well as their spouses and children follow consecutively in the official record.

43. *RBIC*, 1889, 150.

44. Edson Briggs's first survey, as reported by Fletcher, is of the township and range in which Reubens wanted to claim land (ACF to CIA, 20 June 1889, 17003, NAB).

45. Fletcher, "Ethnologic Gleanings," 29, 30. Sappington and Carley suggest that the pole in this photograph is such an honor pole, noting, "In her original notes, Fletcher refers to the honor poles as Death poles" (Fletcher, "Ethnologic Gleanings," 47n48).

46. Fletcher, "Ethnologic Gleanings," 30.

47. *Treaties*, 47.

48. Ts., Josiah Redwolf Folder, box 4, Swayne Collection, ISPARL.

Part 2. Introduction

1. *ARCIA*, 1890, xviii.

2. *ARCIA*, 1890, clxviii.

3. Shannon Jackson, *Professing Performance*, 13.

4. *ARCIA*, 1890, clxviii, clxvii.

5. Roach, *Cities*, 5.

6. "Grand Celebration of the Anniversary of American Independence at Lewiston, I. T., July 4, 1889," *Lewiston Teller*, 27 June 1889. For purposes of this study I focus my analysis on the Native/white dimensions of the day's celebration in Lewiston and Lapwai. This is not to imply, however, that the occasion was observed only by these two groups. In fact, the record of various area festivities in 1889 demonstrates that northwest Idaho was already a cosmopolitan crossroads. For example, those assembled at Lewiston would have included Chinese workers from the silver mines near the neighboring community of Orofino. The town of Grangeville promised a "minstrel troupe" performance to commemorate the day ("City Jots," *Lewiston Teller*, 4 July 1889).

7. Morrill and Morrill, "Talmaks," 6.

8. Roach, *Cities*, 4, 3.

9. "City Jots," *Lewiston Teller*, 13 June 1889.

10. "Grand Celebration," *Lewiston Teller*, 27 June 1889; "Independence Day, Fourth of July. A Grand Celebration at Lewiston: An Immense Gathering of People and All Happy. An Elaborate Programme Successfully Carried Out," *Lewiston Teller*, 11 July 1889; "City Jots" *Lewiston Teller*, 13 June 1889.

11. "Grand Celebration," *Lewiston Teller*, 27 June 1889.

12. "Independence Day," *Lewiston Teller*, 11 July 1889.

13. "Grand Celebration," *Lewiston Teller*, 27 June 1889; "Independence Day," *Lewiston Teller*, 11 July 1889.

14. "Independence Day," *Lewiston Teller*, 11 July 1889.

15. "The Indian Allotment. In Fifteen Months the Reservation to Be Opened," *Grangeville (ID) Free Press*, 14 June 1889.

16. Untitled news note, *Grangeville (ID) Free Press*, 15 July 1892.

17. Kate C. McBeth, Diary, 4 July 1889, "Kate McBeth's Papers," *Kate and Sue McBeth*, University of Idaho website.

18. "Return of Reuben," *Lewiston Teller*, 11 July 1889.

3. "The Square Idea"

1. Dirlik, "Place-Based Imagination," 22, 22–23, 21; emphasis added.

2. According to Greenwald, the northwest portion of the reservation in the Lapwai/Lewiston area is the only place on the Nez Perce Reservation where the allotments approximated the orderly rectilinear plots imagined

by the Dawes Act, although they were not interspersed with white claims, as allotment's early theorists had planned (*Reconfiguring*, 71–73).

3. "Nez Perce Reservation to be Allotted at Once," *Lewiston Teller*, 30 May 1889. Any estimate of how long allotment might take to accomplish was made more complex by the fact that field work could be done only in fair weather (usually May through October). Thus Fletcher's estimate of fifteen months implied three summer seasons. In four summers between 1889 and 1892 she spent about twenty-five months in the field.

4. ACF to CIA, 5 Oct. 1889, 29030, NAB.

5. "Tellings of the Week," *Lewiston Teller*, 1 May 1890.

6. RBIC, 1885, 46.

7. ACF to CIA, 19 July 1889, 20969, NAB.

8. ACF to CIA, 8 June 1889, 15976, NAB.

9. ACF to Isabel Barrows, 10 Sept. 1889, Samuel J. and Isabel Barrows Papers, bMS Am 1807.1 (175), folder 1, Houghton Library, Harvard University.

10. John Greer to Alonzo Leland, *Lewiston Teller*, 12 Dec. 1889.

11. ACF to CIA, 26 June 1890, 20774, NAB.

12. ACF to CIA, 2 Aug. 1889, 22323, NAB.

13. At least one letter discussing allotment seems to indicate an initial plan to move all the on-reservation Nez Perces into close proximity. Agent George W. Norris wrote to Commissioner J. D. C. Atkins, "In my judgment the most favorable portion of the reservation for bringing together the indians for allotment lies in the Northwesterly part South of the Clearwater river.... I think that one half the indians upon this reserve now reside within this territory. [I]t is well watered and furnishes a variety of land, and opportunity for choice and satisfaction to all" (15 June 1887, 16423, NAB). It is unclear whether this plan was seriously discussed, or whether Norris had misunderstood the intent of the law.

14. ACF to CIA, 2 Aug. 1889, 22323, NAB.

15. ACF to CIA, 26 Aug. 1889, 25370, NAB.

16. ACF to CIA, 26 Aug. 1889.

17. For several of my foundational assumptions here I am indebted to Kelsey's "Viewing the Archive," which offers a detailed account of the photographic archive associated with the western surveys.

18. ACF to CIA, 19 July 1889, 20969, NAB.

19. Briggs, "Field Notes of the Survey of Western Boundary Line of Nez Perce Indian Reservation," September 1889, in *Nez Perce Reservation, Idaho, Plat Maps and Survey Notes, 1870–1995*, BLM Survey vol. 3, 69.

20. In describing this album as private, I follow Sandweiss's distinction

between public and private images. "Where We Camped," a small handmade photograph album, was not made with the intent "to be distributed through exhibition, publication, or sale" (*Print the Legend*, 4).

21. Gay, "Where We Camped," 3–6, SLHWA.

22. Kelsey, "Viewing the Archive," 708.

23. In 1882 and 1883 Cushing had published a three-part series in *Century* magazine titled "My Adventures in Zuñi," a mixture of participant-observational anthropology and dashing adventure. In the early 1890s, as Fletcher was in Idaho working on allotment, she was drafting the first of a similar series of essays based on her ethnographic researches among the Omahas, which was later published in *Century* under the general title "Personal Studies of Indian Life." Less overtly crafted to appeal to adventure and suspense, her anthropological accounts were illustrated with engravings, some of which followed photographs made by Jane Gay. For an analysis of the importance of such popular accounts, see Visweswaran, "'Wild West' Anthropology," 91–93.

24. The small albums made by Jane Gay are all similar in size, shape, material, and design. The Schlesinger Library on the History of Women in America holds three such albums, two of them related to the Idaho experience, titled "Reminiscent Bits" and "Where We Camped." The Lawyer collection, a recent bequest to the Nez Perce National Historical Park Archives, contains two similar albums, one of them also titled "Reminiscent Bits," that was likely the property of Kate McBeth (Acc. 632). The contents of this album differ from those in the album of the same title held by the Schlesinger. The Lawyer collection also includes loose pages from other similar albums, and individual photographs that duplicate many that Gay later collected in *Choup-nit-ki*.

25. I assume that Gay shared Fletcher's social circles, and vice versa. Gay's friends included Jean Margaret Davenport Lander, wife of Frederick West Lander, whose expedition surveyed a possible route for a Pacific railroad. Frederick Lander died in 1862; his wife's friendship with Gay endured into the early twentieth century. Cushing had visited Fletcher in Washington in 1882; and Powell was a professional acquaintance of Fletcher.

26. For the purposes of this chapter I have identified as landscape photographs those images in which the primary purpose seems to have been to show locale or terrain. Many of these images contain buildings or human figures, but those details are, for the most part, incidental to or supportive of the representation of land. Human figures or buildings may occupy the foreground to add an illusion of depth or scale or to establish a

level plane against which the slope of a piece of land may be emphasized. Landscape images comprise approximately one-fourth of Gay's oeuvre.

27. Mary Louise Pratt calls these "[p]romontory descriptions," often describing an expedition's arrival and initial survey from above, "the monarch-of-all-I-survey" scenes (*Imperial Eyes*, 198, 197).

28. Kelsey, "Viewing the Archive," 708.

29. Dirlik, "Place-Based Imagination," 18.

30. ACF to CIA, 5 Oct. 1889, 29030, NAB.

31. In *Choup-nit-ki*, this photograph has been retouched with darkened lines that delineate clouds, add form to the tent's features, and give to the whole the air of an on-site pencil sketch (317). The uneven finish proclaims that the fixative did not spread equally over the print's surface and bleached-out areas remain a distinguishing feature of this amended image.

32. ACF to CIA, 26 Aug. 1889, 25370, NAB.

33. In this line of thinking I follow Jeanne Holland, who has argued that Emily Dickinson's fascicles, which she fair copied and bound, but did not print, nevertheless constitute a form of publication and that those "domestic technologies of publication" can inform the readings and interpretation of her work ("Scraps, Stamps, and Cutouts").

34. Kelsey, "Viewing the Archive," 713.

35. E. Jane Gay, "Brave Woman Allotting," 6.

4. Ethnographic Knowledge and Native Cartography

1. ACF to FWP, 20 Jan. 1890, HUG 1717.2.1, box 6, folder F, Pusey Library. Courtesy of the Harvard University Archives.

2. ACF, Diary, 28 Mar. 1890, PACF.

3. In reporting the transfer of Thaw monies to Harvard and the Peabody, the *Christian Register* reported, "During her work among the Indians, Miss Fletcher has been associated with the museum as a special assistant, and has achieved such results in exploration that no one questions the appropriateness of making her a Fellow of the university for which she has done so much. The fund amounts to $30,000, and was given by Mrs Mary C. Thaw of Pittsburg, Pa., in memory of her husband, who was much interested in the philanthropic and scientific labors of Miss Fletcher" (untitled news note, 70, no. 5 [29 Jan. 1891]: 65).

4. ACF to FWP, 17 Aug. 1890; emphasis added. Frederick W. Putnam Director's Records, Peabody Museum of Archaeology and Ethnology, Harvard University.

[363]

5. ACF to FWP, 20 Aug. 1890, UAV 677.38, box 10, Pusey Library. Courtesy of the Harvard University Archives.

6. ACF to FWP, 28 Sept. 1890, UAV 677.38, box 10, Pusey Library. Courtesy of the Harvard University Archives.

7. ACF to CIA, 8 Oct. 1890, 32432, NAB.

8. Victor Turner, *From Ritual to Theatre*, 13.

9. Taylor, *Archive*, 3, 2. Fletcher used the information she gathered in these interviews as the basis of two monographs she worked on for the next several decades but did not publish (both were eventually published in 1995 in *Northwest Anthropological Research Notes*). Her "Ethnologic Gleanings among the Nez Perces" is a two-part study that contains "ethnographic data" about names, social structures, and customs, and transcribed oral narratives (11). "The Nez Perce Country," a longer study, contains information that Fletcher deemed to be factual and thus historical, relating to the location of villages, settlement patterns, and political organization of the Nimiipuu.

10. Fletcher's field notes to this interview more clearly differentiate the identities of the two women involved in this transaction: "Mrs. Celia Reubens... brings basket & stone pounder. These were made by Kocksatparlo 96 years or thereabouts who remembers the descent of Lewis & Clark" (11 Dec. 1889, Nez Perce Field Notebook, Informants 1889–1891, PACF).

11. ACF to FWP, 1 Jan. [1890], UAV 677.38, box 9, Pusey Library. Courtesy of the Harvard University Archives. The letter is mistakenly dated 1 January 1889. It was surely written a year later, since Fletcher had not yet been to the Nez Perce Reservation in January 1889.

12. Sappington and Carley, Editors' introduction to Fletcher, "Ethnologic Gleanings," 5.

13. Gay printed two views of this location and included both in *Choupnit-ki*. See also page 191, where the image is titled "South Fork of Clearwater River" and Gay's annotation reads, "Depressions in earth made by ancient dwellings." See also ISHS prints 63-221.57a and 63-221.57b.

14. Sappington et al., in Fletcher, "The Nez Perce Country," 206.

15. This series of plats shows signs of heavy wear, the traces of how subsequent users have consulted and employed them. Although I reproduce them here in black and white, on the original the plots have been coded with colored pencil and the entire document has been repeatedly overwritten and annotated by many different hands.

16. Fletcher's idea for this paper may have been part of a comparative

project. In 1890 she was completing a long ethnographic study of the Omahas in which an analysis of political structures had been central.

17. ACF to FWP, 27 July 1890, Frederick W. Putnam Director's Records, Peabody Museum of Archaeology and Ethnology, Harvard University.

18. The whites who lived on and near the reservation called Kew-kew'-lu-yah Jonathan or Billy or Uncle Billy Williams. According to Fletcher, he was also known as "Business Billy" because of "his promptitude in attending to all matters committed to his care" (Sappington et al., in Fletcher, "The Nez Perce Country," 180). All subsequent quotations from "The Nez Perce Country," Fletcher's unpublished monograph that resulted from this encounter, refer to the annotated version of the manuscript published in 1995, as edited by Sappington and colleagues, with emendations and commentary.

Here I use Kew-kew'-lu-yah's Nimiipuu name to indicate information that can reasonably be attributed to this Native intellectual and some version of his anglicized name to suggest instances in which the information he proffered seems to have been filtered through Fletcher's assumptions.

19. Since 1891, when this map was drawn, several other Native maps of Nimiipuu territory, made at earlier moments, have been identified. Map Rock, a petroglyph located near Givens Hot Springs along the Snake River, represents "the territory of the Shoshone Indians" and includes the courses of the Salmon and the Snake rivers (Warhus, *Another America*, 20; the map is reproduced as Image 7, page 19). According to Trafzer, Chief Walammottinin (Twisted Hair) used charcoal to draw a map on an elk hide to show Lewis and Clark how to follow a canoe route from Nimiipuu lands to the Pacific Ocean (*Nez Perce*, 15). Several informants have alluded to the existence of a map of the Wallowa country drawn either by Joseph or by Ollokot as a rebuttal to one made by General O. O. Howard. On this document was inscribed a representation of contested territories that established the non-treaty bands' claim to an "area ... much larger than that of the reservation as established by the Executive Order June 1873" (qtd. in McWhorter, *Hear Me*, 157; see also Nabokov, "Orientations," 242–43).

20. ACF to FWP, 22 June 1891; HUG 677.38, box 9, folder F, Pusey Library. Courtesy of the Harvard University Archives.

21. Warhus, *Another America*, 3. See also Basso, whose work exemplifies his contention that "place-making is ... a form of *cultural* activity [that] can be grasped only in relation to the ideas and practices with which it is accomplished" (*Wisdom*, 7).

22. Fletcher's most notable collaborator was Omaha scholar Francis

La Flesche. Mark notes that Fletcher "used his work to promote herself" rather than to mentor her informant ("Francis La Flesche," 508). Ultimately, however, at La Flesche's insistence, Fletcher finally did include his name as co-author of *The Omaha Tribe*.

23. Fletcher's field diary indicates that the interviews lasted over three days. On Tuesday, 9 June, Fletcher attended a local trial involving a land dispute and "Miss Gay [was] working with Billy." On the next two days, Fletcher apparently joined the group.

24. ACF to FWP, 22 June 1891; HUG 677.38, box 9, folder F, Pusey Library. Courtesy of the Harvard University Archives. Fletcher's notes from these interviews are filed in series 20 and 21, box 20, PACF.

25. These accounts include Fletcher's field diary entries for June and August 1891; her letters to F. W. Putnam on 22 June and 6 August 1891; Gay's Letter 24 (dated 15 August 1891, C, 380–400); and McBeth, *Nez Perces*, 239. McBeth also published an account of the 1832 Nez Perce delegation to St. Louis, based on information she gathered in this interview, in the *Church at Home and Abroad* in April 1894.

26. It is difficult to establish how many village locations might originally have been identified and discussed. According to Gay, Kew-kew'-lu-yah identified "nearly a hundred villages" (C, 381).

27. In her remarks accompanying the map, Fletcher writes, "During the four years that I was among the Nez Perces I found comparatively few who could orient themselves. . . . The people traveled by topography, and this map proves they had the power of making a general picture from detached details, as there was no vantage point from which a bird's-eye view of the country could be obtained" (Fletcher, "The Nez Perce Country," 188).

28. See Fletcher, "The Nez Perce Country," 179–80 for a thorough description of the various emendations to Fletcher's manuscript copy of the map.

29. Barthes, *Camera Lucida*, 42.

30. Nabokov, "Orientations," 241. Warhus also argues that Native informants "used their knowledge to barter advantages from the Europeans" (*Another America*, 4).

31. Nabokov, "Orientations," 242.

32. Dirlik, "Place-Based Imagination," 22.

33. McBeth, *Nez Perces*, 98; see also 186.

34. Greenwald's study of allotment patterns on the Nez Perce Reservation also bears out this contention (*Reconfiguring*, 78).

35. ACF to FWP, 17 May 1890, Frederick W. Putnam Director's Records, Peabody Museum of Archaeology and Ethnology, Harvard University.

36. ACF to CIA, 20 July 1891, Letterbook 1, PACF.

37. Shannon Jackson, *Professing Performance*, 13.

38. Roach, *Cities*, 26.

39. Margaret Currier, "Memorandum on Nez Perce map by 'Billy' Williams made for Alice C. Fletcher around 1893[,] Supposedly given to the Peabody Museum," 26 Mar. 1955, Acc. 92-1, Peabody Museum of Archaeology and Ethnology, Harvard University.

40. Frank H. H. Roberts Jr., Associate Director of the Bureau of American Ethnology, to Margaret Currier, 3 June 1955, Acc. 92-1, Peabody Museum of Archaeology and Ethnology, Harvard University.

41. Horr, "General Nature," 9.

42. C. Marc Miller to the Peabody Museum, 1 May 1953, Acc. 92-1, Peabody Museum of Archaeology and Ethnology, Harvard University.

43. The cartographic evidence gathered in support of the suit, notably Edward Curtis's list of aboriginal groups and village locations, established the accuracy of Kew-kew'-lu-yah's map and indirectly attested to its importance as a foundational Native representation of aboriginal lands. For a list of the documents submitted as evidence in Docket No. 175, *The Nez Perce Tribe of Indians v. The United States of America*, see "Commission Findings," 286–88.

44. Another reproduction of Fletcher's copy of the map, without additional notations, is included in Lohse and Sprague, "History of Research," 14.

45. Gene Eastman, e-mail communication to author, 13 April 2011.

46. Ralph Space, "The Indians," ts., Ralph Space Papers, University of Idaho Special Collections. I thank Dennis Baird for directing me to this map and to Space's work, and Gene Eastman and Mollie Eastman for adding their interpretation of its significance.

47. Space, "The Indians."

48. Some of Space's identifications were inaccurate. Gene Eastman has corrected his work and has verified the location of three of the village sites (e-mail, 13 April 2011).

49. Gene and Mollie Eastman have researched and written about the Lolo Trail for the past eleven years. They have published two books, *Bitterroot Crossing: Lewis and Clark across the Lolo Trail*, volumes 1 and 2.

Part 3. Introduction

1. Saler, "Empire for Liberty," 366, 368. I thank Maureen Konkle for calling this source to my attention.

2. Before the mid-nineteenth century, federal policy aimed to separate

indigenes from whites, either by removing them from territories about to be admitted as states or by containing them within reservations. Allotment policy recognized the futility of these separatist measures and aimed at assimilation instead. See Price and Clinton, *Law and the American Indian*, 76.

3. Cruikshank, *Will to Empower*, 1. For other investigations of "technologies of citizenship," see the essays collected by Castronovo and Nelson in *Materializing Democracy*.

4. Thomson, *Extraordinary Bodies*, 43.

5. Cruikshank, *Will to Empower*, 42, 19.

6. Qtd. in Price, *Law*, 544.

7. The first small Catholic church on the Nez Perce Reservation was dedicated in late 1874; soon thereafter, in early 1875, three Catholic missionaries, Father A. Morillo, Brother A. Cagiagno, and Father Cataldo, "[began] the Nez Percés Mission" (Regis, "Sketch," 117). For a useful summary of the history of Catholicism among the Nimiipuu, see Regis. I thank Dennis Baird for sharing this source with me.

8. Regis, "Sketch," 49.

9. On 11 June 1890, Father Joseph N. Guidi forwarded to Alice C. Fletcher a "petition of the Catholic Nez Perce Indians . . . ask[ing] one mile square of land for the missionaries' buildings and school, etc." that had originally been sent "sometimes in the year 1874 or 1875." He requested that she would "interest herself" in fulfilling this longstanding request (Guidi to ACF, 11 June 1890, 22654, Special case 143, NAB).

10. Walker, *Conflict and Schism*, 135.

11. Charles E. Monteith to J. C. Atkins, 21 July 1885, 17131, NAB.

12. Susan McBeth called her school the New Carlisle, a name signifying her claim to offer a program of Indian education modeled after Richard H. Pratt's Carlisle Indian School.

13. Previous scholars have not connected the ongoing ill will between the missionaries directly to the division of the Kamiah Presbyterian congregations. For example, in their notes to this passage, Hoxie and Mark comment simply, "This falling out with Fletcher and the McBeth sisters may have contributed to Lawyer's decision to oppose allotment and argue against the 1893 surplus land sale" (*With the Nez Perces*, 182–83, n. 20). Nor does Mark, in her biography of Fletcher, connect the problem to the McBeth feud. Rather, she blames Jane Gay for exacerbating an unbreachable and long-lasting split between these groups, first by spearheading repairs on the Kamiah First Presbyterian Church and then by demanding that traditional celebrations of the Fourth of July in 1891 in Lapwai

be forbidden. As I demonstrate, Alice Fletcher was more culpable in both cases than was Gay.

14. Morgan, ARCIA, 1891, 8–9.

5. Technologies of Citizenship

1. Fletcher, "Fourth of July," 496.
2. ARCIA, 1890, xviii, xix.
3. ACF to CIA, 2 Jan. 1890, 373, Sp. case 145, NAB.
4. ACF to CIA, 12 July 1890, 22804, NAB; emphasis added. In the description as published in the *Christian Register*, Fletcher describes the celebrants as "groups of Indians living in this vicinity" (496).
5. Fletcher apparently did attempt to include Lapwai Nimiipuu in the voting, although she did not report its numerical outcome to Morgan. According to a field diary entry dated 28 June 1890, she "sent evidence to Agt to read to Ind. July 4th." Whether this "evidence" was read to both traditional and Presbyterian celebrants at Lapwai is unclear. Even had it been read to both groups, the "vote" taken would not have represented a numerical majority of those concerned.
6. Kate C. McBeth, Diary, 4 July 1890, "Kate McBeth's Papers," *Kate and Sue McBeth*, University of Idaho website.
7. Gay, "Life on the Reservation," 173. I assume spelling of "Tal-lik-lykl" in the *Choup-nit-ki* caption is likely a transcription error (uncrossed final *t*).
8. Untitled news note, *Lewiston Teller*, 19 June 1890.
9. Gay, "Life on the Reservation," 173.
10. ACF, Diary, 6 July 1892, PACF.
11. Morgan to Indian Agents and Superintendents of Indian Schools, 28 Jan. 1890, Letters Received, North Idaho Agency, National Archives and Records Administration, Pacific Alaska Region, Seattle WA (hereafter cited as NARA Pacific Alaska Region (Seattle).
12. RBIC, 1888, 126.
13. RBIC, 1888, 50.
14. In 1886 Agent Charles Monteith had been ordered to make a tribal census. He refused to do so, writing, "Under date of May 17, 1886, I was instructed to take a census of this tribe, and as no funds were available to pay for the expenses connected therewith, I must use such employés as ... could be spared. There being no employés who could be spared from their respective duties, no census has been taken. It is utterly impossible to take a census of this tribe without considerable expense, and I consider it monumental cheek on the part of Congress to expect a census to be taken with-

out expense" (ARCIA, 1886, 232). To my knowledge, no tribal census had been taken before Fletcher arrived in Lapwai in 1889, nor did she conduct a census during her work. In 1890 the Eleventh Census of the United States appointed a special agent in charge of overseeing the census of Natives, whose results were reported in 1894. See Pezzati, "Thomas C. Donaldson."

15. ARCIA, 1890, xlix.
16. ACF to CIA, 2 Jan. 1890, 373, Sp. case 145, NAB.
17. ARCIA, 1890, lxxvi.
18. Jaimes, "Federal," 123.
19. Royster, "Legacy of Allotment."
20. Putnam and Boas, Instructions for taking measurements, 1, F. W. Putnam Papers, HUG 1717.2.14, box 37, Pusey Library. Courtesy of the Harvard University Archives.
21. ACF to FWP, 6 Aug. 1891, UAV 677.38, box 11, Pusey Library. Courtesy of the Harvard University Archives.
22. ACF to FWP, 6 Aug. 1891.
23. ACF to CIA, 8 Oct. 1890, 32432, NAB.
24. Gay's "Jeshuran" was likely a variant of "Jeshurun," a prophet in the Hebrew Bible and a synonym for Israel. Both Jeshuran and Highlander are sassy rejoinders that play with the idea of tribalism.
25. Putnam and Boas, Instructions for taking measurements, 1, F. W. Putnam Papers, HUG 1717.2.14, box 37, Pusey Library. Courtesy of the Harvard University Archives.
26. Questionnaire, series 10, PACF.
27. Morgan's directive in the 1892 *Report of the Commissioner of Indian Affairs* announced federal policies regulating the "exhibition of Indians" and designed to curb the participation of Native subjects in so-called Wild West exhibits, such as those populating the Midway at the Chicago fair, as well as those who worked for Buffalo Bill's Wild West Show. The directives also delimited the ways Natives could be used in the lifeways displays associated with the anthropological and federal exhibits. Morgan writes, "During the past year numerous applications have been received asking for authority to take Indians from reservations for exhibition purposes. I have steadily refused to countenance in any way anything of the 'Wild West' character.... [I]t is unwise for Indians to be allowed to appear before the public exhibiting their savage characteristics" (105).
28. McGovern, *Halligan's Illustrated World's Fair*, n.p.
29. Gay herself had made photographic images in this anthropological documentary mode. See, for example, C, 120. This photograph, likely

made long before the women came to Idaho, and which Gay captioned "Scraping Deer Skins," illustrated Fletcher's *Omaha Tribe*, vol. 2, 344.

30. Of these seven images, two are of the Author, three of the Cook, and two of the Photographer. According to Gay's grand-niece Jane Gay Dodge, "Years later, when the two Misses Gay were selecting the letters [to be included in *Choup-nit-ki*], they improvised background and costume for pictures of the two personalities described as 'The Cook' and 'The Photographer' in the *Letters*. There was no reason at the time of the experience to take such photographs, even supposing there had been any person along who could have done so" ("Brief Biography," 6, SLHWA). I assume these images to be self-portraits, although it is unclear who actually made them. Gay likely posed in a collaboratively planned setting and her niece operated the camera.

31. For an incisive analysis of dioramas and habitat groups in this period, see Haraway, *Primate Visions*, 29–30 and passim.

32. I know of no photographs of Gay or Fletcher made in Idaho in which they are shown in other than standing or seated postures. The kneeling posture I discuss here should recall my analysis of James Stuart's kneeling pose in Image 1.

33. In 1891 the *Red Man* published two of Gay's letters under the same title, "Camp Life Experiences." One appeared in volume 11 (April–May); the other appeared later that year in volume 12 (October–November). All quotations here are taken from the first of these columns (hereafter cited as "CLE," with page numbers). The *Red Man* version of this letter contains several suggestive passages that do not appear in *Choup-nit-ki*, where parts of it comprise letter eight. Gay apparently first wrote a version of this letter to Henrietta Bradley, her and Fletcher's intimate friend and a member of the same reform circles, in September 1889.

34. Other writers and speakers continued to use the figure of allotment policy as a machine—perhaps with little thought to its violent tenor, or perhaps with full intent—to signify the futility of resistance to Indian policy. The phrase "a mighty pulverizing engine for breaking up the tribal mass" has been attributed to and/or used by Commissioner of Indian Affairs William Jones, Merrill E. Gates, and Theodore Roosevelt.

35. ACF to CIA, 16 Sept. 1889, 27011, NAB.

36. ACF to CIA, 2 Aug. 1889, 22323, NAB.

37. RBIC, 1889, 149.

38. RBIC, 1889, 150, 151.

39. See Greenwald, *Reconfiguring*, 73, for a map showing the location of

the Reubens allotments; see *Family History of Allottees* for details related to the Stuart and Corbett allotments (vol. 13668, 20–21, Records of the BIA, North Idaho Agency, 1901, RG 75, NARA Pacific Alaska Region (Seattle).

6. Fictions of Coherence

1. See Tonkovich, "Lost," 58–67. Others who have written about Gay's tactic of constructing multiple personae include Jacox, "Cook"; Mark, SNL, 191–92; Hoxie and Mark, Introduction, xxix–xxx; and Simonsen, "Cook."

2. Qtd. in Priest, *Uncle Sam's Stepchildren*, 249.

3. Of the church repair, Mark writes, "Jane Gay thought the restoration of the church a great success, but for the cause of allotment it was in fact a serious error" (SNL, 187). At the very least, in this passage, the pronouns should be plural, for *both* women were involved in the church's restoration and both were responsible for its negative results, as I demonstrate in the balance of this chapter.

4. Carley has published transcriptions of a number of letters Fletcher wrote to the commissioner of Indian affairs and to Frederick W. Putnam in 1889–92 ("Letters," parts 1 and 2). This valuable effort does not, however, represent a full record. Other correspondence, including Fletcher's letters to women friends, offers an important supplement to these letters.

5. Mark's reflections on writing Fletcher's biography seem to suggest that she has taken a similar approach. She writes, "[T]he different selves that Alice Fletcher seemed to be were not simply roles she played nor adaptive postures crafted to help her get what she needed" (SNL, xvii). In the balance of her book, however, Mark does not fully explore the implications of Fletcher's "different selves." This is most apparent in her decision to write of Fletcher's developing anthropological reputation and the Thaw Fellowship in a separate chapter that interrupts and is fundamentally unrelated to those devoted to the Nez Perce allotment.

6. ACF, Diary, 27 June 1889 and 26 June 1889, PACF.

7. ACF, Diary, 27 June 1889.

8. Allgor, "Lady Will Have," 49.

9. ACF to Electa Sanderson Dawes, 2 Oct. 1890, box 10, Henry L. Dawes Papers, 1833–1933, LC.

10. ACF to Electa Sanderson Dawes, 2 Oct. 1890.

11. ACF to Isabel Barrows, 10 Sept. 1889, Samuel J. and Isabel Barrows Papers, bMS Am 1807.1 (175), folder 1, Widener Library, Harvard University.

12. ACF to TJM, 27 Aug. 1889, Letterbook 1, PACF; emphasis added. The poor quality of this manuscript makes it extremely difficult to read.

It is a letter-press copy and is creased, torn, and water-stained. Here and in similar transcriptions that follow, I indicate indecipherable words with two bracketed question marks and follow those I have guessed at with a single bracketed question mark.

13. Caroline Morgan to ACF, 15 June 1891, box 1, Incoming correspondence, PACF.

14. TJM to ACF, 15 June 1891, box 1, Incoming correspondence, PACF.

15. ACF to CIA, 10 Oct. 1889, 29872, Sp. case 147, NAB.

16. ACF to TJM, 12 [?] Oct. 1889, Letterbook 1, PACF.

17. ACF to TJM, 26 Oct. 1891, Outgoing correspondence, PACF. How this issue was resolved is unclear; I have been unable to locate Morgan's reply. Briggs appears to have been a highly skilled surveyor, although his records were repeatedly challenged after allotment concluded. There is no evidence that he intentionally or inadvertently extended his work. Fletcher's objections here should be taken in the context of her own impatience to close the allotment so she could take up her anthropological work.

Yet Briggs was not a disinterested employee. He was married to the daughter of Sewell Truax, a military officer stationed at Fort Lapwai who later became a trader in the area. Still later in life, Truax became a "wealthy wheat farmer along the lower Snake River" (Dennis Baird, e-mail to author, 28 June 2008). Briggs was one of the first white men to claim land when the reservation was opened, filing a claim shortly after noon on 18 November 1895 ("Lewiston in '95. 500,000 Acres of Choice Indian Land Thrown Open to Settlement," unsourced newspaper account in scrapbook, box 1, Swayne collection, ISPARL).

18. Fletcher, "Missionary Work," 54.

19. Gay, "Camp Life Experiences," *Red Man* 12, no. 3 (October–November 1891): 6. Because this is the second article with this title, I refer to it hereafter as "Camp Life Experiences [II]."

20. Morrill and Morrill claim that Gay, Fletcher, and Thaw (then Mary Copley) "had shared . . . a house in Washington DC, until [Copley's] marriage in 1867" ("Old Church," 16). They offer no documentary support for this assertion, nor have I found evidence to support it.

21. ACF, Diary, 29 Aug. 1889, PACF. [August] corrects Fletcher's mistaken entry, which reads "Mr. Thaw died Sept. 17 in Paris." Thaw, according to the notice in the *New York Times*, had "owned $200,000 worth of lands along the Northern Pacific Road, and held large blocks of Northern Pacific stock" ("Liberal in His Charity," 21 Aug. 1889). Among other bequests, Thaw left approximately $70,000 to Presbyterian charities. This

was over and above the smaller amounts given by his wife from her own part of the fortune (³⁄₁₆ of the estate; "William Thaw's Will," *New York Times*, 3 Sept. 1889).

22. Gay, "Camp Life Experiences [II}," 6. Mark's condemnation of Gay as the principal offender in the remodeling project likely stems from the fact that the major accounts of the work are hers. As I show, Fletcher was careful to obscure her own involvement.

23. Gay, "Camp Life Experiences [II}," 6–7.

24. Gay, "Camp Life Experiences [II}," 7. This passage has been omitted from Hoxie and Mark's edition of Gay's letters.

25. ACF, Diary, 28 Mar. 1890, PACF.

26. ACF, Diary, 31 Mar. 1890, PACF.

27. ACF, Diary, 14 and 15 May 1890, PACF.

28. ACF to CIA, 2 Feb. 1891, 4406, Sp. case 143 (Mission), NAB. The letter carries an endorsement from Daniel Dorchester, the superintendent of Indian schools, that reads, in part, "I have visited the locality & Church refered to in this paper, and myself aided in the contributions for repairing & refitting the church."

29. ACF, Diary, 7 Aug. 1890, PACF.

30. ACF to CIA, 12 July 1890, 22804, NAB.

31. ACF to CIA, 26 July 1890, 24086, Sp. Case 147, NAB; emphasis added.

32. ACF to CIA, 26 July 1890.

33. ACF to FWP, 18 June 1890, FWP Director's Records, Peabody Museum of Archaeology and Ethnology, Harvard University (hereafter cited as PMAE).

34. Hoxie and Mark did not include this episode in *With the Nez Perces*, a serious omission, since it demonstrates the degree to which Fletcher was forced to confront the outcomes of her theories.

35. ACF to CIA, 2 Aug. 1889, 22323, NAB.

36. ACF to CIA, 14 June 1890, 19277, NAB.

37. For a series of affidavits in this case, see Letters Received by the Commissioner of Indian Affairs, 4 and 5 Aug. 1890, 22575 and 22534, NAB.

38. ACF to CIA, 12 Sept. 1891, 34143, NAB; emphasis added. Fletcher's workers had also struck for higher wages earlier in the allotment work, on 25 September 1889 (ACF, Diary, PACF).

39. James Reubens to ACF, undated, Incoming correspondence 1888–1890, PACF.

40. Levi Jonas to ACF, 20 Aug. 1895, Incoming correspondence, PACF.

Part 4. Introduction

1. ACF to CIA, 13 Sept. 1892, 34158, NAB.
2. Charlie Savage, "U.S. Will Settle Indian Lawsuit for $3.4 Billion. Long, Complex Battle over Land Trusts," *New York Times*, 9 Dec. 2009.

7. Irresolutions and Incompletions

1. Edward Conner to CIA, 8 June 1891, 21415, NAB.
2. CIA to Warren D. Robbins, 15 June 1891; CIA to Edward McConville, 15 June 1891. Both in Letters Sent, vol. 110, Records of the Office of the CIA, NAB.
3. This account was published as "Life on the Reservation... II," *Christian Register*, 17 Mar. 1892, 173.
4. Hoxie and Mark, *With the Nez Perces*, 183n24.
5. ACF, Diary, 6 July 1892. One of those "stealth" images may well be the photograph of the war procession Gay included in *Choup-nit-ki* with her account of the Kamiah celebration held two years earlier (358). See figure 36.
6. ARCIA, 1892, 662.
7. *Idaho County Free Press*, 15 July 1892.
8. Darwin James to CIA, 12 Aug. 1892, 30743, NAB.
9. TJM to Miss Fletcher, 15 June 1891, box 1, Incoming correspondence, PACF. This letter departs from Morgan's usual practice of opening official correspondence to Fletcher with the salutation *Madam:*. Typewritten on Office of Indian Affairs letterhead, the letter opens, "My Dear Miss Fletcher:—"; this document is clearly a part of the unofficial correspondence the two maintained about agency affairs.
10. The schools at the agency and at Fort Lapwai were combined under McConville's direction in 1892 (Thompson, *Historic Resource Study, Spalding*, 173). This action was due in no small part to Fletcher's support of McConville and opposition to Robbins.
11. The characterization of McBeth's home is misleading. Jane Gay captioned a photograph of this structure as "Miss Kate's Root House." It shows a board-and-batten structure that appears not to be measurably less comfortable than other buildings at the fort, most of which had fallen into disrepair after the government abandoned the post in 1884 (C, 322). At some point, Presbyterian Indian friends had "boarded" its dirt floor, and Kate herself papered the walls of the "shanty" (Fraser, *Peaka Soyapu*, chap. 1). In 1890 Fletcher arranged for "four men" to work "for two days" on the missionary's house, repairing the porch and removing par-

titions (Kate McBeth, Diary, 5 Oct. 1890, "Kate McBeth's Papers," *Kate and Sue McBeth*, University of Idaho website). Whether these men were directly in Fletcher's employ and thus paid from federal funds is unclear.

McBeth lived here by choice, having been offered "a far better house on the campus" of the Fort Lapwai Industrial School. But because the campus was fenced and locked in the evening, and because the missionary wished to be available to "the Indians . . . whenever they sought her," she chose a location outside the school grounds (Fraser, *Peaka Soyapu*, chap. 1).

12. ACF to CIA, 15 June 1891, 22697, Letterbook 1, PACF. In making her argument to Morgan, Fletcher admitted that the Hay Reservation lands were "unfavorable to growths of any kind" and furnished "very poor pasture." Her advocacy of this exchange thus is inconsistent with her public claims that Indian clients should always receive the most productive and valuable lands. But see also a map made in 1870 titled "The Military & Hay Reservations, at Fort Lapwai, Idaho," whereon a handwritten annotation next to the Hay Reservation reads, "These hills are thickly covered with excellent grass" (Thompson, *Historic Resource Study, Fort Lapwai*, map 3, facing 198). These differing claims only emphasize that descriptions used in grading land were imprecise, unscientific, and subject to seasonal variation, local climate conditions, and political intent.

13. This suggestive phrase is inexplicably omitted from Hoxie and Mark's edition of Gay's letters.

14. Although they did not publicly admit it, these three women were also interested in establishing the site of the original Spalding settlement as a monument to Presbyterian mission activities and had begun to lay plans for appropriate memorial structures. See, for example, *Choup-nit-ki* 389, where Gay discusses how the millstone from the original settlement might be preserved. According to Thompson, "in the late 1920s . . . [t]he old mill race and the mill site were still plainly visible; the Indians told the observer that one of the original mill burrs [likely the one mentioned by Gay] was buried there" (*Historic Resource Study, Spalding*, 180). The Spalding site was marked with a memorial stone (not a millstone) as part of the centennial celebrations of 1936, which also created Spalding State Park. I thank Jason W. Lyon, the integrated resources program manager at the Nez Perce National Historical Park, for sharing information about the Spalding site with me and for pointing out the site of Thaw Cottage.

15. ACF to CIA, 17 Mar. 1890, 8772, NAB; see also Letterbook 1, PACF.

16. As early as 1871 Agent John Monteith had informed the Indian Office that the Nez Perces in the area had gathered fuel wood from the boom

grounds "from time immemorial" and that the site was still used both by the agency and by area residents (Monteith to CIA, 8 July 1871, Monteith Papers, vol. 1, Ms. 19, ISPARL).

17. ACF to CIA, 2 Jan. 1890, 374, NAB.

18. ACF to CIA, 22 June 1891, 23212, Record Group 48, National Archives and Records Administration, College Park MD (hereafter cited as NACP). I am grateful to Dennis Baird for sharing this letter with me. Although the letter bears a chronological number, and although it was at one time assigned to case 147, it is now filed in Record Group 48 in the NACP.

19. Because of the details included in figure 39, I suspect it was adapted from the hand-drawn map Fletcher enclosed in her letter recommending against Moses's allotment, which has since been separated from the letter.

20. "Synopsis of Report of Inspector Miller, Nez Perce Agency, 26 Dec. 1891," RG 48E682, M 10707, roll 30, Inspections, NAB.

21. Gilbert, Luxenberg, and Tolon, *Historic Landscape Report*, 45.

22. CIA to Robbins, 3 July 1891, Letters Sent, vol. 110, Records of the Office of the CIA, NAB.

23. Withholding rations and food was a common tactic to compel Natives to comply with federal edicts. Families reluctant to send their children to federal boarding schools were routinely threatened with reduced rations. For a history of this practice, see Adams, *Education for Extinction*, 63–64.

Was Fletcher aware that her suggestion that the Nez Perces be forbidden to leave the reservation for the hunt had precedent in the administrative philosophies of Charles E. Monteith? In 1886 he recommended that the Indian Office "[i]ssue an order prohibiting Indians from leaving their crops during growing season to go off on hunting and fishing excursions, and in case any Indian or Indians fail to obey the order, they shall be arrested by the police, tried by the Indian court, and fined not less than 10.$ nor more than 20.$ for each and every offense. This is the only way to . . . break up their nomadic habits" (CEM to CIA, 21 Apr. 1886, 6798, NAB).

24. ACF to CIA, 17 Sept. 1891, 34916, NAB.

25. For a summary of the charges against Ryan and the more general issues of which it was a part, see Fletcher's letter to Darwin James, 19 July 1892, 30743, NAB.

26. ACF to General Morgan, 2 Nov. 1891, box 2, Outgoing Correspondence, PACF.

27. Given the plethora of documents related to this period of her life, it is likely that some further evidence exists but is misfiled or otherwise difficult to locate.

28. The literature on the World's Columbian Exposition is massive. For useful secondary analyses of exhibits featuring Native cultures, see especially Bank, "Representing History"; Trennert, "Selling Indian Education"; and Fagin, "Closed Collections." For an insightful reading of Native participation in Wild West shows of the era, see Philip J. Deloria, *IUP*, 61–71.

29. Turner, "Significance," 199; emphasis added.

30. Qtd. in Bank, "Representing History," 603.

31. McGovern, *Halligan's Illustrated World's Fair*, n.p.

32. Boas, "Ethnology at the Exposition," 609.

33. See, for example, Rydell, *All the World's*, and Hinsley, "World as Marketplace."

34. Hibbard, "Chicago 1893," 26.

35. Trennert, "Selling Indian Education," 205.

36. Trennert, "Selling Indian Education," 206, 208.

37. Fagin, "Closed Collections," 250.

38. ACF to CIA, 8 Oct. 1890, 32432, NAB.

39. Fagin compares Powell's display, based on the "closed" collections of the three agencies whose collaboration he headed, to Putnam's "open" exhibit.

40. Davis and Putnam, *World's Columbian Exposition*, 5.

41. Boas, "Ethnology at the Exposition," 608.

42. *Rand McNally and Company's Handbook*, 90.

43. Boas, "Ethnology at the Exposition," 609.

44. Davis and Putnam, *World's Columbian Exposition*, 8.

45. Davis and Putnam, *World's Columbian Exposition*, 9.

46. For photographs of the interior of the Anthropology Building, see Fagin, "Closed Collections," 258, 259, and 261.

47. Handy, *World's*, 8.

48. "Awards in Department of Ethnology of the World's Columbian Exposition." Ts. WCE Misc. Papers, F. W. Putnam Papers, HUG 1717.2.14, box 37, Pusey Library. Courtesy of the Harvard University Archives.

49. Secretary of the Interior to CIA, 16 Jan. 1892, 2102, NAB.

50. Bank, "Representing History," 592.

51. "Indian Office Exhibit at the World's Columbian Exposition." Ts. 30 Jan. 1892. WCE Misc. Papers, F. W. Putnam Papers, HUG 1717.2.14, box 37, Pusey Library. Courtesy of the Harvard University Archives.

52. ACF, Diary, 1 Feb. 1892, PACF.

53. FWP to ACF, 25 July 1891, box 1, Incoming correspondence, PACF.

54. Although Allen Conrad Morrill and Eleanor Dunlap Morrill claim

that Susan McBeth "was already writing numerous letters to open the paths that would lead to" Robert Williams's being taken by Fletcher to the World's Fair, they offer no documentation in support of the claim (*Out*, 329).

55. Susan L. McBeth to Mr. H. Erickson, 16 Dec. 1891, Sue McBeth's Papers, Personal Documents, *Kate and Sue McBeth*, University of Idaho website.

56. Susan L. McBeth to Kate C. McBeth, 26 Jan. 1892, Sue McBeth's Papers, Personal Documents, *Kate and Sue McBeth*, University of Idaho website.

57. ACF to FWP, 30 Apr. 1892, HUG 1717.2.1, box 9, Pusey Library. Courtesy of the Harvard University Archives.

58. ACF to FWP, 31 July 1892, UAV 677.38, box 12, Pusey Library. Courtesy of the Harvard University Archives.

59. ACF to FWP, 13 July 1891, HUG 1717.2.1, box 9, Pusey Library. Courtesy of the Harvard University Archives.

60. FWP to ACF, 25 July 1891, box 1, Incoming correspondence, PACF.

61. ACF to FWP, 30 Nov. 1892, HUG 1717.2.1, box 9, Pusey Library. Courtesy of the Harvard University Archives.

62. The issue of how Fletcher was to acknowledge La Flesche's collaboration with her Omaha work became pressing in early 1893. She wrote to Putnam, "I find that Francis has a good deal of feeling concerning the recognition of his share in the work involved in this monograph. He wants his name to appear on the title page so as to read 'aided by Francis La Flesche'" (13 Apr. 1893, UAV 677.38, box 13, Pusey Library. Courtesy of the Harvard University Archives.).

63. "Ethnologic Gleanings among the Nez Perce" was published in 1995, edited and with commentary by Robert Lee Sappington and Caroline D. Carley.

64. ACF to FWP, 4 Apr. 1891, UAV 677.38, box 11, Pusey Library. Courtesy of the Harvard University Archives.

65. FWP to ACF, 13 May 1891, box 1, Incoming correspondence, PACF.

66. ACF to FWP 13 July 1891, HUG 1717.2.1, box 9, and ACF to FWP, 6 Aug. 1891, UAV 677.38, box 11, Pusey Library. Courtesy of the Harvard University Archives.

67. ACF to FWP, 11 Sept. 1892, UAV 677.38, box 12, Pusey Library. Courtesy of the Harvard University Archives.

68. ACF to FWP, 31 July 1892, UAV 677.38, box 12, Pusey Library. Courtesy of the Harvard University Archives.

69. *Lewiston Morning Tribune*, 7 Sept. 1901. I thank Dick Storch for

this information, sent to me in an e-mail on 5 May 2011. Henry Fair's collection of Nez Perce basketry and beadwork shown in figure 41 was probably not displayed at the 1893 fair. For more information on area collectors of artifacts and "curios," see Grafe, "The Moorhouse Curio Collection," in *Peoples of the Plateau*, 38–40.

70. ACF to FWP, 11 Sept. 1892, UAV 677.38, box 12, Pusey Library. Courtesy of the Harvard University Archives.

71. ACF to CIA, 13 Sept. 1892, 34158, NAB; emphasis added.

72. ACF to FWP, 3 Oct. 1892, HUG 1717.2.1, box 9, Pusey Library. Courtesy of the Harvard University Archives.

73. A survey of the *Chicago Daily Tribune* for 1893 suggests that a number of individual Nez Perces participated in various exhibits related to the World's Columbian Exhibition: as participants in the Wild West show ("Buffalo and Indians for Exhibition," *Chicago Daily Tribune*, 24 Mar. 1893), or living in habitat displays under the sponsorship of private exhibitors ("Shows Many Customs: Ethnological and Archaeological Display Excellent," *Chicago Daily Tribune*, 30 Apr. 1893).

74. ACF, untitled handwritten list, "General Ethnography," box 19, PACF.

8. The Ends of Nez Perce Allotment

1. ACF to Gen'l Morgan, 2 June 1891, 21013, NAB.
2. ACF to CIA, 21 Oct. 1891, 40434, NAB.
3. John C. Beelle to CIA, 20 Aug. 1892, 31097, NAB.
4. ACF to CIA, 16 Aug. 1892, 30860, NAB; emphasis added.
5. ACF to CIA, 16 Aug. 1892, 30888, NAB.
6. John C. Beelle to CIA, 20 Aug. 1892, 31097, NAB.
7. CIA to ACF, 29 July 1892, Letters Sent, vol. 110, Records of the Office of the CIA, NAB.
8. ACF to Edson Briggs, 5 Aug. 1892, Letterbook 2, PACF.
9. ACF to CIA, 20 Aug. 1892, 31172, NAB.
10. ACF to CIA, 17 Sept. 1891, 34916, NAB.
11. ACF to CIA, 13 Sept. 1892, 34158, NAB.
12. ACF to CIA, 13 Sept. 1892.
13. ACF to CIA, 21 Dec. 1892, 45423, NAB.
14. ACF to CIA, 23 June 1893, 22681, NAB.
15. J. A. Stephan to Grover Cleveland, 8 May 1895, 5227, RG 48, NACP. I thank Dennis Baird for locating and sharing this letter. See also RBIC 1891, Government Documents, *Kate and Sue McBeth*, University of Idaho website.
16. CIA to Secretary of the Interior, 11 Dec. 1895, RG 48, NACP.

17. *ARCIA*, 1898, 147. This is the sole evidence I have located that some Nimiipuu resented and resisted the intrusive family register Alice C. Fletcher attempted to compile; emphasis added.

18. C. T. Stranahan to CIA, 29 Dec. 1899, 532, NAB.

19. William W. Junkin, "Synopsis of Report of Inspector," 4 Jan. 1893, RG 48E682, M 10707, roll 30, Inspections, NAB.

20. Warren D. Robbins to CIA, 13 Feb. 1892, 2007, NAB, and 16 Feb. 1892, 7701, NAB.

21. Robert Schleicher, James F. Allen, and Cyrus Beede to CIA, 1 Apr. 1893, 12712, NAB.

22. A. B. Lawyer et al. to CIA, Apr. 1893, 12755, NAB.

23. R. V. Belt, Acting CIA, to Robbins, 18 Apr. 1892, Letters Sent, vol. 118, Records of the Office of the CIA, NAB; emphasis added.

24. CIA to Robbins, 29 Apr. 1892, Letters Sent, vol. 118, Records of the Office of the CIA, NAB.

25. ACF to CIA, 10 May 1892, 18712, Special Case 147, NAB.

26. ACF to CIA, 9 May 1892, Letterbook 2, PACF.

27. ACF to Gen'l and Mrs. Morgan, 12 May 1892, box 2, Outgoing Correspondence, 1890–1892, PACF.

28. For a study of the abuses of post-allotment land policy, see McDonnell, *Dispossession*.

29. ACF to CIA, 26 June 1890, box 4, Correspondence on . . . Nez Perce Allotment, outgoing, 1889–1891, PACF.

30. The mail stations and the associated privileges claimed by their operators were matters James Reubens had laid before the president in June 1889, and even at that time it was an old issue. See, for example, Charles E. Monteith's attempt in 1885 to have the federal government purchase Caldwell's "improvements . . . and convert said place into a school farm" (Monteith to CIA, 19 Mar. 1885, 6457, NAB.)

31. CIA to Robbins, 29 Oct. 1892, Letters Sent, vol. 124, Records of the Office of the CIA, NAB. As part of the civilization programs associated with allotment, mail stations and ferries, when their services could be shown to be important, were to be transferred to Natives.

32. ACF to CIA, 17 Aug. 1892, 30889, NAB. Not incidentally, perhaps, Silcott had testified in support of Fletcher's chainman, Tim Ryan, who was then on trial for illegally selling liquor on the reservation (ACF, Diary, 13 Aug. 1892, PACF).

33. See the sketch of "Silcott Ferry" in Stranahan, *Pioneer Stories*, 5.

34. ACF to Kate McBeth, 3 Aug. 1893, McBeth Crawford Collection,

MS 370, ISPARL; ACF to CIA, 6 Feb. 1894, Letterbook 2, PACF. The interrelated business dealings of Caldwell and Phinney were of long standing. For example, in 1890, Inspector Gardner wrote, "A Mr. Caldwell has some 500 or 600 head of cattle grazing on the reserve. He has made a sham sale of them to one Finney, a man who married a mixed-blood. Finney claims these cattle, but he is impecunious and has not the means of purchasing six head of steers, much less 600 head" ("Synopsis of Report of Inspector Gardner on the Nez Perce Agency, Idaho [Robbins], 19 Aug. 1890," RG 48E682, M 10707, roll 30, Inspections, NAB).

35. Political appointments varied with the party holding national power. In the years in which Fletcher was closely involved with allotment policy, federal control was especially volatile, passing between the major political parties every four years, from the Democratic Cleveland administration in 1885, back and forth to the Republican McKinley in 1897.

36. Record Group 75 contains these special case categories: mail stations and railroads (19), the Langford claim (37), churches and missions (143), allotment in severalty (147), irrigation (190), sale of inherited lands (203), and leases (191).

37. For a useful summary of the history of the Langford claim, see Thompson, *Historic Resource Study, Spalding*, 120–23, 153–56, 168–70, and passim.

38. CIA to ACF, 31 Aug. 1892, Letters Sent, vol. 122, Records of the Office of the CIA, NAB. In the CIA outgoing correspondence files most of the letters are typewritten. This handwritten letter is an unusual exception, suggesting, perhaps, the acting commissioner's haste to inform Fletcher of the decision that would allow her to close her work.

39. ACF to CIA, 7 Sept. 1892, 32450, NAB.

40. Thompson, *Historic Resource Study, Spalding*, 156.

41. Among the letters containing summaries of issues related to the Cox case not gathered into the Special Case 147 files are these: ACF to Julia Cox, 14 June 1889, Letterbook 1, PACF; ACF to John Allen (marked "confidential"), 27 Apr. 1891, box 2, outgoing correspondence, PACF; ACF to CIA, 13 May 1891, Letterbook 1, PACF; ACF to CIA, 18 July 1891, Letterbook 1, PACF; ACF to CIA, 2 Nov. 1891, box 2, outgoing correspondence, PACF; ACF to CIA, 9 May 1892, Letterbook 2, PACF; ACF to "My dear Gen'l and Mrs. Morgan," 12 May 1892, box 2, outgoing correspondence, PACF. In the National Archives the outgoing correspondence of the commissioner of Indian affairs also contains several letters related to the Cox case. See,

for example, CIA to Secretary of the Interior, 11 June 1892 (Letters Sent, vol. 120), probably the fullest summary of the legal issues raised by the case, and CIA to Secretary of the Interior, 11 October 1892 (Letters Sent, vol. 123). This is by no means an exhaustive list.

42. ACF to Julia Cox, 14 June 1889, Letterbook 1, PACF.

43. ACF to CIA, 13 May 1891, Letterbook 1, PACF.

44. ACF to CIA, 18 July 1891, Letterbook 1, PACF.

45. ACF to Gen'l and Mrs. Morgan, 12 May 1892, box 2, Outgoing Correspondence, 1890–1892, PACF.

46. Willis Sweet, no friend to federal initiatives in Idaho, was the state's first congressional representative. A Republican, he served from 1890 to 1895.

47. CIA to Secretary of the Interior, 11 June 1892.

48. CIA to Secretary of the Interior, 14 Oct. 1892.

49. This comment may in fact not be prescient. Gay likely added it sometime between May 1891, when she wrote the letter that ostensibly contained it, and January 1904, the date she finished *Choup-nit-ki*. Surely by that time she would have known that Special Indian Agent John Lane, with a stroke of his pen, had reversed the previous five years' decisions of tribal and federal courts.

50. John Lane to CIA, 14 Dec. 1893, 47771, NAB.

51. John Lane to CIA, 14 Dec. 1893.

52. ACF to CIA, 9 May 1892, Letterbook 2, PACF.

Part 5. Introduction

1. "With the Indians: Religious Element Held a Celebration at Kamiah," *Lewiston Morning Tribune*, 7 July 1903.

2. "Kamiah," unsourced and undated newspaper clipping, Kate McBeth's scrapbook, MS 370, ISPARL.

3. "With the Indians."

4. I thank Nakia Williamson-Cloud for pointing out this salient detail.

5. McBeth, *Nez Perces*, 166.

6. These three news stories are titled "Kamiah," "With the Indians: Religious Element Held a Celebration at Kamiah," and "Will Dance Again: Indians at Lapwai to Give a Second Parade." Unattributed and undated, they are pasted side by side in Kate McBeth's scrapbook (MS 370, ISPARL). "With the Indians" and "Will Dance Again" were originally printed on page 5 of the *Lewiston Morning Tribune*, 7 July 1903. I have been unable to locate the original publication of "Kamiah," but because McBeth pasted the three columns next to each other on the same page, and be-

cause they recount similar details, I assume they refer to celebrations held in the same year.

7. "Will Dance Again: Indians at Lapwai to Give a Second Parade," *Lewiston Morning Tribune*, 7 July 1903.

8. "Will Dance Again"; emphasis added.

9. I have not been able to establish definitively that Joseph led the 1903 parade at Nespelem. According to Gidley's biographical chronology, Joseph attended the 1904 Nespelem celebration just after his return from a trip to the East Coast (*Kopet*, 38–39). I assume the leader was also present in 1903. Edward Latham's undated images, central to my analysis here, represent the major components of celebrations held there during those two years.

10. Gidley, *Kopet*, caption to Image 28.

11. Latham's photographs of the Nespelem Fourth of July celebrations are not precisely dated. In the Lindsley Collection of the Suzzallo Library of the University of Washington, Seattle, his images of Fourth of July celebrations are labeled as having been made between 1900 and 1910.

12. According to Gidley, the photograph "may have been given its title by L. D. Lindsley rather than by Edward Latham" (*With One Sky*, 149).

13. Here I use language that invokes Victor Turner, *From Ritual*; Taylor, *Archive*; and Roach, *Cities*, 3, all of whom see performance as central to cultural preservation.

9. After-Words

1. Aoki, *Nez Perce Dictionary*, 835.

2. ACF to FWP, 17 Aug. 1890, FWP Director's Records, PMAE, Harvard University. Fletcher's disregard of the cultural damage her investigations might inflict ("I must have skulls") typifies standard field procedures of her era.

3. For an insightful critique of Fletcher's work in ethnomusicology, see Philip J. Deloria, *IUP*, 188–204.

4. See ACF, Diary, 9 Jan. 1891, PACF.

5. The recordings are now a part of the Nez Perce Music Archive, Smithsonian Institution, Bureau of American Ethnology.

6. ACF, Diary, 29 Apr. 1897, PACF.

7. ACF to Kate C. McBeth, 27 Sept. 1898; McBeth Crawford Correspondence, MS 370, ISPARL.

8. I assume the testimonies comprising Maxwell's *Memorial* were offered at a Fourth of July gathering, since the dates of the depositions span a period from 6 to 17 July 1911. On such an occasion, Nimíipuu from var-

ious locations would have been gathered in one place, facilitating the process of taking testimonies. For a biography of Maxwell, see Mallickan, *Born*, and Mallickan, Introduction.

9. John McConville, in Maxwell, *Memorial*, 84 (hereafter cited with the name of the deponent, followed by *M* and page numbers).

10. *Black's Law Dictionary*, 6th ed., 440.

11. *Black's Law Dictionary*, 6th ed., 985.

12. "Recall of Judges," qtd. in Murphy, *Lion among the Liberals*.

13. Janiewski, "Learning to Live," 175.

14. James, "Allotment Period," 19.

15. Lipps, *Laws and Regulations*, 43.

16. Carlson, *Indians, Bureaucrats, and Land*, 13, 38.

17. RBIC, 1888, 50.

18. *Black's Law Dictionary*, 6th ed., 500.

19. Diane Mallickan has pointed out an ironic outcome of competency evaluations: properties allotted to owners who were evaluated as Class C and thus deemed incompetent to control or sell their lands remained in their families and are still owned by the descendants of those "incompetent" allottees today (e-mail to author, 4 May 2011).

20. "Report on Application of [ ] for a Patent in Fee." Trust Responsibilities, Fee Patent Correspondence, Fort Lapwai Agency, 1895–1912, Patent Receipts, RG 75, NARA Pacific Alaska Region (Seattle). In deference to the living descendants of the persons examined in these hearings, I have deleted any identifying information from the material I quote here.

21. Application for patent in fee, Patent Receipts, RG 75, NARA Pacific Alaska Region (Seattle).

22. Acting CIA to Superintendent of the Fort Lapwai School, 8 June 1907, 52502, Patent Receipts, RG 75, NARA Pacific Alaska Region (Seattle).

23. Walker writes of a committee formed "to assist in the division of lands." Whether this commission was, in fact, the competency commission established after 1906 is unclear. However, the affiliations of a number of similar nine-member councils, beginning with the group named in 1893 as consultants to the land sale, follow the demographic Walker describes: "Of the nine members chosen, there were three Presbyterian preachers, four Presbyterian elders, one ex-Presbyterian elder who out of a disagreement had established his own schismatic Methodist church, and one Presbyterian layman. Of the two alternates, one was a Presbyterian elder, the other a Catholic. The Presbyterian domination of this first executive committee was more than an expression of numerical superiority. It was an expres-

sion of a strong tradition. Presbyterians had control of the agency practically from its inception, since even the early government-supported chiefs had been predominantly Presbyterian" (Walker, "Some Limitations," 157).

24. *Black's Law Dictionary*, 6th ed., 500.

25. "Report on Application of [ ] for a Patent in Fee." Trust Responsibilities, Fee Patent Correspondence, Fort Lapwai Agency, 1895–1912, Patent Receipts, RG 75, NARA Pacific Alaska Region (Seattle).

26. "Congress Shortchanges the Indians," *New York Times*, 15 March 2010.

10. After-Images

1. Dennis Baird, telephone interview with the author, 26 Feb. 2010.

2. de Certeau, *Practice*, xviii, xiv–xv.

3. Baird, telephone interview, 26 Feb. 2010.

4. Series List, Oliver Otis Howard Papers, 1833–1912, Manuscript Collections, George J. Mitchell Department of Special Collections and Archives, Bowdoin College, Brunswick ME. Web.

5. The Northwest Historical Manuscript Series includes these volumes that relate to nineteenth-century Nez Perce history: *Reports on the Aftermath of the 1863 Nez Perce Treaty by Chief Lawyer, Governor Caleb Lyon, General Benjamin Alvord, and Indian Agent James O'Neill* (1999); *Faithful to Their Tribe: Samuel Black's 1829 Fort Nez Perces Report* (2000); and *"The Treaty of 1855 has not been lived up to and we have no faith that this will be lived up to": The 1867 Nez Perce Treaty Council* (2001). Other volumes in the series reprint historical geographic, survey, railroad, and forest service records from the area.

6. Ott, Tucker, and Buckler, "Introduction," 3.

7. Ott, Tucker, and Buckler, "Introduction," 19.

8. Garvey, "Scissoring and Scrapbooks," 208, 209.

9. Ott, Tucker, and Buckler, "Introduction," 282n10.

10. Corbett Lawyer scrapbook, Accession 632, Lawyer Collection, NPNHPA.

11. The draft manuscript of *Choup-nit-ki* is held by the Idaho State Historical Society, stored there by Elizabeth Jacox, to whom the document has been loaned by Frederick B. Chenevert, the grand-nephew of Emma J. Gay's companion Edith Emerson.

12. Gay made at least three images on this occasion. See ISHS 63-221.218 and ISHS 63-221.221 of the Jane Gay Photograph Collection and a loose photograph contained in Accession 632, Lawyer Collection, NPNHPA.

13. Catlin, *Manners*, plates 207 and 208.

14. From time to time, these albums migrate to become part of public archives, donated by family members who wish to find more secure locations for their holdings, or sold to brokers, agents, or rare book dealers and then resold to archives, some of them located far from the places of the album's making. Several archives in northwest Idaho hold such albums in their collections. I base much of what I write here on my perusal of albums held by the University of Idaho Special Collections and by the Nez Perce National Historical Park Archives.

15. Among those who have written about the significance of family albums, see Hirsch, *Family Frames*; Garvey, "Scissoring and Scrapbooks"; several of the essays collected in Tucker, Ott, and Buckler's *Scrapbook in American Life*; and Tonkovich, "Genealogy."

16. Ott, Tucker, and Buckler, "Introduction," 3.

17. See, for example, several postcards in the scrapbooks comprising collection PG-100, Nez Perce Photographs, Historical Photograph Collection, University of Idaho Special Collections and Archives, Moscow ID.

18. I cannot be sure of this assertion because the album itself no longer exists in its original form. Following standard curatorial practice, archivists disassembled the album and placed each photograph into a plastic sleeve. It is thus impossible to determine the context in which this image might originally have been placed, where in the album it lay, or whether the photograph had been captioned on the page. (Here, as throughout this chapter, I use the term *caption* to refer to documentation written in the album, not on the photograph.) I assume that had captions been part of the scrapbook, archivists would have attempted to document and preserve them. The album was first acquired by a rare books dealer in San Anselmo, California, who subsequently sold it to the University of Idaho Library in 1998 (Accession Records, Historical Photograph Collection, University of Idaho Special Collections and Archives, Moscow ID).

19. Richard Storch, e-mail to author, 5 May 2011, and telephone conversation with author, 22 May 2011.

20. I thank Nakia Williamson-Cloud for drawing my attention to these studios and their cultural and historical importance and Richard Storch for answering my questions about some of the studios and their products.

21. Richard Storch, e-mail to author, 5 May 2011, and telephone conversation with author, 22 May 2011.

22. For a representative sample of such studio images made by a white

[387]

photographer in Pocatello, Idaho, in roughly this same period, see Scherer, *Danish Photographer.*

23. See, for example, many of the images made by Major Lee Moorhouse, the agent at the Umatilla Reservation from 1889 to 1891, whose photographic archive has recently been carefully catalogued by Steven L. Grafe. According to Grafe, "During much of his life . . . Moorhouse defined himself as an authority on local Indian culture" and amassed a large curio collection, which he displayed in local and regional fairs, where he allowed white visitors to don Native regalia and pose for souvenir photographs (*People of the Plateau*, 29, 46–47). Buttressed by Grafe's scholarship, which identifies sitters and carefully describes regalia and artifacts, Native descendants of the people in Moorhouse's photographs can read past the exoticizing intent of their first making to strengthen family continuity, to reinsert such images into family knowledge, and to reclaim, if virtually, the riches of the cultural items displayed in his photographs.

24. *Indian Helper*, 9 Jan. 1891, 4. For the past decade, Barbara Landis, the Carlisle Indian School biographer for the Cumberland County Historical Society, has transcribed and shared the content of the *Indian Helper* with list-serve subscribers. Her work has made available to family members, scholars, and interested supporters the words of Carlisle students and has vivified the context in which they lived and were educated. See Landis's website, *Carlisle Indian Industrial School (1879–1918).*

25. Wexler, *Tender Violence*, 10. Wexler contrasts these institutional images with similar photographs made in other contexts, such as Gertrude Käsebier's studio and the decks and wardrooms of Admiral George Dewey's flagship *Olympia.*

26. Ott, Buckler, and Tucker, "Introduction," 19.

Bibliography

Unpublished and Archival Sources

Houghton Library, Harvard University, Cambridge MA.
    Samuel J. and Isabel Barrows Papers. bMS Am 1807.1 (175).
Idaho State Public Archives and Research Library, Boise ID.
    Gay, E. Jane. Draft ms. of *Choup-nit-ki*.
    E. Jane Gay Photograph Collection.
    Lapwai Agency Files.
    McBeth-Crawford correspondence collection. MS 370.
    Swayne Collection.
Library of Congress. Washington DC.
    Andrew Johnson Papers, Series 1
    Henry L. Dawes Papers, 1833–1933.
National Anthropological Archives, Smithsonian Institution,
        Washington DC.
    Papers of Alice Cunningham Fletcher (1838–1923) and Francis
        La Flesche (1859–1923). Ms. 4558.
    Records of the Bureau of American Ethnology.
National Archives of the United States, Washington DC.
    Record Group 75.
        Letters Received by the Commissioner of Indian Affairs.
        Letters Sent by the Commissioner of Indian Affairs.
    Record Group 95.
        Council Proceedings.
    Record Group 393, Department of the Columbia.

National Archives and Records Administration, College Park MD.
    Record Group 48.
        Indian Division, Letters received.
National Archives and Records Administration, Pacific Alaska Region, Seattle WA
    Record Group 75.
        Letters Received, Northern Idaho Agency.
        Survey Maps.
        Trust Responsibilities.
Nebraska State Historical Society Photographic Collection, Lincoln NE.
    E. Jane Gay collection.
Nez Perce National Historical Park, Spalding ID.
    Accession 632. Lawyer Collection (restricted access).
Peabody Museum, Harvard University, Cambridge MA.
    Accession File #92-1.
    Frederick W. Putnam Director's Records.
Pusey Library, Harvard University Archives, Cambridge MA.
    Records of the Harvard College Observatory, UAV 677.38.
    Papers of Frederick Ward Putnam, HUG 1717.2.1.
Schlesinger Library on the History of Women in America, Radcliffe Institute, Harvard University, Cambridge MA.
    Jane Gay Dodge Papers, 1861–1951.
    Dodge, Jane Gay. "Brief Biography of E. Jane Gay." 1951. Ts. A-20.
    Dodge, Jane Gay. "Sketch of My First Meeting with Alice C. Fletcher in 1888." 1939. Ts. A-20.
    Gay, E. Jane. *Choup-nit-ki, With the Nez Percés*. Washington DC, n.p., 1909. Ms. A-20.
    Gay, E. Jane. "Reminiscent Bits." Ms. A-20. Folder 6.
    Gay, E. Jane. "Where We Camped." Ms. A-20. Folder 6.
University of Idaho Library website.
    Kate and Sue McBeth: Missionary Teachers to the Nez Percé. http://www.lib.uidaho.edu/mcbeth/.
University of Idaho Special Collections. Moscow ID.
    Accession records, Historical Photograph Collection.
    Historical Photograph Collection.
        Stephen Shawley Collection.
    United States Bureau of Indian Affairs, Lapwai Agency. MG 5066.
        Letters, 1864–1904.
University of Washington, Seattle. Special collections.
    Lindsley photograph collection.

Published Sources

Adams, David Wallace. *Education for Extinction: American Indians and the Boarding School Experience, 1875–1928*. Lawrence: University Press of Kansas, 1995.

Aldama, Arturo J. *Disrupting Savagism: Intersecting Chicana/o, Mexican Immigrant, and Native American Struggles for Self-Representation*. Durham: Duke University Press, 2001.

Allgor, Catherine. "'A Lady Will Have More Influence': Women and Patronage in Early Washington City." In *Women and the Unstable State in Nineteenth-Century America*, ed. Alison M. Parker and Stephanie Cole. College Station: Texas A&M University Press, 2000. 37–60.

Annual Report of the Board of Indian Commissioners. Washington DC: Government Printing Office, 1884, 1885, 1886, 1887, 1888, 1889, 1890, 1891.

Annual Report of the Commissioner of Indian Affairs to the Secretary of the Interior. Washington DC: Government Printing Office, 1873, 1882, 1883, 1885, 1886, 1887, 1888, 1889, 1890, 1891, 1892, 1898, 1900.

Aoki, Haruo. *Nez Perce Dictionary*. Berkeley: University of California Press, 1994.

Appadurai, Arjun. "The Heart of Whiteness." *Callaloo* 16, no. 4 (1993): 796–807.

Axtell, Horace, and Margo Aragon. *A Little Bit of Wisdom: Conversations with a Nez Perce Elder*. Norman: University of Oklahoma Press, 1997.

Baird, Dennis, and Lynn Baird, comps. and eds. *In Nez Perce Country: Accounts of the Bitterroots and the Clearwater After Lewis and Clark*. Moscow: University of Idaho Library, 2003.

Baird, Dennis, Diane Mallickan, and W. R. Swagerty, eds. *The Nez Perce Nation Divided: Firsthand Accounts of Events Leading to the 1863 Treaty*. Moscow: University of Idaho Press, 2002.

Ballantyne, Tony, and Antoinette M. Burton, eds. *Bodies in Contact: Rethinking Colonial Encounters in World History*. Durham: Duke University Press, 2005.

Bank, Rosemarie K. "Representing History: Performing the Columbian Exposition." *Theatre Journal* 54, no. 4 (2002): 589–606.

Barthes, Roland. *Camera Lucida: Reflections on Photography.* Translated by Richard Howard. New York: Hill and Wang, 1981.

Basso, Keith H. *Wisdom Sits in Places: Landscape and Language Among the Western Apache.* Albuquerque: University of New Mexico Press, 1996.

Beck, David. *The Struggle for Self-Determination: History of the Menominee Indians since 1854.* Lincoln: University of Nebraska Press, 2005.

Bernardin, Susan, Melody Graulich, Lisa MacFarlane, and Nicole Tonkovich. *Trading Gazes: Euro-American Women Photographers and Native North Americans, 1880–1940.* New Brunswick: Rutgers University Press, 2003.

Biolsi, Thomas. *Organizing the Lakota: The Political Economy of the New Deal on the Pine Ridge and Rosebud Reservations.* Tucson: University of Arizona Press, 1992.

Boas, Franz. "Ethnology at the Exhibition." *Cosmopolitan* 15 (September 1893): 607–09.

Browman, David L. "The Peabody Museum, Frederic W. Putnam, and the Rise of U.S. Anthropology, 1866–1903." *American Anthropologist* 104, no. 2 (2002): 508–17.

Burton, Antoinette. "Introduction: On the Inadequacy and the Indispensability of the Nation." In *After the Imperial Turn: Thinking with and through the Nation*, edited by Antoinette Burton. Durham: Duke University Press, 2003. 1–23.

Carley, Caroline D. "Letters from the Field: Alice Cunningham Fletcher in Nez Perce Country, 1889–1892. Part 1: Commissioner, 1889–1890." *Northwest Anthropological Research Notes* 35, no. 1 (2001): 55–133.

———. "Letters from the Field: Alice Cunningham Fletcher in Nez Perce Country, 1889–1892. Part 2: Commissioner, 1891–1892, and Putnam, 1889–1892." *Northwest Anthropological Research Notes* 35, no. 2 (2001): 135–209.

Carlson, Leonard A. *Indians, Bureaucrats, and Land: The Dawes Act and the Decline of Indian Farming.* Westport CT: Greenwood, 1981.

Castronovo, Ross, and Dana D. Nelson, eds. *Materializing Democracy: Toward a Revitalized Cultural Politics.* Durham: Duke University Press, 2002.

Catlin, George. *The Manners, Customs, and Condition of the North American Indians.* London, 1892.

de Certeau, Michel. *The Practice of Everyday Life.* Vol. 1. Translated by Steven F. Rendall. Berkeley: University of California Press, 1984.

Chalfant, Stuart A. *Aboriginal Territory of the Nez Perce Indians.* In *Nez Perce Indians*, 25–163.

"Commission Findings." In *Nez Perce Indians*, 269–401.

Cruikshank, Barbara. *The Will to Empower: Democratic Citizens and Other Subjects.* Ithaca: Cornell University Press, 1999.

Curiel, Barbara Brinson, et al. Introduction to *Post-Nationalist American Studies*, edited by John Carlos Rowe. Berkeley: University of California Press, 2000. 1–22.

Cushing, Frank Hamilton. "My Adventures in Zuñi." *Century* December 1882, 191–207; February 1883, 500–11; May 1883, 28–47.

Davis, George R., and F. W. Putnam. *World's Columbian Exposition Chicago, U.S.A. 1893. Plan and Classification Department M. Ethnology, Archaeology, History, Cartography, Latin American Bureau, Collective and Isolated Exhibits.* Chicago, 1892.

Davis, Lennard J. *Resisting Novels: Ideology and Fiction.* New York: Methuen, 1987.

Dawson, Lillian, comp. *Jane Gay Photograph Collection Catalog.* Boise: Idaho State Historical Society, 1980.

Deffenbaugh, G[eorge] L. "Report of Missionary at Nez Perce Agency," 14 August 1885. In *Annual Report of the Commissioner of Indian Affairs to the Secretary of the Interior for the Year 1885.* Washington DC: Office of the Commissioner of Indian Affairs, 1885. 72–73.

———. "The Return of the Nez Perces." *Foreign Missionary* 44 (July 1885): 71–72.

Deloria, Philip J. *Indians in Unexpected Places.* Lawrence: University Press of Kansas, 2004.

Deloria, Vine Jr. "Revision and Reversion." In *The American Indian and the Problem of History*, ed. Calvin Martin. New York: Oxford University Press, 1987. 84–90.

DeMallie, Raymond J. "Nicholas Black Elk and John G. Neihardt: An Introduction." In *The Sixth Grandfather: Black Elk's Teachings Given to John G. Neihardt*, edited by Raymond J. DeMallie. Lincoln: University of Nebraska Press, 1984. 1–74.

Dirlik, Arif. "History without a Center? Reflections on Eurocentrism." In *Across Cultural Borders: Historiography in Global Perspective*, ed. Eckhardt Fuchs and Benedikt Stuchtey. Lanham MD: Rowman and Littlefield, 2002. 247–84.

———. "The Past as Legacy and Project: Postcolonial Criticism in the Perspective of Indigenous Historicism." *American Indian Culture and Research Journal* 20, no. 2 (1996): 1–31.

———. "Place-Based Imagination: Globalism and the Politics of Place." In *Places and Politics in an Age of Globalization*, ed. Roxann Prazniak and Arif Dirlik. Lanham MD: Rowman and Littlefield, 2001. 15–51.

"Documents from the Cornerstone of the Nez Perce and Ponca Indian School." *Chronicles of Oklahoma* 12, no. 3 (September 1934): 359–63.

Dozier, Jack. "1885: A Nez Perce Homecoming." *Idaho Yesterdays* 7, no. 3 (1963): 22–25.

Dudziak, Mary L., and Leti Volpp, eds. Introduction to *Legal Borderlands: Law and the Construction of American Borders*. Special issue, *American Quarterly* 57, no. 3 (September 2005): 593–610.

Eastman, Gene, and Mollie Eastman. *Bitterroot Crossing: Lewis and Clark across the Lolo Trail*. 2nd Ed.. Moscow: University of Idaho Library, 2005.

———. *Bitterroot Crossing: Lewis & Clark across the Lolo Trail*. Vol. 2. Privately published.

Echo-Hawk, Walter R. *In the Courts of the Conqueror: The Ten Worst Indian Law Cases Ever Decided*. Golden CO: Fulcrum, 2010.

Ellinwood, F. F. "Descriptive Sketches of Missions. No. III: The Nez Perces." *Foreign Missionary* 44, no. 9 (February 1886): 416–23.

Elliott, Michael A. "Indians, Incorporated." *American Literary History* 19, no. 1 (2007): 141–59.

Fagin, Nancy L. "Closed Collections and Open Appeals: The Two Anthropology Exhibits at the Chicago World's Columbian Exposition of 1893." *Curator* 27, no. 4 (1984): 249–64.

Fixico, Donald. "Federal and State Policies and American Indians." In *A Companion to American Indian History*, ed. Philip J. Deloria and Neal Salisbury. Malden MA: Blackwell, 2004. 379–96.

Fleming, Paula Richardson, and Judith Lynn Luskey. *Grand Endeavors of American Indian Photography*. Washington DC: Smithsonian Institution Press, 1993.

Fletcher, Alice C. "Among the Nez Perces." *Red Man* 9, no. 9 (September 1889): 1.

———. "Composite Portraits of American Indians." *Science* 7 (1886): 408–09.

———. "Ethnologic Gleanings among the Nez Perces." In "Alice Cunningham Fletcher's 'Ethnologic Gleanings among the Nez Perces,'" edited by Robert Lee Sappington and Caroline D. Carley. *Northwest Anthropological Research Notes* 29, no. 1 (1995): 1–50 (including editors' introduction).

———. "Fourth of July among the Indians." *Christian Register* 44, no. 31 (31 July 1890): 496.

———. *Historical Sketch of the Omaha Tribe of Indians in Nebraska.* Washington DC: Bureau of Indian Affairs, 1885.

———. "Home Life among the Indians: Records of Personal Experience." *Century* 54, no. 2 (June 1897): 252–63.

———. "Hunting Customs of the Omahas: Personal Studies of Indian Life." *Century* 50, no. 5 (September 1895): 691–702.

———. *Indian Education and Civilization: A Report in Answer to Senate Resolution of February 23, 1885.* Washington DC: United States Office of Education, 1888.

———. "Indian Songs: Personal Stories of Indian Life." *Century* 47, no. 3 (January 1894): 421–31.

———. "Missionary Work among the Indians." *Christian Register* 49, no. 4 (23 January 1890): 54.

———. "More Indian Canards." *Red Man* 8 (November 1890): 6.

———. "The Nez Perce Country." In "Alice Cunningham Fletcher's 'The Nez Perce Country,'" edited by Robert Lee Sappington, Caroline D. Carley, Kenneth C. Reid, and James D. Gallison. *Northwest Anthropological Research Notes* 29, no. 2 (1995): 177–220 (including editors' introduction).

———. "Open Letters: On Indian Education and Self Support." *Century* 26, no. 2 (June 1883): 312–15.

———. "Personal Studies of Indian Life: Politics and 'Pipe-Dancing.'" *Century* 45, no. 3 (January 1893): 441–55.

———. "The Preparation of the Indian for Citizenship." *Lend a Hand* 9, no. 5 (1892): 190–98.

———. "Tribal Life among the Omahas: Personal Studies of Indian Life." *Century* 51, no. 3 (January 1896): 450–61.

Fletcher, Alice C., and Francis La Flesche. *The Omaha Tribe.* 2 vols. Lincoln: University of Nebraska Press, 1911.

Fowler, Loretta A. *Arapahoe Politics, 1851–1978: Symbols in Crises of Authority.* Lincoln: University of Nebraska Press, 1982.

Fraser, Julia. *Peaka Soyapu: The White Mother of the Nez Perces.* Kate

Christine McBeth, A Memoir. Kate and Sue McBeth, Missionary Teachers to the Nez Perce. University of Idaho website. http://www.lib.uidaho.edu/mcbeth/.

Garraghan, Gilbert J., S.J. *The Jesuits of the Middle United States.* Vol. 2. New York: America Press, 1938.

Garvey, Ellen Gruber. "Scissorizing and Scrapbooks: Nineteenth-Century Reading, Remaking, and Recirculating." In *New Media, 1740–1915*, ed. Lisa Gitelman and Geoffrey B. Pingree. Cambridge: MIT Press, 2004. 207–27.

Gates, Paul W. "Indian Allotments Preceding the Dawes Act." In *The Frontier Challenge: Responses to the Trans-Mississippi West*, ed. John G. Clark. Lawrence: University Press of Kansas, 1971. 141–70.

[Gay, E. Jane]. "Among the Indians: Miss Alice Fletcher's Work." *Christian Register* 69, no. 29 (17 July 1890): 457–58.

[———]. "A Best Room in Nebraska." *Christian Register* 9, no. 25 (19 June 1890): 394.

[———]. "A Brave Woman Allotting Lands to Indians in Idaho: Novel and Interesting Experiences, as Told by the Companion of Miss Fletcher." *Red Man* 10, no. 5 (April 1890): 2–3, 6–7.

[———]. "Brave Women in the Field: Another Interesting Letter from Miss Gay, Who Is Associated with Miss Fletcher in the Work of Allotting Lands to the Nez Perces, in Idaho." *Red Man* 10, no. 9 (December 1890–January 1891): 1–3.

Gay, E. Jane. "Camp Life Experiences." *Red Man* 11, no. 11 (April–May 1891): 6–7.

———. "Camp Life Experiences." *Red Man* 11, no. 12 (June 1891): 6–7.

———. "Camp Life Experiences." *Red Man* 12, no. 1 (July–Aug. 1891): 6–7.

———. "Camp Life Experiences." *Red Man* 12, no. 2 (September 1891): 6–7.

———. "Camp Life Experiences." *Red Man* 12, no. 3 (October–November 1891): 6–7.

———. *Choup-nit-ki: With the Nez Perces.* "Women Working, 1800–1930." Jane Gay Dodge Papers, 1861–1951. *Open Collections Program, Harvard University Library.* http://nrs.harvard.edu/urn-3:RAD.SCHL:744844.

———. "Experiences in Allotting Land." *Lend a Hand* 9, no. 4 (1892): 241–51.

[———]. "Life on the Reservation I: Experiences in Allotting Land in Idaho." *Christian Register* 71, no. 10 (10 March 1892): 157–58.

[———]. E. J. G. "Life on the Reservation: Experiences in Allotting Land in Idaho. II." *Christian Register* 71, no. 11 (17 March 1892): 173.

[———]. "Miss Fletcher and Miss Gay. Incidental Experiences in Allotting Indian Lands." *Red Man* 10, no. 6 (July–August 1890): 3.

———. *With the Nez Perces: Alice Fletcher in the Field, 1889–1892*. Ed. Frederick E. Hoxie and Joan T. Mark. Lincoln: University of Nebraska Press, 1981.

[———]. E. J. G. "A Woman Allotting Lands to Indians: A Rich and Racy View of a Trying Situation." *Red Man* 9, no. 11 (November 1889): 5, 8.

Gidley, M. *Kopet: A Documentary Narrative of Chief Joseph's Last Years*. Chicago: Contemporary Books, 1981.

———. *With One Sky above Us: Life on an American Indian Reservation at the Turn of the Century*. Seattle: University of Washington Press, 1979.

Gilbert, Cathy A., Gretchen A. Luxenberg, and Marsha R. Tolon. *Historic Landscape Report: Spalding Unit, Nez Perce National Historical Park, Idaho*. Seattle: National Park Service, 1990.

Grafe, Steven L. *Peoples of the Plateau: The Indian Photographs of Lee Moorhouse, 1898–1915*. Norman: University of Oklahoma Press, 2005.

Greenwald, Emily. *Reconfiguring the Reservation: The Nez Perces, Jicarilla Apaches, and the Dawes Act*. Albuquerque: University of New Mexico Press, 2002.

Gulick, Bill. *Chief Joseph Country: Land of the Nez Perce*. 2nd ed. Caldwell: Caxton, 1994.

Hagan, William T. "United States Indian Policies, 1860–1900." In *Handbook of North American Indians*, vol. 4: *History of Indian-White Relations*, ed. Wilcomb E. Washburn. Washington DC: Smithsonian Institution Press, 1988. 51–65.

Haines, Francis. *The Nez Percés: Tribesmen of the Columbia Plateau*. Norman: University of Oklahoma Press, 1955.

Handy, M. P., ed. *World's Columbian Exposition 1893 Official Catalogue. Part XII: Anthropological Building, Midway Plaisance, and Isolated Exhibits. Department M. Ethnology, Archaeology, Progress of Labor and Invention, Isolated and Collective Exhibits*. Chicago, 1893.

Haraway, Donna J. *Primate Visions: Gender, Race, and Nature in the World of Modern Science.* New York: Routledge, 1989.

Harley, J. B. "Deconstructing the Map." *Cartographica* 26, no. 2 (1989): 1–20.

Hibbard, Don. "Chicago 1893: Idaho at the World's Columbian Exposition." *Idaho Yesterdays* 24, no. 2 (1980): 24–29.

Hinsley, Curtis M. "The World as Marketplace: Commodification of the Exotic at the World's Columbian Exposition, Chicago, 1893." In *Exhibiting Cultures: The Poetics and Politics of Museum Display,* ed. Ivan Karp and Steven D. Lavine. Washington DC: Smithsonian Institution Press, 1991. 344–65.

Hirsch, Marianne. *Family Frames: Photography, Narrative, and Postmemory.* Cambridge: Harvard University Press, 1997.

Holland, Jeanne. "Scraps, Stamps, and Cutouts: Emily Dickinson's Domestic Technologies of Publication." In *Cultural Artifacts and the Production of Meaning: The Page, the Image, and the Body,* ed. Margaret J. M. Ezell and Katherine O'Brien O'Keeffe. Ann Arbor: University of Michigan Press, 1994. 139–81.

Horr, David Agee. "General Nature and Content of the Series." In *Nez Perce Indians,* 9–11.

Hoxie, Frederick E. "Exploring a Cultural Borderland: Native American Journeys of Discovery in the Early Twentieth Century." *Journal of American History* 79, no. 3 (December 1992): 969–95.

——. *A Final Promise: The Campaign to Assimilate the Indians, 1880–1920.* 1984; Lincoln: University of Nebraska Press, 2001.

——. *Parading through History: The Making of the Crow Nation in America, 1805–1935.* Cambridge: Cambridge University Press, 1995.

Hoxie, Frederick E., and Joan T. Mark. Introduction to *With the Nez Perces: Alice Fletcher in the Field, 1889–92,* by E. Jane Gay, edited by Frederick E. Hoxie and Joan T. Mark. Lincoln: University of Nebraska Press, 1981. xiii–xxxvii.

Huhndorf, Shari M. *Mapping the Americas: The Transnational Politics of Contemporary Native Culture.* Ithaca: Cornell University Press, 2009.

——. "Picture Revolution: Transnationalism, American Studies, and the Politics of Contemporary Native Culture." *American Quarterly* 61, no. 2 (2009): 359–81.

Huskey, Rosemary. "'A Disgrace to the Cause They Represent': The Disputes of Kate and Sue McBeth, Missionary Teachers to the Nez Perce." MA thesis, University of Idaho, 2000.

Iverson, Peter, ed. *"For Our Navajo People": Diné Letters, Speeches, and Petitions, 1900–1960.* Albuquerque: University of New Mexico Press, 2002.

Jackson, John Brinckerhoff. *Landscape in Sight: Looking at America.* Ed. Helen Lefkowitz Horowitz. New Haven: Yale University Press, 1997.

Jackson, Shannon. *Professing Performance: Theatre in the Academy from Philology to Performativity.* Cambridge: Cambridge University Press, 2004.

Jacox, Elizabeth. "'Cook, Photographer, and Friend': Jane Gay's Photographs, 1889–1892." *Idaho Yesterdays* 28, no. 1 (Spring 1984): 18–23.

Jaimes, M. Annette. "Federal Indian Identification Policy: A Usurpation of Indigenous Sovereignty in North America." In *The State of Native America: Genocide, Colonization, and Resistance*, edited by M. Annette Jaimes. Boston: South End Press, 1992. 123–38.

James, Elizabeth. "The Allotment Period on the Nez Perce Reservation: Encroachments, Obstacles, and Reactions." *Idaho Yesterdays* 37, no. 1 (1993): 11–23.

Janiewski, Dolores. "Learning to Live 'Just Like White Folks': Gender, Ethnicity, and the State in the Inland Northwest." In *Gendered Domains: Rethinking Public and Private in Women's History*, edited by Dorothy O. Helly and Susan M. Reverby. Ithaca: Cornell University Press, 1992. 167–80.

Johnson, Janis. "Hidden Nation: Nez Perce Identity and American Indian Sovereignty." PhD diss., Tulane University, New Orleans LA, 1999.

Chief Joseph. "An Indian's View of Indian Affairs." *North American Review* 128 (April 1879): 412–33.

Josephy, Alvin M. Jr. *500 Nations: An Illustrated History of North American Indians.* New York: Knopf, 1994.

———. *Nez Perce Country.* Lincoln: University of Nebraska Press, 2007.

———. *The Nez Perce Indians and the Opening of the Northwest.* New Haven: Yale University Press, 1965.

Kaplan, Amy. *The Anarchy of Empire in the Making of U.S. Culture.* Cambridge: Harvard University Press, 2005.

Kelsey, Robin E. *Archive Style: Photographs and Illustration for U.S.*

Surveys, 1850–1890. Berkeley: University of California Press, 2007.

———. "Viewing the Archive: Timothy O'Sullivan's Photographs for the Wheeler Survey, 1871–74." *Art Bulletin* 85, no. 4 (2003): 702–23.

Kinney, J. P. *A Continent Lost—A Civilization Won: Indian Land Tenure in America.* New York: Octagon, 1975.

Lambert, Valerie. *Choctaw Nation: A Story of American Indian Resurgence.* Lincoln: University of Nebraska Press, 2007.

"Leave No Tribe Behind: NARF Takes on a Class Action for Billions of Dollars of Government Mismanagement of Tribal Trust Funds," *Native American Rights Fund Legal Review* 32, no. 1 (2007): 1–6.

Leibhardt, Barbara. "Allotment Policy in an Incongruous Legal System: The Yakima Indian Nation as a Case Study, 1887–1934." *Agricultural History* 65, no. 4 (1991): 78–103.

Lewis, David Rich. "Reservation Leadership and the Progressive-Traditional Dichotomy: William Wash and the Northern Utes, 1865–1928." *Ethnohistory* 38 (1991): 124–42.

Lewis, Malcolm, ed. *Cartographic Encounters.* Chicago: University of Chicago Press, 1998.

Lipps, Oscar H., comp. *Laws and Regulations Relating to Indians and Their Lands.* Lewiston: Lewiston Printing and Binding, 1913.

Lohse, E. S, and Roderick Sprague. "History of Research." In *Handbook of North American Indians,* vol. 12: *Plateau,* ed. Deward E. Walker, William Sturtevant, and Deward E. Walker Jr. Washington DC: Smithsonian Institution Press, 1998.

Lowe, Lisa. *Immigrant Acts: On Asian American Cultural Politics.* Durham: Duke University Press, 1996.

McBeth, Kate [C.]. *The Nez Perces since Lewis and Clark.* 1908. Moscow: University of Idaho Press, 1993.

McClintock, Anne. *Imperial Leather: Race, Gender, and Sexuality in the Colonial Contest.* New York: Routledge, 1995.

McCoy, Robert R. *Chief Joseph, Yellow Wolf, and the Creation of Nez Perce History in the Pacific Northwest.* New York: Routledge, 2004.

McDonnell, Janet A. *The Dispossession of the American Indian, 1887–1934.* Bloomington: Indiana University Press, 1991.

McGovern, John, ed. *Halligan's Illustrated World's Fair: A Pictorial and Literary History of the World's Columbian Exposition.* Portfolio no. 4. Chicago, 1893.

McLaughlin, Michael R. "The Dawes Act, or Indian General Allotment Act of 1887: The Continuing Burden of Allotment. A Selective Annotated Bibliography." *American Indian Culture and Research Journal* 20, no. 2 (1996): 59–105.

McMillen, Christian W. *Making Indian Law: The Hualapai Land Case and the Birth of Ethnohistory.* New Haven: Yale University Press, 2007.

McWhorter, L[ucullus] V. *Hear Me, My Chiefs! Nez Perce Legend and History.* Edited by Ruth Bordin. Caldwell: Caxton, 1992.

———. *Yellow Wolf: His Own Story.* 1940. Caldwell: Caxton, 1995.

Mallickan, Diane. *Born Under a Star: Starr Jacob Maxwell, 1870–1940.* Spalding: Nez Perce National Historical Park, 1998.

———. Introduction to Maxwell, *Memorial,* i–iv.

Mark, Joan. "Francis La Flesche: The American Indian as Anthropologist." *Isis* 73, no. 4 (1982): 496–510.

———. *A Stranger in Her Native Land: Alice Fletcher and the American Indians.* Lincoln: University of Nebraska Press, 1988.

Maxwell, Starr J., comp. *Memorial of the Nez Perce Indians Residing in the State of Idaho to the Congress of the United States.* Presented by Mr. Borah, 14 August 1911. Moscow: University of Idaho Library, 2000.

"Missionary Work among the Indians." *Christian Register,* 23 January 1890, 54.

Morrill, Allen, and Eleanor Morrill. "J. P. Vollmer and James S. Reuben." *Idaho Yesterdays* 18, no. 4 (1974–75): 4–24.

———. "Old Church Made New." *Idaho Yesterdays* 16, no. 2 (1972): 16–25.

———. "Talmaks." *Idaho Yesterdays* 8, no. 3 (1964): 2–15.

———. *Out of the Blanket: The Story of Sue and Kate McBeth, Missionaries to the Nez Perces.* Moscow: University Press of Idaho, 1978.

Murphy, Kevin C. "The Lion of Idaho: Borah's Intellectual Anatomy." *A Lion among the Liberals: Senator William Edgar Borah and the Rise of New Deal Liberalism. Ghost in the Machine* weblog, http://www.ghostinthemachine.net/.

Nabokov, Peter. "Orientations from Their Side: Dimensions of Native American Cartographic Discourse." In *Cartographic Encounters,* ed. G. Malcolm Lewis. Chicago: University of Chicago Press, 1998. 241–67.

Nelson, Dana D. *National Manhood: Capitalist Citizenship and the*

Imagined Fraternity of White Men. Durham: Duke University Press, 1998.

Nerburn, Kent. *Chief Joseph and the Flight of the Nez Perce: The Untold Story of an American Tragedy.* San Francisco: Harper, 2005.

Nez Perce Indians: Commission Findings. Comp. David Agee Horr. American Indian Ethnohistory: Indians of the Northwest. New York: Garland, 1974.

Nora, Pierre. "Between Memory and History: *Les Lieux de Mémoire.*" *Representations* 26 (1989): 7–24.

Olsen, Loran. *Qillóowawya: Hitting the Rawhide. Serenade Songs from the Nez Perce Music Archive.* Seattle: Northwest Interpretive Association, 2001.

Olund, Eric N. "From Savage Space to Governable Space: The Extension of United States Judicial Sovereignty over Indian Country in the Nineteenth Century." *Cultural Geographies* 9, no. 2 (2002): 129–57.

O'Neal, Larry, and Dennis Baird, eds. *A Collection of Primary Sources on the Nez Perce Exile in Canada, the Indian Territory, and Their Return to the Northwest: 1877–1886.* [Moscow]: University of Idaho Library, 2005.

Otis, D. S. *The Dawes Act and the Allotment of Indian Lands.* Edited by Francis Paul Prucha. Norman: University of Oklahoma Press, 1973.

Ott, Katherine, Susan Tucker, and Patricia P. Buckler. "An Introduction to the History of Scrapbooks." In Tucker, Ott, and Buckler, eds., *The Scrapbook in American Life.* Philadelphia: Temple University Press, 2006. 1–25.

Pearson, J. Diane. *The Nez Perces in the Indian Territory: Nimiipuu Survival.* Norman: University of Oklahoma Press, 2008.

Perry, Adele. *On the Edge of Empire: Gender, Race, and the Making of British Columbia, 1849–1871.* Toronto: University of Toronto Press, 2001.

Pezzati, Alex. "Thomas C. Donaldson and the 1890 U. S. Census." *Expedition* 42, no. 1 (2000): 5.

Pfister, Joel. *Individuality Incorporated: Indians and the Multicultural Modern.* Durham: Duke University Press, 2004.

Ponziglione, Paul Mary, S.J. "Indian Missions." Letter. *Woodstock Letters* 9 (1880): 118–24.

Pratt, Mary Louise. *Imperial Eyes: Travel Writing and Transculturation.* 2nd ed. New York: Routledge, 2008.
Price, Monroe E. *Law and the American Indian: Readings, Notes, and Cases.* Indianapolis: Bobbs-Merrill, 1973.
Price, Monroe E., and Robert N. Clinton. *Law and the American Indian: Readings, Notes, and Cases.* 2nd ed. Charlottesville VA: Michie, 1983.
Priest, Loring Benson. *Uncle Sam's Stepchildren: The Reformation of United States Indian Policy, 1865–1887.* 1942. New York: Octagon, 1969.
"Proceedings at the Council. 29 May 1855." U.S. Department of the Interior. Bureau of Indian Affairs. *Certified Copy of the Original Minutes of the Official Proceedings at the Council in Walla Walla Valley, Which Culminated in the Stevens Treaty of 1855.* Portland, Oregon: Bureau of Indian Affairs, 1953. Government Documents. *Kate and Sue McBeth.* University of Idaho website.
Prucha, Francis Paul. *American Indian Policy in Crisis: Christian Reformers and the Indian, 1865–1900.* Norman: University of Oklahoma Press, 1976.
Prucha, Francis Paul, ed. *Americanizing the American Indians: Writings by the "Friends of the Indian," 1880–1900.* 1973. Lincoln: University of Nebraska Press, 1978.
Rafael, Vicente L. *White Love and Other Events in Filipino History.* Durham: Duke University Press, 2000.
Rand, Jacki Thompson. "Primary Sources: Indian Goods and the History of American Colonialism and the 19th-Century Reservation." In *Clearing a Path: Theorizing the Past in Native American Studies,* edited by Nancy Shoemaker. New York: Routledge, 2002, 137–57.
Rand McNally and Company's Handbook of the World's Columbian Exposition with Special Descriptive Articles. Chicago, 1893.
Redwolf, Josiah. Interview by Zoe Swayne and Doug Marsh. 14 October 1965. Swayne Collection, Idaho State Historical Society.
Regis, St. Francis. "Sketch of the Nez Percés Indians." *Woodstock Letters* 9 (1880): 43–50, 109–18, 191–99; 10 (1881): 71–77, 198–204.
Reubens, James. "The Nez Perces Indians." In "Documents from the Cornerstone of the Nez Perce and Ponca Indian School," *Chronicles of Oklahoma* 12, no. 3 (September 1934): 359–63.
Reynolds, Henry. *Aboriginal Sovereignty: Reflections on Race, State, and Nation.* St. Leonards, NSW: Allen and Unwin, 1996.

Ridington, Robin. "Omaha Survival: A Vanishing Indian Tribe That Would Not Vanish." *American Indian Quarterly* 11, no. 1 (1987): 37–51.

Riley, Robert James. "The Nez Perce Struggle for Self Government: A History of Nez Perce Governing Bodies, 1842–1960." MA thesis, University of Idaho, 1961.

Roach, Joseph. *Cities of the Dead: Circum-Atlantic Performance*. New York: Columbia University Press, 1996.

Roosevelt, Theodore. President's Message. 3 December 1901. *Congressional Record*. 57th Congress, 1st session, part 1.

Rosier, Paul C. *Rebirth of the Blackfeet Nation, 1912–1954*. Lincoln: University of Nebraska Press, 2001.

Rowe, John Carlos. *Literary Culture and U.S. Imperialism from the Revolution to World War II*. New York: Oxford University Press, 2000.

Royster, Judith V. "The Legacy of Allotment." *Arizona State Law Journal* 27 (Spring 1995): 1–78.

Ruby, Robert H., and John A. Brown. *Half-Sun on the Columbia: A Biography of Chief Moses*. Norman: University of Oklahoma Press, 1965.

Rydell, Robert W. *All the World's a Fair: Visions of Empire at American International Expositions, 1876–1916*. Chicago: University of Chicago Press, 1984.

Saler, Bethel. "An Empire for Liberty, a State for Empire: The U.S. National State before and after the Revolution of 1800." In *The Revolution of 1800: Democracy, Race, and the New Republic*, edited by James Horn, Jan Ellen Lewis, and Peter S. Onuf. Charlottesville: University of Virginia Press, 2002. 360–82.

Sandweiss, Martha A. *Print the Legend: Photography and the American West*. New Haven: Yale University Press, 2002.

Sappington, Robert Lee, and Caroline D. Carley, eds. "Alice Cunningham Fletcher's 'Ethnologic Gleanings among the Nez Perces.'" With editors' introduction. *Northwest Anthropological Research Notes* 29, no. 1 (1995): 1–50.

Sappington, Robert Lee, Caroline D. Carley, Kenneth C. Reid, and James D. Gallison, eds. "Alice Cunningham Fletcher's 'The Nez Perce Country.'" With editors' introduction. *Northwest Anthropological Research Notes* 29, no. 2 (1995): 177–220.

Scherer, Joanna Cohan. *A Danish Photographer of Idaho Indians: Benedicte Wrensted*. Norman: University of Oklahoma Press, 2006.

Sekula, Alan. "The Body and the Archive." 1986. In *The Contest of Meaning: Critical Histories of Photography*, edited by Richard Bolton. Cambridge: MIT Press, 1992. 343–79.

Senier, Siobhan. *Voices of American Indian Assimilation and Resistance: Helen Hunt Jackson, Sarah Winnemucca, and Victoria Howard*. Norman: University of Oklahoma Press, 2001.

Simonsen, Jane E. "The Cook, the Photographer, and Her Majesty, the Allotting Agent: Unsettling Domestic Spaces in E. Jane Gay's *With the Nez Perces*." *Arizona Quarterly* 58, no. 2 (2002): 53–87.

——. *Making Home Work: Domesticity and Native American Assimilation in the American West, 1860–1919*. Chapel Hill: University of North Carolina Press, 2006.

Slickpoo, Allen P. Sr. *Noon Nee-Me-Poo (We, the Nez Perces): Culture and History of the Nez Perces*. Lapwai ID: Nez Perce Tribe of Idaho, 1973.

Space, Ralph S. "The Indians." Weippe folder, Ralph S. Space Papers, 1922–1976, MA 2000–18. University of Idaho Special Collections. Ts.

Starr, Frederick. "Anthropology at the World's Fair." *Popular Science Monthly* 43 (1893): 610–21.

Steedman, Carolyn. *Dust: The Archive and Cultural History*. New Brunswick: Rutgers University Press, 2001.

Stern, Madeleine B. "The First American Woman Stenographic Reporter for Congressional Committees: Isabel C. Barrows, 1871." In *We the Women: Career Firsts of Nineteenth-Century America*. New York: Schulte, 1963. 178–204.

Stoler, Ann Laura. *Carnal Knowledge and Imperial Power: Race and the Intimate in Colonial Rule*. Berkeley: University of California Press, 2002.

——. "Tense and Tender Ties: The Politics of Comparison in North American History and (Post) Colonial Studies." In *Haunted by Empire: Geographies of Intimacy in North American History*, edited by Ann Laura Stoler. Durham: Duke University Press, 2006. 23–67.

Stranahan, C. T. *Pioneer Stories*. Lewiston: n.p., 1947.

Sugden, Henry L., ed. *Seventy-Five Years Presbyterian Camp Meetings of the Nez Perce Indians, 1897–1972*. Pamphlet, Nez Perce National Historical Park collections.

Szasz, Margaret. *Between Indian and White Worlds: The Cultural Broker.* Norman: University of Oklahoma Press, 1994.

Taylor, Diana. *The Archive and the Repertoire: Performing Cultural Memory in the Americas.* Durham: Duke University Press, 2003.

Thompson, Erwin N. *Historic Resource Study, Fort Lapwai, Nez Perce National Historical Park, Idaho.* Denver: U.S. Department of the Interior, 1978.

———. *Historic Resource Study, Spalding Area, Nez Perce National Historical Park, Idaho.* Denver: U.S. Department of the Interior, 1972.

Thomson, Rosemarie Garland. *Extraordinary Bodies: Figuring Physical Disability in American Culture and Literature.* New York: Columbia University Press, 1997.

Tonkovich, Nicole. "Genealogy, Genre, Gender: Edith Maude Eaton's 'Leaves from the Mental Portfolio of a Eurasian.'" In *Beyond the Binary: Reconstructing a Multicultural Sense of "American" Identity,* edited by Timothy B. Powell. New Brunswick: Rutgers University Press, 1999. 236–60.

———. "'Lost in the General Wreckage of the Far West': The Photographs and Writings of Jane Gay." In *Trading Gazes: Euro-American Women Photographers and Native North Americans, 1880–1940,* by Susan Bernardin, Melody Graulich, Lisa MacFarlane, and Nicole Tonkovich. New Brunswick: Rutgers University Press, 2003. 33–72.

Trafzer, Clifford E. *The Nez Perce.* New York: Chelsea, 1992.

Trafzer, Clifford E., ed. *The Northwest Tribes in Exile: Modoc, Nez Perce, and Palouse Removal to the Indian Territory.* Sacramento: Sierra Oaks, 1987.

Treaties: Nez Perce Perspectives. N.p.: Nez Perce Tribe, 2003.

Trennert, Robert A. Jr. "Selling Indian Education at World's Fairs and Expositions, 1893–1904." *American Indian Quarterly* 11, no. 3 (1987): 203–20.

Tucker, Susan, Katherine Ott, and Patricia P. Buckler, eds. *The Scrapbook in American Life.* Philadelphia: Temple University Press, 2006.

Turner, Frederick Jackson. "The Significance of the Frontier in American History." *Annual Report of the American Historical Association for the Year 1893.* 1894. N.p.: Readex, 1966.

Turner, Victor. *From Ritual to Theatre: The Human Seriousness of Play.* New York: Performing Arts Journal, 1982.

Visweswaran, Kamala. "'Wild West' Anthropology and the Disciplining of Gender." In *Gender and American Social Science: The Formative Years*, edited by Helene Silverberg. Princeton: Princeton University Press, 1998. 86–123.

Vizenor, Gerald. *Manifest Manners: Narratives on Postindian Survivance*. Lincoln: University of Nebraska Press, 1994.

Walker, Deward E. Jr. *Conflict and Schism in Nez Perce Acculturation: A Study of Religion and Politics*. 1968. Moscow: University of Idaho Press, 1985.

———. "Some Limitations of the Renascence Concept in Acculturation: The Nez Perce Case." *Midcontinent American Studies Journal* 6, no. 2 (1965): 135–48.

Warhus, Mark. *Another America: Native American Maps and the History of Our Land*. New York: St. Martin's, 1997.

Welch, Rebecca Hancock. "Alice Cunningham Fletcher, Anthropologist and Indian Rights Reformer." PhD diss., George Washington University, 1980.

Wexler, Laura. *Tender Violence: Domestic Visions in an Age of U.S. Imperialism*. Chapel Hill: University of North Carolina Press, 2000.

White, Hayden. *Metahistory: The Historical Imagination in Nineteenth-Century Europe*. Baltimore: Johns Hopkins University Press, 1973.

———. "The Value of Narrativity in the Representation of Reality." In *On Narrative*, edited by W. J. T. Mitchell. Chicago: University of Chicago Press, 1980. 1–24.

Index

Page numbers in italic indicate illustrations.

agrarianism, 215, 242
Ah-kaht-tse 'ween settlement, 140
Aldama, Arturo J., 35
Allen, James F., 257
Allgor, Catherine, 203
allotment: as act of violence, 153–54, 193, 195; Alice C. Fletcher's modification of, 105–8, 112–13, 135, 153–54, 156; and assimilation, 257, 367n2; boundary lines in, 215, 222; Charles Monteith on, 46, 339n15, 350n17, 352n7, 354n30; and citizenship, 167–68, 177–78, 184–85, 193, 286; disciplinary tactics of, 168; early trumpeting of, 55–56, 352n2; E. Jane Gay's documentation of, 32, 118–20, 129, 222–23, 306, 308–9; efforts to delay and modify, 34–35, 59, 65, 66, 76–78, 99, 256–57; errors in, 53, 59–71, 62, 64–65, 77, 105, 255; failure of, 10, 11–12, 18, 35, 200, 285, 298, 339n15; family grouping system in, 89–90, 195–96, 215; favoritism in, 251, 255; federal agents' role in, 261, 341n36, 382n35; federal repudiation of, 224, 256; first areas chosen for, 6, 349n13; gendered character of work in, 104–5, 129, 132–33; goals of, 5, 103, 196; inconsistency in, 168; initial work by Alice C. Fletcher, 62–63, 68, 69, 110–12, 361n13; James Reubens and, 78, 83, 89–91, 92; lack of consultation with Nimiipuu, 7, 253–54, 339n15; land equivalency in, 10–11; leading to loss of Nez Perce lands, 8, 196, 285–87; leasing of lands to white settlers, 257–59, 286–87, 289, 294; legal provisions of, 8, 10, 11, 257, 262–63, 286; as machine, 194, 371n34; Nimiipuu discussion and understanding of, 56–57, 59, 67, 82–83, 353n9; Nimiipuu resistance to, 3, 4–5, 11–12, 25, 105, 138, 163, 215, 221–22; phases of, 340n21; Presbyterian Church and, 45, 52–53; of rectilinear plots, 105, 360–61n2; refusal to accept plots, 203, 215; for returning internees, 46–47; and spatialization, 104, 111, 114, 115, 121; and split properties, 155–56; surveying work for, 73, 79–80, 105, 106, 110–12, 361n13; technologies of, 14, 69, 195, 214, 257, 300; time estimates for accomplishing, 106–7, 138, 213, 221, 252, 361n3; and treaties of 1855 and 1863, 56, 352nn6–7; unfinished character of, 224, 236, 252; as volatile issue, 157, 266; white settlers and, 66–67, 355–56n49
America Indian Trust Fund Management Reform Act, xi
anthropology, 114, 136, 240, 300
Appadurai, Arjun, 13

[409]

INDEX

archival record, 31–35, 118–19; Alice C. Fletcher and, 31–32, 114–15; counter-archives and, 119, 282, 299–300, 303; E. Jane Gay's photographs as, 33, 119–34, 309–10, 347n83; family albums and, 310–33, 387n14, 387n18; as ideologically determined, 31; *Memorial of the Nez Perce Indians* as, 281–89, 296–302; memory palaces, 7, 339n16; Nimiipuu maintenance of, 12, 34–35; performance as, 35–36; scrapbooks as, 302–6; voice recordings as, 279–80

Arthur Andersen LLP, xi–xii

assimilation, 2, 180, 216, 300, 327, 333; allotment policy and, 257, 367n2; Nimiipuu sovereignty and, 178–79

Baird, Dennis, 301

Barrows, Isabel Chapin, 118, 202, 210; Alice C. Fletcher's letters to, 58, 108, 118, 177, 179, 181, 204; and Alice C. Fletcher's parlor network, 203, 204, 207

Basso, Keith H., 365n21

Beall, Alfred T., 60

Beede, Cyrus, 257

Beele, John C., 252

Belt, R. V., 258–59

Biolsi, Thomas, 338n13

Boas, Franz, 187–89, 237, 240, 244, 246

Borah, William Edgar, 285

Bowdoin College Library, 301

Bradley, Henrietta, 22, 210

Bredell, Noah, 288

Briggs, Edson, 69, 70, 73, 80, 211; about, 373n17; and Alice C. Fletcher, 15, 206–7; surveying work of, 110, 116, 129; survey maps of, 117, 127, 142, 364n15

Brooks, Abraham, 267

Brown, John A., 49

Browning, D. M., 255

Bureau of Indian Affairs, xi, xii, 239

Burke Act (1906), 11, 287, 292

Burton, Antoinette, 31

Cagiagno, Brother A., 368n7

Caldwell, William, 61, 261, 354n24, 382n34

Camas Prairie, 56, 85, 156, 352n2

Carley, Caroline D., 160

Carlisle Indian School, 238, 327, 388n24

Carlson, Leonard A., 339n14, 346n73

Carter, Billy, 280

Cataldo, Father, 368n7

Catholic Church, 156, 170, 254, 368n7

census, 186, 369n14

Century (magazine), 32

chainmen, 123; Alice C. Fletcher's supervision of, 194–95; strike for higher wages by, 216–17

charity, 200, 208, 214

Choate, John N., 327, 328

Choup-nit-ki: With the Nez Perces (Gay), 15, 179, 182, 183; about, 32–33; as documentation of allotment, 32, 129, 222–23, 306, 308–9; draft manuscript of, 129, 305; illustrations from, 119, 307, 308, 309; presentation of images in, 116, 121, 140–41; "Writer's Note" in, 273, 275, 314–15

Christian Register (newspaper), 31, 33, 177, 181, 202, 207

Chronicles of Oklahoma (journal), 28–31

Churchill, Ward, 187

citizenship, 218, 290; allotment and, 167–68, 177–78, 184–85, 193, 286; and holiday celebrations, 178, 282; technologies of, 185, 257

Clearwater River, 62, 109, 110, 112, 218, 229, 231; photographs of, *113*, *141*

Cleveland, Grover, 354n31

Clinton, Robert, 224

Cloud, Katherine, 310, *311*, 313

Cobell v. Salazar, xii, xiii, 224, 298, 333

Cody, Buffalo Bill, 238

Cold Spring, 73, 76–78, 87–88

A Collection of Primary Sources on the Nez Perce Exile in Canada, the Indian Territory, and Their Return to the Northwest: 1877–1886 (O'Neal & Baird, eds.), 302

colonialism, 13–14, 341n34

Colville Reservation, 43, 49, 50

communal property and resources, 7–8, 52, 154, 168, 214

competency commissions, 292–94, 385n23

Conant, Claudius Buchanan, 19

Conner, Edward, 257, 267

Corbett, Felix, 216

Corbett, Nancy, 27, 137

corruption: Alice C. Fletcher and, 62–63, 67, 77; by federal Indian agents, 60–61, 168–69, 296, 353n21

[410]

Cottonwood Creek, 116
counter-memory, 35–36, 348n86
Cox case, 262–67
Craig claim, 157, 261
Crawford, Mazie, 229
Cruikshank, Barbara, 168
Cushing, Frank Hamilton, 32, 119, 120, 362n23

Davis, Lennard J., 36
Dawes, Electa Sanderson, 3–4, 203–4
Dawes, Henry, 200, 339n18, 341n36, 349n15
Dawes General Allotment Act, 11, 58, 289; and erasure of Native rights and culture, xii, 8; inconsistencies in, 168; Nimiipuu and, 66–67, 256–57; railroad interests and, 55, 339n18
de Certeau, Michel, 299–300
Deffenbaugh, George L., 41–42, 50–51
Deloria, Philip J., 12–13, 242, 310, 337n7, 342n42
Deloria, Vine, Jr., 6, 346n73
Department of the Interior, xi
Dickinson, Emily, 363n33
Dickson-Cloud family album, *313, 316–17, 318, 321, 329, 330, 331, 332*
Dirlik, Arif, 36, 103–4, 123, 153, 348n87
Dodge, Jane Gay, 32, 120, 344n61, 371n30
Dudziak, Mary L., 341n31
Durham, Jimmie, 187

Eastman, Gene, 162
education and schools: boarding schools for Natives, 238, 296, 327; E. Jane Gay on, 194; on Nez Perce Reservation, 60–61, 228
Ellenwood, Phillip, 288
Ellinwood, F. F., 48, 64
Elliott, Michael A., 12
Emerson, Edith, 347n83
Eneas, Paul, *280*

Fair, Henry, 247, 248
family albums, 310–33, 387n14, 387n18; archival value of, 310, 330, 333; as form of resistance, 319; and oral tradition, 320–21
Fillmore, John Comfort, 244
Fisher, S. G., 255

Fletcher, Alice C.: appointment as Indian agent, 6–7, 18–19; and archival record, 31–32, 114–15; banning Nimiipuu from leaving reservation, 234, 377n23; biographical information on, 19; as bureaucrat, 23, 61, 104, 188, 215; on cession of "surplus lands," 253; character traits of, 114, 233, 254, 343n52; and Charles Monteith, 61–62, 79, 81, 84–85, 206, 232; on Chief Joseph, 3–4, 203; complaints about, 234, 256; correspondence of, 201–2, 204–6; and corruption, 62–63, 67, 77; and Cox case, 263–67; and Dawes Act, 1, 6; deciding to work in Kamiah, 68–69, 137–38; and divisions among Nez Perce, 177, 251; doubts by, 202, 204, 213; E. Jane Gay on, 18, 64, 69, 139, 199; E. Jane Gay's relationship with, 23; and Edson Briggs, 15, 206–7; as "educator" of Natives, 67, 155, 193, 194–95; end of field work by, 223, 254, 256, 287, 289; ethnographic work of, 35, 90–91, 135–37, 143, 147, 160–61, 279, 359n45, 365–66nn22–23; and F. W. Putnam, 19, 21–22, 88, 135, 202, 213; family-grouping system of, 89–90, 195–96, 215; favoritism and partisanship of, 196–97, 209–10, 212, 232–33, 243, 251, 255, 284; on Fourth of July celebrations, 177–78, 180, 226, 227; and Francis La Flesche, 19, 202, 245, 342n40, 365n22, 379n62; and gender, 14, 15, 24, 104, 200; impatience of, 221, 234; imperiousness of, 212, 221, 253–54; inconsistency of, 201, 212, 217, 273n5; initial allotment work by, 58–59, 62–63, 68–69, 73–74, 110–12, 361n13; initial errors and missteps, 53, 59, 62, 64–65, 77, 105; and James Moses, 25, 232–34, 267; and James Reubens, 25–26, 79, 80, 85, 87–89, 217, 245; and James Stuart, 5, 25, 26–27, 147, 148, 160, 197, 271; and Kate McBeth, 147, 149, 160, 172, 212, 228, 229, 249; and Kew-kew'-lu-yah's map, 143–44, 148–49, 153, 158, 366n27; kinship documentation by, 139, 185, 287; and Langford claim, 63–64, 157–58, 261–62, 287; letters to Isabel Barrows, 58, 108, 118, 177, 179, 181, 204; limits to objectivity of, 14, 105,

[411]

INDEX

Fletcher, Alice C. (*continued*) 200, 233; modification of allotment policy by, 105–8, 112–13, 135, 153–54, 156; Native artifacts obtained by, 136, 140; as negotiator, 80, 90; and New Orleans World Exposition, 20; official reports by, 65–66, 108, 118, 201, 204, 211–12; parlor network of, 202–3; personal-professional border blurred by, 14, 209–10; photographs and drawings of, 1, 2, 4, 15, *16*, *17*, 69, *70*, *134*; and photography, 20, 343n49; and Presbyterian Church, 21, 63, 69–71, 200, 201, 207–12, 217, 227–28; as reformer, 193, 199, 204; and religion, 343n51; on Richard Henry Pratt, 84–85; and Robert Williams, 209, 212; supported by Mary Copley Thaw, 21, 136, 200–201, 213, 214, 363n3; and Susan McBeth, 59, 62, 68, 85, 136–37, 143, 172, 207, 212, 249, 279, 281; Thomas Jefferson Morgan's correspondence with, 61–62, 202, 205–6, 252–53, 275n9; time estimates for allotment work, 106–7, 138, 213, 221, 252, 361n3; on topography, 115–16, 352n2; torn between duties and scholarship, 136, 212; on tribal identity, 186; view of Native people, 185, 187, 214, 215; and voice recordings, 281; and white settlers, 58, 60, 62, 77, 109; and World's Columbian Exposition (1893), 138, 187–89, 236–37, 239, 241–46, 248, 250
—writings: "Composite Portraits of American Indians," 20; "Ethnologic Gleanings among the Nez Perces," 245, 364n9; "Fourth of July among the Indians," 177–78; *Historical Sketch of the Omaha Tribe of Indians in Nebraska*, 20; "Missionary Work among the Indians," 207; "The Nez Perce Country," 159, 364n9, 365n18; "Personal Studies of Indian Life," 32, 362n23; *Report on Indian Education and Civilization*, 20
Foreign Missionary, 48, 50
Fort Lapwai. *See* Lapwai, Idaho
Fountain, D. S., 260
Fourth of July celebrations: in 1883, 47–49; in 1885, 41; in 1889, 96–101, 360n6; in 1890, 175–84; in 1891, 225–26, 235; in 1892, 226–27; in 1903, 271, 274–77;

Alice C. Fletcher on, 177–78, 180, 226, 227; Chief Joseph at, 182, 215, 277, 384n9; and divisions among Nez Perce, 183–84; E. Jane Gay and, 179–83, 225–26, 227; James Reubens as orator at, 47–49, 97, 100–101, 226; Kate McBeth and, 47, 100, 181, 227, 228, 274; photographs of, *276*, *319*; prohibition of activities at, 226–27, 228, 234–35; significance for Nimiipuu of, 42, 43–44, 96, 139, 282; war processions in, 146–47, 182, 215, 226–27, 228, 277
Fowler, Loretta A., 338n13

Gallison, James D., 160
Galton, Francis, 20
Garvey, Ellen Gruber, 303
Gay, E. Jane, 188–89, 216, 355n42; albums of, 129–32, 306–7, 362n24; as Alice C. Fletcher's photographer, 3, 23–24, 344n61; on allotment work, 64, 69, 73–74, 76–77, 221, 222–23; anthropological documentation by, 135, 314, 344n60; and archival record of allotment, 3, 33, 119–34, 309–10, 347n83; biographical information on, 22; character of, 343n52; correspondence of, 32, 34; on Cox case, 266, 383n49; depictions of Alice C. Fletcher by, 18, 68–69, *134*, *139*, 199, 214; on disputes among reservation officials, 61; and divisions among Nimiipuu, 177, 201, 208, 368n13, 374n22; as ethnographic collaborator, 147, 160, 366n23; and Fourth of July celebrations, 179–83, 225–26, 227, 273, 275; and gender, 15, 24, 129, 131, 133; income of, 344n61; on James Stuart, 27, 275; landscapes and panoramas by, 120–21, 123, 125–26, 337n10; later life of, 348n83; on Mary Thaw, 208, 229; and Presbyterian Church refurbishment, 207–9, 210–11; racialization by, 192; and relationship with Alice C. Fletcher, 23; wet-plate process of, 123, 125; on white settlers, 355n49; and World's Columbian Exposition, 246
—photographs: "The Barbecue," 183, *307*; "Behold the Cook," *191*, 192; "Box Case," 263, *264*, *265*; "Camp at Lapwai. Tlal-lik-lykl. July 4," 183, *184*; "Camp

[412]

Bearing Tree," 131, *132*; "Camp Meeting at Lapwai, July 4," 273, 274; "Chief Joseph with Alice C. Fletcher . . . ," 1, 2, 3, 4–5, 203, 215; "Clearwater River at Kamiah," 112, *113*; "Clearwater River—Nicodemus' Home on the Left," 140, *141*; "The Damp Thermopylae," 123, 125, *126*, 363n31; Fort Lapwai, 121, 123, *124*; Harriet Stuart and Annie Parnell Little, 324; "Leaving Camp. Kamiah, July 4th," 183; Lewiston, Idaho, 121, *122*; "North Fork of the Clearwater," 123, *125*; "Old Billy Williams," 149, *150*, 151; "Salmon Feast," 307; self-portraits, 190, 371n30; "Squirrel Camp," 116, *118*, *119*, 133; "They Donned War Bonnets," 74, *75*, 76, 89, *90–91*, 203, 327, 357nn1–2; "Where Dick Fell," 126–27, *128*; "Where We Gathered Indian Songs," *130*
—writings: "Camp Life Experiences," 193–95, 371n33; in *Red Man*, 64, 66, 70, 133, 193–94, 208, 371n33; "Where We Camped," 117, 133; "Writers Note," 273, 275, 314–15. *See also Choup-nit-ki: With the Nez Perces* (Gay)
Gay, Emma J., 306
gender: Alice C. Fletcher and, 14, 15, 24, 104, 200; E. Jane Gay's photography mediated by, 24, 129, 131, 133; and gendered ideals, 13–14, 104–5, 341n34; hierarchies of, 128–29; and identity, 18
Grafe, Steven L., 388n23
Grangeville Free Press, 55, 56
Grant, James, 301
Greenwald, Emily, 28, 360n2
Greer, John, 109
Guidi, Joseph N., 368n9

Hagan, William T., 10–11
Haines, Francis, 347n75
Half Moon, Charley, 295
Harvard University, 213, 363n3
Hayes, Harry, 281
Hayes, James, 281
Hay Reservation, 228, 262, 376n12
Heth, Henry, 57, 61, 88
He-yume-toke-te-nikt (Mabel Halfmoon), 294, 300
He-yum-ka-yon-mi, 295

Hill, Tom, 51
Hines, James, 267
holidays, 95–96, 100. *See also* Fourth of July celebrations
Holland, Jeanne, 363n33
Hoona, Solomon, 293
How-pa-loo village, 156–57
Hoxie, Frederick E.: *Final Promise*, 339n14, 340n21; *Parading through History*, 338n13; *With the Nez Perces: Alice Fletcher in the Field*, 32–33, 42, 58–59, 127, 368n13
hunt, annual fall, 65, 216, 234–35, 265, 318

Idaho, 56, 167, 175
Il-law-kart-'part-poo village, 155
Im-nee-wo-ton-my, 297
Inauzakamma (Ellis), 169, 170
Indian Claims Commission, 159
Indian Helper (newspaper), 327, 388n24
Indian Reorganization Act, 13
Indian Rights Act, 256
Indian Rights Association, 19
Indians in Unexpected Places (Deloria), 12–13
intercultural communication, 97, 101, 164, 345n65
intermarriage, 62, 186, 354n31
internment: Nez Perce effecting end to, 43; returning internees, 5–6, 44, 46–47, 49, 50–51, 350nn17–18
intersubjectivity, 7
Its-ah-ha-yam (Captain Pierce), 255
Iverson, Peter, 338n13

Jackson, John Brinckerhoff, 337n10
Jackson, Paul, 288
Jackson, Shannon, 95–96
Jacox, Elizabeth, 347n83
Jaimes, M. Annette, 187
James, Darwin, 226–27
James, Elizabeth, 285–86
Janiewski, Dolores, 285
Johnson, Andrew, 22, 343n54
Jonas, Levi, 218, 281
Joseph, Chief, 49, 281; Alice C. Fletcher on, 3–4, 203; Fourth of July war processions led by, 182, 215, 277, 384n9; James Reubens's alliance with, 44, 349n10; and

Joseph, Chief (*continued*)
  Nez Perce War, 2, 29–30; photographs of, 1, 2, 3, 4, 309; resistance to allotment by, 5, 25, 215
Joseph War, 2, 29–30, 297–98, 337n5; and Nez Perce scout payment, 59, 82, 296, 358n17
Josephy, Alvin M., 28
July Fourth. *See* Fourth of July celebrations
Junkin, William W., 65, 256

Kamiah, Idaho: as Alice C. Fletcher's base of operations, 25, 53, 59, 62, 137; allotment work in, 15, 68–69, 110, 112–13, 137, 140, 195, 215, 233; church refurbishment project in, 172, 201, 207–12, 217; early inhabitants of, 156; Fourth of July celebrations in, 25, 175–81, 271; and Nimiipuu at Lapwai, 43, 52, 170–71; photographs of, 70, *113*, *274*; Presbyterian congregation in, 43, 52, 69–70, 86, 90, 201
Kaplan, Amy, 340n28
Kelsey, Robin E., 118–19, 131
Kew-kew'-lu-yah (Billy Williams), 27, 137, 143, 365n18; biographical information on, 151–52; photograph of, 149, *150*, *151*
Kew-kew'-lu-yah's map, 143–59; accuracy of, 147, 367n43; chronological dimension of, 160; subsequent history of, 158–59, 160
Kinney, J. P. A., 339n14
kinship: Alice C. Fletcher's efforts to document, 139, 185, 287; Nez Perce system of, 154–55
Kooskia, Idaho, 27, 140, 312

La Flesche, Francis: Alice C. Fletcher and, 19, 202, 245, 342n40, 365n22, 379n62; James Reubens and, 80, 81
La Flesche, Suzette, 19
Lake Mohonk Conference, 168–69
Lambert, Valerie, 338n13
land: communal use of, 52, 154, 214; conceptualized as space, 103; for farming and for grazing, 108; mineral and timber resources of, 10–11, 83, 121, 288–89; and Native mapping practices, 152; Nimiipuu view of, 143, 156–57, 161

Lander, Frederick West, 120, 362n25
Landis, Barbara, 388n24
Lane, John, 266, 267, 383n49
Langford claim, 63–64, 87, 157–58, 261–62, 287
Lapwai, Idaho, 206, 209, 252, 259; Alice C. Fletcher and E. Jane Gay moving from, 68, 105; allotment work in, 53, 59, 62–63, 65, 69, 105, 138, 157, 221, 232, 234–35, 262, 360n2; Catholics in, 170, 254; Fourth of July celebrations in, 5, 41, 49, 100–101, 175, 181–83, 225–26, 274–77, 279; and Nimiipuu at Kamiah, 43, 50, 52, 170–71; photographs of, *124*, *184*; Presbyterian congregation in, 46, 170, 226–27, 255; returning internees in, 26, 42, 46–47, 49, 50, 51
Lapwai River and Creek, 63, 100
Latham, Edward, 277
Lawyer, Archie, 44, 212, 257; opposition to allotment by, 208, 368n13; photographs of, 44, *45*, *75*, *76*; Susan McBeth and, 171–72
Lawyer, Chief (Tlu-la-lal-quil-soot), 161, 169
Lawyer, Corbett, 161–62, 285
Lawyer, James, 171–72
Lawyer, Mylie, 351n34
Lend a Hand (magazine), 31, 33
Lewis and Clark, 140, 143, 162
Lewiston, Idaho, 26, 56, 66, 87, 122, 175; Fourth of July celebrations in, 97–100, 226
Lewiston Morning Tribune, 274–75
Lewiston Teller (newspaper), 46, 67, 99, 182, 356n51; on Alice C. Fletcher, 60, 106–7; on James Reubens, 83, 86, 87, 101; and white settlers, 57–58, 109
Lindsley, Thomas, 293
Lipps, Oscar H., 285–86, 290
Little, Annie Parnell, 324
Lowe, Lisa, 348n89
Lowrie, J. C., 64

mail stations, 260–61, 381nn30–31
Mallickan, Diane, 301
Manifest Destiny, 36, 56
manifest domesticity, 6, 13–14, 18, 24, 338n12

[414]

The Manners, Customs, and Condition of the North American Indians, 308
maps and map making, 153; by Corbett Lawyer, 161, 162; as cross-cultural argument, 151; by Edson Briggs, 117, 127, 142, 364n15; by Kew-kew'-lu-yah, 143–49, 152–53, 155–59, 160, 367n43; Native practices of, 152, 365n19
Marcum, T. D., 353n21, 354n24
Mark, Joan: on E. Jane Gay, 208, 343n52, 347n83, 374n22; *A Stranger in Her Native Land*, 15, 20, 21, 33, 42, 58, 65, 201, 343n50, 368n13; *With the Nez Perces: Alice Fletcher in the Field*, 32–33, 42, 58–59, 127, 368n13
marriage, 62, 186, 354n31
matrilineality, 187–88
Matt, Jim (Kol-Kol-Chaw-hin), 288
Maxwell, Starr J., 281–82, 283, 284, 289, 296, 300
McBeth, Kate C., 63, 129, 256, 303; as Alice C. Fletcher's ethnographic collaborator, 147, 149, 160; feud with sister, 170–71; and Fourth of July celebrations, 47, 100, 181, 227, 228, 274; home of, 228, 229, 375n11; and James Reubens, 47–48; *The Nez Perces since Lewis and Clark* by, 47, 273–74; and returning internees, 46–47, 51–52, 351n34
McBeth, Susan L., 15, 68, 85, 351n34, 368n12; and divisions among Nez Perce, 178, 180–81; feud with sister, 170–71; and support of Alice C. Fletcher, 59, 62, 136–37, 143, 207, 279, 281; and World's Columbian Exposition, 244, 379n54
McConville, Edward, 85, 226, 228
McCoy, Robert R., 347n75
McFarland, Philip, 287
McMillen, Christian W., 338n13
Mellikin, Utsin, 257
Melville, Catherine, 22
Memorial of the Nez Perce Indians Residing in the State of Idaho to the Congress of the United States, 281–302; presented to Congress, 285; subsequent fate of, 301
Miller, C. Marc, 159–60
Miller, E. H., 15, 16
Miller, James, 234
Monteith, Charles E., 62, 229, 353n17, 369n14; Alice C. Fletcher and, 61–62, 79, 81, 84–85, 206, 232; on allotment process, 46, 339n15, 350n17, 352n7, 354n30; and McBeth sisters, 170–71, 180–81; Nimiipuu opposition to, 59–60, 71, 80–81, 86; relieved of duties, 81, 86–87, 101, 202; slandering James Reubens, 89; support of white settlers by, 61, 258–59, 261, 353n11, 353n19, 354n24, 381n30
Monteith, James B., 44, 45, 170
Moorhouse, Lee, 326, 388n23
Morgan, Caroline S., 203, 205–6, 210
Morgan, Thomas Jefferson, 186, 210; Alice C. Fletcher's correspondence with, 61–62, 202, 205–6, 252–53, 275n9; on allotment and citizenship, 184–85; annual reports by, 172–73, 178–79, 370n27; on holiday celebrations, 95, 227; and World's Columbian Exposition, 138, 236, 237, 238, 239, 241–42
Morillo, Father A., 368n7
Morning Star (newspaper), 31
Morrill, Allen Conrad, 52, 86, 149
Morrill, Eleanor Dunlap, 52, 86, 149
Morris, Sam (Sik-Um-Chets-Kun-In), 279, 280
Moses, Chief, 49–50
Moses, George, 257
Moses, James, 25, 65, 229, 232–34, 267
Mox Mox, Annie, 286
Mt. Idaho, 68, 85, 137, 171

Nabokov, Peter, 151, 152
National Anthropological Archives, 33, 301
Nelson, Dana D., 147
Nespelem, Washington, 5, 271, 277, 384n9
Nez Perce Home and Farm Association, 27
The Nez Perce Indians and the Opening of the Northwest (Josephy), 28
Nez Perce Music Archive, 279
Nez Perce National Historical Park Achives, 33
The Nez Perce Nation Divided: Reports on the Aftermath of the 1863 Treaty (Baird et al., eds.), 302
Nez Perce News, 55
Nez Perce Reservation: boundaries of, 109–10, 115–16, 153, 222; census of, 186, 369n14; chaos and corruption at, 60–61, 353n21; discussion of allotment at, 6,

[415]

INDEX

Nez Perce Reservation (*continued*) 56–57, 223, 353n9; and Lapwai Agency, 59, 61, 68, 353n21, 354n25; Presbyterian administration of, 43, 50, 207; and railroads, 55–56, 99; schools on, 60–61, 228, 243; terrain of, 121; tribal council of, 27, 99; tribal identity debated at, 178–79, 186, 369n5; white settlers' cattle grazing on, 57–58, 108, 257–58, 353n11. *See also* Nimiipuu

The Nez Perces in the Indian Territory (Pearson), 6, 28, 338n13

The Nez Perces since Lewis and Clark (McBeth), 47, 273–74

Nez Perce Tribe, et al. v. Kempthorne, et al., xii, xiii

Nimiipuu: active agency of, 6, 71, 76–78, 214; annual fall hunt by, 65, 216, 234–35, 318; and assimilation, 178–79, 180, 216, 333; attempts to erase culture of, xii, 5, 11, 37, 243; and Catholicism, 156, 170, 368n7, 368n9; cession of "surplus lands" of, 253, 257; communal land and resources of, 7–8, 52, 154, 214; divisions among, 30, 43, 50, 169–70, 172, 177, 178, 180–81, 183–84, 201, 217–18, 232, 263; history of, 27–31, 346–47nn73–75; and Joseph War, 2, 29–30, 297–98, 337n5; and Kew-kew'-lu-yah's map, 143–59, 367n43; kinship systems of, 154–55; and land, 143, 156–57, 161; lawsuits by, 159–60; letter-writing by, 221–22, 263; loss of land through allotment, 8, 196, 285–87; and *Memorial of the Nez Perce Indians Residing in the State of Idaho*, 281–98; and performance, 43–44, 95, 139, 179; place-based political structures of, 156; and Presbyterian Church, 41, 42, 43, 50, 59, 151, 156, 216, 348n1, 351n34; reparations money owed to, 83, 358n19; resistance to allotment by, 3, 4–5, 6, 11–12, 25, 34–35, 59, 65, 66, 76–78, 99, 105, 138, 163, 215, 221–22, 256–57; seasonal living patterns of, 105–6, 113, 154, 215–16; as skilled negotiators, 90; sovereignty of, 101, 105, 143, 178–79; survivance of, 43–44, 152, 158, 243, 277, 281; understanding of allotment by, 56–57, 59, 67, 82–83, 353n9; whites' characterization of, 56; women, 345n65. *See also* Nez Perce Reservation

Noble, John W., 81
Noon Nee-Me-Poo (Slickpoo), 28, 347n75
Nora, Pierre, 339n16
Norris, George W., 57, 353n9, 361n13
Northwest Historical Manuscripts Series, 301
Northwest Ordinance (1787), 167

Oberly, John H., 185
Office of Indian Affairs, 10, 60, 65, 86, 104, 173, 217
Olsen, Loran, 279
Olund, Eric N., 12
Omahas, 214
O'Neill, E., 64
oral tradition, 320–21
Orofino, Idaho, 194, 216, 360n6
O'Sullivan, Timothy S., 121, 129
Otis, D. S., 338n14
Ou-na-ne-we-nan-ny (Celia Reubens), 139–40, 246
Out of the Blanket (Morrill and Morrill), 52, 86, 149

Page, J. W., 354n25
Pa-lote-pe village, 157
Parker, Aaron F., 51
patronage, 42, 200, 203
Peabody Museum of Archaeology and Ethnology, 15, 137, 140, 144–45, 158–59
Pearson, J. Diane, 6, 28, 50, 338n13, 350n17, 350n25
Pellicin, Kip Kip, 257
performance, 95–96, 139, 179; and archival record, 35–36; strategic, 43–44
photography: Alice C. Fletcher and, 20, 343n49; and archival record, 119–34, 302, 309–10; "doubled pictures," 330, 333; E. Jane Gay's approach to, 3, 23, 120–21, 123, 125, 337n10, 344n60, 384n83; and ethnographic research, 20; in family albums, 310–33, 387n14, 387n18; landscape, 120–21, 362n26; Natives and, 69, 356n54
Pile of Clouds, 290, 291
place, 145, 156; place-making, 365n21; and space, 103–4, 106, 123, 128, 134, 146
Plessy v. Ferguson, 186–87
plots, 36
polygamy, 186

[416]

INDEX

post-nationalist American Studies, 12–13, 340n28, 341n31
Powell, John Wesley, 88, 120, 239, 362n25
The Practice of Everyday Life (de Certeau), 299–300
Pratt, Mary Louise, 363n27
Pratt, Richard Henry, 84–85, 133, 210, 238, 239
Presbyterian Church: and administration of Nez Perce Reservation, 43, 50, 207; Alice C. Fletcher and, 21, 63, 200, 201, 207–12, 217, 227–28; and allotment, 45, 52–53; attire of Native members of, 48, 350n25; and Catholics, 169–70; and competency commissions, 385n23; divisions within, 170–71, 172, 208, 217–18, 368n13; and Fourth of July celebration behavior, 227, 228; Nez Perces in, 41, 42, 43, 50, 59, 151, 156, 348n1, 351n34; refurbishment of, in Kamiah, 207–12, 217; Robert Williams and, 70–71, 171, 172, 293; supporting Charles Monteith, 353n17
Price, Hiram, 45–46, 349n13
Priest, Loring Benson, 8, 200, 339n14, 339n18
progressivism, 181, 239
property: communal, 7–8, 52, 154, 214; patrilineal transfer of, 185
Prucha, Francis Paul, 339n14
Putnam, F. W.: and Alice C. Fletcher, 19, 21–22, 88, 135, 202, 213; and World's Columbian Exposition, 187–88, 236, 237, 240, 241, 242, 243, 246

racial identity: blood and, 182, 187–88; hierarchies of, 128–29
railroads, 8, 55–56, 99, 339n18
Rand, Jacki Thompson, 13–14
Reconfiguring the Reservation (Greenwald), 28
Red Man (newspaper), 31, 33, 202; E. Jane Gay's articles in, 64, 66, 70, 133, 193–94, 208, 371n33
Red Wolf, Harrison, 287–88, 300
Redwolf, Josiah, 91, 92
Reid, Kenneth C., 160
religion, traditional, 43, 50
Reubens, James, 218, 257, 267, 296, 381n30; about, 25–26, 44; and Alice C. Fletcher, 25–26, 79, 80, 85, 87–89, 217, 245; allotment claim of, 89–91; and Charles Monteith, 89, 358n24; and Chief Joseph, 44, 349n10; history of Nez Perce by, 28–31; and inception of allotment, 78, 83, 92; and J. P. Vollmer, 79, 357n5; as orator at Fourth of July celebrations, 47–49, 97, 100–101, 226; photographs of, 44, 45, 75, 76, 326; and Presbyterian Church, 45; representation of Nimiipuu in Washington, 65, 77–82, 85–86, 101, 355n42
Reubens, Stephen, 75, 89
Ridington, Robin, 338n13
Riley, Robert James, 347n75
Roach, Joseph, 43–44, 96, 158, 348n86
Robbins, Warren D., 228, 234, 258, 260
Roller, Charles, 288
Rosier, Paul C., 338n13
Ruby, Robert H., 49
Ryan, Timothy, 235, 252, 381n32

Saler, Bethel, 167
Salmon Valley, 169
Sappington, Robert Lee, 140, 153, 160
savagism, 182
Schleicher, Robert, 257
Schlesinger Library on the History of Women in America, 32, 33, 120, 362n24
schools. *See* education and schools
The Scrapbook in American Life (Tucker et al., eds.), 304
scrapbooks, 302–6
Sells, Cato, 187
Senier, Siobhan, 18
Seth, Annie, 294–95
"The Significance of the Frontier in American History" (Turner), 237
Silcott, Jane, 260, 267, 381n32
Slickpoo, Allen P., 27, 28, 43, 49, 347n75
Smith, Edward P., 7–8
Snake River, 365n19, 373n17
Sorosis, 19
Southern Workman (magazine), 31, 202
space, 121, 152; and place, 103–4, 106, 123, 128, 146
Space, Ralph, 161, 162
Spalding, Henry, 63, 64, 169, 170, 179
Spalding claim, 157, 158, 229, 230, 231, 232, 234, 376n14
Steedman, Carolyn, 35
Stephan, J. A., 254–55
Stevens, Isaac, 169, 179, 352n6
St. Joseph's Mission, 43

[417]

INDEX

Storch, Richard, 320
Stot-ka-i, 297
Stranahan, C. T., 255–56
A Stranger in Her Native Land (Mark), 15, 20, 21, 33, 42, 58, 65, 201, 343n50, 368n13
Stuart, Harriet Mary, 147, 271, 272, 324, 345n65
Stuart, James, 129, 216, 267; and Alice C. Fletcher, 5, 25, 26–27, 147, 148, 160, 197, 271; as allotment supporter, 56–57, 73; E. Jane Gay on, 27, 275; photographs of, 1, 2, 3, 69, 70, 272, 312; and World's Columbian Exposition, 241, 248, 249–50
Suck-ko'-ly-e-kin-ma village, 157
Supreme Court, xi
survivance, 30; and Nimiipuu, 43–44, 152, 158, 243, 277, 281
Sweet, Willis, 266

Tah'mawiinúnmy, 291
Taylor, Diana, 139
Thaw, Mary Copley, 88, 229; as Alice C. Fletcher's benefactor, 21, 136, 200–201, 213, 214, 363n3; support to Presbyterian Church by, 21, 208, 209
Thaw, William, 21, 208, 373n21
Thompson, David P., 115, 376n14
Thomson, Rosemarie Garland, 168
Three Eagles, 297
Tibbles, Thomas Henry, 19
Tlu-la-lal-quil-soot (Chief Lawyer), 161, 169
Treaty of 1855, 56, 154, 352n6
Treaty of 1863, 56, 83, 110, 115, 154, 352n7
Trennert, Robert A., Jr., 239
tribal identity, 186, 189, 265; voting on, 178–79, 369n5
tribalism, 168, 214–15, 370n24
Truax, Sewell, 373n17
Turner, Frederick Jackson, 237
Turner, Victoria, 139

Vizenor, Gerald, 30
Vollmer, J. P., 78–79, 98, 99
Volpp, Leti, 341n31

Walker, Deward E., Jr., 159, 385n23
Wal-la-mot-kin (Hair tied on forehead), 29
Wallowa Valley, 5, 44, 169, 215, 296, 297–98, 365n19

Warhus, Mark, 145
Washington Indian Association, 132–33
Wa-to-lina, Charlie, 297–98
Weippe Prairie, 161, 162, 163
Well-'eyou-way-we village, 157
Wexler, Laura, 3, 327, 341n34, 388n25
We-yah-la-hom, 294
Wheeler, Harry, 161
Wheeler, William, 257
White, Elijah, 169, 179
white settlers: Alice C. Fletcher and, 58, 60, 62, 77, 109; and allotment process, 66–67, 355n49; business dealings of, 260–61, 382n34; cattle grazing on reservation lands by, 57–58, 108, 257–58, 353n11; Charles Monteith's support of, 61, 258–59, 261, 353n11, 353n19, 354n24, 381n30; marrying Native women, 62, 354n31; Nimiipuu conflicts with, 18; and reservation borders, 109–10; and squatter sovereignty, 288
Whitman, Silas D., 271, 273; and *Memorial of the Nez Perce Indians*, 281, 285, 287–88, 289, 290, 293
Wild West Shows, 238, 370n27
Williams, Billy. *See* Kew-kew'-lu-yah (Billy Williams)
Williams, Mark, 44, 45
Williams, Robert, 178; Alice C. Fletcher and, 209, 212; as Presbyterian pastor, 70–71, 171, 172, 293; and World's Columbian Exposition, 244, 379n54
Williamson-Cloud, Nakia, 319
Winnebagos, 214
With the Nez Perces: Alice Fletcher in the Field (Hoxie and Mark), 32–33, 42, 58–59, 127, 368n13
women. *See* gender
"Women and Patronage in Early Washington City" (Allgor), 203
Women's Indian Association, 19, 22
Woodin, Lewellyn E., 350n18
World's Columbian Exposition (Chicago, 1893), 138, 187–89, 190, 236–42, 245–50; Nimiipuu representation at, 240–41, 243–44, 245, 248–49, 380n73
World's Industrial and Centennial Cotton Exposition (New Orleans, 1884), 20

Yellow Bull, 215
Yellow Wolf, 50, 337n5

[418]

Author's Previous Works

Trading Gazes: Anglo-American Women Photographers among North American Indians.
With Melody Graulich, Lisa MacFarlane, and Susan Bernardin.
New Brunswick NJ: Rutgers University Press, 2003.

American Woman's Home
by Catharine Beecher and Harriet Beecher Stowe. 1869.
Ed. Nicole Tonkovich. New Brunswick NJ:
Rutgers University Press, 2002.

Domesticity with a Difference:
The Nonfiction of Catharine Beecher, Sarah Josepha Hale,
Fanny Fern and Margaret Fuller.
Jackson: University Press of Mississippi, 1997.

www.ingramcontent.com/pod-product-compliance
Lightning Source LLC
Chambersburg PA
CBHW021140240426
43661CB00075B/1593